Francis J. Moloney, S.D.B.

M000249734

SIGNS AND SHADOWS

Reading John 5–12

FORTRESS PRESS
MINNEAPOLIS

SIGNS AND SHADOWS
READING JOHN 5–12

Copyright © 1996 Augsburg Fortress. All rights reserved. Except for brief quotations in critical articles or reviews, no part of this book may be reproduced in any
manner without prior written permission from the publisher. Write to: Permis-
sions, Augsburg Fortress, 426 S. Fifth St., Box 1209, Minneapolis, MN 55440.

Interior design: The HK Scriptorium, Inc.
Cover art: *Prophet* by Emil Nolde. Used by permission of The Museum of Modern
   Art, New York, NY

Library of Congress Cataloging-in-Publication Data

Moloney, Francis J.
      Signs and shadows : reading John 5–12 / Francis J. Moloney.
         p.   cm.
      Includes bibliographical references and index.
      ISBN 0-8006-2936-1 (alk. paper)
      1. Bible. N.T. John V–XII—Criticism, Narrative.   2. Narration
in the Bible.   I. Title.
      BS2615.2.M573   1996   96-11618
                                                             CIP

The paper used in this publication meets the minimum requirements of American
National Standard for Information Sciences—Permanence of Paper for Printed
Library Materials, ANSI Z329.48-1984.

Manufactured in the U.S.A.   AF 1-2936
00   99   98   97   96   1   2   3   4   5   6   7   8   9   10

For the
Melbourne College of Divinity

Contents

Preface

¶ AS IN THE FIRST VOLUME of my narrative commentary on the Fourth Gospel, I am pursuing a reading of the text of the Fourth Gospel that attempts to blend traditional historical critical scholarship and the more contemporary reader-oriented approaches to a narrative text.[1] Tracing the evolving reader is but one way of approaching a narrative text. It disassociates itself from the widespread attempts to seek unity in the putative thought of the Evangelist who is long since dead as it attempts to demonstrate unity at the level of the interplay between the author and the reader in a text whose present readership keeps it alive.

In some ways a study of John 5-12 could be a monograph in its own right. It must be recognized, however, that the reader in 5:1 is a product of John 1-4. The title, *Signs and Shadows*, is drawn from a homily of Leo the Great: "Lord, you drew all things to yourself so that all nations everywhere in their dedication to you might celebrate in a full, clear sacramental rite, what was done only in the Jewish Temple and in signs and shadows" (*Sermon 8 on the Passion of the Lord*).[2] It suggests that John 5-10 presents Jesus as the perfection of Jewish liturgy and theology, and that John 11-12 points to a "lifting up" that will attract all nations.

---

[1] See F. J. Moloney, *Belief in the Word: Reading John 1-4* (Minneapolis: Fortress Press, 1993) ix-x.

[2] "Traxasti, Domine, omnia ad te, ut quod in uno Judaeae [or Judaeorum] templo obumbratis significationibus agebatur, pleno apertoque sacramento, universarum ubique devotio celebraret" (PL 54:341B). For the textual difficulty, see CCSL 138A 358:175-90.

I am indebted to many people who support and encourage me, especially the Salesians of the Province of Australia, and my confrere in the
community at Chadstone. Dr. Mark Coleridge and Nerina M. Zanardo,
F.S.P., have read this text in its entirety. Henry Bertels, S.J., and his staff at
the library of the Pontifical Biblical Institute in Rome, where I was the
Catholic Biblical Association Visiting Professor for 1993–94, made a final
text possible. The Catholic Biblical Association of America has again
enabled my continued research and writing.

I am dedicating *Signs and Shadows* to the ecumenical Melbourne
College of Divinity, where I have taught and been taught for the past
twenty years. The dedication is a token of gratitude offered to all who
have given so much to the Melbourne College of Divinity: students, fac-
ulty, and administrators.

Abbreviations

The abbreviations for the biblical books follow those provided by the *NJBC*, xxxi–xxxii. References to the Mishnah name the tractate, without any prefix, while references to the Babylonian Talmud have the prefix *b.* before the tractate and references to the Jerusalem Talmud have the prefix *j.* before the tractate. The *Midrashim Rabbah* are indicated by the abbreviation of the biblical book, followed by *R* (e.g., *ExodR*). All other references to Jewish, intertestamental, and patristic literature not mentioned below are given in full.

AB	Anchor Bible
ABD	D. N. Freedman, ed. *The Anchor Bible Dictionary*. 6 vols. New York: Doubleday, 1992.
ABRL	Anchor Bible Reference Library
AnBib	Analecta Biblica
ANRW	W. Haase and H. Temporini, eds. *Aufstieg und Niedergang der römischen Welt Teil II: Principat—Religion*. Berlin: Walter de Gruyter, 1979–84.
Aug	*Augustinianum*
AusBR	*Australian Biblical Review*
BAGD	W. Bauer, W. F. Arndt, F. W. Gingrich, and F. W. Danker, *A Greek-English Lexicon of the New Testament and Other Early Christian Literature*. 2d ed. Chicago: University of Chicago Press, 1979.

BBB   Bonner Biblische Beiträge
BBET   Beiträge zur biblischen Exegese und Theologie
BDF   F. Blass, A. Debrunner, and R. W. Funk, *A Greek Grammar of the New Testament and Other Early Christian Literature.* Chicago: University of Chicago Press, 1961.
BEB   Biblioteca Escuela Bíblica
BETL   Bibliotheca Ephemeridum Theologicae Lovaniensis
Bib   *Biblica*
BibInt   *Biblical Interpretation*
BibIntS Biblical Interpretation Series
BibOr   *Bibbia e Oriente*
BJ   Bible de Jérusalem
BK   *Bibel und Kirche*
BT   *The Bible Translator*
BTB   *Biblical Theology Bulletin*
BTS   Biblische theologische Studien
BZ   *Biblische Zeitschrift*
BZNW   Beihefte zur Zeitschrift für die Neutestamentliche Wissenschaft
CahRB   Cahiers de la Revue Biblique
CBQ   *Catholic Biblical Quarterly*
CCSL   Corpus Christianorum Series Latina. Turnhout: Brepols.
CD   Damascus Document
ConNT   Coniectanea Neotestamentica
DRev   *Downside Review*
Ebib   *Etudes bibliques*
ETL   *Ephemerides Theologicae Lovaniensis*
ETR   *Etudes théologiques et religieuses*
EvQ   *Evangelical Quarterly*
ExpT   *Expository Times*
FRLANT   Forschungen zur Religion und Literatur des Alten und Neuen Testaments
FThSt   Frankfurter theologische Studien
Greg   *Gregorianum*
HeyJ   *Heythrop Journal*
HKNT   Handkommentar zum Neuen Testament
HTCNT   Herder's Theological Commentary on the New Testament
HZNT   Handbuch zum Neuen Testament
ICC   International Critical Commentary
Int   *Interpretation*
JAAR   *Journal of the American Academy of Religion*
JB   Jerusalem Bible

JBL	*Journal of Biblical Literature*
JSNT	*Journal for the Study of the New Testament*
JSNTSup	Journal for the Study of the New Testament Supplement Series
JSOTSup	Journal for the Study of the Old Testament Supplement Series
JTS	*Journal of Theological Studies*
ktl.	Greek: *kai ta loipa* = et cetera
LAB	*Liber Antiquitatum Biblicarum*
LAS	Libreria Ateneo Salesiano
LD	Lectio Divina
LSJ	H. Liddell, R. Scott, and H. S. Jones, *A Greek-English Lexicon.* Oxford: Clarendon, 1968.
LTP	*Laval théologique et philosophique*
LXX	Septuagint
MSR	*Mélanges de Science Religieuse*
MT	Masoretic text
NCB	New Century Bible
NEchtB	Die neue Echter Bibel
Neot	*Neotestamentica*
NICNT	The New International Commentary on the New Testament
NJB	New Jerusalem Bible
NJBC	R. E. Brown, J. A. Fitzmyer, and R. E. Murphy, eds. *The New Jerome Biblical Commentary.* Englewood Cliffs: Prentice Hall, 1989.
NovT	*Novum Testamentum*
NovTSup	Supplements to Novum Testamentum
NRSV	New Revised Standard Version
NRT	*Nouvelle revue théologique*
NTAbh	Neutestamentliche Abhandlungen
NTS	*New Testament Studies*
NVB	Nuovissima Versione della Bibbia
ÖBS	Österreichisches Biblische Studien
ÖTB	Ökumenischer Taschenbuchkommentar zum Neuen Testament
PL	J. P. Migne, ed. Patrologiae cursus completus, series latina.
PNTC	Pelican New Testament Commentaries
RB	*Revue Biblique*
RevExp	*Review and Expositor*
RevScRel	*Revue des Sciences Religieuses*
RevThom	*Revue Thomiste*
RHPR	*Revue d'histoire et de philosophie religieuses*

RivBib	*Rivista Biblica*
RSR	*Recherche de science religieuse*
RSV	Revised Standard Version
RTL	*Revue Théologique de Louvain*
SANT	Studien zum Alten und Neuen Testament
SBB	Stuttgarter biblische Beiträge
SBFA	Studium Biblicum Franciscanum Analecta
SBLDS	Society of Biblical Literature Dissertation Series
SBLMS	Society of Biblical Literature Monograph Series
SBS	Stuttgarter Bibelstudien
SBT	Studies in Biblical Theology
ScEs	*Science et Esprit*
Sem	*Semeia*
SJLA	Studies in Judaism and Late Antiquity
SJT	*Scottish Journal of Theology*
SNTSMS	Society for New Testament Studies Monograph Series
SNTU	Studien zum Neuen Testament und seiner Umwelt
Str-B	H. Strack and P. Billerbeck, *Kommentar zum Neuen Testament aus Talmud und Midrasch.* 6 vols. Munich: C. H. Beck, 1922–61.
s.v.	sub voce
Tanḥ	*Midrash Tanḥuma*
TDNT	G. Kittel and G. Friedrich, eds. *Theological Dictionary of the New Testament.* 10 vols. Grand Rapids: Eerdmans, 1964–76.
Test	*Testament*
TOB	Traduction Oecuménique de la Bible
TS	*Theological Studies*
TTZ	*Trierer Theologische Zeitschrift*
TynBul	*Tyndale Bulletin*
UBSGNT	*Greek New Testament.* United Bible Society
VC	*Vigiliae Christianae*
VD	*Verbum Domini*
WBC	Word Biblical Commentary
WUNT	Wissenschaftliche Untersuchungen zum Neuen Testament
ZNW	*Zeitschrift für die Neutestamentliche Wissenschaft*

Chapter One

Jesus and the Sabbath
John 5:1-47

THE PROLOGUE (1:1-18) affirms that God's former gift through the Law of Moses is perfected by the fullness of the gift of the truth in Jesus Christ (1:16-17). There is no conflict between the two gifts; one leads to the other, but the latter gift of the truth through Jesus Christ surpasses the gift of the Law through Moses. It is the fullness of God's gracious gifts. In a journey from Cana to Cana (2:1—4:54) the reader learned that belief in Jesus is universally possible, both within and beyond Judaism. But how does Jesus relate to Israel's traditional approach to YHWH? For the Johannine Christians this is a serious question. While their former friends from Judaism are celebrating "the feasts of the Jews" (Sabbath, Passover, Tabernacles, and Dedication), they are barred from such celebrations.[1]

The celebration of a Jewish feast is a *zikkārôn,* which recalls God's active presence to his people in the past, *rendered present* in the liturgical celebration of the feast.[2] Had belief in Jesus of Nazareth, as the Christ, sepa-

---

[1] I place the expression "the Jews" (*hoi Ioudaioi*) in quotation marks to indicate that they are not the Jewish people. "The Jews" are one side of a christological debate. See F. J. Moloney, *Belief in the Word: Reading John 1–4* (Minneapolis: Fortress Press, 1993) 14–17. One must "recognise in these hot-tempered exchanges the type of family row in which the participants face one another across the room of a house which all have shared and all call home" (J. Ashton, *Understanding the Fourth Gospel* [Oxford: Clarendon Press, 1991] 151).

[2] See F. Chenderlin, *"Do This as My Memorial": The Semantic and Conceptual Background and Value of Anamnēsis in 1 Corinthians 11:24-25* (AnBib 99; Rome: Biblical Institute Press, 1982) 88–167.

rated the Johannine Christians from their traditional celebration of the presence of YHWH to his people, a celebration ordered by YHWH himself?[3] But the Johannine Christians were not the only ones who had to rethink the celebrations of Israel's experience of God. After the loss of the Temple in the post-70s of the first century, the survival of the Pharisees led to a shift from Temple to synagogue-centered worship.[4] Postwar Judaism had to rethink and restructure its celebrations. "The liturgical feasts of the temple and the piety of the people were in a state of transition and adaptation. The old order and way of life having gone for the most part, the new order under the Pharisees labored and strained to find authority and acceptance in the wider Jewish community."[5] This is the background for the narrator's indications of the celebration of major feasts in John 5–10 (see 5:9b; 6:4; 7:2; 10:22). Within this broader context of feasts, the narrative of 5:1-47, set on a Sabbath (see v. 9b), unfolds in three stages: (1) vv. 1-18: the miracle and its consequences; (2) vv. 19-30: a discourse on Jesus' Sabbath activity; (3) vv. 31-47: a discourse on witness and accusation.[6]

I. JESUS' HEALING WORK ON A SABBATH: 5:1-18

THE SHAPE OF THE NARRATIVE

The first words the reader encounters indicate that there was a feast of the Jews. There have been many attempts to resolve the question of what feast is indicated by this comment from the narrator.[7] No precise feast is either mentioned or intended, as 5:1a introduces the *theme* of feasts. If a feast must be attached to v. 1, then it is the Sabbath. But rather than an introduction to the feast behind the story of 5:1-47, "the feast of the Jews" announced in 5:1 is the narrator's way of indicating to the reader that a

---

[3] See ibid., 107.

[4] See W. D. Davies, *The Setting of the Sermon on the Mount* (Cambridge: Cambridge University Press, 1966) 256–72, on the post-Jamnian situation.

[5] G. A. Yee, *Jewish Feasts and the Gospel of John* (Zacchaeus Studies: New Testament; Wilmington: Michael Glazier, 1989) 21.

[6] This is a widely accepted division of the material. For a survey, see F. J. Moloney, *The Johannine Son of Man* (2d ed.; Biblioteca de Scienze Religiose 14; Rome: LAS, 1978) 70–77; and especially M. J. J. Menken, *Numerical Literary Techniques in John: The Fourth Evangelist's Use of Numbers of Words and Syllables* (NovTSup 55; Leiden: E. J. Brill, 1985) 114–15, 133–34 n. 51, 137. On the tradition history of 5:1-18, see L. T. Witkamp, "The Use of Traditions in John 5.1-18," *JSNT* 25 (1985) 19–31.

[7] The suggestions are: Tabernacles, Passover, Pentecost, Purim, and Rosh Hashanah. For a documented survey, see Moloney, *Son of Man*, 68 n. 3.

major change of direction is occurring. The issue of belief in Jesus has been dealt with (2:1–4:54); now the story must face other questions.[8]

Having established the theme of the feast (v. 1a) and located Jesus in Jerusalem (v. 1b), the narrator provides the setting of the pool of Bethesda and the reason for its importance (vv. 2-3).[9] Within this setting, the characters are introduced: a certain sick man (v. 5) and Jesus (v. 6), who dialogues with the sick man (vv. 6-8). This section leads to the miracle, associated with Jesus' command: "Rise, take up your pallet, and walk" (v. 8). The man wordlessly follows Jesus' commands (v. 9a). This description is immediately followed by a comment providing information crucial for the reader's appreciation of the dialogues and the monologue that follow: "Now that day was the Sabbath" (v. 9b). The Sabbath theme dominates the account of the miracle and its aftermath. Following the words and actions of any two active characters,[10] five scenes emerge. Four of the five scenes mention the Sabbath and the narrative has the following overall shape:[11]

I. *Verses 1-4:* Introduction
   (a) *Verse 1a:* Introduction to both 5:1-47 and the whole of 5:1—10:42.
   (b) *Verses 1b-4:* The setting for 5:1-47.
II. *Verses 5-18:* The Sabbath events
   (a) *Verses 5-9:* Jesus and the man. The miracle, concluding: "Now that day was a Sabbath."
   (b) *Verses 10-13:* "The Jews" and the man. The interrogation of a man who carried his pallet on a Sabbath.

---

[8] Against J. Becker, *Das Evangelium des Johannes* (2 vols.; ÖTB 4/1-2; Gütersloh: Gerd Mohn; Würzburg: Echter-Verlag, 1979, 1981) 1:230: "Das Fest is für Joh 5 sonst ohne Bedeutung."

[9] Archeological activity and the copper scroll from Qumran (3Q15 11:12) have led to an increasing agreement that "Bethesda" is to be preferred. See J. Jeremias, *Die Wiederentdeckung von Bethesda* (Göttingen: Vandenhoeck & Ruprecht, 1966); D. J. Weiand, "John V.2 and the Pool of Bethesda," *NTS* 12 (1965–66) 392–404; and especially A. Duprez, *Jésus et les dieux guérisseurs: A Propos de Jean V* (CahRB 12; Paris: Gabalda, 1970) 57–127. For a summary of the discussion, see W. D. Davies, *The Gospel and the Land: Early Christianity and Jewish Territorial Doctrine* (Berkeley: University of California Press, 1974) 302–13. It is generally agreed that vv. 3b-4 should be omitted. For a summary, see B. M. Metzger, *A Textual Commentary on the Greek New Testament* (London and New York: United Bible Society, 1971) 209. But some (e.g., Duprez, *Jésus,* 128–30; M.-E. Boismard and A. Lamouille, *L'Evangile de Jean* [Synopse des Quatres Evangiles en Français III; Paris: Cerf, 1977] 152–53) argue for their authenticity.

[10] See J. L. Martyn, *History and Theology in the Fourth Gospel* (Nashville: Abingdon, 1979) 26–27.

[11] See also R. A. Culpepper, "John 5.1-18: A Sample of Narrative Critical Commentary," in *The Gospel of John as Literature: An Anthology of Twentieth Century Perspectives,* ed. M. W. G. Stibbe (NT Tools and Studies 17; Leiden: E. J. Brill, 1993) 198-202.

(c) *Verse 14:* Jesus and the man. Separated from the rest of the action by the expression *meta tauta,* this encounter makes no mention of the Sabbath.

(d) *Verse 15:* "The Jews" and the man. The man informs "the Jews" that Jesus performed the miracle on the Sabbath.

(e) *Verses 16-18:* Jesus and "the Jews." "The Jews" put Jesus on trial, seeking to kill him for his Sabbath offense.

Sabbath is crucial to the story. "The Jews" have one understanding of the right way to worship God on the Sabbath, but Jesus has another.

READING THE NARRATIVE

The expression *meta tauta* (5:1; see 2:12; 3:22; 4:43) indicates that the story is taking a new direction.[12] This is further reinforced by the general indication that *ēn heortē tōn Ioudaiōn,*[13] and that Jesus has gone up from Cana in Galilee (see 4:46-54) to Jerusalem (v. 1). The reader has been taken from the Galilean setting of a miracle in 4:46-54, where a Gentile displayed his belief in the word of Jesus, to another context: a Jewish feast in Jerusalem. The action is suspended briefly, as a precise location in Jerusalem is described: "Now at the Sheep-Pool in Jerusalem there is a place with five colonnades. Its name in the language of the Jews is Bethesda."[14] Despite the difficulties involved in deciding on the accuracy of the detail of the description,[15] the existence of a pool long associated with healing, including pagan healing, at the northern corner of Jerusalem opposite the Antonia Fortress, is now well established.[16] The further

---

[12] See ibid., 196–97.

[13] Reading the text without a definite article, as do almost all scholars. See W. Bauer, *Das Johannesevangelium erklärt* (3d ed.; HKNT 6; Tübingen: J. C. B. Mohr [Paul Siebeck] 1933) 79–81.

[14] This translation, following R. E. Brown, *The Gospel According to John* (2 vols.; AB 29, 29A; Garden City, N.Y.: Doubleday, 1966, 1970) 1:206, is based on the text as it is found in P66, P75, and Vaticanus. There is considerable disturbance of the text here, due to the scribal insertion of vv. 3b-4. See the discussion in C. K. Barrett, *The Gospel According to St John* (2d ed.; London: SPCK, 1978) 251, and G. D. Fee, "On the Inauthenticity of John 5:3b-4," *EvQ* 54 (1982) 207–18.

[15] R. Schnackenburg, *The Gospel according to St John* (3 vols.; HTCNT 4/1-3; London: Burns & Oates; New York: Crossroad, 1968–82) 2:94, accepts Jeremias's conclusions, but J. A. T. Robinson, *The Priority of John* (London: SCM Press, 1985) 54, describes them as "a construct of the imagination." For a symbolic interpretation of the colonnades see J. Marsh, *The Gospel of Saint John* (PNTC; Harmondsworth: Penguin Books, 1968) 245–46; but against symbolism in 5:1-18, see H. van der Loos, *The Miracles of Jesus* (NovTSup 8; Leiden: E. J. Brill, 1961) 461–63.

[16] See Duprez, *Jésus,* 57–127.

description of the people gathered in the colonnades as invalids, blind, lame, and paralyzed (v. 4) "clearly suggests its continuity as a place of healing (going perhaps right back to Canaanite times)."[17] It is within this context of a Jewish feast and a traditional healing site that Jesus saw a man who had been ill for thirty-eight years (vv. 5-6). A miraculous knowledge of the man's situation recalls to the reader Jesus' encounter with Nathanael in 1:47-48, and with the Samaritan woman in 4:18. Jesus' question, after v. 5, seems superfluous: "*theleis hygiēs genesthai?*" (v. 6b), but it raises the possibility of a healing that, in turn, enables a dialogue.

The man's response to Jesus shows his unawareness of who Jesus is.[18] The reader sees ignorance in the man who responds to Jesus: *kyrie, anthrōpon ouk echō* (v. 7). The man seeks another human being who can see to his physical needs so that the healing might happen.[19] The reader knows who Jesus is and what he can do (see 4:46-54).[20] The irony of the limitations of the man's response is obvious.[21] Jesus' command, "Rise, take up your pallet, and walk" (v. 8), is followed by the exact repetition of those words in the description of the man's response (v. 9b). But between the command and the response there is an indication that something happened, *egeneto hygiēs*: the man was made well (v. 9a) through the word of Jesus.[22] The reader recalls the same chain of events in the previous miracle story. Jesus told the royal official that his son was alive, and the man accepted the word of Jesus and set off for home, to find his son cured (4:50-53). There are some preliminary indications in this man's story that he may be on a journey to true faith. Although he began without understanding who Jesus was and what he could offer (v. 7), he has responded unquestioningly to the word of Jesus (v. 9b).[23]

[17] Robinson, *Priority,* 57.

[18] See Barrett, *St John,* 254.

[19] Bauer, *Johannesevangelium,* 51, points out that *anthrōpos* may mean "slave." On the movement of the water and the placing of the sick in it, see Robinson, *Priority,* 57–59.

[20] On the links between 4:46-54 and 5:1-18 see C. H. Dodd, *The Interpretation of the Fourth Gospel* (Cambridge: Cambridge University Press, 1953) 318–20; A. Feuillet, "La signification du second miracle de Cana (Jean IV, 46-54)," in *Etudes Johanniques* (Bruges: Desclée, 1962) 34–46.

[21] See R. A. Culpepper, *Anatomy of the Fourth Gospel: A Study in Literary Design* (Foundation and Facets; Philadelphia: Fortress Press, 1983) 171; S. van Tilborg, *Imaginative Love in John* (BibIntS 2; Leiden: E. J. Brill, 1993) 215–16.

[22] The word *hygiēs* is found in John only in 5:11, 14, 15, and 7:23, which looks back to the miracle in John 5. On the relationship between John 5 and 7:14-24, see S. Pancaro, *The Law in the Fourth Gospel: The Torah and the Gospel, Moses and Jesus, Judaism and Christianity according to John* (NovTSup 42; Leiden: E. J. Brill, 1975) 169–74.

[23] D. R. Beck, "The Narrative Function of Anonymity in Fourth Gospel Characterization," *Sem* 63 (1993) 143–58, argues that anonymous characters draw the reader into the narrative and an identification with the character, culminating with the anonymous Beloved Disciple

The narrator's comment, which closes the account of the miracle, "Now that day was the Sabbath" (v. 9c), warns the reader that difficulties could arise from the events reported: the man carried his pallet in obedience to the command of Jesus (vv. 8-9).[24] The incipient faith of the man will surely be put to the test as he has carried his pallet on a Sabbath. This is unacceptable (see *Shabbat* 7:2; see also 10:5; Exod 20:8-11; Jer 17:19-27).[25] "The Jews" enter the story accusing the man of unlawful Sabbath work (v. 10). But the man will not accept responsibility for his actions; he did what he was asked to do by the stranger who commanded him to take up his pallet and walk (v. 11). The central issue emerges: the person of Jesus.[26] "The Jews" want to know *tis estin ho anthrōpos*; (v. 12), but the narrator can only report that the cured man *ouk ēdei tis estin* (v. 13a). Two issues crucial to the narrative have now emerged: the celebration of the Sabbath and the identity of Jesus.[27]

The only scene in the drama that does not mention the Sabbath follows (v. 14). It opens with *meta tauta* (see 2:12; 3:22; 4:43; 5:1), a Johannine indication of time that separates the brief encounter between Jesus and the cured man in the Temple from the surrounding narrative. Jesus takes the initiative and finds the man in the Temple. The Jewish institution of the Sabbath is laid to one side for a moment, and in its place one finds the Jewish institution of the Temple. His words to the cured man recall the initial question of Jesus (v. 6) and the report of the miracle (v. 11): "See you are made well" (*ide hygiēs gegonas*).[28] Jesus does not dwell on the man's physical condition, but transcends the issues raised by the miracle. He commands: "Sin no more." Sin will lead the man to be worse off than before. Someone more than "a man" (see v. 7), more than a miracle worker, speaks in the Temple with an authority that transcends human authority. Jesus is transcending the chronological (v. 9c), theological, and legal (v. 10) Sabbath background of the reported events. The reader accepts Jesus' association of the physical healing of the man with his greater offer of eternal life (see 1:4; 3:15-16, 36; 4:14, 36). The rabbis associated sin with

---

from chap. 13 onward. On "the man" in John 5, see p. 151, but by v. 15 the reader would no longer identify with a character who is in league with "the Jews."

[24] On this, see J. L. Staley, "Stumbling in the Dark, Reaching for the Light: Reading Characters in John 5 and 9," *Sem* 53 (1991) 59-60. J. Painter, *The Quest for the Messiah: The History, Literature and Theology of the Johannine Community* (2d ed.; Edinburgh: T. & T. Clark, 1993) 216, shows the importance of this comment.

[25] See J. C. Thomas, "The Fourth Gospel and Rabbinic Judaism," *ZNW* 82 (1991) 169-72.

[26] See Staley, "Stumbling in the Dark," 60–61.

[27] Pancaro, *Law*, 9–16, shows that a traditional miracle story has been rewritten to make central the relationship between Jesus, the Law, and the Sabbath.

[28] See X. Léon-Dufour, *Lecture de l'Evangile selon Jean* (3 vols.; Paris: Seuil, 1988–93) 2:22.

God's punishment through suffering and death,[29] but Jesus, on the basis of what has already been said of him in the prologue (see 1:4) and the promise of his own words (see 3:15-16; 4:14, 36), shows an authority as life-giver and judge.[30] The reader senses that Jesus has been granted functions traditionally allowed to God alone. Thus Jesus proclaims that the man who is now whole physically must not sin if he wishes to retain his wholeness into eternal life.[31] In the house of God (see 2:16) Jesus speaks in the name of God. The characters in the story will continue to debate the Sabbath issue, but the reader of the story has been reminded that such issues are transcended by Jesus.

The narrator separates Jesus and the man by reporting that the latter "went away" (v. 15a: *apēlthen ho anthrōpos*). There is no hint of the man's "following" Jesus (see 1:37, 38, 40, 43), or accepting his word (see 2:5; 3:29; 4:42, 50). The man goes away from Jesus to report to "the Jews" that their question now has an answer: "It was Jesus who had healed him" (v. 15). The man is making no progress. Unlike the characters portrayed in the journeys of faith in the Cana to Cana section of the Gospel (2:1–4:54), this man goes away from Jesus, and is thus only able to speak of "Jesus" to protagonists called "the Jews."[32] Their hostility to Jesus has already been glimpsed in their rejection of his word in a scene in the Temple (see 2:18-20). The man who has been cured is only able to provide "the Jews" with the name of a human being, without any further qualification or manifestation of belief in his word or person, despite Jesus' authoritative intervention in the Temple. There he revealed himself to the man as someone who transcends both Sabbath and Temple (v. 14), but the words of Jesus from this encounter are not recalled. The possibilities offered to the man in the Temple disappear from his story. The reader is aware of a failure in faith. The man has not moved since his original response to Jesus in v. 7. There he said, *kyrie, anthrōpon ouk echō*, and in his report to "the Jews" he tells *hoti Iēsous estin ho poiēsas auton hygiē* (v. 15). The man Jesus made him well.[33]

The narrator introduces the final section dealing with the miracle and its aftermath with a comment upon the decision of "the Jews": *kai dia*

---

[29] See Schnackenburg, *St John,* 2:461 n. 20.

[30] See B. Lindars, *The Gospel of John* (NCB; London: Oliphants, 1972) 217.

[31] Admittedly, the expressions "life" or "eternal life" are not found here. However, the idea lies behind the threat of death involved in *hina mē cheiron soi ti genētai.* See R. H. Lightfoot, *St. John's Gospel,* ed. C. F. Evans (Oxford: Oxford University Press, 1956) 141.

[32] See Culpepper, "John 5.1-18," 204–5.

[33] Staley, "Stumbling in the Dark," 58–64, shows that the reader understands the man as going nowhere in faith, but rightly insists on his subordination to a plot that is highlighted by Jesus' transcending the Sabbath.

touto ediōkon hoi Ioudaioi ton Iēsoun (v. 16). The verb *diōkein* is universally translated as "to persecute."[34] But this is not the only meaning of the word. The verb is used to mean "to bring a charge against," "to prosecute."[35] Given the use of the word to mean "persecute" across the New Testament,[36] a subtle insinuation of both meanings may be involved here. Jesus has offended against the Jewish Law, and it was the responsibility of the religious authorities to bring a charge against him, to convict him, and to punish him.[37] This leads to a constant persecution of Jesus,[38] because he did these things (*tauta*) on a Sabbath. It is not simply his command to the man to carry his pallet, so clearly an offense, but also his healing miracle, giving life to the sick man, which is performed on a Sabbath. A trial is under way, and Jesus' response to the beginnings of his trial and the persecution of the Jews is the linchpin for the chapter,[39] and it depends upon Jewish Sabbath theology. Jesus answers: "My Father is working still, and I am working" (v. 17).[40] It was clear to Jewish thinkers that God could not rest on the Sabbath; as his creation continued, people died and were thus judged, children were born, and thus life was given. God could not cease to be active, even on the Sabbath, or else history would come to an end (see especially *b. Taʿanit* 2a). But this prerogative of God could not be usurped by any creature. Sabbath exists for the worship of the Deity and the public recognition of his unique lordship.[41]

But Jesus includes himself under the rubric of his Father who works on the Sabbath: "My Father is working still, and I am working." The claim of Jesus is blasphemy to "the Jews" (see Gen 3:5; Isa 14:14; Ezekiel 28; Dan 11:31-36; 2 Macc 9:12), but not to the reader who knows that Jesus is the Word become flesh, who has taken up his dwelling among us (see 1:14).

[34] See, for example, the translations of RSV, NRSV, JB, NJB, BJ, TOB.

[35] See LSJ, 440, s.v., para. IV.

[36] See BAGD, 201, s.v., para. 2.

[37] For this interpretation of *diōkein* in v. 16, see A. E. Harvey, *Jesus on Trial: A Study in the Fourth Gospel* (London: SPCK, 1976) 50–51.

[38] The verb is in the imperfect tense, and thus indicates a repeated action.

[39] See Pancaro, *Law*, 54–56.

[40] For the following, see *Mekilta Shabbata* 2:25; *GenR* 11:5, 10, 12; *ExodR* 30:6, 9; *b. Taʿanit* 2a. See also Philo, *De Cherubim* 86-90; *Legum Allegoria* 1.5-6; *Letter of Aristeas* 210. See Dodd, *Interpretation*, 320–23, and the comprehensive excursus in J. Bernard, "La guérison de Bethesda: Harmoniques judéo-hellénistiques d'un récit de miracle un jour de sabbat," *MSR* 33 (1976) 13–34.

[41] For good syntheses of the biblical and rabbinic understanding of Sabbath, see J. Morgenstern, "Sabbath," *IDB* 4 (1962) 135–41; G. F. Hasel, "Sabbath," *ABD* 5:849–56. Detailed bibliography is provided in these studies. Sabbath was a "memory" (*zakkôr*: see Exod 20:8) of a creating (see Gen 2:2-3; Exod 20:8-11) and redeeming (see Deut 5:15) God that rendered that God present to his people. It celebrated his lordship as creator and redeemer, and called on the people to recognize publicly this lordship.

For the reader, Jesus' claims are not a refusal of the Jewish Sabbath traditions, but the Johannine rereading of them. Jesus has claimed that *his
Father* works on the Sabbath. He points out that the Father is working *heōs
arti*: until now, the present time. It is not as if God has stopped working.[42]
YHWH remains God of the Sabbath, but the issue is one of relationship.
Jesus' claim to work on the Sabbath depends upon his relationship with
the God of Israel, whom he calls "my Father" (v. 17).[43]

"The Jews" interpret Jesus' actions and words accurately. According to
the criteria that they use in the process of judging Jesus, he offends on
three scores:

1. He has broken the Sabbath by telling the man to carry his pallet and
   by healing (v. 18b).[44]
2. He has called God his own Father by claiming that the one who
   works on the Sabbath is his Father (v. 18c).
3. He has made himself equal to God by claiming that just as God is
   able to work on the Sabbath, so is he (v. 18d).

It is Jesus' relationship with God that demands a new way of understanding the Sabbath. Jesus' encounter with the cured man in the Temple has
already shown that he transcends the Sabbath (v. 14). It is the logical consequence of the authoritative word of the narrator in the prologue (1:1-
18), of Jesus' authoritative word in his response to Nicodemus (3:11-21),
and of the narrator's authoritative commentary upon the final witness of
John the Baptist (3:31-36).[45]

The response of Jesus to "the Jews" in v. 17 and their *correct* understanding of it in their terms in v. 18 paves the way for the discourse that follows
in vv. 19-47. "They can only understand equality with God as independence from God, whereas for Jesus it means the very opposite, as is
brought out immediately in v. 19."[46] Ironically, "the Jews" have expressed
a true understanding of Jesus. He cannot be controlled by the Sabbath

[42] See G. Ferraro, "Il senso di *heōs arti* in Giov. 5,17," *RivBib* 20 (1972) 529–45.

[43] As Brown, *John*, 1:213, has pointed out, only here and in v. 19 is the verb *apokrinasthai*
used in the middle voice.

[44] If the verb *elyen* means "he did away with" rather than "he loosened" or "he broke,"
"the Jews" would be wrong. He is not abolishing the Sabbath; he is interpreting it in terms of
his relationship to the Father.

[45] Jesus and the narrator are the most authoritative voices in the story. See D. Foster, "John
Come Lately: The Belated Evangelist," in *The Bible and the Narrative Tradition*, ed. F.
McConnell (New York: Oxford University Press, 1986) 113–31.

[46] See R. Bultmann, *The Gospel of John: A Commentary* (Oxford: Blackwell, 1971) 245. On
the development and significance of this claim for the Johannine community, see W. A.
Meeks, "Equal to God," in *The Conversation Continues: Studies in Paul & John: In Honor of
J. Louis Martyn*, ed. R. T. Fortna and B. R. Gaventa (Nashville: Abingdon Press, 1990) 309–21.

laws; God is his Father, and he can lay claim to equality with God.[47] The reader knows that these claims are true from 1:2: "What God was, the Word also was." But "the Jews," on the basis of their understanding of Jesus' words and actions within the limitations of their traditional Sabbath laws and practices, "sought all the more to kill him" (v. 18a). Within the Jewish legal system Jesus' claim to be equal to God is blasphemous. He must be executed (see Lev 24:10-16; Num 15:30-31).[48] The possibilities of violence and death (vv. 16-18) have replaced the earlier attitude of hostility and the rejection of his word (see 2:18-20). The reader will see the relationship between Jesus and "the Jews" deteriorate steadily from this point on.

A trial has been set in motion in which the two sides have different answers to the same question. Jesus has reinterpreted the Sabbath traditions on the basis of his relationship with the God of Israel, his Father. "The Jews" seek to kill him. The reader follows a crisis created by the clash between the Jewish and the Christian understanding of the Sabbath and the Lord of the Sabbath. Jesus claims to be the Son of God, able to give life and to judge.[49] From the perspective of "the Jews," there is only one God, YHWH the Lord of the Sabbath, life-giver and judge. "The one acting with the authority of God comes into conflict with the human custodians and exponents of God's law."[50] During the court scene that follows, Jesus may be the only one who speaks, but "the Jews" are always present.

II. LIFE AND JUDGMENT: 5:19-30

THE SHAPE OF THE NARRATIVE

In vv. 19-47 Jesus speaks his own defense.[51] It opens with a concentration upon the themes of life and judgment (see v. 21: life; v. 22: judgment; v. 24: life and judgment; v. 25: life; v. 26: life; v. 27: judgment; vv. 28-29: life and judgment). On arrival at v. 30 the reader meets, although now spoken in

---

[47] See Culpepper, Anatomy, 171.

[48] On Sabbath and blasphemy legislation, and the Johannine tendency to have Jesus breach it, see Harvey, Trial, 67–81.

[49] The themes of giving life and judging, so closely linked to the theme of the Sabbath, play little role in T. L. Brodie's analysis of vv. 19-29 in the light of creation (rather than Sabbath) themes (The Gospel According to John: A Literary and Theological Commentary [New York: Oxford University Press, 1993] 246–50).

[50] Schnackenburg, St John, 2:97.

[51] Léon-Dufour, Lecture, 2:40–42, describes vv. 19-47 as a "plaidoirie." See also Harvey, Trial, 46–66.

the first person, a repetition of what Jesus said of the Son and the Father in v. 19:

v. 19: The son can do nothing of his own accord.
       ou dynatai ho huios poiein aph' heautou ouden.
v. 30: I can do nothing on my own accord.
       ou dynamai egō poiein ap' emautou ouden.

But despite the unity of theme, critical problems emerge. Apparently conflicting eschatological perspectives appear in vv. 24-25 and vv. 28-29: vv. 24-25 presuppose a thoroughly Johannine realized eschatology, while vv. 28-29 resort to a traditional end-time eschatology.[52] There have been many attempts to see vv. 19-30 as a chiasm,[53] but the consistent discussion of life and judgment is interrupted in v. 23, where Jesus speaks directly to his audience about the honor due to the Son of the Father.[54] The interplay of ideas and themes produces a discourse shaped as follows:

(a) *Verses 19-20*: Theological introduction: the relationship of love that exists between the Father and the Son produces a dependence of the Son upon the Father. This relationship and dependence could bear fruit for those listening to the discourse.

(b) *Verse 21*: As the Father gives life, so also the Son *exercises* an authority to give life. The key expression is the verb *zōiopoiein:* to give life.

(c) *Verse 22*: The *basis* of the Son's authority to judge is explained: The Father has given all judgment to the Son: *ho patēr . . . dedōken.*

(d) *Verse 23*: Theological reflection: The themes of life and judgment disappear, as Jesus speaks directly to his audience. He pauses to remind them that the God whom they honor is his Father, and that the honor they give to the Father of the Son must also be given to the Son.

---

[52] For the discussion, see Moloney, *Son of Man,* 72–74, and A. Stimpfle, *Blinde sehen: Die Eschatologie im traditionsgeschichtlichen Prozess des Johannesevangeliums* (BZNW 57; Berlin: de Gruyter, 1990) 74–93.

[53] For a critical survey, see Moloney, *Son of Man,* 74–76. Since then, see Bernard, "La guérison," *MSR* 34 (1977) 17–20; S. A. Panimolle, *Lettura Pastorale del Vangelo di Giovanni* (3 vols.; Bologna: Dehoniane, 1978–84) 2:29–30; P. F. Ellis, *The Genius of John: A Composition-Critical Commentary on the Fourth Gospel* (Collegeville: Liturgical Press, 1984) 90–93; G. Mlakuzhyil, *The Christocentric Literary Structure of the Fourth Gospel* (AnBib 117; Rome: Biblical Institute Press, 1987) 126–28.

[54] Not even the carefully constructed chiasm of A. Vanhoye, "La composition de Jean 5,19-30," in *Mélanges Bibliques en hommage au R. P. Béda Rigaux,* ed. A. Descamps and A. de Halleux (Gembloux: Duculot, 1970) 270–74, escapes the difficulty of v. 23. His C (vv. 21-23) leaves v. 23 without any genuine parallel in his C¹ (vv. 26-27).

(e) *Verses 24-25*: The Son is presented as the one who gives life, but closely associated with his life-giving is the subtheme of judgment. The urgency of the situation is expressed by the words *erchetai hōra . . . akousousin tēs phonēs*.

(f) *Verse 26*: The *basis* of the Son's authority to give life is explained: The Father has granted the Son to have life in himself: *ho patēr . . . edōken*.

(g) *Verse 27*: The Father no longer judges, as he has now granted the Son the authority to *exercise* all judgment, as the Son of Man. The key expression is *krisin poiein*.

(h) *Verses 28-29*: The Son is presented as the one who judges, but closely associated with his judging is the subtheme of his giving life. The urgency of the situation is expressed by the words *erchetai hōra . . . akousousin tēs phonēs*.

(i) *Verse 30*: Theological conclusion: The relationship between the one who sends and the sent one produces a total dependence of the latter upon the former. This relationship and dependence could bear the fruit of just judgment for those who are listening to the discourse.

The reader accepts that Jesus is the best person to answer the questions that arise directly from the Sabbath miracle.[55] No one has ever seen God, but his only begotten Son tells his story (see 1:18). The literary form shifts from a narrative built upon action and dialogue (vv. 5-18) to a monologue (vv. 19-30). However, there are still two players in the drama: Jesus who speaks the discourse, and "the Jews" who are addressed.

READING THE NARRATIVE

The words of v. 19 respond directly to the problem that Jesus' Sabbath activity created for "the Jews" (v. 18).[56] Jesus argues his defense on the basis of truths about a relationship between the Son and the Father that are not entirely new for the reader, but that offend "the Jews." Toward the end of the prologue the terms used to express the relationship between *ho theos* and *ho logos* (see 1:1-5) became *ho pater* and *ho huios* (1:14, 18). The Son was identified as Jesus Christ (1:17) who now delivers this discourse, speaking in the third person of the Son and the Father. Further informa-

---

[55] Against Lindars, *John,* 219, who claims that vv. 19-47 leave the Sabbath issue to one side.

[56] The use of *oun* by the narrator indicates to the reader that what follows is linked to what has just been read. The double "amen," found only in the Fourth Gospel (24 times), introduces a statement that links what has been said and done to what follows. On this, see J. H. Bernard, *A Critical and Exegetical Commentary on the Gospel According to St. John* (2 vols.; ICC; Edinburgh: T. & T. Clark, 1928) 1:67.

tion on the Father-Son relationship was provided in two parallel mono-
logues that concluded Jesus' encounter with Nicodemus (3:16, 17, 18) and
the final witness of the Baptist (3:35, 36). Now the author elaborates,
through the discourse beginning with 5:19, on *how* Jesus is the Son of the
Father and the activity and authority that this relationship generates.[57]

For Israel there was only one Lord of the Sabbath, and the celebration of
the Sabbath existed to render honor and praise to YHWH. Jesus' defense
does not eliminate the necessity for the Sabbath God. God, whom Jesus
now calls Father, does not lose any of his authority. Jesus does not claim to
replace God in any way. For "the Jews" Jesus' claim to equality was a claim
to independence from the Father's authority, to equality of status, "as if
Jesus were setting himself up as a rival to God."[58] But the term *isos*, used
by "the Jews" to accuse Jesus of making himself equal to God (v. 18), never
appears on Jesus' lips. It would be inappropriate.[59] All that the Son is and
does flows from his Father. The negative structure of the sentence, *ou
dynatai ho huios poiein aph' heautou ouden*, strikes this chord in the reader.
The stress is upon the *ouden*: the Son can do *nothing*. The Son is not
another Sabbath God, but totally dependent. God remains the Lord of the
Sabbath.[60] However, Sonship allows Jesus the privilege of intimacy. He sees
what the Father does, and is thus able to do exactly what the Father has
done. The use of the expression *ho huios homoiōs poiei* looks back to v. 17:
"My Father is working still, and I am working." The reader has no illusions
about the primacy of God. The Father is working *heōs arti* (see v. 17). However, the Son of the Father has entered the human story (see 1:14; 3:16),
and thus something new is happening. As the Father does, so also does the
Son (v. 19b).

The nature of the relationship between the Father and the Son is
described as one of love (v. 20). It is not every father who shows his son all
that he is doing (*panta deiknysin autō autos poiei*). In this relationship
there are no secrets.[61] Because of the relationship of love between the
Father and his Son "greater works" (*meizona*) than the works already wit-

---

[57] Many scholars (e.g., Dodd, Gächter, Brown, Lindars, Panimolle, Talbert) have seen a traditional parable on a son's relationship to his father behind this passage. See Moloney, *Son of
Man*, 72–75. Whatever the tradition behind the passage, the absolute use of *ho huios* points to
one of the author's most important christological claims for Jesus. See G. Segalla, *Giovanni*
(NVB; Rome: Edizioni Paoline, 1976) 213; and especially Ashton, *Understanding*, 292–329.

[58] Pancaro, *Law*, 55.

[59] See Léon-Dufour, *Lecture*, 2:40.

[60] The use of *ekeinos* instead of *houtos* to say "whatever he does" in reference to God in
v. 19c "lays stress on the separate divine Person" (Barrett, *St John*, 259).

[61] Reflected in the use of *panta*. See Barrett, *St John*, 259. See also E. C. Hoskyns, *The Fourth
Gospel*, ed. F. N. Davey (London: Faber & Faber, 1947) 267–68, on the importance of the love
relationship.

nessed will be shown to the Son, so that "you (*hymeis*) may marvel" (v. 20b). The explicit use of the second person plural pronoun addresses the audience of "the Jews." They are offered the possibility of being drawn into the relationship of love between the Father and the Son that is not self-contained. There is more to be seen and more to be marveled at as Jesus' listeners are promised they could be part of a revelation of God that reaches beyond their Sabbath expectations.[62]

The wonders that Jesus' listeners might eventually witness are explained. Formerly, only the God of Israel was understood as having the privilege of raising the dead and giving life (see 1 Sam 2:6; Deut 32:39; Isa 25:8; Wis 16:13; 2 Kgs 5:7). In the miracle, Jesus commanded the sick man "rise" (v. 8: *egeire*). But the authority to raise the dead (v. 21a: *egeirei*) belongs to the Father. Only the Lord of the Sabbath is the master of life and death, but because of the relationship that exists between the Father and the Son, God has passed this privilege on to the Son. The Son exercises the authority to give life (v. 21b: *zōiopoiein*). From this statement of the Son's exercising Sabbath authority, Jesus passes on to explain the basis of a further authority. God also judges (see Pss 67:5; 94:2; 105:7; Isa 2:4; 26:9; 33:22; Mic 4:3; Ezek 30:3), but Jesus affirms that the Father judges no one (v. 22). In a shift from traditional Jewish thought, the reader is now informed that all judgment has been given over to the Son (v. 22: *ho patēr . . . tēn krisin pasan dedōken tǭ huiǭ*). Two major Sabbath activities have now been associated with Jesus, as the Son of the Father. He exercises a life-giving authority (v. 21), and the exercising of judgment has been given to him (v. 22).[63]

Jesus' argument in defense of his claim to be working as his Father is working (v. 17) pauses, as he addresses—almost accuses—his audience. The trial, the persecution, and the plot to kill Jesus (see vv. 16 and 18) lie behind Jesus' threat. Israel claims to honor God, life-giver and judge, on the Sabbath. But "the Jews" are trying, persecuting, and plotting to kill his Son. This is an impossible contradiction. Jesus' authority to give life and to judge has been granted to him by God, his Father, so that the honor which "the Jews" claim to give to God will also be given to Jesus. In attempting to kill Jesus, they are honoring neither the Son, nor the Father. Their claims to the proper observance of the Sabbath are empty.[64]

---

[62] Some interpreters claim that the *meizona* refer to Jesus' more spectacular works (healing of the blind man [chap. 9] and the raising of Lazarus [chap. 11]). The "greater works" are not Jesus' further miracles, but the life and judgment that he brings. See Schnackenburg, *St John*, 2:104–5.

[63] See Léon-Dufour, *Lecture*, 2:48–53.

[64] See C. H. Talbert, *Reading John: A Literary and Theological Commentary on the Fourth Gospel and the Johannine Epistles* (New York: Crossroad, 1992) 126.

Jesus now returns to a further development of his exercising of the authority to give life. Associated with the twofold use of the double "amen" is the indication that Jesus is still speaking to "the Jews": *legō hymin*. The section running from Cana to Cana (2:1—4:54) has taught the reader that the believer listens to the word of Jesus, the Sent One of God (see 3:17, 48; 4:34). Hearing the word of Jesus and having faith in the one who sent him produces eternal life (5:24). It is not surprising that now the participles *akouōn* and *pisteuōn* are applied to the person who has *zōē aiōnion* (v. 24).[65] However, the teaching of Jesus on life cannot be detached from his teaching on judgment that enters here, in this Sabbath discourse, as a subtheme. To have eternal life through hearing the word of Jesus means that there can be no judgment. The believer has already passed from death to life (see also 3:15-16, 17-18, 19).[66] Those who listen to the voice of the Son of God will pass from death to life (v. 25).[67] This passage from death to life is not a future promise; it happens now. The hour is coming, and is already present. There is no need to wait for the traditional end time for the fullness of life. The passage from death to life is a passage from sinfulness, ignorance, and the world where God is not properly God, to a right understanding of God and his ways in the human story. Jesus is the one who offers light and life in such darkness (see 1:4). Here we have a clear expression of Johannine realized eschatology. The hour is coming, and now is. The event of Jesus Christ does not remove the celebration of the Sabbath, but on the Sabbath festival (see 5:9b) Jesus is proclaimed as the source of life and judgment—now (v. 25).[68]

Jesus now indicates the basis of the Son's authority. The Jewish tradition has no difficulty with the first part of Jesus' teaching: the Father has life in himself. The difficulty arises from the *hōsper gar . . . houtōs kai*.[69] What is traditionally accepted of God has now been given to Jesus. On the theological basis of v. 19, Jesus affirms that, as with judgment (see v. 22), the Father has granted to the Son also to have life in himself (*ho patēr . . . tǭ huiǭ edōken zōēn echein en heautǭ*). Jesus speaks first of the Son's exercising of his life-giving authority (v. 21: *zōiopoiein*) and only toward the end

---

[65] See Schnackenburg, *St John*, 2:108–9; Panimolle, *Giovanni*, 2:45. On "life" and "eternal life," see J. G. van der Watt, "The Use of *aiōnios* in the Concept *zōē aiōnios* in John's Gospel," *NovT* 31 (1989) 217–28.

[66] See G. R. Beasley-Murray, *John* (WBC 36; Waco: Word Books, 1987) 76: "The strongest affirmation of realized eschatology . . . in the NT."

[67] Stimpfle, *Blinde sehen*, 84, rightly points to the use of the future tense (*akousousin, zēsousin*) in vv. 24-25 as already looking toward vv. 28-29.

[68] See J. Blank, *Krisis: Untersuchungen zur johanneischen Christologie und Eschatologie* (Freiburg: Lambertus-Verlag, 1964) 134–40.

[69] See Barrett, *St John*, 260, 262.

of this discussion on life-giving and judgment does he provide the theological basis for such activity (v. 26: the Father). He has dealt with the
judgment theme by first providing the basis of the Son's authority to
judge (v. 22: the Father), and only toward the end of the discourse does he
present the Son's judging activity (v. 27: *krisin poiein*).[70]

The introduction of the Son's exercising his function as judge (v. 27)
leads into another eschatological perspective. In speaking of the Son's life-
giving authority, a realized eschatological perspective taught that life was
available *now*: the hour is coming *and now is* (vv. 24-25). The Son's authority as judge (v. 27) introduces a section that looks toward a future coming
of the hour, the future resurrection of the dead: the hour is coming (vv.
28-29).[71] Whatever may have been the history of the traditions that stand
behind the juxtaposition of eschatological perspectives in vv. 25-29,[72] the
author placed them side by side intentionally. The Father has given
authority to execute judgment. As with the Father's life-giving authority,
this does not mean that God does not maintain his Sabbath Lordship, but
the judging *function* has now been passed on to the Son: "because he is
Son of Man." The reader recalls that in the Son of Man the heavenly will
be made visible (1:50-51). Only the Son of Man, who has come from
heaven, is able to reveal the heavenly things (3:13). However, this revelation will take place through his being lifted up, as Moses had lifted up the
serpent on a stake, so that all who believed in him might have eternal life
(3:14-15; see Num 21:8-9). In 5:27, a further feature of Jesus as the Son of
Man is added that develops the suggestion of 3:15. If the revelation of God
through the lifting up of the Son of Man can bring eternal life, it might
also produce death and darkness. Not only does Jesus, the Son of Man,
make God known (1:51; 3:13-14) and bring eternal life to those who
believe in him (3:15); his presence produces a *krisis*, a division between
those who accept the revelation of God in and through Jesus and those
who refuse it. The realized eschatology of vv. 24-25 is continued into v.
27. Life or death is to be had *now*, in the acceptance or refusal of the revelation of God in Jesus of Nazareth.[73] God no longer actively judges (v. 22)
because he makes himself known in Jesus, the Son of Man.[74]

---

[70] On the interplay between the basis of Jesus' authority and his exercising of such authority, see Blank, *Krisis,* 174–76.

[71] On v. 27 as a "bridge," see Stimpfle, *Blinde sehen,* 84. The change in perspective is particularly clear in the deliberate omission of the words *kai nyn estin* in v. 28.

[72] See Moloney, *Son of Man,* 72–74, 77–81. More recently, see J. G. van der Watt, "A New
Look at John 5:25-29 in the Light of the Term 'eternal life' in the Gospel According to John,"
Neot 19 (1985) 71–76.

[73] See Blank, *Krisis,* 158–64; Stimpfle, *Blinde sehen,* 78–80.

[74] For a full discussion of "Son of Man" in 5:27, see Moloney, *Son of Man,* 77–86. See also

But judgment does not only take place *now*. "The Jews" are told not to marvel at what Jesus has said to them (v. 28a). The fact that all authority to judge and to give life has been passed on to the Son does not take away from the traditional understanding of the end time, with its associated judgment unto life or death. Jesus' teaching in vv. 28b-29 matches traditional Jewish and early Christian eschatological expectations. The hour is coming, some time in the future, when those physically dead, those in the tombs, will hear the voice of the Son and come forth into either the resurrection of life or the resurrection of judgment. The criterion for their post-tomb experience is their performance during their pre-tomb lives. The reader is comforted by these words on the final resurrection from the tomb. The words "do not marvel at this" are a guide to the reader, as well as an instruction to "the Jews."[75] The narrative is read within the limitations of time where one event is sure to take place: death. A reader may be challenged by the realized eschatology of v. 24, but "must come to terms with . . . the fact that the ordinary patterns of human life and death continue despite the 'eternal life' which they claim to possess as his gift."[76]

There must also be a word addressing the other side of death.[77] Those who believe in the word of Jesus may have "eternal life," but they still die. Within the context of a debate over the Sabbath authority of Jesus to work as God works, Jesus' *present* authority must be stressed. YHWH is the Lord of the Sabbath, and as such gives life and judges. Jesus, the Son of the Sabbath Lord, whom he called Father, claims the same authority and honor (see v. 23). But the lordship of the God honored by the celebration of the Sabbath reaches beyond the limitations of time. God is the Lord of all creation, both here and hereafter. Although the author's main concern, throughout Jesus' presentation of himself as the life-giver and judge, is his *present* authority, his role as the future judge cannot be neglected in this Sabbath encounter with "the Jews." To eliminate any reference to a future judgment would be to leave the reader wondering about the physical reality of life and death, as much the domain of a Sabbath God as his present role as life-giver and judge.[78] Acceptance and refusal of the Son *now* must be in some way related to life on the other side of the tomb. The Son gives

---

D. R. A. Hare, *The Son of Man Tradition* (Minneapolis: Fortress Press, 1990) 90–96. For a very different interpretation, see Ashton, *Understanding,* 357–63.

[75] See N. A. Dahl, "'Do Not Wonder!' John 5:28-29 and Johannine Eschatology Once More," in *The Conversation Continues,* 322–36; Stimpfle, *Blinde sehen,* 96–99.

[76] B. J. Byrne, *Lazarus: A Contemporary Reading of John 11:1-46* (Zacchaeus Studies: New Testament; Collegeville: Liturgical Press, 1991) 15.

[77] For a convincing linguistic and stylistic analysis that defends the unity of vv. 19-30, see Vanhoye, "La composition," 262–68.

[78] See Stimpfle, *Blinde sehen,* 99–101.

life (v. 24) and judges (v. 27) *now* as he frees people from their sin. But he will also give life and judge *in the future*, summoning people from their graves. Those who hear the voice of the Son and have life *now* are spared neither the need to endure the vicissitudes of life nor the reality of physical death, but they will be summoned from their graves.[79] YHWH's lordship over the Sabbath is but a particular aspect of his lordship over the whole of creation (see Gen 1:1—2:4a). He is Lord of creation and its history. Jesus' closing words on life and judgment on the other side of death (vv. 28-29) associate the Son with the Father in that wider lordship upon which, ultimately, the honor given to YHWH on the Sabbath depends.

On arrival at v. 30, the reader senses that this section of the discourse is coming to a conclusion. In v. 19 Jesus spoke in the third person about the total dependence of the Son upon the Father. Here the third person becomes first person. Jesus, the Son, is totally dependent, hearing and judging according to the will of the one who sent him. The reader is by now familiar with the presentation of Jesus as "the one sent" (see 3:17, 34, with the verb *apostellō*; 4:34, with *pempō*). As the discourse has unfolded the terms "Father" and "Son" have been gradually replaced by "the one who sent me." Jesus has already referred to "the Father" as *ho pempsantos me* in vv. 23 and 24. Just as the reader has been familiar with the language of Father-Son in reference to Jesus since the prologue (see 1:14-18), the reader also has a growing familiarity with the language of "the one who sent me" in reference to God who sends and Jesus who is sent.[80] The reader, who has a growing acceptance that Jesus is the Sent One of God, now begins to understand what this means in the action of his story: as God is life-giver and judge, so also is Jesus life-giver and judge.[81] This belief allows the author to reread traditional Jewish Sabbath theology and practice. The action of the narrative has been set within the celebration of the Sabbath (vv. 9b, 10, 16, 18). There is a trial in progress, where "the Jews" are the accusers (see v. 18) and Jesus is the defendant (vv. 19-30). The issue at stake is Jesus' person and role as the Son of the Father, authorized

---

[79] See Painter, *Quest,* 233–34; J. T. Carroll, "Present and Future in Fourth Gospel 'Eschatology,'" *BTB* 19 (1989) 63–69. Léon-Dufour, *Lecture,* 2:61–62, expands on this, claiming that this text refers to all those who have come before Jesus and those who have come after him, but never heard of him. They too will have their moment of judgment. See also van der Watt, "New Look," 76–85. This interpretation reads too much into the passage and its context.

[80] On the choice of two verbs *apostellō* and *pempō* to speak of Jesus as the Sent One (and also the Baptist; see 1:6), see K. Rengstorf, "*apostellō (pempō) ktl.,*" *TDNT* 1:404–5.

[81] See Harvey, *Trial,* 90–92. In the Semitic world, the one sent becomes the presence of the one who sends. Jesus' claim to be the Sent One of the Father fits into this scheme. See especially J.-A. Bühner, *Der Gesandte und sein Weg im 4. Evangelium* (WUNT 2/2; Tübingen: J. C. B. Mohr [Paul Siebeck], 1977) 181–267.

to work on the Sabbath as "the Jews" allowed God to work (vv. 17-18). But now "the Jews" are being accused of not understanding the revelation of the Sabbath action of God in Jesus. He has not replaced God, nor has he done away with the Sabbath celebration. He has broadened its understanding by claiming that he brings into the human story the life-giving and judging activity previously reserved to a more distant God. In the trial of Jesus over Sabbath observance, the accusers are becoming the accused, and the accused is becoming the accuser.

III. WITNESS AND ACCUSATION: 5:31-47

THE SHAPE OF THE NARRATIVE

Why view the Sabbath from the perspective of a man who, claiming to be Son of God, breaks the Law (vv. 16-18), arguing that he has received from his Father Sabbath authority to give life and to judge (vv. 19-30)? "The Jews" have every right to ask for more from Jesus before they withdraw their accusations and turn to honor him.[82] The second part of the discourse (vv. 31-47) continues the trial.[83] Although Jesus speaks, "the Jews" are addressed throughout (*hymeis*: vv. 33, 34, 35, 38, 39, 42, 44, 45). Verbs in the second person plural are aimed at a specific audience (vv. 37, 40, 43, 46, 47). "The Jews" become the accused through a discourse that unfolds as follows:[84]

(a) *Verses 31-32*: The problem of an acceptable witness to Jesus is raised by Jesus himself.
(b) *Verses 33-40*: A series of witnesses are presented to "the Jews." They are:
   (i)   John the Baptist (vv. 33-35)
   (ii) the works of Jesus (v. 36)
   (iii) the word of the unseen Father (vv. 37-40).
(c) *Verses 41-44*: Jesus presents two contrasting understandings of *doxa*.
(d) *Verses 45-47*: "The Jews" are accused by the writings of Moses.

In the first part of the discourse (vv. 19-30) there was a close link between the beginning and the end of Jesus' defense of his actions on the Sabbath

---

[82] See Bultmann, *John*, 263.

[83] See Becker, *Johannes*, 1:249–51, on the literary form of a *Rechtstreit*. On the rabbinic background, see Thomas, "Fourth Gospel," 174–77.

[84] See J. Beutler, *Martyria: Traditionsgeschichtliche Untersuchungen zum Zeugnisthema bei Johannes* (FThSt 10; Frankfurt: Josef Knecht, 1972) 255–56.

(v. 19 and v. 30). In the second (vv. 31-47), Jesus' words open with an admission that he cannot bear witness to himself but that he has "another" to bear witness (vv. 31-32), and they close indicating to "the Jews" that he does not accuse them, but "the writings of Moses" do (vv. 45-47).

READING THE NARRATIVE

Jesus points out that the witness he has borne to himself thus far in his encounter with "the Jews" is not able to be verified (v. 31: *ouk estin alēthēs*).[85] According to Jewish practice, the "truth" was established via witnesses. It was not sufficient for the accused to prove the *facts* as *true* in the modern sense. It was essential in the Jewish legal system to call witnesses whose word could be trusted.[86] Thus far, Jesus has spoken for himself. His accusers require more from him, as they demand that he fit their established conventions (see Deut 19:15; *Rosh Hashanah* 3:1; *Ketubot* 2:9; Josephus, *Antiquities* 4:219).[87] Jesus accepts this situation and points enigmatically toward another (*allos*) who bears witness to him, a continuous witness of lasting value (present tense: *martyrei*).[88] The enigma, however, is for "the Jews." The reader knows that John the Baptist has already given witness to Jesus as the Lamb *of God* and the Son *of God* (see 1:6-8, 19-34).[89] Jesus has spoken of his relationship to God as that of a son and a sent one (see 3:16, 17, 18; 5:17, 19-30). The narrator has spoken of Jesus as the Son of God (see 3:35-36). The reader knows that Jesus does not speak of his own accord. He has come to tell the story of the unseen God (see 1:18, 51; 3:11-12, 32-34). Jesus does not come to do his own deeds but to accomplish the work (*to ergon*) of the one who sent him (4:34). The *allos* must be God, and Jesus claims certain knowledge that his witness is true (v. 32).[90]

But the case must proceed before "the Jews." Thus Jesus systematically proceeds to present "witnesses": John the Baptist (vv. 33-35), his works

[85] For this translation, see Brown, *John,* 1:222.

[86] On this process, see Harvey, *Trial,* 19–20. It is often pointed out that there is a contradiction between 5:1 and 8:14, where Jesus speaks of the truth of the witness which he bears to himself. See, for example, Barrett, *St John,* 264. The reader of 5:31 has no knowledge of 8:14, and will eventually read 8:14 within its own context.

[87] See Bultmann, *John,* 263–64.

[88] See M.-J. Lagrange, *Évangile selon saint Jean* (Ebib; Paris: Gabalda, 1936) 150–51.

[89] Chrysostom interpreted the *allos* as John the Baptist. As Bernard, *St. John,* 1:248, points out, this "makes havoc of the argument that follows."

[90] See Beutler, *Martyria,* 256–57. Some textual evidence (the Western readings of Original Sinaiticus, Bezae, Old Latin, Curetonian Syriac, Armenian and Georgian) reads "you know" (*oidate*) rather than "I know" (*oida*). This is a scribal tendency to heighten the argument, and should be rejected.

(v. 36), and the word of God (vv. 37-40).[91] The first of the witnesses to be presented in detail, after the enigma of the *allos* of v. 32, is John the Baptist. Unlike the witness of the *allos*, described by means of a verb in the present tense (v. 32: *martyrei*), the witness of the Baptist is past (v. 33: *memartyrēken*).[92] Jesus reminds "the Jews" that they "sent to John" (v. 33, see 1:19, 24). The truth of John's witnessing to Jesus as Lamb *of God* (see 1:29, 35) and Son *of God* (1:34) is affirmed.[93] If Jesus is "of God," then the claims of vv. 19-30 need no further defending. Because he is "of God," Jesus has no need of *martyria* from a human being. But he is dealing with human beings, and is prepared to subject himself to their processes (v. 34a; see 1:14; 3:16-17).[94] Jesus is prepared to submit himself to the messiness of the human situation, including the trial now in process, so that his questioners might be saved (v. 34b). There may be conflict, and even a trial that seeks the death of Jesus (vv. 16-18), but Jesus has not eliminated "the Jews" from his saving mission (*hina hymeis sōthēte*).

Jesus describes the Baptist as "a lamp that is kindled and shining." The reader recalls that the Baptist was sent by God to bear witness (1:6). The light he bears is the result of someone else's initiative. The passive form of the participle (*ho kaiomenos*) is used to describe the light as "kindled." It is possible that the reader also recalls the reference to a lamp that becomes a witness to the Messiah alluded to in LXX Ps 131:16b-17: "Her faithful will shout for joy (*agalliasei agalliasontai*). There I will cause a horn to sprout up for David; I have prepared a lamp for my anointed one (*lychnon tǭ christǭ mou*)." Primitive messianic concepts are behind the idea of a lamp that becomes a witness to the Messiah (see also Sir 48:1).[95] This is the lamp that gave a light (*phainōn*) that caused joy. "The Jews" were prepared (*ēthelēsate*) to be joyful (*agalliathēnai*) over John the Baptist, but, as the present context of trial and a plot for the death of Jesus demonstrates, their joy stopped there. The problem for "the Jews" was not the witness of the Baptist, which they were prepared to accept as the light that paved the way for the coming of the Messiah. They were unable to accept the one to whom he gave witness (see 1:11).[96] "The Jews," in their joy over the light

---

[91] Pancaro, *Law,* 209–10, separates vv. 37-38 (witness of the Old Testament revelation) from vv. 39-40 (witness of the Scriptures).

[92] Lagrange, *Saint Jean,* 151. It is, however, in the perfect tense. The witness has been given, but its significance endures.

[93] See Boismard and Lamouille, *Jean,* 175.

[94] See Lagrange, *Saint Jean,* 151.

[95] See, on this, F. Neugebauer, "Miszelle zu Joh 5,35," *ZNW* 52 (1961) 130; Beutler, *Martyria,* 258; Léon-Dufour, *Lecture,* 2:68 n. 124. Some scholars refuse to accept this link. See, for example, Becker, *Johannes,* 1:253.

[96] In the Fourth Gospel there is no rejection of the Baptist, and no account of his death at the hands of Herod. The reader knows of his witness subordinated to Jesus, not rejected. See

of the lamp that shone for the coming Messiah, should have been able to receive the witness of the Baptist as a true witness to Jesus' claims, but they were not prepared to look beyond the reflected light of the Baptist to see him to whom he bore witness. Jesus speaks of their willingness to accept the revelation of God in their terms: *hymeis de* (v. 35; see also v. 33), but now he passes to another of his witnesses, which surpasses that of the Baptist, his works: *egō de . . . echō tēn martyrian meizō tou Iōannou* (v. 36a; see also v. 34).

On an earlier occasion Jesus announced that he came to bring to perfection the work (*ton ergon*) his Father gave him (4:34). As Jesus began the defense of his Sabbath behavior, he spoke of the Son who does what the Father shows him, and who will do even greater works (5:20: *ta erga*). Now these two notions are combined. Jesus has a task (*to ergon*) to perform that has its origins in God (see 4:34), but that task will be performed through Jesus' continual response to the one who sent him. This response is reflected in the many works (*ta erga*) that Jesus accomplishes (5:36a; see v. 20).[97] The use of the verb *teleioun* tells the reader that Jesus does not simply perform works; he does them perfectly.[98] Jesus does not witness to himself; his perfect accomplishment of his tasks witnesses to the truth that he is the Sent One of the Father.[99]

Finally, Jesus calls upon the witness of the Father (vv. 37-40). After the vague reference to the *allos* in v. 32, there has been a logical progression from John the Baptist (vv. 33-35), to the works of Jesus (v. 36), to the Father (vv. 37-40).[100] In many ways, v. 37 clarifies for the reader what was initially suggested in v. 32. The Father who sent Jesus bears witness to him, but the question arises: How? The witness of John the Baptist and the deeds of Jesus of Nazareth were there to be seen and heard, but such is not

---

M. Stowasser, *Johannes der Täufer im Vierten Evangelium* (ÖBS 12; Klosterneuberg: Österreichisches Katholisches Bibelwerk, 1992). On 5:33-36, see pp. 221-331.

[97] Contrary to Bultmann, *John,* 265; and Becker, *Johannes,* 1:253-54, there is a distinction between the singular *to ergon* and the plural *ta erga.* The singular is a more theological concept that speaks of the whole of Jesus' mission, consummated on the cross (see especially 4:34; 17:4; 19:30). The plural refers to the many individual deeds of Jesus that lead to Jesus' consummation of the *ergon.* They reflect Jesus' being the Sent One of the Father. On this, see A. Vanhoye, "L'oeuvre du Christ, don du Père (Jn. 5,36 et 17,4)," *RSR* 48 (1960) 415-19; Beutler, *Martyria,* 259-60.

[98] See Vanhoye, "L'oeuvre," 409-15.

[99] This point is made stronger by the syntax, where the subject is again repeated after a relative: *auta ta erga ha poiō.* Never in the Fourth Gospel does Jesus speak of "*my* works." See Vanhoye, "L'oeuvre," 394-408; J. Bernard, "Témoignage pour Jésus Christ: Jean 5:13-47," *MSR* 36 (1979) 21-26.

[100] This progression is missed by those who regard vv. 37-40 as referring to the Old Testament. See especially Pancaro, *Law,* 216-31.

the case with the *martyria* of the Father. "The Jews" have never heard his voice (*phōnēn autou*), and they have never seen his form (*eidos autou*). This is not merely a statement of fact, looking back on "the Jews'" lack of a true understanding of their own Scriptures, as is often supposed by interpreters.[101] There is accusation in the words of Jesus, spelled out in what the reader would regard as a further explanation of *phōnē* and *eidos* in v. 38b: *hoti hon apesteilen ekeinos, toutō hymeis ou pisteuete*. It is taken for granted by "the Jews" that they have the word of God abiding in them in their Scriptures (v. 38a). Jesus tells them that this is presumptuous, because they do not believe in the one sent by God (v. 38b). He is the *phōnē* and the *eidos* of God among them, but they do not hear or see him as such.[102] This is the only use of *eidos* in the Fourth Gospel. But side by side with the negative affirmation in 1:18a, that no one has ever seen God, a point repeated in the present context in 5:37, the prologue has affirmed positively that his only begotten Son tells his story (1:18b). We have seen the glory of the only begotten Son of God (1:14). While the expression *eidos* is not found, the reader understands Jesus as the *eidos* of God. He is not the Father, but he is the one sent by the Father, making the Father visibly present to the human story.[103] The reader accepts that the *phōnē* of God is the *logos* of Jesus.[104] The presumption that all is well for "the Jews" has been denied. They think they have the Word of God among them, but they do not, because they have refused to believe in Jesus, the Sent One of the Father, God's *eidos* and *phōnē*.[105]

The attack upon "the Jews" continues in vv. 39-40. The Jewish practice of study and reflection upon the Scriptures is regarded as a life-giving end in itself (v. 39).[106] But "the Jews" miss the life-giving power of the Scriptures that comes only through recognition that the biblical word bears

---

[101] See, for example, Lagrange, *Saint Jean*, 152–53; Léon-Dufour, *Lecture*, 2:69–72.

[102] See Stimpfle, *Blinde sehen*, 102–3. This possibility is not taken into account by Pancaro, *Law*, 216–26. Pancaro argues that *eidos* and *phōnē* refer to Sinai, and thus in vv. 37-38 Jesus presents the testimony given by the Father to Moses and Israel on Mount Sinai, i.e., the Old Testament revelation.

[103] As Segalla, *Giovanni*, 219, points out, there is a hint of the Old Testament tradition of the inaccessibility of God (see Deut 4:12, 15), only overcome by the Son.

[104] See U. C. von Wahlde, "The Witnesses to Jesus in John 5:31-40 and Belief in the Fourth Gospel," *CBQ* 43 (1981) 385–95; Panimolle, *Lettura*, 2:55–56; Painter, *Quest*, 240–41; M. M. Thompson, "'God's Voice You Have Never Heard, God's Form You Have Never Seen': The Characterization of God in the Gospel of John," *Sem* 63 (1993) 177–204.

[105] Thus also Bultmann, *John*, 266–67.

[106] This practice is behind the use of the verb *eraunate*, "you search," which corresponds to Hebrew *dāraš*, the technical term for biblical study and exposition. See Dodd, *Interpretation*, 329–30 n. 1, showing that the verb is indicative, not imperative. Jesus is not telling "the Jews" to do something; he is chastising them for their incorrect use of the Scriptures.

witness to Jesus. Their decision to try and to kill Jesus is based upon their scrutiny of the Scriptures. But it is in the Scriptures that one finds the witness which the Father gives to Jesus. It has taken some time to arrive at this clarification of Jesus' original affirmation: "And the Father who sent me has himself born witness to me" (v. 37a). The Scriptures do give life, but only to those who are prepared to come to Jesus (see 1:47; 3:2; 4:30, 40, 47). The Scriptures, used by "the Jews" to try and to condemn Jesus, are in fact the witness of the unseen God to Jesus (v. 37). The Scriptures point to Jesus as the voice and the form of God, and belief in him leads to and reflects the presence of the word of God dwelling in the believer (v. 38). "The Jews," who mistakenly believe that they have life from their traditional study of the Scriptures (v. 39),[107] in their decision to try Jesus and to kill him for his blasphemous interpretation of the Sabbath (vv. 16-18), have refused to come to him (v. 40a). They are thus excluding themselves from the life-giving presence of Jesus (v. 40b; see vv. 21, 24).[108]

A procession of witnesses (vv. 33-40) has now affirmed the truthfulness of Jesus' testimony (vv. 31-32), that he is the Son of the Father and, as such, has authority to give life and to judge on the Sabbath (vv. 19-30). It is impossible to read vv. 31-40 without the context of the Sabbath miracle and its consequences. The trial against Jesus, initiated by "the Jews" after his offensive Sabbath miracle (vv. 16-18), is now turning in Jesus' favor. As Jesus' summoning of witnesses draws to a conclusion, "the Jews" are told that in rejecting Jesus they have refused life (vv. 39-40). Ironically, this process began with a Jewish decision that Jesus must die (v. 18). Now the tables are being turned. The position taken by "the Jews" condemns them to death. The accusers are becoming the accused.

Jesus now assesses the basis of the two cases being presented in the court case.[109] He first speaks of himself (v. 41). The expression *doxa* has a secular and a biblical meaning.[110] In common usage, the expression refers to the esteem, praise, and glory that come from human achievement. This meaning emerges for the reader here, as Jesus indicates he has no interest in the *doxa tōn anthrōpōn*. The source of all Jesus is and does comes "from above," from God, and this gives him a certainty (v. 42: *egnōka*) that "the Jews" do not have the love of God in them. Scholars discuss whether the expression *tēn agapēn tou theou* (v. 42) means "you do not love God"

---

[107] Psalm 119; Deut 8:3; Sir 17:11; 45:5. For further rabbinic material, see Str-B 2:467. Particularly instructive are *Pirke Abot* 2:8; 6:7. See Bernard, "Témoignage," 35–42.

[108] See Hoskyns, *Fourth Gospel*, 273: "Being the witness of God to his Son, the Scriptures are prophetic, not life-giving."

[109] It is important to see that two sides are being presented. The section is well described as "une sorte de réciprocité" by Léon-Dufour, *Lecture*, 2:73–74.

[110] On this, see Moloney, *Belief*, 55–57; Pancaro, *Law*, 234–39.

(objective genitive) or "you are not people whom God loves" (subjective genitive).[111] As "the Jews'" active reading of the Scriptures and their rejection of Jesus on the basis of that reading has been at the center of the argument, I read it as an objective genitive. From his intimate knowledge of God (*egnōka*), Jesus reproaches "the Jews" because, whatever their claims to life from the Scriptures might be, they do not show this sign of loving God.[112] Love of God flows from an adequate response to the Word and produces children of God (see 1:12-13). "The Jews'" response to the word of Jesus, which has led them to the decision that he must die (see v. 18), has been far from adequate. On the one hand Jesus, the accused, does not seek human recognition (v. 41), while on the other, the accusers do not love God (v. 42). This leads to the rejection of the one sent in the Father's name (v. 43a) and the easy acceptance of anyone who comes in his own name (v. 43b). There is no need for the reader to identify any single messianic claimant whom "the Jews" uncritically accepted.[113] The contrast is between *en tǭ onomati tou patros mou* and *en tǭ onomati tǭ idiǭ*. Two radically different perspectives are emerging. Jesus looks to God as the one who sends him and whose mission he accomplishes, while "the Jews" judge only according to external appearances. "The failure to accept Jesus is really the preference of self."[114]

In v. 44 there is a further play on the secular and the biblical meaning of *doxa*. It is impossible for "the Jews" to come to authentic belief, because they receive the *doxa* that comes from their fellow humans (*doxan para allēlōn*). They seek to see and to judge according to criteria that they can measure and touch, accepting mutual human praise and esteem as worthy reward for such an approach. They are thus unable to seek out the *doxan tēn para tou monou theou*. Jesus Christ, the Word become flesh, is the *doxa* of God. This has been explicitly stated for the reader in 1:14. In 2:11 the reader was informed that in a repetition of God's gift of the Law at Sinai, through the first miracle at Cana, the glory of God was seen by the disciples. "The Jews" have failed to seek the revelation of the one and only God in Jesus. Indeed, they seek to kill him (see v. 18). In a lawsuit over Sabbath worship (5:44), it is not the *doxa tou theou* that "the Jews" seek, lost as they are in the *doxa tōn anthrōpōn*. Jesus reveals the glory of the one and only God (*tēn doxan tēn para tou monou theou*),[115] Lord of the Sabbath, the

[111] For a summary, see Lindars, *John,* 231.

[112] See Pancaro, *Law,* 239-40. Schnackenburg, *John,* 2:127; and Brodie, *John,* 254, attempt to marry both the subjective and objective meanings.

[113] See Lagrange, *Saint Jean,* 155.

[114] Brown, *John,* 1:228.

[115] Some very good witnesses (P[66], P[75], Vaticanus, Freer Gospels, Origen, and Eusebius) omit *theou.* For this reading, see Lagrange, *Saint Jean,* 156. It should be retained. See Barrett, *St John,* 269; Metzger, *Textual Commentary,* 211.

Father of Jesus, who has shown the Son all he does so that the Son may repeat these works, and even greater works (see v. 20). In rejecting the revelation of the one and only God in his Son, "the Jews" have rejected the Sabbath God they claim to be defending (see vv. 16-18). The overall unity of the chapter, created by the Sabbath theme, is continued into the culmination of the encounter that Jesus has had with "the Jews" by means of this discourse, given as his defense at a trial (see v. 16). Jesus began the presentation of his witnesses by admitting that his word alone was not *alēthēs* (v. 31). He concludes by pointing away from himself once more. He no longer produces witnesses to defend himself against his accusers. He introduces Moses, the one upon whom Israel set its hope, as the accuser of "the Jews." The roles in the trial have been reversed.[116]

According to Jewish thought, Moses was regarded as the mediator between God and Israel, the one who intercedes before God for Jews (see Exod 32:11-14, 30-33; Deut 9:18-29; *ExodR* 18:3; *Test Moses* 11:17; *Jubilees* 1:19-21; Josephus, *Antiquities* 4:194-95).[117] The Law had come to Israel through Moses (1:17a). This was God's first great gift. However, God's gifts have continued and been perfected (1:16). The fullness of a gift that is the Truth has come through Jesus Christ (1:17b).[118] There is no conflict between the two gifts, as one takes the place of the other in God's design.[119] Because "the Jews" have rejected the fullness of God's gifts, Jesus Christ, Moses accuses them. The use of the verb *kategoreō* keeps the discussion within the setting of a legal process.[120]

A theme treated in v. 39b returns in vv. 46-47: the Scriptures bear witness to Jesus. There is irony in Jesus' charge: "If you believed Moses" (v. 46a). The conflict between Jesus and "the Jews" comes from the Jewish understanding of the Mosaic tradition concerning the Sabbath. On the basis of their interpretation of the Mosaic Torah "the Jews" condemn Jesus (see v. 18), but they are wrong. Jesus does not point to any particular Mosaic passage; he simply declares that the Mosaic writings are *peri gar emou* (v. 46b). Their great intercessor must turn against "the Jews" to condemn them. There is a continuity between the writings of Moses and the

---

[116] See R. Kysar, *John's Story of Jesus* (Philadelphia: Fortress Press, 1984) 36.

[117] Str-B 2:561; J. Jeremias, "*Mōysēs*," *TDNT* 4 (1967) 848-73; W. A. Meeks, *The Prophet-King: Moses Traditions and the Johannine Christology* (NovTSup 14; Leiden: E. J. Brill, 1967) 159-61.

[118] For this reading of John 1:16-17, see Moloney, *Belief,* 46-48.

[119] The *anti* in 1:16 is not a rejection of the gift of the Law. Against those who argue that the truth of Jesus Christ replaces "that which Judaism meant to offer, but failed to provide" (Dodd, *Interpretation,* 86).

[120] BAGD, 422, s.v.; LSJ, 926-27, s.v. On the rabbinic (and legal) use of this verb, and the derived nouns *katēgoros* and *katēgōr,* see Barrett, *St John,* 270.

word of Jesus, which perfects all that had been said by Moses (see 1:16-17). The contrast between *ekeinou grammasin* and *emois rhēmasin* highlights the failure of "the Jews": if you do not believe Moses, how will you believe the Christ (v. 47)? Fresh from the experience of reading the Cana to Cana section of the narrative (2:1—4:54), the reader is able to judge "the Jews" as having no faith. "The Jews" have begun this discussion as the accusers of Jesus. Jesus has presented his witnesses, and at the end of the discussion "the Jews" have been accused to the Father by Moses himself, and they are judged as having no faith because they refuse the words of Jesus. He has earlier warned this same audience: "He who hears my word and believes him who sent me has eternal life; he does not come into judgment but has passed from death to life" (v. 24). The need to read 5:1-47 as a whole is again evident. In defense of his Sabbath authority (vv. 1-18), Jesus' words on life and judgment (vv. 19-30) guide the reader's understanding of Jesus' words on witness and accusation (vv. 31-47).[121]

CONCLUSION

The celebration of the Sabbath festival is essential literary and theological background for John 5. A miracle worked on a Sabbath creates difficulties (vv. 1-13). After an encounter between Jesus and the cured man which suggests that Jesus cannot be limited to the expected Sabbath behavior (v. 14), a trial opens (vv. 15-16), and a verdict is taken, that Jesus must die (vv. 17-18). Jesus' defense of his Sabbath activity as the Son of the Father who can exercise the Sabbath function of life-giver and judge depends entirely upon the Jewish understanding of YHWH as the only one who can give life and who judges on the Sabbath (vv. 19-30). But it is not enough for Jesus to affirm that he is the Son of the Father and does everything the Father teaches him to do (vv. 19 and 30). He must face the normal processes of a trial and bring other witnesses (vv. 31-32). John the Baptist (vv. 33-35), the works of Jesus, the Sent One of the Father (v. 36), and the Father himself (vv. 37-40) bear witness to his Sabbath authority. The inability of "the Jews" to see and accept these witnesses leads to an ironic change in the direction of the trial: the accusers become the accused. Their search for human esteem cannot match Jesus' authority as the revelation of the glory of the one and only Sabbath God (*ho monos theos*; see v. 44; 2 Kgs 19:15, 19; Ps 85:10; Isa 37:20; Dan 3:25). Because of their superficiality, they stand condemned, unable to believe the words of

---

[121] See D. A. Lee, *The Symbolic Narratives of the Fourth Gospel: The Interplay of Form and Meaning* (JSNTSup 95; Sheffield: JSOT Press, 1994) 108–25.

Jesus (vv. 41-47). The reader knows that life and freedom come from acceptance of the word of Jesus (v. 24), the Son of the Father, Lord of the Sabbath (vv. 19 and 30).

The original readers of this text belonged to a community cast out from the synagogue (see 9:22; 12:42; 16:2). They were struggling to understand how they were to relate to the God of Israel, a God who was worshiped as the one and only creator God through the Jewish celebration of the Sabbath. Their ex-friends and fellow Jews were also coming to grips with their changed situation, without a priesthood, a holy city, or a temple. But the Johannine community was asked to believe that Jesus was the Son of God, the one whose word brought life and freed from judgment (see 5:24). Jesus was the perfection of the Mosaic tradition on the Sabbath God and the Sabbath Law (see 1:16). The Johannine Christians could not join "the Jews" in their attempts to restructure and rethink the Sabbath celebration of YHWH. Jesus, the Son of God, made a difference. Indeed, he was the stumbling block that led to division and conflict between the emerging Johannine community and the emerging postwar synagogue.[122] What had been done in the Jewish Temple on the Sabbath was but a sign and a shadow of the perfection of the gift of God in the person of Jesus Christ (1:16-17), life-giver and judge (5:19-30), the bringer of eternal life to all who would believe his word (5:24). To judge Jesus otherwise, as did "the Jews" (vv. 16-18), could only lead to judgment and death.

The Johannine community has not lost contact with the celebration of the Sabbath, the *zikkarōn* of God's creating, life-giving, and judging presence to his people. In Jesus Christ the Sabbath traditions have become enfleshed, not destroyed. The Johannine community belongs to the Mosaic tradition, now perfected in the fullness of the gift of Jesus Christ (1:17). A serious problem for a community that had its roots in Judaism, but that had been driven from its matrix because of its faith in Jesus as the Christ, has been faced and resolved.

The Johannine community is one with an emerging implied reader as the story indicates that those who would use the Mosaic tradition to sit in judgment on Jesus are, in the end, judged and found wanting.[123] The accuser remains the same: Mosaic traditions were used for the condemnation of Jesus' Sabbath practice (vv. 16-18), but Moses himself accuses "the Jews" (v. 45). Like Jesus, the Johannine Christians have been condemned and expelled from the place where the traditions of Moses were celebrated on the Sabbath. But, as the narrative of John 5 shows, it is "the Jews" who have lost their way and who are judged. The absolute lordship of God is

[122] See especially Pancaro, *Law*, 241-53.
[123] On the importance of a mutuality between the real reader *of the text* and the heuristic device of an implied reader *in the text*, see Moloney, *Belief*, 9-21.

now part of the human story as his only begotten Son makes him known (see 1:18). "The Jews" who do not honor the Son do not honor the Father (v. 23). They do not accept Jesus' offer: to pass from death to life (v. 24). But as Jesus perfects the signs and shadows of the feasts of traditional Israel, he also enters into conflict with "the Jews." His behavior on the Sabbath initiates a process that promises to be fatal. The implied reader suspects that the conflict which emerges from the encounter between Jesus and "the Jews" may lead to his death. But the conflict between Johannine Christianity and "the Jews" also led to death (see 16:2).

Chapter Two

Jesus and the Passover
John 6:1-71

¶ The expression *meta tauta* (6:1) leads the reader to a new place (v. 1: the Sea of Galilee, which is the Sea of Tiberias), to the introduction of a new set of characters (v. 2: a multitude; v. 3: the disciples), and a change of time (v. 4: the Passover). The reader is informed that "the Passover, the feast of the Jews, was at hand" (6:4). After the general indication of the theme of feasts in 5:1, the fundamental observance of the celebration of Sabbath (see 5:9b) follows logically. Other Jewish feasts then appear, following the passing of a year: 6:1-71: Passover (celebrated for 7 days in the first month of the year), 7:1—10:21: Tabernacles (celebrated for 7 days in the seventh month of the year), and 10:22-42: Dedication (celebrated for 8 days in the ninth month of the year).[1]

The celebration of Passover contains elements commemorating the passage from winter to spring and the dramatic liberation of the Jewish people from Egypt, and it affirms liberation from every form of enslavement.[2] Two independent feasts, Passover (originally associated with the slaying of a sheep or a goat in a pastoral community) and Unleavened Bread (originally associated with eating unleavened bread in a community producing a barley harvest) were joined soon after Israel's settlement of Canaan. These feasts were then historicized and associated with God's

---

[1] See *Mekilta* on Exod 16:25: "If you will succeed in keeping the Sabbath, the Holy One, blessed be He, will give you three festivals, Passover, Pentecost, and Tabernacles." On the order of John 4–7, see Moloney, *Son of Man*, 87–89.

[2] See J. C. Rylaarsdam, "Passover and Feast of Unleavened Bread," *IDB* 3:663–68; B. M. Bokser, "Unleavened Bread and Passover, Feasts of," *ABD* 6:755–65.

30

deliverance of Israel from Egypt. Although only part of the celebration, two elements were fundamental to it. The slaying of the Passover lamb recalled God's action in protecting the firstborn of the Israelites in Egypt (see Exod 11:1-10; 12:29-51), and the eating of unleavened bread recalled God's nourishing of Israel in the wilderness with the manna (see Exod 16:1-36), regarded as "bread from heaven" (see Exod 16:4; Neh 9:15). After the loss of the Temple and the possibility of ritual sacrifice, postwar Judaism adapted and domesticated these rituals.[3]

John 6, equally the product of a postwar Jewish world, is shaped as follows:[4]

I.   *Verses 1-4*: An introduction to the narrative (where? when? who? why?).
II.   *Verses 5-15*: The account of the miracle of the loaves and fishes and its aftermath.
III. *Verses 16-21*: Jesus comes to his disciples across a stormy sea.
IV.   *Verses 22-24*: A second introduction (where? when? who? why?).
V.   *Verses 25-59*: The discourse on the bread from heaven.
VI.   *Verses 60-71*: A *krisis* is created by the word of Jesus:
      (a) *Verses 60-66*: Many disciples leave Jesus.
      (b) *Verses 67-71*: Peter, in the name of the Twelve, confesses true faith, but Jesus warns of Judas's future betrayal.

The epoch-making study of P. Borgen convinces me that the so-called discourse is a homiletic midrash on a text provided by Jesus' interlocutors in v. 31: "He gave them bread from heaven to eat."[5] The first part of the

---

[3] See Bokser, "Unleavened Bread," 763–64

[4] For a survey of scholarly opinion on the structure of John 6, see M. Roberge, "Le discours sur le pain de vie (Jean 6,22-59): Problèmes d'interpretation," *LTP* 38 (1982) 265–99; Menken, *Numerical*, 186–88.

[5] No Old Testament passage states explicitly: "He gave them bread from heaven to eat," and various suggestions have been made. Borgen (and others) claim that Exod 16:4, 15 are combined to form the text, while Exod 16:2 is used in the midrashic paraphrase (P. Borgen, *Bread from Heaven: An Exegetical Study of the Conception of Manna in the Gospel of John and the Writings of Philo* [NovTSup 10; Leiden: E. J. Brill, 1965] 40–42). Many disagree. C. K. Barrett, "The Flesh of the Son of Man," in *Essays on John* (London, SPCK, 1982) 39–40; G. Geiger, "Aufruf an Rückkehre: Zum Sinn des Zitats von Ps 78,24b in Joh 6,31," *Bib* 65 (1984) 449–64; M. J. Menken, "The Provenance and Meaning of the Old Testament Quotation of John 6:31," *NovT* 30 (1988) 39–56; Painter, *Quest*, 271–72; U. Schnelle, *Antidocetic Christology in the Gospel of John: An Investigation of the Fourth Gospel in the Johannine School* (Minneapolis: Fortress Press, 1992) 196 n. 129; and B. G. Schuchard, *Scripture Within Scripture: The Interrelationship between Form and Function in the Explicit Old Testament Citations in the Gospel of John* (SBLDS 133; Atlanta: Scholars Press, 1992) 33–46, have argued for Ps 78:24. Rightly, F. Manns comments: "Il s'agit vraisemblablement de text d'Ex 16,4 et 16,15, passage qui sera médité dans le Ps 78,24 et en Ne 9,15" (*L'Evangile de Jean à la lumière du Judaïsme* [SBFA 33; Jerusalem: Franciscan Printing Press, 1991] 153).

discourse (vv. 32-48) is a midrashic paraphrase of the words of Scripture: "He gave them bread from heaven," while the latter part (vv. 49-58) is a midrashic paraphrase of the words of Scripture: "to eat." Over the latter part of the discourse, a paraphrase of the earlier words ("he gave them bread from heaven") continues, but the paraphrase of the action of eating ("to eat") predominates.[6] Whatever its prehistory, once the discourse is in existence it has its own life. The emerging reader takes the text as an entity that has its own shape and message. The discourse does not start in v. 31, and there is no new beginning at v. 49, where the midrashic paraphrase of the words "to eat" commences.[7] The rhythm of question and answer directs the reading process.

I. AN INTRODUCTION: 6:1-4

THE SHAPE OF THE NARRATIVE

In 6:1-4 the reader is provided with information concerning:

(a) the presence of Jesus (v. 1), the disciples (v. 3), and a multitude (v. 2);
(b) the approaching Passover (v. 4);
(c) events on the other side of the Sea of Galilee, which is the Sea of Tiberias, and on the mountain (v. 1);
(d) the multitude's following Jesus "because they saw the signs that he did on those who were diseased" (v. 2).

READING THE NARRATIVE

Jesus, a multitude, and the disciples assemble on the other side of the Sea of Galilee.[8] The crowds are following him, but he ascends an unnamed mountain (*eis to oros*) and seats himself there with his disciples. The use of

[6] See Borgen, *Bread from Heaven*, 28–57. For a summary, see Moloney, *Son of Man*, 95–98. For a rejection of Borgen's thesis, see Becker, *Johannes*, 1:199–203. But now see Borgen, "John 6: Tradition, Interpretation and Composition," in *From Jesus to John: Essays on Jesus and New Testament Christology in Honour of Marinus de Jonge*, ed. M. C. de Boer (JSNTSup 84; Sheffield: JSOT Press, 1993) 279–85.

[7] For this division, see M. Gourgues, "Section christologique et section eucharistique en Jean VI: Une proposition," *RB* 88 (1981) 516–19; Léon-Dufour, *Lecture*, 2:128–29.

[8] The expression "to the other side" (*peran*) creates problems: the other side from where? "To the other side" may simply indicate a given place at the north end of the lake, close to Tiberias. See E. Delebecque, *Evangile de Jean: Texte traduit et annoté* (CahRB 23; Paris: Gabalda, 1987) 157–58.

the definite article, to indicate "the mountain," may be a first hint for the
reader that Jesus is adopting a position parallel to that of Moses, who
received the Law on a mountain (see Exod 19:20; 14:1-2; Isa 34:2-4).[9] The
reader is told that the crowds are continually following Jesus "because
they saw the signs that he did" (v. 2). The experience of Nathanael (see
1:49-51), Nicodemus (see 3:1-11), and the Samaritan woman (see 4:16-26),
and the narrator's comment in 2:23-25 instruct the reader that such faith is
limited. These events take place as "the Passover, the feast of the Jews, was
at hand" (v. 4).[10] The reader suspects that a story which begins with the
crowd following Jesus for the wrong reasons, as the Jewish feast of the
Passover draws near, may lead to another encounter between Jesus and the
traditional celebrations of the memory of God's presence to his chosen
people.

II. THE MIRACLE OF THE LOAVES AND FISHES: 6:5-15

THE SHAPE OF THE NARRATIVE

If one incorporates the introduction (vv. 1-4) into this section of the narrative, the following shape emerges:

(a) *Verses 1-4:* Setting the scene and the characters.
(b) *Verses 5-9:* A problem is posed by Jesus, and remains unresolved by
the disciples.
(c) *Verses 10-11:* A miracle takes place through the words and actions of
Jesus.
(d) *Verses 12-15:* The aftermath of the miracle.

This account largely follows the traditional shape of a miracle, but the
author insinuates a unique point of view into the telling of this traditional
story.[11]

READING THE NARRATIVE

The distinction between the three participants in the events (Jesus, disciples, and the crowd) is carefully maintained. The narrator reports that

[9] See, for example, Schnackenburg, *St John*, 2:18; Brown, *John*, 1:232; Segalla, *Giovanni*,
224. Against this, see Becker, *Johannes*, 1:191.
[10] On the uniqueness of this indication of time, see J. D. Crossan, "It Is Written: A Structuralist Analysis of John 6," *Sem* 26 (1983) 5.
[11] See L. T. Witkamp, "Some Specific Johannine Features in John 6.1-21," *JSNT* 40 (1990)
46–51.

Jesus, lifting up his eyes, saw the multitude coming to him (v. 5). Earlier the reader was told that the multitude "followed him" (v. 2), but he was with his disciples on the mountain (v. 3). Jesus turns to one of the disciples, Philip (see 1:43), with a question concerning the purchase of bread to feed the people (v. 5). Jesus takes the initiative (contrast Mark 6:37; 8:4; Matt 15:33), indicating his concern that the multitudes be nourished. The question asked by Moses of YHWH in the desert is recalled (see Num 11:13),[12] but here the question is rhetorical; Jesus already knew what he would do (v. 6b). The question tests the faith of the disciples (v. 6a). Jesus' rhetorical question to Philip tests whether his disciples have progressed in their understanding of who he is and what he can do. The christological question has been raised in terms of a gift of bread (see v. 5) as "the Passover, the feast of the Jews, was at hand" (v. 4).

Philip's response indicates that no progress has been made since the disciples' puzzled reaction to Jesus' words on the food that nourished him (see 4:32-34). Philip still responds in terms of material bread and the concrete reality of the number of denarii needed to buy bread to feed such a multitude. The reader looks forward to a solution to the problem that transcends the limitations of money and quantities of bread, something that Jesus will do (v. 6). Andrew joins Philip in pointing to the paucity of the food: a lad is at hand with five barley loaves and two fish. Andrew and Philip, who have been with Jesus from the first days (see 1:43), point out to Jesus that such meager provisions can do nothing for such an immense crowd (vv. 8-9).[13] Will the disciples never learn (see 1:35-51)? The raw material for the events that follow has been provided: the loaves and the fish.

Jesus commands the disciples to have the people lie down, as if for a meal. The reader notices that, while Jesus "sat down" (*ekathēto*) in v. 3, he tells his disciples to instruct the people to take up a physical position that prepares for a meal (*anapesein*) in v. 10.[14] The narrator comments that there was much grass in the place, which enables the men to lie down for the meal. The insinuation, which has been with the reader since vv. 5-6, that Jesus will eventually provide bread for the multitude suggests that the abundance of grass links the passage with Ps 23:2: "He makes me lie down

---

[12] Num 11:13: "Where am I to get the meat to give all this people?"

[13] On the disciples' failure, see Lee, *Symbolic Narratives*, 138–39. For possible links between this story and Elisha's feeding one hundred men in 2 Kings 4:42-44, see Bauer, *Johannes-evangelium*, 92. Bauer calls the text from 2 Kings the "Urmuster unserer Erzählung." See also J.-M. Léonard, "Multiplication des pains: 2 Rois 4/42-44 et Jean 6/1-13," *ETR* 55 (1980) 265–70.

[14] See BAGD, 59.

(LXX Ps 22:2: *ekei me kateskenōsen*) in green pastures."[15] With this passage in mind, the reader waits for Jesus to provide nourishment for his flock in the way promised by the psalm: "The Lord is my shepherd, I shall not want" (Ps 23:1). The number of five thousand men indicates the immensity of the crowd, and thus heightens the impact of the subsequent miracle.[16] For the moment, in the light of the narrator's comment in v. 6, the reader looks forward to a great sign from Jesus.

The reader is not disappointed. The narrator describes the actions of Jesus, taking (*elaben*) the loaves, giving thanks (*eucharistēsas*), and distributing (*diedōken*) them to the people stretched out for the meal (*tois anakeimenois*).[17] In words that recall the formal setting of a eucharistic celebration, Jesus distributes the loaves (v. 11a). He does the same with the fish (v. 11b), and the narrator concludes that they all had as much as they wanted (v. 11c), an allusion to the satisfaction given by YHWH to the people in Ps 23:1: "The Lord is my shepherd, I shall not want (LXX Ps 22:1: *ouden me hysterēsei*)."[18] The greatness of the miracle is indicated as the reader is told that all had their fill, but Jesus now adds a further command to the disciples: "Gather up (*synēgagon*) the fragments (*ta klasmata*) left over, that nothing may be lost (*hina mē ti apolētai*)" (v. 12).[19] The account of the gathering of fragments uses words found in the early church to speak of the eucharistic assemblies. The *Didache* (9:4), *1 Clement* (34:7), and Ignatius (*Letter to Polycarp* 4:2) use the verb *synagein* in ways that indicate the gathering of the faithful at the Eucharist. Similarly, *ta klasmata* was used to speak of the fragments of bread at the Eucharist (*Didache* 9:3, 4).[20] Some connection with the celebration of the Eucharist is present, but we must not lose contact with the flow of the story. While it is sometimes claimed that the text indicates "the gathering

---

[15] See Schnackenburg, *St John*, 2:16. Many commentators link the grass with the Passover, held in spring. See, for example, B. F. Westcott, *The Gospel According to Saint John* (London: John Murray, 1908) 97.

[16] The singling out of "men" (*andres*) in the number given, in contrast to "the people" (*anthrōpous*) who are made to lie down, indicates the patriarchy of the times.

[17] Sinaiticus, Bezae, and the Old Latin have *eucharistēsen kai edōken*, which is closer to liturgical celebrations, and must be rejected as such.

[18] There are no verbal links, but the context makes links for the reader.

[19] It is widely recognized that Jewish tradition ruled against waste. See especially *b. Ḥullin* 105b; *b. Berakot* 50b; *b. Shabbat* 147b. On this, see E. D. Johnston, "The Johannine Version of the Feeding of the Five Thousand—an Independent Tradition?" *NTS* 8 (1962) 153-54. Again 2 Kings 4:42-44 may be part of the background. After one hundred men ate from the barley loaves, they "had some left" (v. 44).

[20] On the close relationship between the Johannine details and the eucharistic prayer in the *Didache*, see C. F. D. Moule, "A Note on Didache IX 4," *JTS* 6 (1955) 240-43.

by God of his elect,"[21] the reader finds nothing more than the gathering of the *klasmata* by the disciples.[22]

Jesus has fed a vast multitude in a way that recalls a Christian celebration of the Eucharist, and this feeding has taken place at Passover time, which celebrates the gift of the manna. The disciples are commanded to gather the fragments of this original meal, *hina mē ti apolētai*. The Passover and the Eucharist blend as the author uses language that recalls the practice of the Exodus people, gathering the manna each day, and eating it until they have had their fill (see Exod 16:8, 12, 16, 18, 21).[23] Jesus shows no interest in gathering the fragments of *ta opsaria*, only of *ta klasmata* (contrast Mark 6:43). However, in the desert, Moses commanded that the manna was *not* to be stored. Any manna that was collected and put away perished (Exod 16:19-20). But the bread provided by Jesus will not perish.[24] Here we have the first suggestion of the encounter between Jesus' gift of bread and the gift of the manna, commemorated at the celebration of the Passover. Jesus' gift to people who come to him in search of bread (see v. 5) must not be lost, and the disciples are to see to its preservation.[25]

In Johannine material that has hints of a Christian sacrament, the author is often concerned to show that the reader, now distant from the events *in the story*, is still *part of the story*.[26] The language used by the narrator makes clear to the reader that an abundance of *klasmata* is still available, coming directly from this feeding miracle as "the Passover, the feast of the Jews, was at hand" (v. 4). Looking back to the fundamental text of Exodus 16, the reader is informed that, unlike the manna in the desert given by God to the ancestors of Israel, the *klasmata* given by Jesus on the occasion of the Passover feast have not perished; they are still available. The traditional number 12 indicates a collection complete in itself (see also Mark 6:43; Matt 14:20; Luke 9:17), and this collection of *klasmata* is gathered by the disciples, obedient to the command of Jesus (v. 13).

[21] Barrett, *St John*, 277. See also J. M. Perry, "The Evolution of the Johannine Eucharist," *NTS* 39 (1993) 25.

[22] Too much is sometimes made of the Jewish notion of God's blessing in the gift of the surplus. See D. Daube, *The New Testament and Rabbinic Judaism* (London: Athlone, 1956) 36–51; C. H. Dodd, *Historical Tradition in the Fourth Gospel* (Cambridge: Cambridge University Press, 1963) 424 n. 4. This is not part of the context.

[23] The verb *synagein* is used by Moses as he directs the Israelites to gather manna in LXX Exod 16:16. See also 16:5, 21.

[24] Different verbs are used. In LXX Exod 16:21 the bread is described as breeding worms and becoming foul (*kai exesesen skōlēkas kai epōzesen*).

[25] See Crossan, "It Is Written," 20. Witkamp, "Some Specific Johannine Features," 49, also sees the prolepsis, but understands the *klasmata* as the members of the gathered community who must not be lost.

[26] See F. J. Moloney, "When Is John Talking about Sacraments?" *AusBR* 30 (1982) 10–33.

The sight of the miracle leads the people to a profession of faith: "This is indeed the prophet who is to come into the world" (v. 14). In a way that parallels the first movement of the disciples toward Jesus (1:35-49), Nicodemus's conditioned confession of Jesus (see 3:2), and the Samaritan woman's hesitant preparedness to accept Jesus as prophet (see 4:19) and Messiah (see 4:25, 29), a sign has led to a limited understanding of Jesus. As the narrator commented to the reader in 2:23-25, many came to Jesus when they saw the signs that Jesus did, but he did not entrust himself to them. The reader is aware that the people have not moved beyond the faith that originally drew them to follow Jesus, "because they saw the signs that he did" (6:2). They are still looking for a figure who would satisfy their needs and expectations. Here, their hopes for a Moses-like prophet who would return to usher in the messianic era are fulfilled, a hope based on the word of YHWH to Moses in Deut 18:15-18.[27]

First-century Jewish literature links the gift of a second manna to the coming of the Messiah: "And it shall come to pass at that self-same time that the treasury of manna shall again descend from on high, and they will eat of it in those years, because these are they who have come to the consummation of time" (2 Baruch 29:8).[28] Jesus' gift of bread has led to the arousal of a messianic expectation that he is not prepared to accept. He earlier corrected the messianic confessions of Nathanael (1:49-51) and of the Samaritan woman (4:25-26) with further words; here Jesus' actions show that he is not prepared to accept their acclamation. Seeing that they are about to come and impose their royal messianic expectations upon him (*harpazein auton hina poiēsōsin basileia*),[29] Jesus goes away from them, retiring to the mountain from which he had descended to feed the multitude (v. 15).[30]

The reader senses from the beginning of the narrative (vv. 5-6) that the feeding is linked to a food that only Jesus can give. But the disciples are

---

[27] For a discussion of the evidence for a first-century messianic interpretation of Deut 18:15-18, see W. Bittner, *Jesu Zeichen im Johannesevangelium: Die Messias-Erkenntnis im Johannesevangelium vor ihrem jüdischen Hintergrund* (WUNT 2/26; Tübingen: J. C. B. Mohr [Paul Siebeck], 1987) 155–58. For the case against such an identification, see Schnelle, *Antidocetic Christology*, 103–4. Recent scholarship, following R. A. Horsley, "Popular Messianic Movements around the Time of Jesus," *CBQ* 46 (1984) 471–95, has looked to a more general notion of a prophetlike Messiah. See, for example, Painter, *Quest*, 260-64; Beasley-Murray, *John*, 88–89.

[28] *2 Baruch* is roughly contemporaneous with the Fourth Gospel. See also *Mekilta* on Exod 16:25; *EcclR* 1:9; *Tanḥ Shemot* 4:24.

[29] The use of the verb *harpazein* indicates that they are about to impose their will upon him. See Brown, *John*, 1:235.

[30] This must be understood, as the reader has never been explicitly told that he came down from the mountain of v. 3. See Bauer, *Johannesevangelium*, 93.

unable to transcend the purely physical impossibility of feeding such a crowd (vv. 5, 7). Paralleling and yet surpassing the gift of the manna in the desert (see Exodus 16; Leviticus 11), Jesus feeds the multitude, and begins a feeding that endures, as the fragments are gathered into twelve baskets. There are no indications in the text that the disciples have made any progress in their understanding of who Jesus is and what he does. How do Jesus' person and actions relate to the Passover traditions of Israel? The Passover context of the miracle (see v. 4) and the background of Exodus 16 (and Leviticus 11) to the theme of the gathering of the fragments force the question. The people claim that he is the prophet who is to come, the one who repeats the Mosaic gift of the manna (vv. 14-15). The reader is aware that any attempt to impose traditional Jewish messianic categories on Jesus will never be satisfactory (see also 1:35-49, 49-51; 2:23-25; 3:2-11; 4:16-29).

The story of the multiplication of the loaves and fishes as the Jewish Passover feast is at hand (v. 4) raises more questions than it answers, but it has plunged the reader into Jewish beliefs about the Exodus and the bread provided in the desert. It has also indicated to the reader that the bread which Jesus gives surpasses that provided for the ancestors of Israel in the desert. The reader senses the Christian celebration of the Eucharist, but only in its relationship with Jesus' nourishment of the people and the parallel gift of the manna in the desert. The primary focus of the reader's attention is on the comparison between the bread provided by Jesus on the occasion of the Jewish Passover, and the celebration of the gift of the manna through Moses, recalled at the Passover feast. But the manna of Moses was not to be kept. It bred worms and became foul (Exod 16:19-20). The bread provided by Jesus has been gathered into twelve baskets by the disciples so that it would not perish (John 6:12-13). The author has introduced a prolepsis, an unresolved gathering of the *klasmata*, presumably for some future "feeding." This obliges the reader to look further into the narrative.[31]

III. THE MIRACLE ON THE SEA: 6:16-21

THE SHAPE OF THE NARRATIVE

A further miracle story (vv. 16-21) matching the shape of the miracle of the multiplication follows:

[31] On prolepsis see G. Genette, *Narrative Discourse: An Essay in Method* (Ithaca: Cornell University Press, 1980) 33–84; S. Rimmon-Kenan, *Narrative Fiction: Contemporary Poetics* (New Accents; London: Methuen, 1983) 46–51.

(a) *Verses 16-17:* Setting of the scene and the characters.
(b) *Verse 18:* The problem of the storm is presented.
(c) *Verses 19-20:* Jesus miraculously comes to the disciples across the stormy waters.
(d) *Verse 21:* The response of the disciples is reported as "receiving" Jesus.

READING THE NARRATIVE

The account opens with the coming of the evening and the disciples' descent from the mountain to the sea. The characters mentioned in vv. 1-4 have been separated.[32] *Jesus* (see v. 1) has fled from the crowd "to the mountain by himself" (v. 15). *The disciples* (see v. 3) have come down to the sea and set out across the lake to Capernaum in a boat (vv. 16-17). The reader takes for granted that *the multitude* (see v. 2) remains by the lake.

Time passes and the disciples struggle across the lake: *kai skotia ēdē egegonei,*[33] while the narrator remarks: "and Jesus had *not yet* (*oupō*) come to them" (v. 17). As the disciples cross the lake in the darkness, the reader is aware that Jesus will come to them. The disciples see Jesus, walking *epi tēs thalassēs,* drawing close to their boat. There have been attempts to read *epi tēs thalassēs* as "beside the sea."[34] The drama of the sea journey in the stormy night (vv. 16-19a), the fear of the disciples (v. 19c), and Jesus' subsequent command to cease from fear associated with his self-revelation (v. 21) make this interpretation unacceptable. Jesus' coming to his disciples across the waters repeats an Old Testament literary form for a theophany (see, for example, Gen 15:1; 26:24; 46:3; Isa 41:13-14; 43:1, 3), and the reader is aware of YHWH's unique authority over the terror of the sea (see, for example, Exodus 14-15; Deut 7:2-7; Job 9:8; 38:16; Pss 29:3; 65:8; 77:20; 89:10; 93:3-4; Isa 43:1-5; 51:9-10).[35] It is as Lord that Jesus comes across the waters, reveals himself with the formula *egō eimi,* and tells his

---

[32] See Witkamp, "Some Specific Johannine Features," 51-52.

[33] As Barrett, *St John,* 280, points out, the durative or the conative force of the imperfect *ērchonto* must be given weight: "they were trying to go." The use of *skotia* is dramatic, but not symbolic as, for example, Léon-Dufour, *Lecture,* 2:120, would maintain.

[34] Grammatically, this is a possible translation. See BAGD, 286, s.v. *epi.* It is also the meaning of the expression in 21:1. For this, see Bernard, *St John,* 1:185-86; Talbert, *John,* 133; A. Nisin, *Histoire de Jésus* (Paris: Seuil, 1961) 275-76. For Boismard and Lamouille, *Jean,* 188, an original "by the sea" became "on the sea" in the final form of the Gospel.

[35] On this, see A. Feuillet, "Les *Ego eimi* christologiques du quatrième évangile," *RSR* 54 (1966) 19-21. Becker, *Johannes,* 1:194, remarks rightly, "Alles ist auf die Epiphanie des seewandelnden Jesus konzentriert." There is also a recalling of the Exodus tradition concerning the crossing of the Reed Sea found in Ps 77:18-19. See, for example, Kysar, *John's Story,* 40-41.

disciples not to fear (v. 20).[36] Their response is to receive him gladly (*ēthelon oun labein auton*), and they find themselves "at the land to which they were going" (v. 21). As earlier in the story (see 2:1-12; 4:46-54; 5:2-9a), an acceptance of the word of Jesus leads to a miracle.[37] The order of events is familiar to the reader. As in earlier miracles, the seemingly insurmountable problem of the stormy sea (see vv. 17-19a) is solved as disciples "receive" Jesus (see 2:1-12; 4:46-54; 5:2-9).[38]

But the crowds have been left behind, limited by their messianic expectations (vv. 14-15). For the second time in the story, Jesus has made himself known as *egō eimi* (see 4:26). Here Jesus' self-revelation has been accepted. The crowds' response to the multiplication of the bread in vv. 14-15 indicates a determination to impose their categories on Jesus. The disciples have been provided with a correct understanding of who Jesus is, while the multitude has not.[39] The people, therefore, remain locked within the Mosaic hopes that they had expressed, as a result of the gift of bread, in vv. 14-15. However, they will eventually be the recipients of the word of Jesus, revealing himself to them through the *egō eimi* formula. On four occasions during the discourse that Jesus will deliver to them at Capernaum he will reveal himself as the living bread, the bread that has come down from heaven (vv. 35, 41, 48, 51). *The reader* will encounter these words of Jesus with the *egō eimi* of v. 20 in mind. But *the crowds* were not privy to that moment of self-revelation. A correction of false messianic hopes has been made through Jesus' revelation of himself as *egō eimi* to the disciples.[40] From this point on the reader watches the performance of the disciples, who know the truth about Jesus. Strangely, they will disappear from center stage for some time, as Jesus speaks to the multitude and "the Jews" (vv. 25-59), but they will return, and the quality of their faith will again be tested (vv. 60-71).

---

[36] Not all would accept that *egō eimi* is being used as the revelatory formula here; some see it simply as self-identification: "It's me, don't worry." See, for example, Bernard, *St John*, 1:187; Barrett, *St John*, 281. J. P. Heil, *Jesus Walking on the Sea: Meaning and Gospel Functions of Matt 14:22-33, Mark 6:45-52 and John 6:15b-21* (AnBib 87; Rome: Biblical Institute Press, 1981) 79–80, goes halfway: "Jesus as the one acting on behalf of Yahweh," (p. 79), but "not to reveal" (p. 80).

[37] There may be a hint of the fulfillment of Ps 107:23-32, especially v. 30: "And he brought them to their desired haven." See Heil, *Jesus Walking*, 82.

[38] The verb *lambanein* is used. As the reader has learned from the prologue (1:12-13), this verb can reflect the authentic reception of Jesus. See Moloney, *Belief*, 38–39.

[39] The role of vv. 16-21 has been seen by C. H. Giblin, "The Miraculous Crossing of the Sea (John 6.16-21)," *NTS* 29 (1983) 96–103. For the importance of the separation between crowd and disciples, see Borgen, "John 6," 269–71.

[40] See also Brown, *John*, 1:254–55. Brown also suggests (pp. 255–56) that there may be a Passover link between Jesus' crossing the waters and Moses' crossing the Reed Sea. For a strong Mosaic reading of 6:1-21 as a whole, see Perry, "Evolution," 22–26.

IV. A SECOND INTRODUCTION: 6:22-24

THE SHAPE OF THE NARRATIVE

By means of a second introductory passage,[41] matching vv. 1-4, the reader learns that:

(a) Jesus (vv. 22, 24), the disciples (vv. 22, 24), and "the people who remained on the other side," who had eaten the bread (vv. 22, 23), are again assembled.
(b) It is "the next day" (v. 22).
(c) They are at Capernaum (v. 24).
(d) The multitude was "seeking Jesus" (v. 24).

READING THE NARRATIVE

"The people who remained on the other side" (v. 22), those who "ate the bread after the Lord had given thanks" (v. 23), are aware that Jesus and the disciples have been separated.[42] They had observed on the day before that there was only one boat, but that Jesus had not departed with his disciples (v. 22).[43] Yet neither Jesus nor his disciples are "there" (*ouk estin ekei*), present with them. This introduces an element of wonder and confusion into the narrative. Jesus should be with them, as he did not depart with the disciples, but he is not to be found. Has another miracle happened? The people who had eaten the bread are puzzled; they hail boats passing by

---

[41] This brief passage is not only confusing, but it is also confused from a textual point of view. The original hand of Sinaiticus, the *Diatessaron*, Chrysostom, and the early versions give evidence of an extremely varied textual tradition. On this, see M.-E. Boismard, "Problèmes de critique textuelle concernant le Quatrième Evangile," *RB* 60 (1953) 359–71; L. Schenke, "Das Szenarium von Joh 6,1-25," *TTZ* 92 (1983) 191–203; M. Roberge, "Jean VI,22-24: Un problème de critique textuelle?" *LTP* 34 (1978) 275–89; idem, "Jean VI,22-24: Un problème de critique littéraire," *LTP* 35 (1979) 139–51. For an exhaustive survey of the discussion, see F. Neirynck, "L'*epanalepsis* et la critique littéraire. A propos de l'évangile de Jean," *ETL* 56 (1980) 325–32. Léon-Dufour, *Lecture*, 2:124–27, after noting the obscurity of vv. 22-23, comments upon vv. 24-25 as "l'essentiel s'y trouve" (p. 125). On the originality of vv. 22-24, see Schnelle, *Antidocetic Christology*, 110–11.

[42] Not only does this recall the events of the day before, but the singular *ton arton* is a eucharistic allusion. See Léon-Dufour, *Lecture*, 2:125–26. The Western text (Bezae, Old Latin, Sinaitic Syriac, Curetonian Syriac) omits *eucharistēsantos tou kyriou*, but see Schnelle, *Antidocetic Christology*, 110–11.

[43] This understanding of the text must read *eidon* and *ēn* in v. 22 as pluperfects. On this, see Lagrange, *Saint Jean*, 170; Barrett, *St John*, 285.

from Tiberias,[44] and set off for Capernaum, *zētountes ton Iēsoun*.[45] Confusion and wonder reign. He has already worked one miracle (see v. 23); what else has he done? The reader observes the crowd hustling and bustling into boats in order to find their miracle-man (see vv. 14-15).[46] That was where the reader left the people, but by now the disciples and the reader know more than the crowd. The eucharistic hints in the bread miracle (especially v. 11), have reappeared in v. 23. The issue of the *klasmata* remains unresolved. The place for the assembly is Capernaum (v. 24; see vv. 16 and 21). The reader is told that it is "the next day," an indication of time following Jesus' encounter with his disciples during the night (see vv. 16-17). However, if the first introduction was given as "the Passover, the feast of the Jews, was at hand" (v. 4), "the next day" brings the discourse and the events that are about to be reported closer to the celebration of the feast.

V. THE DISCOURSE ON THE BREAD FROM HEAVEN: 6:25-59

THE SHAPE OF THE NARRATIVE

Five interventions from the crowd or "the Jews" give the following discourse its shape:[47]

(a) *Verses 25-29:* "Rabbi, when did you come here?" (v. 25). This trivial question leads Jesus to instruct on the need to search for the food that endures to eternal life: belief in the one whom God has sent.
(b) *Verses 30-33:* "Then what sign do you do?" (v. 30). Jesus is asked for miracle-working credentials that surpass Moses' gift of manna in

[44] Understanding "boats from Tiberias" as passing by, and not there by accident, "blown out of harbour" (Westcott, *St John*, 99; Bernard, *St John*, 1:189; Barrett, *St John*, 285) by the overnight storm. Several commentators (see, for example, Bauer, *Johannesevangelium*, 94, citing Wellhausen) remark that this is a *deus ex machina* solution. But such solutions are not foreign to the Fourth Gospel (see 2:6, 15; 3:25; 4:6-7, 45).

[45] It is often pointed out that the whole crowd could not be intended. It would take a flotilla of boats from Tiberias to carry the "5000 men" (see v. 10). The issue is that people who had witnessed the miracle and expressed their messianic hopes (see v. 14) are still seeking Jesus.

[46] Against Schnackenburg, *St John*, 2:18, who claims that the acclamations of vv. 14-15 disappear from the narrative.

[47] This is not to accept the suggestions of B. Gärtner, *John 6 and the Jewish Passover* (ConNT 17; Lund, Gleerup, 1959); E. J. Kilmartin, "Liturgical Influence on John 6," *CBQ* 22 (1960) 183–91; and Daube, *New Testament and Rabbinic Literature*, 36–51, 158–69, that the questions and answers echo the Jewish Passover Haggadah. They form part of the Johannine misunderstanding technique. On this, see Brown, *John*, 1:266-67.

the wilderness (vv. 30-31). He points to the gift of another bread from heaven, *the true bread from heaven.*

(c) *Verses 34-40:* "Lord, give us this bread always" (v. 34). Jesus presents *himself* as the *true bread from heaven,* the only one able to make God known and give eternal life.

(d) *Verses 41-51:* "Is not this Jesus, the son of Joseph, whose father and mother we know? How does he now say, 'I have come down from heaven'?" (v. 42). Jesus raises the question of origins.

(e) *Verses 52-59:* "How can this man give us his flesh to eat?" (v. 52). A final question leads to Jesus' teaching on the need to eat the flesh and drink the blood of the Son of Man.

The reader follows the words of Jesus as he responds to the queries and objections of his interlocutors.[48]

READING THE NARRATIVE

Verses 25-29
The people arrive at Capernaum asking: "Rabbi, when did you come here?" (v. 25). The reader recognizes an insufficient understanding of Jesus in the title "Rabbi" (see 1:28, 49; 3:2). The question: "When did you get here?" trivializes the crowd's search (see v. 24). When last they were in the presence of Jesus, they wanted to make him king (v. 15); now they are interested in the time of his arrival at Capernaum. A double "amen" introduces words of Jesus crucial for the understanding of the discourse.[49] The sight of Jesus' signs had led the people to follow Jesus (v. 2), to experience the miraculous feeding (vv. 5-13), and to a partial confession of faith in Jesus as the Mosaic prophet (vv. 14-15). But now Jesus interprets their search for him (see v. 24) as having a baser motivation: they enjoyed the food that Jesus provided. They are to work (*ergazesthe*) not for the bread (v. 26: *artos*) that fills their bellies, not a food that perishes (*tēn brōsin tēn apollymenēn*), but for the food that endures (v. 27: *tēn brōsin tēn menousan*).[50] The reader recalls an earlier use of this expression: "I have food

[48] Against Menken, *Numerical*, 159-60, who claims "the interruptions in 6,41-42.52 do not have a function in the progression of the discourse." But see L. Schenke, "Die formale und gedankliche Struktur von Joh 6,26-58," *BZ* 24 (1980) 21-41, who has his own structure but sees a developing argument parallel to mine. See also G. A. Phillips, "'This is a Hard Saying. Who Can Be Listener to It?' Creating a Reader in John 6," *Sem* 6 (1983) 38-44, 49-54, who shows that the questions form different "enunciative posts."

[49] See Barrett, *St John*, 282: "The whole discourse is summarized here."

[50] For F. Grob, "'Vous me cherchez, non parce que vous avez vu des signes . . .' Essai d'explication cohérente de Jean 6/26," *RHPR* 60 (1980) 429-39, Jesus is not critical, but explains

(*brōsin*) to eat of which you do not know. . . . My food (*emon brōma*) is to do the will of him who sent me and to accomplish his work" (4:32, 34). There is a form of nourishment that transcends earthly bread, and this food must be the goal of the people's searching; it is for this they must work. The reader also recalls an event reported by the narrator at the end of the multiplication of the bread that still requires resolution: the gathering of the fragments *hina mē ti apolētai* (v. 12). "What is this *miraculous food*, and where is it to be found?"[51]

Jesus points forward to a food "that the Son of Man will give to you" (v. 27b).[52] Once again the enigmatic title "the Son of Man" is introduced at a crucial stage in the encounter between Jesus and would-be believers. The reader is aware that Jesus is the Son of Man (1:51; 3:13-14; 5:27) and is also aware that the Son of Man is the only revealer who can claim to have come from God (3:13), to make God known (1:51) by means of a "lifting up" (3:14). The acceptance or refusal of this revelation will bring about judgment (5:27). But a great deal of this revelation lies in the future. To the questions of what the food is and where it can be found, the reader asks a further question: When will it be given? Both 1:51 and 3:14 looked to the future for fulfillment. There will be a moment further on in the story when the revelation of God will take place in the lifting up of the Son of Man. Now the reader learns that the food the Son of Man will give will endure for eternal life. The promise of a nourishment that provided life responded to the expectations of Israel. The Law provided life for those who lived by it (see Sir 17:11; 45:5; *Mekilta* on Exod 15:26; *ExodR* 29:9; *DeutR* 8:3; *Tanḥ Shemot* 4:19),[53] and they "labored" (*ergazesthai*) to have this life from the Law. Jesus points to an alternative nourishment as the source of eternal life, the gift of the Son of Man.[54]

Whatever difficulty the characters in the story, and even the reader, may have in fully understanding this promise, Jesus Christ, the Word of God

---

that the crowd does not hunger, because it is "satiated" by the eschatological bread of the miracle. M. Roberge, "Jean 6,26 et le rassasiement eschatologique," *LTP* 45 (1989) 339–49, accepts Grob's explanation of v. 26b, but makes the *zēteite* of v. 26a into an imperative. The crowd is told to seek Jesus not on the basis of signs, but because of the promise of eschatological satisfaction, of which the miracle was a symbol.

[51] Bultmann, *John*, 222.

[52] Many witnesses (Sinaiticus, Bezae, Old Latin, Curetonian Syriac) have the present tense, but P[75] tips the scale in favor of the future. See Manns, *L'Evangile*, 143.

[53] See Borgen, *Bread from Heaven*, 148–49; Léon-Dufour, *Lecture*, 2:132.

[54] Ashton disposes of the complex of "Son of Man" sayings in 6:27, 53, 62, which makes havoc of his overall understanding of the Johannine Son of Man as a heavenly figure (see *Understanding*, 337–73) by making John 6 part of a second edition (see p. 356) that must be understood in the light of the original ascending and descending Son of Man in 3:13 (see p. 368). A reader does not respond to first and second editions.

who became flesh and dwelt among us to make God known (1:14-18), speaks with an unquestionable authority as he affirms that God the Father has set his seal upon the Son of Man: *touton gar ho patēr esphragisen ho theos* (v. 27c).[55] The emphatic use of *houtos* singles out the Son of Man. There is a uniqueness about the nourishment that the Son of Man will give because it is "God the Father who attests the authority and truth of Jesus."[56] As an author puts his own seal on a missive to show its authenticity and to give it authority, so has God the Father done with the Son of Man, his unique mediator between heaven and earth. He is the one who has come down from heaven (see 1:51; 3:13), bearing the credentials of God the Father (6:27c). Whatever difficulties this prolepsis might create for the reader, its promise will be fulfilled. It has been uttered by the most authoritative character in the story.

The crowd attempts to bypass the promise of the Son of Man, asking how they may have direct access to the works of God: "What must we do to be doing the works of God (*hina ergazōmetha ta erga tou theou*)?" (v. 28).[57] They have their Law, given through Moses, and by means of the Law they have direct access to the will of God. The works of God are the things that please God (see CD 2:14-15).[58] Jesus' response indicates that the former access to "doing the works of God" by means of the Law has been surpassed. Access to God is only through the Son who makes God known (see 1:18). Israel may regard itself as having access through the covenant and its Law, but because the Word has become flesh (1:14) there can be no bypassing the one the Father has sent. The only way to do the work of God (*to ergon tou theou*) is to believe in the one whom he has sent (v. 29).[59]

As the Passover feast approaches, Jesus teaches that the nourishment and revelation provided by God in the Law is now to be found in the revelation of God that will take place in the Son of Man, and that the task of the believer is to believe in the one sent by God. Jesus has not spoken in the first person. The work of God is done when one believes in the one sent (v. 29). There will be a gift from God, made available through the Son of Man (v. 27), the one sent by God (v. 29), which surpasses all human food (v. 26). Laboring for the possession of this food (vv. 27, 28-29), believing in

[55] The aorist refers back to the *egeneto* of 1:14, the moment in history when the *logos pros ton theon* (1:1) became flesh. See Moloney, *Son of Man*, 114–15.

[56] Barrett, *St John*, 287. See also Borgen, "John 6," 272–74.

[57] This is the only question interrupting the discourse that does not begin a new subsection. There are too many links across vv. 25-29, highlighted by the movement from *ergazesthe* in v. 27, to *hina ergazōmetha* in v. 28 to Jesus' final words that equate *to ergon tou theou* with *pisteuēte eis hon apesteilen ekeinos* in v. 29.

[58] See Schnackenburg, *St John*, 2:39.

[59] As, among others, Brown, *John*, 1:262, points out, the present subjunctive here has a durative meaning.

the one whom God has sent (v. 29), will produce eternal life (v. 27). The program for the rest of the discourse has been established, and it is closely linked to themes that are important at the celebration of the Passover: nourishment, bread from heaven, and the revelation of God in the Law.

Verses 30-33

The crowd recognizes that Jesus is making claims for himself. Content with their Mosaic traditions and determined to force Jesus into their criteria by the performance of visible signs, they ask: "Then what sign (*sēmeion*) do you do that we may see, and believe you? What work do you perform (*ti ergazē*)? Our fathers ate the manna in the wilderness; as it is written: 'He gave them bread from heaven to eat'" (vv. 30-31). The reader knows that Jesus does the *ergon tou theou* (see 4:34), focusing on what *God* can and will do through the gift of the Son. But the crowd asks Jesus for *his* works. The basis for these demands is the tradition of the gift of the manna. Judaism was familiar with the tradition of confirmatory miracles, and the crowd asks that Jesus conform to this tradition.[60] Moses and the traditions that came from him could call on belief and observance because Moses had worked the miracle of the manna: "He gave them bread from heaven to eat" (v. 31). As C. K. Barrett has commented: "He who makes greater claims than Moses must provide a more striking attestation of his right."[61] Jesus' interlocutors provide the text that will serve as the basis for the rest of the discussion, and they also reintroduce the Passover background central to John 6 (see v. 4).

When Israel looked back to its Mosaic traditions, founded in the Exodus, the people linked Moses and the gift of the manna, understood as a bread from heaven (see Exod 16:4; Pss 78:24; 105:40; Neh 9:15; Wis 16:20), to the never-failing nourishment that God provides. The manna was identified, in both the wisdom and Jewish midrashic traditions, with the gift of the Law.[62] Despite Jesus' warnings and promises (vv. 25-29), the people still attempt to force Jesus into their Mosaic model (vv. 30-31).[63] Moses, the manna, and Torah give life to Israel. What sign can Jesus do to surpass the sign of the gift of the bread in the desert, and all that this gift has come to mean: the life-giving presence of the Torah to God's people? The use of the story of the gift of the manna fixes the reader's attention on an important contrast. Within the context of the Jewish celebration of the Passover, when the gift of the manna was recalled and celebrated, Jesus has sum-

---

[60] On this tradition, see Schnackenburg, *St John*, 2:39-40.

[61] Barrett, *St John*, 288.

[62] See especially Borgen, *Bread from Heaven*, 148-64; Manns, *L'Evangile*, 154-58.

[63] See M. J. Menken, "Some Remarks on the Course of the Dialogue: John 6,25-34," *Bijdragen* 48 (1987) 139-49; Borgen, "John 6," 276-78.

moned the crowd to labor for a bread that does not perish (v. 27; see vv. 12-13). Aroused by these words, the crowd demands that he offer them a sign that will authorize him to challenge the unique authority of Moses and the ongoing presence of the manna reinterpreted as present to the Jewish people in the Torah (vv. 30-31).

Jesus again opens his response with a double "amen" (as in v. 26).[64] He first reminds the crowd not to set so much store by Moses; he did not give the bread from heaven. The people must be reminded that God was responsible for the original gift of the manna. This gift, once given by God (*dedōken*),[65] is surpassed by a bread that God *now gives* (*didōsin*): *ton arton ek tou ouranou ton alēthinon.*[66] However wonderful the former gift of God, the *true bread* from heaven is the gift of the Father of Jesus. The reader knows that the Father of Jesus is the God of Israel (see 5:17-18, 19-30). There is a difference between the bread that was given through Moses and the true bread that God now gives. The latter bread comes down from heaven and gives life to the world (v. 33). While the people of Israel celebrate the Passover, recalling the gift of the manna, rendered present in the gift of the Law, Jesus instructs them that there is another bread, the "true" bread. The use of *alēthinos* sets this bread over against all other breads, even the bread given to the ancestors of Israel through Moses. This is the authentic bread that is and does all that it claims to be and do.[67] Jesus claims that it is the bread "that comes down from heaven" and "gives life to the whole world."[68] This bread is the gift of God, descending from above, and—unlike the Torah—is no longer limited to the nourishment of a chosen people. It is a bread that gives life to the whole world. There is both contrast and continuation here. Moses did not give the bread from heaven, God did. Now this same God, the Father of Jesus, gives the true bread from heaven. The Mosaic manna provided nourishment for Israel; the true bread from heaven gives life to the whole world.

[64] This is an indication that the first two units in the discourse are vv. 25-29 (a question answered with a double "amen") and vv. 30-33 (a question answered with a double "amen"). For the rabbinic nature of this response of Jesus to the question raised in vv. 30-31, see Borgen, *Bread from Heaven*, 61–69.

[65] The perfect tense must be maintained, even though Vaticanus, Bezae, and Clement of Alexandria have *edōken*. See Barrett, *St John*, 289.

[66] The adjective is used emphatically here. See Brown, *John*, 1:262. On the importance of *both* gifts, but the superiority of the latter, see Barrett, *St John*, 290.

[67] On this use of *alēthinos* in the Fourth Gospel, see Moloney, *Belief*, 36, and the references mentioned there. See also H. Leroy, *Rätsel und Missverständnis: Ein Beitrag zur Formgeschichte des Johannesevangeliums* (BBB 30; Bonn: Peter Hanstein, 1968) 103–7.

[68] As Brown, *John*, 1:262–63, points out, the reading could be "that which comes down," which would be a reference to the Law, or "he who comes down," which is christological. Only further reading will make clear that a reference to Jesus is intended.

Verses 34-40

The people at Capernaum now ask, *kyrie pantote dos hymin ton arton tou-ton* (6:34; see 4:15). They misunderstand the nature of the bread and ask Jesus to give them this bread *pantote*. They suggest that the bread of heaven be given again and again. Jesus responds in the first person singular, correcting the misunderstanding and carrying his self-revelation further. He identifies himself as the bread: *egō eimi ho artos tēs zōēs* (v. 35).[69] As with all the *egō eimi* sayings with a predicate, Jesus is not describing who he is, but what he does. He nourishes with a bread that produces life. The idea of a heavenly bread comes from the biblical story of the gift of the manna. The manna came to be interpreted, especially in the wisdom tradition, in terms of God's revelation in word and instruction. The nourishing bread for Israel is Torah.[70] Jesus claims that he is perfecting the former gift of the Torah. Gone are all the limitations of a chosen people, as Jesus promises to satisfy the needs of anyone who would come to him (*ho erchomenos pros eme*); they will not hunger. Anyone who would believe in him (*ho pisteuōn eis eme*) will not thirst. The two expressions "to come to . . . to believe in," set in close parallel, mean the same thing. The reader senses that those who come to Jesus will find rest from the never-ending search for Wisdom: "Those who eat me [Wisdom] will hunger for more, and those who drink me will thirst for more" (Sir 24:21; see also Isa 49:10).

No longer will Moses, the manna, Wisdom, or Torah provide for the deepest needs of humankind, but Jesus will satisfy all hunger and thirst.[71] Jesus will provide both food and drink, *in the future*: "shall not hunger (*ou mē peinasę̄*) . . . shall never thirst (*ou mē dipsēsei pōpote*)." The reader again encounters a prolepsis, a promise that belief in Jesus will provide a never-failing food and drink.[72] When might this happen? What might this food and drink be? The link with wisdom traditions indicates to the reader that the revelation of God in Jesus surpasses and perfects the Law. But the memory of the unresolved prolepses involved in the gathering of the *klasmata* so that they might not perish (vv. 12-13) and the promise that the Son of Man would give a bread that, unlike the bread of Israel's ancestors, would endure to eternal life (v. 27) remain with the reader.

[69] On the christological use of *egō eimi* with a predicate, see, among many, the surveys of Bultmann, *John*, 225–26 n. 3; Barrett, *St John*, 291–93; and Schnackenburg, *St John*, 2:79–89, especially 88–89.

[70] For a discussion, see Dodd, *Interpretation*, 336–37. On the rabbinic nature of vv. 34-40, see Borgen, *Bread from Heaven*, 69–80.

[71] For the wisdom background to v. 35, see M. Scott, *Sophia and the Johannine Jesus* (JSNTSup 71; Sheffield: JSOT Press, 1992) 116–19.

[72] The twofold use of *ou mē* and the use of *pōpote* (subtly correcting the crowd's *pantote*, v. 34) provide the emphasis.

The hostility Jesus showed toward the people when they came in search of him so that they might have more to eat (v. 26) is repeated, but now in a more christological key. Jesus claims to have told them that they have seen and not believed (v. 36).[73] These words that Jesus claims to have said cannot be found earlier in the Gospel. This is a reference back to Jesus' revelation of himself through the miraculous gift of the bread that has been misunderstood in terms of the crowd's Mosaic traditions.[74] Verse 26 provides the key for a correct reading of v. 36. The reader looks back over the context of vv. 1-26. Close to the feast of the Passover (v. 4) Jesus has made himself known to the multitude (see vv. 5-13), and they have not believed in him (see vv. 14-15, 25-26).[75] Jesus is the nourishment of Israel; he replaces the manna that is the Torah, but the crowd has not believed in this revelation, even though they have seen it. The Passover theme, the gift of the manna that is the Law, perfected by the revelation of God in the one whom he has sent (see v. 29), is now at the center of the discussion. Whereas once the Passover recalled the gift of the manna of the Torah, Jesus has identified himself with the true bread from heaven that gives the nourishment essential for life to all who come to him, who believe in him (v. 35). This is what has been *seen*, but not *believed* (v. 36).

It is the Father's initiative that sends those who come to Jesus in faith, and Jesus willingly accepts "everyone" (*pan ho didōsin moi ho patēr*).[76] He will surely not cast out (*ou mē ekballō exō*) anyone or anything given to him by the Father. The universality in this acceptance contrasts with the exclusivity of those who are not prepared to go beyond their Mosaic tradition. The implied reader is being addressed with words that would strike a chord with the intended readers: the members of the Johannine community. They have experienced a "casting out" (see 9:34) because of their faith in Jesus as the Christ. As the word of God (see Isa 55:10-11) and the Law of God were understood as a gift from God that came down from heaven (see Exod 19:11, 20; *Sanhedrin* 10:1; *b. Shabbat* 89b; *Pesikta Rabbati* 53:2; *ExodR* 28:1-3),[77] Jesus presents himself as the perfection of the for-

---

[73] The textual evidence for the presence of *me* (you have seen *me*) is balanced. With Barrett, *St John*, 293 (and against Brown, *John*, 1:270), I am reading the more general affirmation: "You have seen and not believed." It has strong textual support (Sinaiticus, Old Latin, Sinaitic Syriac, Curetonian Syriac), and better suits the argument.

[74] See also Brown, *John*, 1:269.

[75] See Lagrange, *Saint Jean*, 176–77. Against Painter, *Quest*, 269, who does not see v. 26 as a reproach, and claims that there is no hostility in vv. 1-34 (pp. 237–38).

[76] Strangely, the neuter singular *pan* is used where one would expect the masculine plural. This is, however, found elsewhere in the Johannine Gospel and Letters. On this, see Bernard, *St John*, 1:199.

[77] For a discussion of Philo on "a heavenly order reaching down to check the disorderly tendencies of the earth," see Borgen, *Bread from Heaven*, 122–46.

mer gift of the Law. Like the Law, his presence is a reflection of the will of the Father (v. 38; see 4:34). The Father gives (v. 37), the Father sends (v. 38a), and the one who is sent responds totally to the will of the Father who sent him (v. 38b). But formerly the will of God had been given in the gift of the Law. How does Jesus, the true bread from heaven, relate to this former understanding of the will of God, whom he now calls "my Father"?

Jesus answers that question in two stages (vv. 39-40).

1. As the Law was to lead a chosen people so they would belong forever to YHWH, so it is with Jesus. In the new situation, where the Law has been replaced with Jesus and the new people of God is anyone whom the Father gives to him, the will of the Father is that this new people will never be lost, neither now nor hereafter: "I should lose *nothing* of all that he has given me." But some were dying a physical death. Thus follow words essential to a third-generation Christian church, facing the mystery of the death of its members (v. 39b). The promises of God made concrete through the Law of Moses have been perfected in the presence of his Son.

2. Continuing the theme of his relationship to the manna of the Law, Jesus promises eternal life to those who would perfect their adherence to the Law by believing in the Son sent by the Father (v. 40a). But here the relationship to the Law becomes more explicit. It was through the concrete reality of the Law, words of God that spoke to the lived situation of a chosen people, that Israel could find the will of God. This "living presence," the visible assurance that God cares for and guides his people, is no longer found in a written law. It is to be seen and it is to be believed in the presence of the Son: "*Everyone* who sees (*pas ho theōrōn*) the Son and believes (*pisteuōn*) in him should have eternal life."[78] The words of Jesus assure the reader that *all* those the Father had given to him, and *all* those who had believed in him in life, would live forever, as he would "raise him up at the last day" (v. 40b).

Both the temporal dimensions of the Law, guarding and directing a people during its earthly pilgrimage, and the ethnic limitations of the Law, an exclusive covenant between God and the people of Israel, have been perfected in Jesus, who promises life to *everyone*, both *now* and *forever*. The God of the Passover still makes himself known, and he continues to nourish his people, but the former gift of the bread from heaven has been perfected in Jesus, the true bread from heaven.

---

[78] As Brown, *John*, 1:270, has pointed out concerning the action of "seeing" in v. 40: "*theorein* . . . not only physically, but with spiritual insight." The nature of *pisteuein* needs no explanation for the reader, after 2:1—4:54.

Verses 41-51

Repeating the behavior of the ancestors of Israel, who murmured against Moses (Exod 16:2, 7, 8), the previously unspecified multitude (*ho ochlos*) becomes "the Jews." Once "the Jews" emerge from the crowd to pose a question, hostility grows.[79] The presence of the "murmuring," recalling the attitude of the Israelites in the wilderness (see Exod 15:24; 16:2, 7, 12; 17:3), already indicates rebellion. There is nothing naive about the question of "the Jews": "Is not this Jesus, the son of Joseph, whose father and mother we know? How does he now say, 'I have come down from heaven'?" (v. 42). Jesus' claim to be the bread that comes down from heaven, the subject of vv. 35-40, is being challenged. Jesus makes claims that can be understood only in terms of his origins: a descent *from his Father above*. His opponents will not consider such a possibility; they know *his father Joseph*.

Moses had warned the people: "Your complaints are not against us, but against the Lord" (Exod 16:8). Jesus does not defend his claim to have come down from heaven; he points beyond himself to his Father, but Jesus is crucial to the process. The Father sends Jesus, the Father draws believers to him, but it is the response of those drawn to the revelation of the Father in and through Jesus that will be the measure of their everlasting life.[80] It is Jesus who will "raise him up at the last day" (v. 44). While God determines the process, the encounter between the human being and the revelation of God in Jesus determines life, death, and everlasting life. Such claims are possible only because of Jesus' origins. He is not the son of Joseph (vv. 41-42), but the Son of the Father.

Thus Jesus asks "the Jews" to listen to God and to let themselves be taught by him. The prophets had foretold that "they shall all be taught by God" (v. 45a, freely citing Isa 54:13).[81] This affirmation is crucial for Israel's understanding of itself. The gift of the Law is the way in which God has taught and will continue to teach his people. But Jesus, the one who has come down from heaven (see v. 42), is claiming that all those who have truly learned from God, whom he continues to call his Father, will come to him. "The Jews" have no difficulty in accepting the ideas behind Jesus' affirmations about a gift from above that nourishes and instructs a

[79] For Painter, *Quest*, 275–78, the nature of the discourse changes here. While vv. 25-35 can be classified as a "quest story," vv. 36-71 are "rejection stories," with vv. 36-40 as a "transitional addition," bridging vv. 1-40 and vv. 36-71. But see Borgen, "John 6," 283–85.

[80] In the rabbinic sources, the expression "to draw" is used to describe a bringing close to the Torah, and thus to conversion. See *Pirke Abot* 1:12.

[81] The vague reference to "the prophets" is made only here in the Fourth Gospel. On the text from Isaiah, see M. J. J. Menken, "The Old Testament Quotation in John 6,45: Source and Redaction," *ETL* 64 (1988) 164–72; and Schuchard, *Scripture Within Scripture*, 47–57.

people, but Jesus claims that the instruction God gives *to all peoples* (v. 45a: *pantes*) draws them to Jesus (v. 45b: *pas . . . erchetai pros eme*). In fulfill-ment of the prophetic promise (v. 45a), there is a process by which the Father is made known, which leads to the true believer's coming to Jesus (v. 45b). No longer is Israel the object and the Law the source of God's instruction. It is now aimed at all believers, without the limitations of race or nation, and it comes through Jesus.

Jesus is the one who makes the Father known. Recalling words from the prologue (see 1:18), Jesus informs "the Jews" that no one has ever seen the Father, but there is one who has come from the Father; he it is who is able to make the Father known (v. 46). As in 1:16-18, the relationship between Jesus and Moses is in question. No matter how exalted the claims for Moses, there is only one who has ever seen God; not Moses, but the only begotten Son who throughout his human story gazes toward the Father (1:18).[82] The difference between Jesus and Moses is their origins. Jesus' opponents cling to what they know, his father and mother, but the reader is aware that Jesus' origins *pros ton theon* (see 1:1) give him a unique authority to make God known (see 1:18). Because this is the case,[83] the one who believes in the revelation of Jesus, the true bread that has come down from heaven, has eternal life. As throughout the discourse, a com-parison is pursued between the manna of the Law given from heaven by God, and Jesus the true bread from heaven. It is no longer the Law that produces life. The revelation of God, now possible because Jesus, the true bread from heaven, came from the Father to make him known, has sur-passed the former gift of a bread from heaven.

Two "breads" are being compared, as Jesus claims for a second time: "I am the bread of life" (v. 48; see v. 35). If knowledge of God ensures eternal life, as is clear from the Scriptures (v. 45), then it can only be had from being drawn toward the one from God, as one was formerly drawn to the Law and thus to conversion (v. 46), believing in him, rather than the Law, for eternal life (v. 47). The author rests his case by pointing to Jesus, the true bread that comes down from heaven: he is the bread of life (v. 48). The ancestors of Israel ate the bread that came down from heaven in the form of the manna, but they have all died (v. 49); the bread that comes down from heaven, recognized by now as the person of Jesus himself, promises a life that is eternal. There will be no death for those who con-sume that bread (v. 50). The comparison continues between the gift of the manna and the gift of the revelation of God in Jesus.

There is a close parallel between the words of Jesus in v. 50: "This is the

---

[82] For this interpretation of 1:18, see Moloney, *Belief,* 48–51.

[83] The use of the solemn double "amen" in v. 47 lies behind my "because this is the case."

bread that comes down from heaven," and v. 51: "I am the living bread that came down from heaven." Moses pointed to the manna and proclaimed: "This is the bread that the Lord has given you for food" (Exod 16:15). The words "this is the bread" are repeated by Jesus in John 6:50. But the ancestors of Israel ate of the bread, and they died (v. 49). They are no longer present; even the death of Moses is recorded in the Law (see Deut 34:5-8). But now there is another bread from heaven, and *houtos estin ho artos ho ek tou ouranou katabainōn . . . egō eimi ho artos ho zōn ho ek tou ouranou katabas.* As Moses pointed to the manna and said: "This is the bread" (Exod 16:15), now Jesus points to himself saying: "This is the bread" (John 6:50). He then repeats his claim in the first person, but by means of an inceptive aorist (*katabas*) points back to the basis for his claim to be the bread coming from heaven. The enfleshing of the Word, when *ho logos sarx egeneto* (1:14), initiated the presence of Jesus Christ in the human story (1:17). He is the true bread from heaven claiming to provide a nourishment that makes God known. Going beyond anything that the Law could offer, Jesus is the revelation of God, making God known to all who come to him so that they may have eternal life (vv. 46-47). In doing this he perfects the former gift of the manna, the Law (v. 48), and proof of this can be seen in the fact that those who ate of the former manna are now dead (v. 49). The nourishment that Jesus provides will give people everlasting life, because Jesus has come from God to make him known (vv. 50-51ab).

There has been a gradual intensification of the concentration on the person of Jesus: "This is the bread . . ." (v. 50a), "I am the bread . . ." (v. 51a). This focus on Jesus now culminates in a surprising fashion as he introduces a further prolepsis: "The bread that I shall give is my flesh for the life of the world" (v. 51c).[84] Although many elements in v. 51c lead scholars to find contacts with Johannine eucharistic traditions (*ho artos, sarx, egō dōsō, hyper*),[85] the reader recalls 1:14, where *sarx* was used to speak of the presence of the Word among us in the historical human being, Jesus Christ (1:17). After all that has been said to this point, the reader understands that Jesus, the true bread that has come down from heaven, *will* make God known by an unconditional gift of himself for the life of the world.[86] The discourse takes a surprising turn, but Jesus' words

---

[84] Following P[66], P[75], Vaticanus, Bezae, Old Latin, Vulgate, Sinaitic Syriac, Curetonian Syriac, and Sahidic for the future tense.

[85] See, for example, J. Jeremias, *The Eucharistic Words of Jesus* (London: SCM Press, 1966) 106-8.

[86] For a detailed study, coming to this conclusion, see H. Schürmann, "Joh 6,51c—ein Schlüssel zur grossen Brotrede," *BZ* 2 (1958) 244-62. See also Moloney, *Son of Man*, 115; Léon-

affirm that he will give himself totally for the life of the world. When will this be? How will it happen? As in the proleptic statements that point to a future encounter between the darkness and the light (1:5), to the hour of Jesus (2:5), and to his being lifted up (3:14), much remains a mystery to the reader. But there are already some solid hints that Jesus is heading for death at the hands of "the Jews." They rejected him at the Temple in 2:13-23, and the encounter between Jesus and "the Jews" on the occasion of the Sabbath ended in a decision that Jesus must be killed (5:18). However, *how* Jesus' experience of death will provide nourishment for the life of the world remains incomprehensible. The reader accepts the promise of Jesus, the most authoritative character in the story, but "the Jews" do not. A claim to give his flesh for the life of the world can only bring dispute, shock, and horror to the Jewish listeners who take his words on their face value.[87]

The future tense of the verb in Jesus' promise, *ho artos de hon egō dōsō*, must be taken seriously.[88] It is not the first time in the narrative that Jesus has promised a future gift. The words of Jesus, pointing to the future gift of his flesh for the life of the world (v. 51c), remind the reader of three earlier prolepses in the narrative. In 6:12-13 the disciples were commanded to gather the *klasmata* so that they might not be lost. But why are the twelve baskets to be preserved? In 6:27 Jesus urged the crowds not to labor for a nourishment that would perish, but for a food that would endure, to be provided by the Son of Man. Is there a link between the gathering of the *klasmata* so that they might not perish (6:12: *hina mē ti apolētai*), and the future gift of the food of the Son of Man, surpassing all food that perishes (v. 27: *tēn brōsin tēn apollymenēn*)? If so, what might this food be, and when might the gift take place? A further prolepsis occurs in v. 35. Jesus' claim to be the bread of life led to the promise that anyone who comes to him *will not* hunger, and anyone who believes in him *will not* thirst. There is to be a definitive food and drink that will forever satisfy the needs of all who believe in Jesus. Jesus has been arguing throughout his discussion with the crowd and "the Jews" *that* the gift of the nourishment provided by the Law has been surpassed by the gift of the true bread from heaven, the revelation of God in and through Jesus. The reader reasonably awaits some explanation of *how* this will take place.

Dufour, *Lecture*, 2:159–62; M. J. J. Menken, "John 6,51c-58: Eucharist or Christology?" *Bib* 74 (1993) 9–13.

[87] The disputing (*emachonto oun . . . hoi Ioudaioi*) continues the theme of the "grumbling" from Exodus 16. It appears in Exod 17:2, with the same meaning as the verb *gongyzein* in Exod 16:7-8 and John 6:41, 43. See also Num 11:4.

[88] See also Menken, "John 6,51c-58," 13–15.

Verses 52-59

"The Jews" ask that question: "*How* (*pōs*) can this man give us his flesh to eat?" (v. 52). Their certitude about Jesus' parents and family (vv. 41-42) has provided Jesus with the opportunity to address the question of his origins with God, the basis for his ability to make God known (vv. 43-51ab), giving his flesh for the life of the world (v. 51c).[89] The question raised in v. 52 is a rejection of Jesus' outrageous suggestion, but for the reader it is a question that needs to be answered in the further unraveling of Jesus' perfection of the Mosaic bread from heaven through his gift of himself as the true bread from heaven. "The Jews" are not prepared to go beyond what they cannot control or understand, taking Jesus' words to mean physical eating of the body of the person standing before them (see also 3:4). There is profound misunderstanding here.[90] Jesus insists on a gift of flesh and blood for life.[91] He first says it negatively: whoever does not eat of the flesh and drink of the blood of the Son of Man has no life (v. 53); and then positively, identifying himself as "Son of Man": whoever eats the flesh and drinks the blood of Jesus has eternal life now and will be raised up on the last day (v. 54).

The paraphrase of the verb "to eat" in the midrashic exposition of the Exodus passage provided in v. 31 has reached its high point. The use of the physical verb *trōgein* in vv. 54 and 56-57, a word that indicates the action of crunching with the teeth,[92] renders concrete the notion of the eating of the flesh of Jesus. Flesh and blood emphasize that it is the incarnate life of the Son which is life-giving food. It is only the physical body of a real human being that produces flesh and blood.[93] The argument of vv. 25-51 continues into vv. 52-59. The celebration of the feast of the Passover and the contrast between the gift of Moses and the gift of Jesus, the unique revelation of God, so central to the discussion so far, remain at the center of the discussion between Jesus and "the Jews." The reader also senses the culmination of a series of prolepses (see vv. 12-13, 27, 35, 51c): Jesus will

[89] There is no break at v. 48, nor does a new section begin with v. 51c. On this, see Barrett, *St John*, 296. Most commentators and critics, impressed by the eucharistic possibilities of v. 51c, read vv. 51c-58 as a unit.

[90] See Leroy, *Rätsel und Missverständnis*, 121–24.

[91] The presence of the double "amen" at the opening three out of five responses (vv. 26, 32, 53) is an indication of the staged unfolding of the argument.

[92] BAGD, 829; LSJ, 1832. Some would object to this. See, for example, Barrett, *St John*, 299; and Menken, "John 6,51c-58," 16–18. For the position adopted, see especially C. Spicq, "*Trōgein*: Est-il synonyme de *phagein* et d'*esthien* dans le Nouveau Testament?" *NTS* 26 (1979–80) 414–19.

[93] It is often suggested that the vigor of these claims combats emerging docetic ideas about Jesus. See especially Schnelle, *Antidocetic Christology*, 201–8.

provide a bread for the life of the world, and that bread is his flesh. Through the total gift of himself, Jesus will provide a food for the life of the world.

While "the Jews" ask *how* Jesus can give his flesh to eat, the reader asks *how* the total self-gift of Jesus will provide a food that will not perish, but will provide a nourishment for the life of the world. As the ancestors of Israel were nourished by the gift of the Torah, Jesus will nourish the whole world with the gift of himself. Israel was nourished by the eating of the manna, perennially recalled in the nourishment provided for them by their total receptivity to and absorption of the Law.[94] Now "the Jews" are told of the absolute need to eat the flesh and drink the blood of the Son of Man (vv. 53-54). Flesh is to be broken and blood is to be spilled. The reader has been aware for some time that violence is in the air (see 2:13-23; 5:16-18). Jesus now associates the separation of flesh and blood in a violent death as the moment of his total giving of himself. There can be no mistaking the message: Jesus, the Son of Man, will give of his whole self for the life of the world (6:51c) by means of a violent encounter between himself and his enemies (1:5, 11; 2:18-20; 3:14; 5:16-18) in which his body will be broken and his blood poured out (6:53-54). This is the enduring gift that the Son of Man will give, the food that will not perish (v. 27) but will forever satisfy all hunger and thirst (v. 35).

The reader knows of Jesus' crucifixion but is meeting, for the first time, an understanding of this event as a life-giving lifting up of Jesus that makes God known in a way previously performed by the Law. The Son of Man will offer this nourishment not only for the life of Israel, but for the life of the world. There is a growing bank of knowledge that leads the reader further into the narrative in anticipation of a story of broken flesh and blood poured out.[95] As once Israel ate of the manna in the desert, and was nourished by adhesion to the Law given at Sinai, now the world is summoned to accept the further revelation of God that will take place in the broken body and the spilled blood of the Son of Man. In this way all will have life, now and hereafter (vv. 53-54). These claims are further developed through vv. 55-57. Earlier parts of the discourse are recalled as Jesus insists that his flesh *alēthōs estin brōsis* and his blood *alēthōs estin posis*.[96] This play on words recalls Jesus' promise of the *brōsis* that the Son

---

[94] For a collection of Jewish material on this "absorption" of the Law, see H. Odeberg, *The Fourth Gospel Interpreted in Its Relation to Contemporary Religious Currents in Palestine and the Hellenistic-Oriental World* (Uppsala: Almqvist, 1929) 238–47.

[95] For a detailed study of v. 53, arguing for its primary reference being the crucifixion, see Moloney, *Son of Man*, 115–20.

[96] Following the first hand of Sinaiticus, Bezae, Koridethi, Athos, Old Latin, Vulgate, Sinaitic Syriac, Curetonian Syriac, and the Peshitta, I am reading *alēthōs*, rather than *alēthēs*.

of Man would give (v. 27), and his claim that over against all other bread from heaven, and especially the gift of the Law from heaven, the Father gives *ton arton ek tou ouranou alēthinon* (v. 31). He is the true bread from heaven (v. 35). On the basis of the entire discourse Jesus can lay claim to his flesh and his blood as authentically (*alēthōs*) food and drink.

The reader next encounters an expression that will later develop into a major theme: the mutual abiding of Jesus in the believer and the believer in Jesus (v. 56; see 15:4-7). Although the physical verb *trōgein* is used here for the second time (see also v. 54), it is balanced by the more spiritual idea of a mutual indwelling (*menein en*) that results from the commitment of the believer to the revelation Jesus brings. The midrashic explanation of Exod 16:4, 15 (see v. 31) continues: through a total absorption of the revelation of God made available through the bloody death of Jesus, believers will come to a mutuality where they live in Jesus and Jesus lives in them. The mutual indwelling of Jesus in the believer and the believer in Jesus, which results from the acceptance of the revelation of God in the flesh and blood of Jesus (v. 56), flows from the union that exists between the Father and his Son, Jesus (v. 57). Jesus' words play upon the verb "to live" (*zōein*).[97] He refers to the Father as the *"living* Father" (*ho zōn patēr*) who has sent his Son, who has life in him precisely because of this Father–Son link. If the one who sends is "living," then the one who is sent *lives* because of the one who sent him (*kagō zō dia ton patera*) and therefore has an authority to pass on life to those who accept the revelation of the Father in the Son.[98]

This idea of the reception of the revelation of God in and through his Son so that one might have life is not new to the reader (see especially 3:11-21, 31-36). Now the image is changed. No longer is it "belief in" (see 3:12, 15, 18, 36) that is used to speak of the way in which the believer is to relate to Jesus, but "he who eats me" (*ho trōgōn me*, v. 57). The expressions are parallel. Even though the strongly physical verb *trōgein* is again used, to consume Jesus means to believe in him.[99] As throughout the Gospel, life here and hereafter combine: the one who eats the flesh of Jesus *will live* because of him (*kakeinos zēsei di' eme*).

Jesus' final words to "the Jews" return to the theme that has dominated the miracle story (vv. 5-15) and the ensuing discourse (vv. 25-58): the comparison between the bread that Israel's ancestors ate in the desert and

---

[97] This concentration upon the theme of "life" produces the expression *ho zōn patēr*, found only here in the New Testament.

[98] The use of *dia* with the accusative could mean "through, by means of," rather than "because of." For my choice of "because of," see Bernard, *St John*, 1:213–14; Brown, *John*, 1:283. For a contrary view, see Lagrange, *Saint Jean*, 185–86.

[99] See Léon-Dufour, *Lecture*, 2:167–69.

the bread that comes down from heaven (v. 58). Jesus reaffirms that all former gifts from heaven have now been surpassed. Israel has consumed the
bread from heaven commemorated in the celebration of the Passover, the
gift of the Law, but that bread does not provide everlasting life. Playing on
the two possibilities of life—physical life, which the manna could not provide, and eternal life, which the true bread from heaven does give (see vv.
49-50)—Jesus points to the death of Israel's ancestors and promises everlasting life for those who eat of the true bread from heaven. A new possibility has entered the human story. The Law was a gift of God (see 1:17),
but now it has been surpassed by Jesus, the bread from heaven (v. 35), the
gift of the revelation of God in and through the flesh and blood of the Son
of Man (vv. 53-54). He is authentic food and drink (v. 55), promising the
abiding presence of Jesus (v. 56), communicating the life of the Father to
all who consume this true bread (v. 57). There is now another bread from
heaven that eclipses all the original bread offered to the ancestors of Israel
(v. 58).

But what of the eucharistic background to this final part of the discourse, highlighted by the words *artos, brōsis, sarx, haima, trōgein*? While
the author is not primarily concerned with the presence of Jesus in the celebration of the Eucharist, the paraphrasing of "to eat" from v. 31 summons up eucharistic language.[100] There is no break in the argument at v.
51c, as throughout the discourse Jesus is presented as the true bread from
heaven, replacing the former bread from heaven, the manna of the Law.[101]
The reader is asked to be receptive to the revelation of God that will take
place in broken flesh and spilled blood (vv. 53-54), a never-failing (v. 35)
nourishment that the Son of Man will give (v. 27). But the Christian reader
asks: Where do I encounter this revelation of God in the flesh and blood
of the Son of Man? By means of the underlying eucharistic language the
author insinuates an answer: It is in the Eucharistic celebration that one
can encounter the flesh and blood of Jesus the Christ. The use of the
expression *klasmata* to refer to the bread consigned by Jesus to his disciples (vv. 12-13) has lurked behind the story, reminding the reader of
such celebrations.

The author is working at two levels here. The main thrust of the discourse is to point to Jesus as the revelation of God, the true bread from
heaven, perfecting God's former gift, the bread of the manna. The use of
the expression *klasmata* in vv. 12-13, the promise of a future gift of a food
that the Son of Man would give in v. 27, the reference to satisfying food
and drink in v. 35, and the further promise of the gift of the flesh of Jesus

---

[100] See Menken, "John 6,51c-58," 6–9.
[101] Against, for example, Brown, *John*, 1:284.

for the life of the world in v. 51c, however, keep the eucharistic question alive. Thus the eucharistic celebration, recalled through the use of the verb "to eat" in vv. 49-58, plays a secondary but important role. It renders concrete, in the Christian understanding of the implied reader, and in the eucharistic practice of the Johannine community, what the author has spelled out through the discourse. One senses that the Johannine Eucharist was a place where one could come to eternal life. Encountering the flesh and blood of Jesus (vv. 53-54), the believer was called to make a decision for or against the revelation of God in that encounter (vv. 56-58), gaining or losing life because of it (vv. 53-54).[102]

A full understanding of the *klasmata* (vv. 12-13), the future gift of the Son of Man (v. 27), totally satisfying food and drink (v. 35), Jesus' flesh as food for the life of the world, and the eating of the flesh of the Son of Man and drinking his blood (vv. 53-54), still lies ahead. But the reader trusts in Jesus' assuring words that only here can be found a life-giving mutual indwelling between the believer and Jesus, the Sent One of the living God (vv. 56-57). The reader does not question these promises made by the most authoritative character in the story, Jesus Christ, the only begotten Son of the Father, the incarnation of the preexistent Word (see 1:1-18). Such assurances make the need to discover the full truth of these matters more urgent. "Narrative texts implicitly keep promising the reader the great prize of understanding—later."[103] For the moment the author signals to the reader that the discourse has come to an end by repeating the geographical indication with which it opened: "This he said in the synagogue, as he taught at Capernaum" (v. 59; see v. 24). Jesus is in a Jewish center of worship at the Passover season, uttering a message that presupposes, fulfills, and transcends a Jewish Passover tradition.

VI. THE *KRISIS:* RESPONSE TO THE WORD OF JESUS: 6:60-71

THE SHAPE OF THE NARRATIVE

The response to Jesus' words is twofold:

(a) *Verses 60-66:* "Many of the disciples" find Jesus' word hard (v. 60), and after further words from Jesus, including an allusion to the future betrayal of Judas (v. 64), "many disciples" no longer go with Jesus (v. 66).

---

[102] See Hoskyns, *Fourth Gospel*, 297; F. J. Moloney, "John 6 and the Celebration of the Eucharist," *DRev* 93 (1975) 243–51; H. van den Bussche, *Jean: Commentaire de l'Évangile Spirituel* (Bruges: Desclée de Brouwer, 1976) 247–52; Lee, *Symbolic Narrative*, 148–53.

[103] Rimmon-Kenan, *Narrative Fiction*, 125.

(b) *Verses 67-71:* The Twelve, represented by Peter, express authentic belief (vv. 68-69), but Jesus foretells that from among the disciples he has chosen, one will betray him (vv. 70-71).

READING THE NARRATIVE

The disciples have *heard* what has been said (v. 60a: *polloi oun akousantes ek tōn mathētōn*). But it is one thing to hear and see things, and it is another to make them one's own. There has been some debate, linked to decision about the originality of vv. 51c-58, concerning the objection of the disciples. Is the "hard word" (*sklēros estin ho logos houtos*) an objection to Jesus' words on the necessity to eat his flesh and drink his blood (vv. 53-55), or to the earlier part of the discourse (vv. 25-51c)?[104] The reader is aware (see 2:1—4:54) that the disciples have reached a crucial moment. They have heard "the word" of Jesus; how will they respond? On the lake *only the disciples* had been told by Jesus: *egō eimi; mē phobeisthe* (v. 20). They have been shown (vv. 5-13, 16-21) and told (vv. 25-29) *who it is* who speaks to them.

Despite this knowledge, they find the word of Jesus *sklēros:* unacceptable, harsh, offensive.[105] The disciples are being asked to enter a world where the traditional way of coming to know God through the revealing nourishment of the Torah is replaced by the true bread from heaven, the person of Jesus, made concrete in their lives through his broken body and his spilled blood. They find that it is not possible to "listen" (*akouein*) to this word. Despite their knowledge, they are moving toward "the Jews" because of his word (v. 61a). Jesus challenges them with a further word. Do they take offense at what he has said? Although the harshness of the word on eating his flesh and drinking his blood leaps to mind as the offensive element in what Jesus has said, the whole discourse is still in question. He claims to make God known in a way that transcends the revelation of God in the gift of the Torah. Thus, he suggests to his disciples that they may be looking for further support for his claim to be the definitive revealer of God.[106]

---

[104] See, for example, G. Bornkamm, "Die eucharistische Rede im Johannesevangelium," *ZNW* 47 (1956) 161–69; Brown, *John*, 1:299–303, for only vv. 25-51b; and, for example, Barrett, *St John*, 284; L. Schenke, "Das johanneische Schisma und die 'Zwölf' (Johannes 6,60-71)," *NTS* 108–11, for the whole discourse.

[105] Barrett, *St John*, 302. It does not mean "difficult to understand."

[106] Against Brown, *John*, 1:299–303, who offers an interpretation of vv. 60-71 as containing no reference to vv. 51-58, but closely linked to vv. 35-50. In defense of a close link between vv. 60-71 and vv. 51c-58, see Menken, "John 6,51c-58," 23–26.

Jesus' unfinished conditional question: "What if you were to see the Son of Man ascending to where he was before?" is high rhetoric.[107] Understood is the conclusion: Would that satisfy your doubts? Both Jews and Greeks had their speculations about the ascent and descent of a heavenly redeemer.[108] Jesus' question takes for granted information about the Son of Man already provided for the reader in 3:13.[109] There the reader learned that no one had ever gone up to heaven, but the Son of Man, the unique revelation of God, has come down from heaven. The same claim has been made several times throughout Jesus' discourse. He has claimed to be the bread that has come down from heaven (see vv. 32-33, 35, 38, 51a) and as "the Jews" questioned his origins (see vv. 41-42) he affirmed that he comes from God (v. 46). Because of his origins he is able to make God known (see vv. 46-47). The Son of Man has come from heaven, but Jesus asks his disciples if they would like him to conform to *their* expectation of a revealer. Would that satisfy them? The disciples should know that he is from heaven; he was there before (*hopou ēn to proteron*). Jesus suggests that they might like him to ascend into the heavens. Would a gesture that matched the ascent of the traditional revealers, Abraham, Moses, Isaiah, and Enoch, lead them to accept his word? Within the Passover context, it is particularly Moses' ascent that lies behind the half-asked question.[110] But Jesus transcends all that Moses did and said. To make God known Jesus has no need to ascend from earth to heaven (v. 62a). He comes from heaven; he has been there before (v. 62b), and it is on the basis of his previous presence *pros ton theon* (1:1) that his words have ultimate authority.

The evident desire of the disciples that Jesus not lead them into a world which they cannot control produces Jesus' instruction on the life-giving power of his words, warning them against the uselessness of the flesh in v. 63. The use of *sarx* in v. 63 is one of the major elements in the scholarly rejection of the originality of vv. 51c-58. *Sarx* is used six times in vv. 51,

---

[107] For various suggestions concerning the possible apodosis of this protasis, see Brown, *John*, 1:296; Moloney, *Son of Man*, 120-21.

[108] For further discussion and documentation of this, see Moloney, *Son of Man*, 54-55; C. H. Talbert, "The Myth of a Descending-Ascending Redeemer in Mediterranean Antiquity," *NTS* (1975-76) 418-39.

[109] Most interpreters understand Jesus' use of *anabainein* as a reference to the cross or to the ascension, or to both, with the apodosis being that the offense would be even greater. See, for example, Bultmann, *John*, 445; Hoskyns, *Fourth Gospel*, 300-301; Brown, *John*, 1:296; Barrett, *St John*, 304; Becker, *Johannes*, 215; Léon-Dufour, *Lecture*, 2:179-81; Painter, *Quest*, 281-82; Menken, "John 6,51c-58," 24-26; Brodie, *John*, 287. This asks too much of the reader, whose previous contact with *anabainein* was in 1:51 and 3:13, both times in association with the Son of Man. It has to do with a movement between earth and heaven to make God known.

[110] On Moses' ascent to receive the Torah, see, as a sample, *ExodR* 28:1; 40:2; 41:6-7; 43:4; 47:5, 8; *DeutR* 2:36; 3:11; 11:10; *Pesikta Rabbati* 20:4.

52, 53, 54, 55, 56. It is essential for life. Now the reader is told that *hē sarx ouk ōphelei ouden*: the flesh is worthless. But the reader is aware that the *sarx* of vv. 51-56 is the flesh of Jesus, who is the Logos who became *sarx* (see 1:14). The *sarx* of Jesus tells the story of God (1:18). But to judge Jesus' words and actions by the superficial judgment of human expectation is to misunderstand him. Such an understanding is "fleshly," where the *sarx* refers to the superficial knowledge, experience, and understanding of a human being.[111] Jesus' words to the disciples in v. 63 warn them against their "fleshly" lack of courage and understanding when they are faced with his words (see Isa 40:6-8). They are not prepared to accept the "words" of Jesus that are spirit and life (v. 63c). The disciples want Jesus to conform to their expectations, but Jesus rejects their "fleshly" hopes that he might ascend, as Moses was said to have ascended (v. 62). Such an appreciation of Jesus is worthless. It is the life-giving power of the Spirit, made available to the disciples in and through the revelation of God through the word of Jesus, that matters (v. 63). But Jesus is aware that, no matter how much has been revealed to the disciples, some do not believe, and one among them would betray him (v. 64). Violence forms part of the work of the Father (see 4:34; 5:16-18), and Jesus is aware that one of his disciples will hand him over.

The disciples have seen the miracle of the loaves and fishes (vv. 5-15), witnessed Jesus' coming across the waters announcing *egō eimi* (vv. 16-21), and heard the discourse on the true bread from heaven (vv. 25-59). Because of this (*ek toutou*) refusal of the word of Jesus, "many of his disciples" drew away from him.[112] This passage on the disciples (vv. 60-66) opens with a comment from the narrator that "many disciples" murmured against Jesus' word (vv. 60-61), and closes with "many disciples" leaving him (v. 66). The true disciple is the one to whom discipleship is given by the Father, and who believes in the Son (vv. 64-65). The reader has learned an important lesson on discipleship: it is not information that makes a disciple, but a Spirit-filled response to the Father made known in the word of Jesus. The Johannine community and its divisions are behind this presentation of the disciples who have heard and witnessed so much, but no longer go about with Jesus. The centrality of the word of Jesus as the essential nourishment of the community, its spirit and life (v. 63), is strongly affirmed, and the critical reader suspects that some Johannine

[111] See W. Stenger, "'Der Geist ist es, der lebendig macht, das Fleisch nützt nichts' (Joh 6,63)," *TTZ* 85 (1976) 116–22; Schenke, *Antidocetic Christology*, 194–95.

[112] The expression *ek toutou* could mean "for this reason" or "from this time." I am opting for the former, although, as Barrett, *St John*, 306, points out, both meanings may have been in the mind of the author.

disciples were unable to accept this. They would rather have had Jesus conform to the Mosaic pattern of a heavenly revealer (v. 62).

But another response is possible. Jesus questions the Twelve, asking
whether they also (*kai hymeis*) would like to leave him (v. 67) to return to
their own world. Simon Peter answers for them all. The reader knows that
the Father draws the disciples toward Jesus (see v. 65), and recognizes
Peter's inability to look anywhere else as a response to the Father's initiative. They can do no other than go to Jesus. However, Peter's motivation
for the unique attraction of Jesus: "You have the words (*rhēmata*) of eternal life" (v. 68), communicates to the reader the centrality of the unconditional acceptance of the word of Jesus as the criterion for authentic faith.
Peter's confession repeats what was manifested in the responses of the
mother of Jesus (see 2:5), John the Baptist (see 3:28-30), the Samaritan villagers (see 4:42), and the royal official (see 4:50). Peter has rightly interpreted Jesus' words to the larger group of disciples: "The words that I have
spoken to you are spirit and life" (v. 63; see also 5:24).

But Peter goes further. Looking back over the experience of the disciples
(*hēmeis pepisteukamen kai egnōkamen*), he tells Jesus that they have arrived
at belief in him and are living from that faith and knowledge.[113] For the
first time in the narrative a character correctly identifies the reason why
the word of Jesus gives eternal life: his origins. The holiness of Jesus comes
from the fact that he is *of God* (v. 69). The faith and knowledge of the
Twelve is sound because the word of Jesus has its source in God.[114] But
even among this group, failure is possible. There will be a betrayer, Judas,
the son of Simon Iscariot (vv. 70-71). The fragility of the human response
is raised. The Twelve have been able to make a perfect confession of Johannine faith, through the words of Simon Peter, but the reader is warned that
something more will be needed. If there is a betrayer, then there will be a
betrayal. The shadow of a violent death, which has been across much of
this celebration of the Passover (see vv. 12-13, 15, 27, 51, 53-54), emerges
as the account of Jesus' activity on the occasion of the feast comes to a
close (vv. 70-71). The author is working at several levels, telling the reader
that not even correct confessions of faith will make the perfect disciple;
there is also a message of a future betrayal and death that will test the disciples further. The reader suspects that the confession of Simon Peter is
excellent . . . so far! How will this expression of faith survive in the diffi-

---

[113] The two verbs are virtually synonymous. See Brown, *John*, 1:298; Barrett, *St John*, 306.

[114] Recently, W. R. Domeris, "The Confession of Peter according to John 6:69," *TynBul* 44
(1993) 155-67, has argued cogently that the title refers to Jesus' being the "agent of God." See
also H. L. N. Joubert, "'The Holy One of God' (John 6:69)," *Neot* 2 (1968) 57-69. Borgen,
"John 6," 286-87, agrees, drawing together vv. 27, 29, and 68-69 as meaning "consecrated by
God and sent by Him into the world."

cult moments that, by now, the reader knows will conclude this story? How will the Twelve respond to a "lifting up" of the Son of Man (3:14) that will provide a food which will endure to eternal life (6:12-13, 27, 35, 51, 53-54)? Not only the Twelve must face these questions—so also must the reader.

CONCLUSION

Jesus does not deny the Jewish Passover memory of the gift of the manna, present in the nourishment provided by the Law that makes God known to his people. But the reader has been instructed that the revelation of God in the Law is not the end of God's action for his people. "The Jews" and many of the disciples are unable to go further in their response to the ongoing revelation of God, or to accept the further revealing intervention of God. Moses, the manna, and the Law exhaust all possibilities. The reader is aware that to remain with Moses is to stay with the former gift, denying the fullness of the gift of the truth (see 1:16-17). The Johannine community has experienced a definitive separation from Jewish life and its liturgy (see 9:22; 12:32; 16:2). In the synagogue, now without a priesthood and a temple, the focus was on the gift of the Law. But the Johannine Christians are asked to accept Jesus' claim: "I am the bread of life" (6:35; see vv. 41, 48, 51). There is no longer need to celebrate the former gift of the bread from heaven through Moses. Like the reader in the narrative, the members of the Johannine community were summoned to believe that Jesus was the true bread from heaven, the one who gave life to all who believed in him. Jesus is the perfection of the Mosaic tradition, of the Mosaic gift of the bread: he is the true bread from heaven.

As in John 5, Jesus is the stumbling block who leads to division and conflict between the emerging Johannine community and the emerging postwar synagogue. For the Johannine community, what was done in the Jewish celebration of the Passover was but a sign and a shadow of the perfection of the gift of God in the person of Jesus Christ, the true bread from heaven, the bringer of eternal life to all who would believe in him. In Jesus Christ the Passover traditions are enfleshed, not destroyed. The Johannine community belonged to the Mosaic tradition, but that tradition had been brought to its fullness, the fullness of the gift that is the truth (see 1:16). But this solution to the community's relationship with the celebration of the Passover was not without its problems for the internal life and unity of the emerging Johannine community. As the story tells, it brought pain and division to the community itself. It was not only "the Jews" who were outraged by the word of Jesus. Because of Jesus' claim to be the true bread from heaven, "many of the disciples drew back and no longer went about with him" (v. 66).

Chapter Three

Jesus and Tabernacles, 1
John 7:1—8:59

¶ IN 7:1 THE READER again encounters *meta tauta* (see also 5:1, 14; 6:1), and then: "Now the Jews' feast of Tabernacles was at hand" (7:2). There is no further mention of a feast until 10:22: "It was the feast of the Dedication at Jerusalem." Within 7:1—10:21 indications are provided of the passing of time:

1. The first words the reader encounters in 7:1 are *meta tauta*. This expression does not appear again in 7:1—10:21.
2. There is reference to the time of the year as the reader is told that Tabernacles is "at hand" (7:2).
3. Both the brothers and Jesus go up to the feast (v. 10).
4. A series of encounters between Jesus and others takes place "about the middle of the feast" (v. 14).
5. Another series of encounters takes place "on the last day of the feast" (v. 37).
6. The word *palin* reminds the reader that Tabernacles is still being celebrated (8:12).
7. The same expression is used in v. 21: "Again (*palin*) he said to them" (v. 21). In v. 59, as "the Jews" took up stones "Jesus hid himself, and went out of (*exēlthen*) the temple."
8. This leads to 9:1: "Passing by (*paragōn*). . . ." The deliberate association of two verbs of motion, the first in the aorist tense (8:59) and the second a present participle (9:1), links the time during which the action of chaps. 8 and 9 takes place, although the location has changed.

9. The temporal unity that unites 7:1—10:21 is broken in 10:22 with an expression that indicates a new beginning: "It was (*egeneto tote*) the feast of the Dedication."

The reader of 7:1—8:59 follows events that took place at the feast of Tabernacles in the Temple.[1] While the narrative of 9:1—10:21 continues within the temporal framework of the feast of Tabernacles, the change in geographical setting calls for a separate treatment.[2]

TABERNACLES IN THE JEWISH TRADITION

Tabernacles was regarded as the most popular of the three pilgrimage feasts, known as "the feast of YHWH" (Lev 23:39; Judg 21:19), or simply "the feast" (1 Kings 8:2, 65; 2 Chron 7:8; Neh 8:14; Isa 30:29; Ezek 45:23, 25). Josephus describes Tabernacles as "especially sacred and important (*hagiōtatēs kai megistēs*) to the Hebrews" (*Antiquities* 8:101). Tabernacles was associated with the covenant and God's care and guidance during the wilderness experience of the Exodus. But this feast was not only historicized, it was also eschatologized; it was celebrated in terms of the end time.[3] Earlier a feast of ingathering (see Exod 23:16; 34:22), and booths (Hebrew *sukkōt*), it later commemorated God's protection of the people as they dwelt in tents during their sojourn in the wilderness (see Deut 16:13, 16; Lev 23:34; Neh 8:13-19).[4] The essential elements of the celebration are provided by the Mishnah (*Sukkah*) and other rabbinic material.[5] I offer the following description of the feast aware of its speculative nature.[6]

---

[1] It is generally held that the *palin* of 8:12 is a continuation of 7:52. It is almost universally admitted that 7:73—8:11 did not belong to the original text. For a discussion, see Brown, *John,* 1:332–38. For a summary of textual evidence, see S. R. Pickering, ed., "John 7:53—8:11: The Woman Taken in Adultery," *New Testament Textual Research Update* 1 (1993) 6–7.

[2] See also L. Schenke, "Joh 7–10: Eine dramatische Szene," *ZNW* 80 (1989) 172–92, and I. de la Potterie, *La vérité dans saint Jean* (2 vols.; AnBib 73–74; Rome: Biblical Institute Press, 1977) 816–19.

[3] See M. Dacy, "Sukkot: Origins to 500 C.E." (unpublished M.Phil. thesis; Department of Semitic Studies, Sydney University, 1992) 137–42; and especially G. Bienaimé, *Moïse et le don de l'eau dans la tradition juive ancienne: targum et midrash* (AnBib 98; Rome: Biblical Institute Press, 1984) 200-229.

[4] See G. W. MacRae, "The Meaning and Evolution of the Feast of Tabernacles," *CBQ* 22 (1960) 251–76; J. C. Rylaarsdam, "Booths, Feast of," *IDB* 1:455–58. See also Yee, *Jewish Feasts,* 70–77.

[5] See the collection of the relevant material in Str-B 2:774–812. See also P. Goodman, *The Sukkot and Simkah Torah Anthology* (Philadelphia: Jewish Publication Society of America, 1973).

[6] On this, see Manns, *L'Evangile,* 185–94, and the literature cited there. See also G. Vermes,

The celebration of the feast of Tabernacles begins on the 15th day of the seventh month, Tishri (September-October). It is highlighted by the building of "tabernacles," representing the tent experience of the Israelites in the desert, cared for by YHWH, with whom Israel now has a covenant. The men celebrating Tabernacles slept and ate meals in the booth for seven days, the duration of the feast (*Sukkah* 1–2; see Lev 23:42-43; Hos 12:10). Twigs of myrtle, palm, and willow were gathered from around Jerusalem, bound together (along with a citron) to form a *lulab*, to be carried and waved during the joyful daily procession that marked the water libation ceremony (*Sukkah* 3–4; see Lev 23:40).[7] After the seven days of celebration in the booths, there was an additional day, an eighth day, recalling the protection of YHWH during the Exodus period. On this eighth day those celebrating the feast no longer dwelt in their booths, there was no procession, and the water ritual ceased. The eighth day was dedicated to Israel's request for a superabundance of rain as a sign of YHWH's special and continuing care for the people.[8] Three major elements formed the ritual.

THE WATER LIBATION CEREMONY (SUKKAH 4:9-10)

On the morning of each day of the seven days a procession led by priests and singing Levites, accompanied by a milling crowd of people, went down to the Pool of Siloam to gather water in a golden container. A return procession through the Water Gate, accompanied by the milling people and blasts of the *shofar*, led to the Temple area. According to rabbinic literature, the Water Gate had a special eschatological significance. Rabbi Eliezer ben Jacob identified it as the south gate of Ezek 47:1-5, through which the waters of life, issuing from the threshold of the Temple, would flow (Tosefta *Sukkah* 3:2-10; *GenR* 28:18; *Shekalim* 6:3; *Middot* 2:6). Each day there was a joyous procession around the altar, during which the pilgrims sang Psalms 113–118 (the Hallel) and waved the *lulab* at 118:1: "O give thanks to the Lord, for he is good," and again at v. 25: "Save us, we beseech you, O Lord! O Lord, we beseech you, give us success." When the procession reached the altar, the priest whose turn of duty it was, poured water from Siloam and wine into two vessels positioned on the altar, allowing the water and wine to flow out on to the altar (see *Sukkah* 4:9).

"Jewish Literature and New Testament Exegesis: Reflections on Methodology," in *Jesus and the World of Judaism* (London: SCM Press, 1983) 74–88.

[7] See Dacy, "Sukkot," 77–78, 116–19.

[8] See Rylaarsdam, "Booths," 455–56; Yee, *Jewish Feasts*, 74–77; Dacy, "Sukkot," 103–7. The feast of the eighth day was almost a feast in its own right.

On the seventh day of the feast the procession around the altar was repeated seven times (see *Sukkah* 4:5).

The association of water with the celebration of the feast was linked with the association of the feast of Tabernacles with the gift of rain, as it is found in Zechariah 14. This biblical text associates Tabernacles with the end of time.[9] After the destroying plague of the Lord, which will wipe out those who wage war on Jerusalem (14:12), all the surviving nations will go up to Jerusalem for the feast of Tabernacles. If they do not go up, "there will be no rain upon them" (14:17).[10] There is evidence that the water ceremony was also linked with messianic expectation in which a Moses-like teacher (see *Sukkah* 3:3-9) repeats the gift of the well of the Torah (see Num 21:18; CD 6:2-11; Pseudo-Philo, *LAB* 10:7; 11:15; 28:7-8; *Targum Onkelos* on Num 21:18), which follows the Israelites (see targums on Num 21:18; Tosefta *Sukkah* 3:10-12). The targums on Gen 49:10 play on the digging of the scribes to promise a future Messiah who digs from the well of the Torah, a final "giving of water" from the Torah, the well of God.[11] Jewish messianic expectation seems to have linked the Messiah with the definitive gift of water from the well, the interpretation of the Law, as expressed in *EcclR* 1:8:

> As the former redeemer made a well to rise, so will the latter redeemer bring up water, as it is stated, "And a fountain shall come forth of the house of the Lord, and shall water the valley of Shittim" (Joel 4:18).[12]

As Jewish reflection looked to the repetition of the gift of the Mosaic bread in the messianic age, these texts indicate the repetition of the gift of the Mosaic water (see also the *Fragment Targum* on Num 24:17).[13]

---

[9] See de la Potterie, *La vérité*, 2:817–18. On Zechariah 14, see K. Schaefer, "The Ending of the Book of Zechariah," *RB* 100 (1993) 165–238. On Zech 14:16-19, and other parts of Zechariah that point to the messianic nature of Sukkot, see pp. 223–32.

[10] See MacRae, "Meaning and Evolution," 268–70.

[11] The above paragraph draws from the rich study of Bienaimé, *Moïse*, 58–194.

[12] A parallel remark about the Mosaic gift of bread is found earlier in *EcclR* 1:8: "As was the first redeemer so is the latter redeemer . . . as the first redeemer brought down the manna, so will also the latter redeemer bring down the manna." The antiquity of this association of the second Mosaic gift of both bread and water is suggested by its presence in Pseudo-Philo, *LAB* 10:7, which dates from "around the time of Jesus" (see D. J. Harrington, "Pseudo-Philo," in *The Old Testament Pseudepigrapha*, ed. J. H. Charlesworth [2 vols.; London: Darton, Longman & Todd, 1983-85] 2:299). See also the association of the Mosaic gift of bread and water in *Mekilta* on Exod 15:27.

[13] Any messianic reinterpretation of God's gifts must be understood as a "mediation," parallel to that of Moses who gives water in Exod 17:1-7 and the leaders who dig for water at the well of the Lord in Num 21:16-18. God instructs his people through others.

THE CEREMONY OF LIGHT (SUKKAH 5:1-4)

Four menorahs were set up in the center of the court of the women. The men of piety and good works who were celebrating the feast (see *Sukkah* 5:4) danced under the lights, while the Levites sang Psalms 120–134. This celebration lasted most of the night for each of the seven days of the feast. The Mishnah describes the light from the Temple: "There was not a court-yard in Jerusalem that did not reflect the light of the House of the Water Drawing" (*Sukkah* 5:3). Again Zechariah 14 is present:

> On that day there shall not be either cold or frost. And there shall be continu-ous day (it is known to the Lord), not day and not night, for at evening time there shall be light. On that day living waters shall flow out from Jerusalem, half of them to the eastern sea and half of them to the western sea; it shall con-tinue in summer as in winter (Zech 14:6-8).

If there was a connection between the light ceremony and the pillar of fire that led Israel through the wilderness (see Exod 13:21), there may have been a link between this ritual and the expected return of the pillar of fire at the end of time (see Isa 4:5; Bar 5:8-9; *SongR* 1:7, 3). The light ceremony, as well as the water ritual, probably helped in the eschatologization of the celebration of the feast of Tabernacles.[14]

THE RITE OF FACING THE TEMPLE (SUKKAH 5:4)

At cockcrow of each of the seven days the priests proceeded to the East gate of the Temple area and gazed away from the Temple. At the moment of sunrise, they turned west to face the Temple and recited: "Our fathers when they were in this place turned with their backs toward the Temple of the Lord and their faces toward the east, and they worshipped the sun toward the east [see Ezek 8:16]; but as for us, our eyes are turned toward the Lord" (*Sukkah* 5:4). Immediately after the description of the endless day and the water flowing from Jerusalem, Zechariah concludes:

> And the Lord will become king over all the earth;
> on that day the Lord will be one and his name one (Zech 14:9).

Ps 118:28-29 concludes the *Hallel*, and summarizes:

> You are my God, and I will give thanks to you;
> You are my God, I will extol you.

---

[14] See Talbert, *Reading John*, 153.

O give thanks to the Lord, for he is good,
for his steadfast love lasts forever.

Despite the difficulties of dating rabbinic traditions, one can reasonably conclude that the celebration of the feast in the first century was marked by a celebration of a water libation ceremony every day of the feast. By the first century the feast had been associated with eschatological and messianic expectations (Zechariah 14). Great candelabra were lit in the center of the Temple area for a celebration of both light and joy. YHWH was recognized as the one true God to whom all praise and allegiance was due.

THE SHAPE OF THE NARRATIVE

The narrative unfolds in four major sections:

   I. *7:1-9:* Before the feast. A *schisma* arises between Jesus and his brothers about going up to the feast.[15]
   II. *7:10-13:* At the feast in Jerusalem. There is a *schisma* about Jesus: Is he a good man, or does he lead the people astray?
   III. *7:14-36:*
       (a) *7:14-24:* "About the middle of the feast." Jesus teaches in the Temple and *conflict* arises. The question of God as the one who sent Jesus is central, and the events and discussions of John 5 are recalled.[16]
       (b) *7:25-31:* The questions of Jesus' messiahship and his origins cause *schisma*.
       (c) *7:32-36:* A *conflict* arises over the *destiny* of Jesus.
   IV. *7:37—8:59:*
       (a) *7:37-52:* "On the last day of the feast." Jesus' revelation of himself as the living water leads to *schisma*.
       (b) *8:12-30:* Jesus' revelation of himself as "the light of the world."
       (c) *8:31-59:* Jesus and "the Jews" in conflict over *origins*.

Indications of the passing of time during the feast of Tabernacles determine the shape of the narrative. "Chapters 7 and 8 are bound together by their relation to the Feast of Tabernacles."[17]

---

[15] I will use the Johannine word *schisma* (see 7:43; 9:16; 10:19) to speak of the division that Jesus' presence creates, even when the word itself does not appear.

[16] This recalling of chap. 5 has led some scholars to rearrange the material, incorporating parts of chap. 7 within 5:1-47.

[17] Beasley-Murray, *John*, 100.

READING THE NARRATIVE

I. Before the Feast: Jesus and His Brothers: 7:1-9

After the events at the Sea of Tiberias (*meta tauta*; see 5:1, 14; 6:1), because of "the Jews," Jesus remains in Galilee. He does not wish to go to Judea.[18] He continues to go about (*periepatei*) in Galilee.[19] The decision of "the Jews" that Jesus must be killed (see 5:18) still holds.[20]

The Jewish feast of Tabernacles is at hand (v. 2). All male Jews had a duty to go to Jerusalem to celebrate this feast in the Temple (see *Sukkah* 2:8-9), and the brothers of Jesus (*hoi adelphoi autou*; see Mark 6:3; Matt 13:55) ask him to leave Galilee for Judea. The fundamental motivation for this, however, is not given as the feast, but so that the works (*ta erga*) of Jesus might be seen by his disciples.[21] Three groups are involved: Jesus and his brothers in Galilee, and his disciples (*hoi mathētai sou*) in Judea.[22] The reference to *ta erga* is to the miracles at Cana (2:1-11; 4:46-54) and by the Sea of Tiberias (6:1-13, 16-21). The brothers of Jesus have been in the background since journeying from Cana to Capernaum with Jesus, his mother, and his disciples (see 2:12). The reader is aware that they have misunderstood Jesus. His miracles are indeed *erga*, and form part of the larger concept of Jesus' *ergon*: to bring to perfection the task that the Father gave him (see 4:34), but they are not an end in themselves. The brothers rightly state that no person works in secret if he seeks to be known openly (v. 4), but they think that Jesus will come to be known through his *erga*. The faith of the brothers is faulty at two levels. In the first place, their conditioned statement about Jesus' miraculous activity, "If you do these things," indicates that they doubt it is true.[23] And at a deeper level, they misunderstand the purpose of the *erga* of Jesus when they ask him to go to Judea to repeat his works there, so that he might show himself to the world (*phanerōson seau-*

---

[18] The Curetonian Syriac, Old Latin, Freer Gospels, a few other Greek manuscripts, Chrysostom, and Augustine read *eichen exousian*, indicating that Jesus "did not have the ability" to go about. Some scholars accept this reading. In the light of the weight of the evidence (e.g., P[66.75]), it is better to retain the theologically less significant *ēthelen*.

[19] The imperfect is iterative. See BDF, 166, para. 318 (3); 169, para. 325.

[20] Exactly the same words, *ezētoun auton hoi Ioudaioi apokteinai*, are used in both 5:18 and 7:1. This still makes sense if the present order of chaps. 5, 6, and 7 is maintained. Violence is threatened in Jerusalem in chap. 5; misunderstanding, but not violence, is met throughout chap. 6. Thus Jesus continues to go about in Galilee.

[21] The feast, however, is part of the motivation, as is made clear by the use of *oun* to link vv. 2 and 3.

[22] Some of the *mathētai* have just left him (see 6:66). The brothers are urging some miraculous works in Jerusalem to convince such failing disciples.

[23] See Bernard, *St John*, 1:267.

ton tǭ kosmǭ). Jesus has not come to show *himself* to the world, but to make God known to the world.

The narrator confirms the reader's suspicions about Jesus' brothers with his comment: "For even his brothers did not believe in him" (v. 5). The use of the expression *oude gar*, "for even," indicates a wider scenario of disbelief. If his brothers do not believe, then there are many others who do not believe. Jesus' response to his brothers draws a sharp distinction between *ho kairos ho emos* and *ho de kairos ho hymeteros*. The use of *de* indicates to the reader that the two *kairoi* are not the same and that there is some conflict between the two "times."[24] The *kairos* of Jesus is not at hand. There is something measured in the process of Jesus' life. This has already been made clear to the reader in Jesus' response to his mother: "My hour has not yet come" (2:4), and in the frequent indications that Jesus is the Sent One of the Father (see 3:17, 34; 4:34; 5:23, 24, 30, 36, 37, 38; 6:29, 38-39, 44, 57). The reader knows that Jesus is not the master of his own destiny, but (*de*) his brothers are not part of God's initiative to make himself known, and are thus free to do what they want when they want. This is not a further criticism of the brothers, but an indication of the general situation of all "others." It is the author's way of pointing to the singular nature of the story of Jesus, intimately linked with the designs of the Father's direction of that story (see 5:19-30).

Jesus and his brothers belong to different worlds, and this is the seed out of which a great deal of the following episodes will develop.[25] The world of ordinary *kairoi* and ordinary events will not hate the brothers of Jesus, but (*de*) does hate (*misei*) Jesus. Jesus is the light of the world (1:4), locked in bitter conflict with the darkness (1:5), laying bare the evil that people do: "The light has come into the world, and people loved darkness rather than light, because their deeds were evil" (3:19). But the world can reject the light and turn to evil deeds. Jesus bears witness to these evil deeds of the world, and thus conflict and hatred are inevitable (v. 7). The brothers experience none of this hatred, and can proceed to the festival (v. 8a). Jesus is not going up *eis tēn heortēn tautēn* (v. 8b). The indication that he is not going up to *this* feast causes the reader to ask: If he is not going up to *this* feast, does he plan on attending *another* feast? This section of the narrative concludes with the note from the narrator that Jesus did as he said: he remained in Galilee (v. 9). The issue of feasts is central: not *this* feast, because his time has not yet come. Themes emerge from this first *schisma* associated with the feast of the Tabernacles. Jesus' activity is sub-

[24] See BDF, 231–32, para. 447. The word *kairos* appears in John only at 7:6, 8. "It is not distinguishable from the more common *hōra*" (Barrett, *St John*, 312).

[25] Bernard, *St John*, 1:269, points out that the use of *hymas* in v. 7 is emphatic, thus opening the gap between Jesus and his brothers. See also the *hymeis* in v. 8.

ordinated to a plan that is larger than the passing of ordinary time. When his time comes it will be marked by a clash between light and darkness, by evil and the witness of Jesus that lays bare evil deeds, a clash generated by the hatred between Jesus and the powers that oppose him (v. 7). Jesus' decision not to go to *this* feast to show himself to the world (v. 8b; see v. 4) hints to the reader that a moment of revelation will be associated with *another* feast.[26]

II. AT THE FEAST IN JERUSALEM: 7:10-13

The brothers go up to the feast (v. 10a),[27] and Jesus (*kai autos*) makes the pilgrimage. The principal affirmation of the sentence is not the journey of the brothers, but that Jesus went up to Jerusalem *ou phanerōs alla en kryptǫ* (v. 10b).[28] The reader must now accept that this feast, earlier declared as belonging only to the "time" of the brothers, which is always at their disposal, now forms part of the *kairos* of Jesus. As in 2:4-7 and 4:48-50, an initial apparent unwillingness to be part of an action is reversed as Jesus responds to the will of someone greater than his mother (see 2:3), the royal official (see 4:47), and his brothers (see 7:3-4). If Jesus went to the feast, it is because it now forms part of his being sent by the Father.[29] His brothers demanded of Jesus: *phanerōson seauton tǫ kosmǫ* (v. 4). In deliberate contrast to the plans of the brothers, Jesus goes up to the feast *ou phanerōs alla en kryptǫ* (v. 10b). A theme of secrecy has been introduced. The reader is aware of the movements and of the secret of the person of Jesus, but in the discussions and *schismata* that follow, "the Jews" are not.[30] The reader is aware that Jesus is now in the city of Jerusalem, at the feast, while "the Jews" are not. This gives added point to the questions that they now raise (vv. 11-12). The narrator reports that "the Jews" were

---

[26] Some good witnesses read *egō ouk anabainō* as *egō oupō anabainō*. This reading is almost universally rejected as an attempt by early scribes to avoid the difficulty created by Jesus' going to Jerusalem in v. 10.

[27] The technical verb *anabainein* is used twice in v. 10 for "going up" to Jerusalem for the pilgrim feast.

[28] Good witnesses read *hōs en kryptǫ*, but it is omitted by others, probably rightly. It was possibly added to lessen the impression of contradiction and deceit. See Barrett, *St John*, 313.

[29] On this pattern, see C. H. Giblin, "Suggestion, Negative Response and Positive Action in St John's Portrayal of Jesus (John 2.1-11.; 4.46-54.; 7.2-14.; 11.1-44.)," *NTS* 26 (1979–80) 197–211. On 7:2-14, see pp. 206–8. See also J. R. Michaels, "The Temple Discourse in John," in *New Dimensions in New Testament Study*, ed. R. N. Longenecker and M. C. Tenney (Grand Rapids: Zondervan, 1974) 203–4.

[30] Painter, *Quest*, 290–93, sees here the theme of the hiddenness of the Messiah. He points out that Jesus' secret movements are no longer motivated by fear of "the Jews" (pp. 292–93).

looking for him (*ezētoun auton*) at the feast (v. 11a). This search is ominous. It recalls the use of the same verb in 5:18, where the decision was made to kill Jesus (*ezētoun auton hoi Ioudaioi apokteinai*), and in 7:1 to explain to the reader why Jesus remained in Galilee: "the Jews" sought to kill him (*ezētoun auton hoi Ioudaioi apokteinai*). Another crucial theme for the development of the Johannine story of the feast of Tabernacles is raised, unwittingly, by the question asked by "the Jews": *pou estin ekeinos?* The question of where Jesus comes from and where he is going will emerge as the discussion unfolds.

Earlier in the story "the Jews" have "muttered" (*egongyzon*) over Jesus' claims to be the bread that came down from heaven (6:41, 43, 61). Now "the people" join them, muttering (*egongyzen*) over another matter.[31] Is he a good man, or is he leading people astray (v. 12)? Is Jesus a reliable authority (*agathos*) or is his teaching false, in league with the devil, leading the people astray (*planos*)?[32] "The people" remain divided over the issue, but "the Jews" are called back into the story. "The people" are not prepared to speak publicly about Jesus, for fear of "the Jews." The hint given to the reader in v. 11, that "the Jews" were continuing to seek the death of Jesus, returns in v. 13. "The Jews" have made up their minds about Jesus. The question that "the people" have raised in v. 12 has already been answered by "the Jews." This is so obvious that even the people are frightened to manifest their interest in this man whom "the Jews" have already decided to eliminate.[33] Jesus' coming to Jerusalem secretly has led to further secrets. The people wonder, "the Jews" seek to kill him, and the reader is aware that Jesus is present while all this subterfuge is taking place.[34] The scene is set. The question of Jesus' revelation of himself to the world has been raised (vv. 1-9). Jesus, disciples, "the Jews," and "the people" are present at the feast of Tabernacles in Jerusalem (vv. 10-13). The right ques-

---

[31] See Becker, *Johannes*, 1:264. Brodie, *John*, 313, 317–18, strangely interprets "the Jews" and "the crowds" as "allusions to the diversity of the world—Jews and Gentiles" (313). Such an interpretation cannot be pursued into the rest of the narrative. All characters (the crowds, Jerusalemites, Jewish leaders, and "the Jews") are Jews, but some are "the Jews."

[32] On the charge of false teaching, see Pancaro, *Law*, 77–116.

[33] This is another indication that the Fourth Gospel's use of the term "the Jews" is aimed at a group of people who have made a decision about Jesus and the Johannine community. It is not a reference to the Jewish people. In vv. 11-13 "the Jews" and "the people" are all Jews. See Ashton, *Understanding*, 131–59.

[34] The use of different interlocutors within chaps. 7-8 has sometimes been used as a key for rearrangements or as an indication of various strata in the tradition. See, for example, Ashton, *Understanding*, 332–34. Whatever the prehistory of the text, characters play a different but complementary role in the story. See Schenke, "Joh 7–10," 175–78; R. Robert, "Étude littéraire de Jean VIII, 21-59," *RevThom* 89 (1989) 71–84.

tions are being asked: Where is Jesus? (v. 11), What is he doing? (v. 12). The reader knows that a conflict unto death is under way (vv. 10 and 13).

III. About the Middle of the Feast: 7:14-36

John 7:14-36 can be read in three parts.

(a) *Verses 14-24:* The origins of Jesus' teaching and authority are questioned by "the Jews."
(b) *Verses 25-31:* The Jerusalemites wonder whether Jesus can be the Christ; they know of his origins. But many of the people recognize him as the miracle-working Messiah.
(c) *Verses 32-36:* "The Jews" show their inability to understand Jesus' destiny.

The narrative is dense, as the characters involved and the issues debated chop and change. The plot is heavily subordinated to the author's ideological point of view.

Jesus, "the Jews," and "the People": 7:14-24
Through the indication of time, "about the middle of the feast," the narrator draws the reader into the full celebration of Tabernacles (v. 14a).[35] The daily water ritual is being performed and the festive illumination of the Temple is taking place every evening. Each morning the priests are turning their backs on the rising sun to gaze on the Holy of Holies in recognition of YHWH as the one true God. Within this setting, Jesus went up (*anebē*) into the Temple and taught.[36] The reaction to Jesus' teaching comes from "the Jews," whose decision against Jesus has already been made (see 5:18; 7:1, 11). Their question is a rejection of Jesus' teaching authority. The "marveling" (*ethaumazon*) of "the Jews" is not a positive wonder, but an emotional rejection, of Jesus' teaching (v. 15a).[37] "The people," who will enter the action later (see vv. 20-24), are also present. Authoritative teaching, or knowledge of letters (*grammata oiden*), presupposes that one is working from a traditional basis, explaining the Torah.[38] Traditions were passed on authoritatively by the teachers, and a newcomer teaching in the Temple would necessarily be known as a disciple of a cer-

---

[35] This need not be the Sabbath, or any special day. See Barrett, *St John*, 317.
[36] This is the first time Jesus has "taught" in Jerusalem. Michaels, "Temple Discourse," 204-6, suggests that John 7–8 is the teaching of Jesus referred to in 18:19.
[37] See BAGD, 352.
[38] Pancaro, *Law*, 88, 106–8. The use of *houtos* is pejorative.

tain teacher. This method of passing on the tradition became central to post-70 rabbinic Judaism, emerging as the authoritative form of Judaism as the Johannine community was attempting to articulate its understanding of Israel, God, Jesus, and itself. Jesus can lay claim to no authoritative teacher, and therefore there is no authority in what he has to teach (v. 15b). There can be no valid learning without an established teacher, under whom one has studied.[39] The issue raised by "the Jews" is christological, and it concerns "origins"; here, the origins of Jesus' authority. Jesus' response, given in direct speech in vv. 16-24, with only brief further interruption from the people in v. 20, repeats what he has said in chaps. 5-6, especially in 5:19-47.

Everything that Jesus says and does has its origins in his Father (see 5:19-20), thus his teaching is the teaching of the Father who sent him (v. 16b; see 5:23). The issue at stake is not whether "the Jews" accept Jesus, but whether they accept their traditional God, now revealed as the Father of Jesus. The reader is being summoned to take sides. Are "the Jews" correct in their insistence on the traditional ways in which teaching authority is passed on from teacher to pupil? Or rather, is it true that Jesus of Nazareth as the Son of God teaches with divine authority? The will of God is at stake. Is it manifested in the traditions of the rabbis, or in the teaching of Jesus? This is an urgent question for the reader of the Fourth Gospel.[40] In vv. 17-18 "the Jews" are challenged to make their decision. Jesus asks his opponents to assess whether they willfully accept or refuse the intervention of God in the person of his Son: *ean tis thelē to thelēma autou poiein* (v. 17a). Anyone who is genuinely seeking to do the will of God will be able to make their own decision about the origins of Jesus' teaching authority, whether it is "from God" (v. 17b: *ek tou theou*) or whether it is "from Jesus" (*egō ap' emautou lalō*).

In further explanation of this, Jesus plays on the double meaning of the expression *doxa* (v. 18). Within rabbinic Judaism, authority was received from a tradition produced by a human chain, a teaching succession passed on from one ordained rabbi to another. The authoritative utterances of the synagogue, which has definitively ejected the Christians, and thus rejected Jesus as the Christ (see 9:22; 12:42; 16:2), are subtly condemned as seeking their own *doxa*. But there is another *doxa*: one can also seek the *doxa tou theou*, in this context: *tēn doxan tou pempsantos auton*.

---

[39] See Pancaro, *Law*, 82–83.

[40] The reading suggested (see also Lightfoot, *St John*, 178; Schnackenburg, *St John*, 132–33) transcends the debate over the question of "doing the will of God." Ethical performance is not demanded as a measure of true faith. See E. Haenchen, *John* (2 vols.; Hermeneia; Philadelphia: Fortress Press, 1984) 2:13–14.

The reader accepts that Jesus' teaching makes known the story of God (see 1:18). Thus Jesus' being sent by God to make God known, a mission with no trace of a search for self-glory, makes the Son a person who is true (*alethēs estin*). It is the truth that is revealed, and in the one who reveals there is no falsehood (*adikia*).[41] As Pancaro has shown, Jesus' mission as the authentic revealer of God is at stake. "It is because the Jews do not value the teaching of Jesus for what it is (revelation) that they consider him a false prophet, in league with the devil, who leads the people astray, away from the Law and orthodoxy."[42] If Jesus is from God and his teaching is from God, he is all that he claims to be, and there is no shadow of doubt in what he teaches. By now the reader accepts as established that the origin "in God" of the teaching authority of Jesus makes it the complete truth, inevitably accepted by those who will to do the will of God (see v. 17a).

The clash between Jesus and "the Jews," leading to a discussion of Moses (vv. 19-23), from whom the chain of rabbinic teaching authority runs, indicates to the reader that "the Jews" do not accept the origins of Jesus' teaching. The reader is aware that it is incorrect for Jesus to insinuate that the authority for the rabbinic teaching comes from a human succession of ordained rabbis, seeking their own *doxa* (v. 18a). The authority of the rabbis claims to reach back to Moses himself. Moses had his teaching directly from God, and the rabbis claim to continue that tradition.[43] "The Jews" can claim that their teaching authority is "from God," through the mediation of Moses. But "the Jews" have decided to kill Jesus (see 5:18; 7:1, 11). This is a refusal to accept the Law (v. 19). Jesus transcends any rabbinic discussion. Indeed, the stance of "the Jews" over against the word of Jesus puts them in a state of continual breach of the Law (*oudeis ex hymōn poiei ton nomon*). There is a direct line from God, through Moses, to Jesus. The reader is aware of this from 1:16-17: "And from his fullness we have all received a gift in place of a gift. For the Law was given through Moses; the gift of the truth took place through Jesus Christ." God is behind the gift of the Law through Moses and the gift of the truth through Jesus Christ. "The Jews" cannot lay claim to a direct line back to God through the Law that was given through Moses because they

---

[41] This is the only place in the Fourth Gospel where the word *adikia* appears. It is the opposite of *alethēs*.

[42] See Pancaro, *Law*, 92–101, where Pancaro shows that the background to the contrast between *alethēs* and *adikia* is found in Qumran, the *Testaments of the Twelve Patriarchs*, and Jewish wisdom literature: "true revelation" as opposed to "false revelation." For the quote, see p. 100.

[43] See K. Rengstorf, "*didaskō ktl.*," *TDNT* 2 (1964) 137; J. H. Zaiman, "The Traditional Study of the Mishnah," in *The Study of Ancient Judaism*, ed. J. Neusner (2 vols.; New York: KTAV, 1981) 1:27–36.

are violently refusing to accept the gift of the truth offered to them
through Jesus Christ. Jesus can therefore charge "the Jews": "None of you
is keeping (*poiei*) the Law. Why do you seek to kill me?" (v. 19). There is a
link between Jesus' earlier statement to "the Jews" in v. 17 on the need to
do the will of God (*to thelēma autou poiein*) and his charge that they do not
practice the Law in v. 19 (*oudeis ex hymōn poiei ton nomon*). Any attempt to
eliminate the Sent One of God (see v. 16) is a refusal to do the will of God
(v. 17) and thus a breach of the Law of Moses. This is the case because it is
a rejection that separates "the Jews" from the place where the fullness of
the gift of God can be found: in Jesus' teaching, which is the *didachē* of
God (see v. 16). There is an absoluteness about this situation, indicated by
the universal significance of Jesus' address: *oudeis ex hymōn*. "Whereas the
Jews consider belief in Jesus a betrayal of the Law, Jn points out that it is
the will of God and, as accomplishment of the divine will, cannot be
opposed to the Law. . . . Jn is tracing the Law back to its source and doing
away with the opposition between the Law and belief in Jesus."[44]

In v. 20 the interlocutors change, without any introduction, but the
question raised by "the people" (*ho ochlos*) shows that the reader must dis-
tinguish between "the Jews" and "the people." The former have already
decided that Jesus must be killed (see 5:18; 7:1, 11). But "the people," not
aware of this (v. 20), are puzzled by Jesus and his accusation, as they have
no plan to kill him, nor do they know of any. The words "You have a
demon" are not a rejection of Jesus, but an indication that they think he is
insane.[45] Two groups are in dialogue with Jesus. One of those groups, "the
Jews," has settled on the violent elimination of Jesus, while the other, "the
people," has no plot against him. They are able to go one way or the other
in their acceptance or refusal of what Jesus says and does.

Jesus' answer is directed to "them" (v. 21a: *eipen autois*). Are his words,
reported in vv. 21-24, directed to "the people," "the Jews," or both? They
are addressed to all who have been involved in the discussion of Jesus'
authority. Jesus recalls the events of the Sabbath healing and the ensuing
discussions of 5:1-18. He tells them that he did one deed, and they *all* marveled at it (*kai pantes thaumazete*).[46] These words ask the reader to recall
"the Jews" of 5:1-18 and 7:20, as well as "the people" of 7:14-24.

The discussion initiated in v. 19, concerning his opponents' claim to
have Moses as their authority, continues (vv. 22-23). A tradition coming
from God through Moses teaches that if the eighth day after the birth of a
child falls upon a Sabbath, that child is to be circumcised on the Sabbath

---

[44] Pancaro, *Law*, 379.
[45] See Barrett, *St John*, 319.
[46] Reading, with the majority of commentators, *thaumazate dia touto*.

(see *Shabbat* 18:3; 19:2; *Nedarim* 3:11).[47] The gift of circumcision, which Israel claims comes from Moses, even though it was practiced before Moses (see Gen 17:10 for Abraham's use of it), was a sign of entry into a covenanted people, the fulfillment of the Law, and the completion of a person's perfection (see *Nedarim* 3:11). The reader knows that a matter of such life-giving importance overrides the Sabbath observance. This is acceptable to Israel, and also to Jesus, who comes from that tradition (see 4:22). But if a person's wholeness in a covenanted race is to be preserved by insisting that he be circumcised on the Sabbath, why is there an objection to Jesus' activity on a Sabbath when he gives a person his whole humanity (v. 23: *holon anthrōpon hygiē epoiēsa*; see 5:6, 9, 11)? The issue is not so much whether the Law of Moses is right and the actions of Jesus are wrong. Jesus' accusation, leveled against the Jews in v. 19, is at stake. God has made his ways known to his people in the gift of the Law through Moses, and in the fullness of his gift through Jesus Christ. There is no conflict or contradiction between these two gifts, but a progression. Jesus is using a legal argument, moving from a lesser to a greater case (Hebrew *qal waḥōmer*).[48] According to the former gift of the Law, circumcision marked the person's entry into the life of a covenanted people. Now, Jesus comes to restore humanity to its wholeness: *holon anthrōpon hygiē epoiēsa*. Not to see this is to refuse to see the gradual unfolding of the revelation of God, first through Moses and then through Jesus Christ. "Jesus' attitude is not a sentimental liberalizing of a harsh and unpractical law, . . . nor the masterful dealing of an opponent of the Law as such; it is rather the accomplishment of the redemptive purpose of God toward which the Law had pointed."[49]

Jesus' final words in this section of the narrative (v. 24) show that his opponents are totally conditioned by appearances (*kat' opsin*). They are prepared to judge by what they can measure, see, and touch. For them, the former gift of the Law is sufficient. They are not prepared to reach behind what they can control, to accept the word of Jesus, the Son of God. To do that would be to judge with right judgment (*tēn dikaian krisin*). The setting of the feast of Tabernacles enables the reader to appreciate the irony of this charge.[50] Each morning the Priests are turning their backs on the

---

[47] See Thomas, "The Fourth Gospel," 173–74.

[48] See Manns, *L'Evangile*, 313–14.

[49] Barrett, *St John*, 321.

[50] It is an accusation: "Stop judging by appearances, adopt a right judgment." This calls for two forms of the verb *krinein*: *mē krinete . . . krinate*. The verbs have been conformed as present imperatives in some important manuscripts (e.g., P[66], P[75], Vaticanus, Bezae), but present imperative . . . aorist makes better sense and is well attested (e.g., Sinaiticus, Koridethi, Freer Gospels). See Barrett, *St John*, 321.

rising sun, looking toward the Tabernacle, and proclaiming their rejection of all false gods. Now, in their rejection of God as Jesus' authority, they are making a lie of their daily ritual. About the middle of the feast (see v. 14), the question of God has been raised by means of a discussion of the authority of Jesus' teaching. "The Jews" are shown to have lost their way in their adherence to a Mosaic tradition that is not—ultimately—the tradition willed by God (see v. 17). They will not see that, in Jesus, the fullness of the gifts of God is now available to them. In their rejection of Jesus they are rejecting God, whom they are proclaiming as the one true God in their daily liturgy at the feast of Tabernacles. According to the Mishnah, the priests, in turning toward the Temple, proclaimed: "Our fathers when they were in this place turned with their backs toward the Temple of the Lord and their faces toward the east, and they worshipped the sun toward the east; but as for us, our eyes are turned toward the Lord" (*Sukkah* 5:4). The narrative of the Fourth Gospel asks the reader: Which Lord? The traditional question of a renewed and perfected commitment to the ways of the one true God has been raised in vv. 14-24.

The Jerusalemites and "the People": 7:25-31

A further group enters the discussions with the introduction of *tines ek tōn Ierosolymitōn*. While "the people" (*ho ochlos*) knew nothing of the plot against Jesus (see v. 19), some of the people of Jerusalem do. This group, privy to the fact that "the Jews" seek to kill him (*zētousin apokteinai*; see also 5:18, 7:1, 11), are puzzled. Despite the plot, Jesus appears at the feast and speaks openly, but nothing is being said to him (vv. 25-26). How are the people from Jerusalem, who know of the plot to kill Jesus, to interpret this silence from "the Jews"? The authorities should intervene.[51] The people from Jerusalem suspect that "the Jews" know Jesus is the Messiah. Maybe his claim to come from God as the authentic teacher of God is true, and therefore he cannot or must not be silenced. The reader follows a *schisma* over the Messiah.[52]

The people from Jerusalem have no hesitation in declaring that Jesus cannot be the Messiah. The Messiah would be hidden by God, and when he finally appeared, his origins would not be known to anyone.[53] They

---

[51] I am distinguishing between "the people" and "certain people from Jerusalem." But I identify "the authorities," "the Jews," and "the Pharisees," used without distinction in vv. 11, 13, 15, 32, 35, 45, 47-48.

[52] Schnackenburg, *St John*, 2:146, claims that "this instant raising of the messianic question is surprising." Attention to the Tabernacles context makes it less so.

[53] See Isa 7:14-17; Mal 3:1; Dan 7:13; *b. Sanhedrin* 97a; *1 Enoch* 46; 48:2-6; 2 Esdras 7:28; 13:32; *2 Baruch* 29:3; Justin, *Trypho* 8:4; 110:1; Str-B 2:489. On this, see Bernard, *St John*, 1:273-74. For more detail, see S. Mowinckel, *He That Cometh* (Oxford: Blackwell, 1959) 304-8.

"know" (*oidamen*) the Messiah's origins are to be hidden, "not known" (*oudeis ginōskei*). The Jerusalemites therefore "know" that Jesus cannot be the Messiah (v. 27). As they "know" where Jesus comes from, they also "know" that he cannot be the Messiah. The reader is aware that such confident "knowledge" about the Messiah is mistaken (see 1:41, 45; 3:2; 4:25; 6:42). Jesus' response to this certain knowledge opens with a destabilizing question, delivered in the Temple. The feast of Tabernacles forms the background for this discussion: "So Jesus proclaimed, as he taught in the Temple" (v. 28a). The Temple reminds the reader of the celebration of Tabernacles, the setting for the people's discussion of the Messiah, and Jesus' response (*ekraxen*). The Jerusalemites' claim to know where Jesus comes from is false. Whatever their knowledge of the geographical origins of Jesus, they have no notion of who he is or where he comes from. The discussions of vv. 14-24 are still present to the reader. They have led to the messianic question (see vv. 26-27). The question of the origin of the Messiah has been raised, so Jesus describes his origins (v. 28). Jesus comes from God. A refusal to accept what Jesus teaches means that the Jerusalemites do not accept the one who is true (v. 28). There cannot be two true Gods. They celebrate their loyalty to the one true God each morning of the celebration of Tabernacles, but they are rejecting Jesus, the sent one of the one true God. They do not know the one true God (*alēthinos ho pempsas me, hon hymeis ouk oidate*), and thus their morning protestations are a sham.[54] The polemic increases as Jesus strongly affirms his knowledge of God, the one who sent him (v. 29). He has accused the Jerusalemites of ignorance (vv. 28-29), despite their claims to knowledge (v. 27). The tables have been turned against the all-knowing Jerusalemites who dismiss Jesus as a possible Messiah. They are now being accused of ignorance, not only of the Messiah, but also of the God who sends him.

Such an accusation leads to an attempt by the Jerusalemites to arrest him. "The Jews" may not be prepared to move against Jesus (v. 26), but the offended Jerusalemites, who have been told they are ignorant of God and his Messiah (v. 28), take action against a blasphemer who not only accuses them but claims to have an immediate knowledge of God because he has come from him (v. 29). The consequences of their attempted action against Jesus reinforce the reader's impression that God is behind everything that is happening. They are unable to lay hands on Jesus "because his hour has not yet come" (v. 30). The "not yet" (*oupō*) tells the reader that eventually the hour will take place. At Cana (2:5), "the hour" looked forward to some future messianic revelation; in his discussion with his brothers Jesus linked "the hour" with a future Jewish feast (7:6). Now the

---

[54] Reading *alēthinos* in a strong adjectival (rather than an adverbial) sense.

reader is aware that violence will be part of "the hour of Jesus." As yet they are not able to lay hands on him (7:30). At some time in the future, to be determined by God alone, his opponents will have their violent way. But the reader recalls that "the light shines in the darkness, and the darkness has not overcome it" (1:5). The Jerusalemites may have decided that Jesus' claims are unacceptable, but many of "the people" (*ho ochlos*) are being won over.[55] Their openness to Jesus' revelation of God is still present: he may be the miracle-working Messiah.[56] Jesus' claims to be the authoritative teacher of God, sent by God, on the occasion of the feast of Tabernacles, has led to a major *schisma*. The Jerusalemites have decided that action must be taken against him (v. 30), while some of "the people" are prepared to accept that he might be the Messiah because of the signs he did (v. 31). The reader is aware that *both* responses fall short of the ideal.

Jesus and "the Jews": 7:32-36

"The Pharisees" and "the chief priests"[57] are not happy with this division among the people (see vv. 30-31). The reader, understanding the inability of the Jerusalemites to arrest him (*auton piasai*) because his hour had not yet come (v. 30), knows that the Pharisees will also fail in their attempt to do the same by sending officers (*hyperētas*) to arrest him (v. 32: *hina piasōsin auton*).[58] The rubric of "the hour of Jesus" is still in place, determining the temporal aspect of the narrative. Jesus warns his opponents that they are to make the most of the short time that remains for them. There will be a brief future time during which Jesus will be with "the Jews" (v. 33: *meth' hymōn*),[59] but this period of time will conclude when

[55] There is contrast with the Jerusalemites (against Barrett, *St John*, 323), and yet continuation, as the messianic question continues in a different key.

[56] Popular messianism did not associate the Messiah with miracles. For the discussion, see Painter, *Quest*, 294-95; and especially Ashton, *Understanding*, 273-78. See Meeks, *Prophet-King*, 162-64, for the signs and wonders that were to accompany the Mosaic eschatological prophet. Bittner, *Jesu Zeichen*, 245-58, has shown the importance of Isaiah 11 in pointing to a Davidic Messiah who would work miracles to show his goodness.

[57] See Barrett, *St John*, 324: "He simply takes *hoi Ioudaioi* as a general term for the enemies of Jesus, analysing it on occasion into *hoi archiereis* (or *hoi archontes*) together with *hoi Pharisaioi*."

[58] The *hyperētai* were Temple officers, available only to the chief priests. See Bultmann, *John*, 306 n. 6. This is an indication that Jesus is still in the Temple area (see v. 28).

[59] The expressions "a little longer" and "a short time" have Old Testament background (see Isa 10:25; 54:7; 55:6; Jer 51:33; Hos 1:4; Hag 2:6) as does the idea of seeking and not finding (see Deut 4:29; Hos 5:6). See Leroy, *Rätsel und Missverständnis*, 57-58. They also carry a note of apocalyptic urgency. See T. Korteweg, "'You will seek me and you will not find me' (Jn 7,34). An Apocalyptic Pattern in Johannine Theology," in *L'Apocalypse johannique et l'Apocalyptique dans le Nouveau Testament*, ed. J. Lambrecht (BETL 53; Gembloux: Duculot, 1980) 349-54.

Jesus proceeds back to the one who sent him. The reader knows that Jesus is speaking about a future return to the Father. This is part of Jesus' active acceptance of God's design.[60] Because "the Jews" are unable to move outside categories that they can understand and control, they will search (*zētēsete me*) for Jesus from within those categories.[61] "The Jews" will seek Jesus within their world, but he will not be found there.[62] The world of Jesus, the world of the Father, is beyond their ability either to understand or enter (v. 34).[63] As often happens in the Fourth Gospel, the discussion is working on two planes. Jesus addresses his audience on the basis of the union between himself and his Father (see especially 5:19-30), his descent from above to reveal God to the human story (see especially 3:13-14; 6:62), his being the Sent One of the Father and his return to his place of origin (7:33). The discussion of the Messiah preceding this encounter moved within the world of Jewish messianic expectation: the hidden Messiah (vv. 27-28) and the Messiah who works signs (v. 31). "The Jews" are attempting to eliminate Jesus violently from the ordinary events of their story, which they can control as authorities and leaders of the people (see v. 32). They cannot understand that their plot is being thwarted because there is another plane, beyond their control, which is determining the events of the story.

"The Jews" are unable to understand what Jesus is saying. He is speaking of a relationship between heaven and earth, and they are hearing him speak of events that happen on earth. Yet there is an ironic truth in their discussion. There is one place where Jesus would be outside their reach and control. Maybe he has decided to go to the diaspora, the world outside the confines of the sacred land of Israel, so that he might teach the Greeks (v. 35).[64] To go into the diaspora would be a journey into lands outside the confines of Israel, and his teaching of the Greeks would be instructing people who were not Jews. The reader knows that, at one level, "the Jews" have missed the point entirely. Jesus is speaking of his return to the Father, not about some journey into a foreign land. Yet the reader also recalls that the prologue (see 1:9-13) and earlier parts of the narrative promised that

[60] A favorite Johannine word for Jesus' active return to the Father emerges: *hypagō* (see further 8:14, 22; 13:3, 33, 36; 14:4, 5, 28; 16:5, 10, 17).

[61] The use of *zēteō*, describing the action of Jesus' opponents, always has a hint of violence (see 7:1, 11, 19, 20, 25, 34, 36).

[62] Again reading "the Jews" as an all-embracing term, referring to the groups mentioned in v. 32.

[63] This interpretation accentuates place, and does not call for an understanding of *hopou eimi egō* as an allusion to the christological use of *egō eimi*. See Léon-Dufour, *Lecture*, 2:231.

[64] On the background to *hē diaspora tōn hellēnōn*, see especially W. C. van Unnik, *Das Selbstverständnis der jüdischen Diaspora in der hellenistisch-römischen Zeit*, ed. P. W. van der Horst (AGJU 17; Leiden: E. J. Brill, 1993).

Jesus would bring God's saving presence to the whole world, even to those who were not Jews (see 3:16; 4:42; 6:35, 40, 45, 51).[65]

Jesus may not be going into the diaspora, but his going to the one who sent him (v. 33) promises the possibility of life to the whole world. How will this happen? The reference to the teaching of the Gentiles reminds the reader that this project, promised in earlier parts of the Gospel, lies unfulfilled. "The Jews" opened their attack upon Jesus "about the middle" of the feast of Tabernacles by questioning his teaching (vv. 14-15). These encounters close with the same interlocutors wondering whether he will go to teach the Greeks (v. 35). They are confused and puzzled by a teaching that they had initially rejected, and that now, they suggest, Jesus may be taking to the Gentiles. But they will not leave the comfort of their own world. Their words express the puzzlement of "the Jews" and address the reader: "What does he mean?" (v. 36): What is meant by "You will seek me and you will not find me," or "Where I am you cannot come" (v. 36)?

The setting of Tabernacles is essential for a right reading of the passage. The *schisma* that arises over Jesus as a potential Messiah emerges at a celebration marked by traditional messianic expectation (vv. 25-31). The reader finds expressions of messianic expectation, the hidden Messiah (vv. 27-28) and the Messiah who does signs (v. 31) all attempts to understand Jesus in a way that limits him to the Jewish feast. The mystery of Jesus must be understood in terms of his origins in God and his destiny in God (vv. 33-34). Such origins and destiny defy all limitations. Jesus is the Christ (see 1:17), but not according to the categories that his Jewish contemporaries were attempting to pin on him (see vv. 26-27, 31). Jesus' messianic status cannot be understood in traditional Jewish terms (vv. 26-27, 31), but only on the basis of his origins in God and his destiny to return to God (vv. 29, 33-35). His ministry is producing *schismata* (vv. 25-26, 31, 35-36), conflict (vv. 28-29, 33-34), and violent rejection (vv. 30, 32). It is leading toward "the hour" (vv. 6, 30). The presence of Jesus at the Jewish feast of Tabernacles points the reader toward a deeper understanding of the Messiah that does not nullify traditional messianic thought, but transcends and transforms the hopes normally expressed within the context of that feast.

IV. ON THE LAST DAY OF THE FEAST: 7:37—8:59

Jesus, "the People," and the Leaders: 7:37-52
What day is indicated by *en de tȩ eschatȩ hēmerai tȩ megalȩ tēs heortēs* (v. 37a)? The celebration of the libation ritual, the use of the Temple as the light of all Jerusalem, and the turning toward the Temple to profess alle-

[65] See Kysar, *John's Story*, 46.

giance to YHWH ceased on the seventh day of the celebration. The eighth day was a rest day, similar to a Sabbath (see Lev 23:33-43). It was a day of great rejoicing, and the singing of the *Hallel* continued into this eighth day (see *Sukkah* 4:8; Josephus, *Antiquities* 3.245, 247). Throughout the seven days of the feast, water and light had marked the celebrations in the Temple. Once these *symbols* have been taken away from the celebration, and the people rest and rejoice, Jesus announces that he is the provider of water (7:37-38; see 9:7) and the light of the world (8:12; 9:5).[66] The reader makes this link with the Temple liturgy, now ceased, but continued in the person of Jesus.

The narrator calls the last day "the great day," even though there are no grounds for it to be called such. Its greatness comes from the Johannine context. Jesus "stood up" (*eistēkei*) and "proclaimed" (*ekraxen*) in the Temple.[67] This is not the place for a history of the exegesis of 7:37-39,[68] but three major problems are associated with the passage:[69]

1. The question of punctuation: Do the words of Jesus come to a full stop after "come to me and drink"? This would give the RSV translation, based on the text of Nestle-Aland: "If anyone thirst, let him come to me and drink. He who believes in me, as the scripture has said, 'Out of his heart shall flow rivers of living water.'"[70] Or is there a lesser break after "come to me," reading on until "he who believes in me" for the full stop? This would produce: "If anyone thirst, let him come to me, and let him who believes in me drink. As the scripture has said, 'Out of his heart shall flow rivers of living water.'"[71]

---

[66] See, for example, Bauer, *Johannesevangelium*, 112; Hoskyns, *Fourth Gospel*, 320; Barrett, *St John*, 326; Lindars, *John*, 297–98. Against, for example, Str-B 2:490–91; Brown, *John*, 1:320; Schnackenburg, *St John*, 2:152.

[67] Some very good witnesses (the original hand of P66, Sinaiticus, Bezae, and Koridethi) read the imperfect *ekrazen*. This is a less likely reading, and Barrett suggests that it may be original (*St John*, 326). I read *ekraxen*, but the imperfect may indicate (somewhat clumsily in the context) the ongoing proclamation of Jesus as the living water.

[68] See the survey of the patristic data in H. Rahner, "'Flumina de ventre Christi.' Die Patristische Auslegung von Joh 7:37-38," *Bib* 22 (1941) 269–302; J. E. Menard, "L'interprétation patristique de Jo 7:38," *Revue de l'université d'Ottawa* 25 (1955) 5–25; M.-E. Boismard, "De son ventre couleront des fleuves d'eau," *RB* 65 (1958) 523–46.

[69] Most commentators give a survey of the possibilities for 7:37-38. But see especially G. M. Burge, *The Anointed Community: The Holy Spirit in the Johannine Tradition* (Grand Rapids: Eerdmans, 1987) 88–93; A. Pinto da Silva, "Giovanni 7,37-39," *Salesianum* 45 (1983) 575–92; G. Bienaimé, "L'annonce des fleuves d'eau vive," *RTL* 21 (1990) 282–302.

[70] Among modern scholars, this punctuation and subsequent interpretation relating the source of the living water to the believer is favored by Barrett, Bernard, Haenchen, Lightfoot, Léon-Dufour, Lindars, Segalla, RSV, and others, largely on the basis of the punctuation suggested by the second-century P66.

[71] Among modern scholars, this punctuation and subsequent christological interpretation

2. The question of meaning: Out of whose heart does the living water flow? The RSV translation leads to an interpretation that has the living water flowing from the heart of the believer. The punctuation of the NRSV, NJB, and others leaves this question open for the reader. Living water might flow from Jesus, to whom the believer has gone for refreshment. The "heart" (*koilia*) mentioned in the quotation would refer back to Jesus as the provider of drink. This would be the more likely meaning, but it is still possible that living water might flow from inside the one who has gone to Jesus for refreshment, as a result of the association with Jesus.
3. The origins of the biblical text referred to in v. 38.

The reader has already discovered that Jesus, the giver of water that will raise up to eternal life (4:14), is the presence of the creating God of the Sabbath (chap. 5). Jesus has perfected the presence of God's gift of bread from heaven, formerly understood as the Law, at the time of the Passover (chap. 6). Within the context of another Jewish feast marked by libations, and a promise of the coming Messiah who will repeat the Mosaic gift of water, the reader identifies Jesus as the source of living water. The reading experience thus far leads the reader to understand vv. 37-38 christologically. Jesus proposes another source of living water: "If anyone thirst, let him come to me, and let the one who believes in me drink" (v. 37).[72] Jesus changes the source and content of the life-giving water.[73] No longer is there any need to hold daily ritual lustrations, carrying water from the Pool of Siloam. Jesus is the source of living water for *all* who believe in him (*ean tis dipsa . . . ho pisteuōn*); he perfects and transcends the ritual of the Jewish feast. All believers will find life-giving refreshment in Jesus; the only criterion is movement toward Jesus (v. 37: *erchesthō pros me*) and faith in Jesus (v. 38a: *ho pisteuōn eis eme*). Jesus claims that his presence as the giver of life-giving refreshment to whoever believes in him is a fulfillment of the Scriptures (v. 38b). Scholars have great difficulty in discovering

---

is favored by Bauer, Becker, Bultmann, Beasley-Murray, Boismard, Brown, Dodd, Hoskyns, Schnackenburg, Westcott, NEB, JB, BJ, TOB, NJB, NRSV, and others. H. Rahner and Boismard have both shown that the second-century church witnessed to this reading. To this one can now add the *Gospel of Thomas* 13. See R. E. Brown, "The Gospel of Thomas and St John's Gospel," *NTS* 9 (1962–63) 162.

[72] There is some textual evidence against the *pros me* in "let him come to me." It is missing from the first hand of P[66], the first hand of Sinaiticus, Bezae, some Latin witnesses, and others. It is widely agreed that either *pros me* or another form, *pros eme* (found in P[75] and Vaticanus), is original, omitted through scribal oversight in some traditions because of the *eis eme* in v. 38. It should be retained.

[73] For this understanding of the living water as Jesus' revelation and teaching, replacing Torah, see Brown, *John*, 1:327–39; Léon-Dufour, *Lecture*, 2:233–35.

which Scripture is being cited.[74] The reader is told that there is a biblical tradition which Jesus fulfills, promising rivers of living water flowing from within him (v. 38b), quenching the thirst of all who believe in Jesus and come to him (v. 37-38a).

The celebration of the feast of Tabernacles directs the reader's memory to a biblical tradition in which the Temple and Jerusalem are the source of living water, nourishing and giving life to what was previously lifeless. In Ezek 47:1-11, ever-deepening waters flow out from the Temple (vv. 3-6), enlivening the desert regions of the Arabah, via En-gedi and En-eglaim (vv. 8-11). Ezek 47:9 promises: "Everything will live where the river goes." But given the close link between Zechariah 14 and the celebration of the feast of Tabernacles (see Zech 14:16-19), one may also see a reference to Zech 14:8: "On that day living waters shall flow out from Jerusalem, half of them to the eastern sea and half of them to the western sea; it shall continue in summer as in winter" (see also 14:17). An exact verbal link between John 7:38b and these two prophecies is not obvious, but there is a close relationship between them, and there is evidence that a link between the texts from Ezekiel and Zechariah had already been made in pre-Christian times.[75] Jesus transcends all attempts to understand him within the categories of Jewish messianic expectation (see vv. 14-36). In Ezek 47:1-11 the life-giving waters flowed from the Temple, the very center, the navel of Jerusalem and the earth (see Ezek 38:12; *Jubilees* 8:19; *b. Sanhedrin* 37a). Jesus proclaims that the life-giving waters now flow *ek tēs koilias autou* (John 7:38b). There is little need to determine whether the expression means "heart" or "belly," whether it is a translation of an Aramaic *gûph*, a memory of the rock in the wilderness, or a reference to a rock of the Temple.[76] For the reader, the meaning is clear; the living waters flow from within Jesus. "John used this word as a means to transfer the prophecy from the city to a person."[77] His person is now the origin of life-giving water, perfecting all that had been promised by the water celebrations of the feast of Tabernacles, the symbol of the definitive mediator of God's gift of water from the well that is the Torah.

But Jesus' proclamation of himself as the source of living water is in the future tense: "Out of his heart *shall flow* (*rheusousin*) rivers of living water" (v. 38b). The narrator then informs the reader that the gift of the

---

[74] No passage, from either the MT or the LXX, matches John 7:38b. Yet the use of the singular *graphē* would appear to refer to some specific text. See the summary of the discussion in Bienaimé, "L'annonce," 418-31.

[75] See especially P. Grelot, "Jean VII,38: eau du rocher ou source du Temple?" *RB* 70 (1963) 43-51. For a rabbinic combination of these ideas, see Tosefta *Sukkah* 3:18.

[76] For the discussion, see Brown, *John*, 1:323-24.

[77] Barrett, *St John*, 328. He prefaced these words with "It is possible that. . . ."

living water is the future gift of the Spirit (v. 39). Later rabbinic reflection on the feast of Tabernacles asked of the water ceremony: "Why do they call it the house of drawing?" And responded: "Because thence they draw the Holy Spirit" (*GenR* 70:1).[78] This link between the drawing of the water and the gift of the Spirit may lie behind Jesus words, but the perfection of this gift of God lies in the future. The reader knows that the believer is caught up in the mystery of a life in the Spirit (see 3:8), but the story time of John 7 looks forward to a future moment, marked by the glorification of Jesus, when life in the Spirit will be available to those who come to Jesus, those who believe in him (v. 37-38a). It has not yet been given, because Jesus has not yet been glorified (v. 39).

Further puzzling questions emerge for the reader of this prolepsis. How will Jesus "give" the Spirit? Is this gift of the Spirit related to the traditional expectation of the effusion of the Spirit that will take place at the end of time (see Ezek 11:19; 36:26-27; 39:29; Isa 44:3; Joel 2:28; 3:1)? What is the link between the perfection of the messianic symbol of the water, the Spirit, and Jesus' glorification? What does it mean to say that Jesus will be "glorified"? When will this glorification take place? What is its connection with "the hour" of Jesus (see 2:4; 7:6, 30)? Will it be related to Jesus' gift of himself for the life of the world (6:51c)? The reader, familiar with the basic Christian story but hearing the Johannine version of it for the first time, suspects that the growing violence surrounding the story time of the feast of Tabernacles (see 7:1, 19-20, 23, 25, 30, 32) may be linked with the gift of the Spirit, the perfection of the messianic promise, the time, the place, and the nature of Jesus' glorification. But this is a strange way to point forward to a violent death.

The narrator reports the response of the people by means of a participle (*akousantes tōn logōn toutōn*). Jesus' words, revealing himself as the living water, perfecting the Mosaic gift of water, lead to confessions of faith from some of the people who claim that Jesus is "the prophet" (v. 40), and from others who profess, "This is the Christ" (v. 41a). They are following a path already traveled by the Samaritan woman (see 4:13-26). The celebration of the feast of Tabernacles recalled Jewish messianic ideas of a second gift of water, perfecting the Torah. This recollection explains the people's response (in vv. 40-41) to the words of Jesus (in vv. 37-38). Messianic expectations have been articulated in various ways throughout Jesus' presence at the feast (see vv. 26-27, 31), but now that Jesus has presented himself as the source of living water (vv. 37-38), the people and "the Jews" must come to a decision: Is he or is he not the Messiah (vv. 40-52)? The reader knows that he is, but only in terms of the prologue: the gift of the

---

[78] See Dacy, "Sukkot," 150. See also *j. Sukkah* 55a; *RuthR* 4:8.

truth came through Jesus Christ (1:17). The gift of the truth is behind the words of Jesus in vv. 37-38, and then made explicit in the comment from the narrator: the glorification of Jesus will lead to the gift of the Spirit (v. 39).

But the people are not privy to the information of 1:17 and 7:39. They continue their discussion on the basis of the Jewish expectation of the Davidic Messiah (see 2 Sam 7:12-16; Pss 18:50; 80:3-4, 35-37; Isa 11:1, 10; Jer 23:5). The people previously wondered whether Jesus was the hidden Messiah (vv. 26-27) and a worker of great signs (v. 31). The messianic question returns, as some accept Jesus as the Messiah on the basis of his words in vv. 37-38, while others point out that Jesus comes from Galilee, but the Christ is not to come from there (v. 41b). It is part of the biblical tradition that the Messiah would come from the Davidic line, and, the people claim, the Scriptures even indicate the city of his origins: Bethlehem, the village where David was (v. 42; see Mic 5:2).[79] The reader probably knows that Jesus was from Bethlehem,[80] and is aware that Jesus is not *ek tēs Galilaias* (v. 41). Galilee is a place Jesus visits to go away from his own country (4:42). But the irony runs deeper. The reader knows that Jesus is "from God." The prologue established this as the basic characteristic of the Word who became flesh, and the narrative so far has returned repeatedly to insist that Jesus is the revealer of God who comes from God as the Sent One of God whom he calls his Father. The discussion cannot lead the people into the truth because they are using the wrong criteria. There is a uniqueness about who Jesus is and what he is doing that cannot be resolved by Jewish messianic categories. Faced with this uniqueness, the people can only fall into disarray. There is a *schisma* over who Jesus is (v. 43), but part of the people (*tines . . . ex autōn*) join the Jerusalemites (see v. 30) and "the Jews" (see v. 32): they want to arrest him (v. 44a). The reader is not surprised to learn that they are unsuccessful in their attempts, because his hour had not yet come (see v. 30).

The reader has followed the Jerusalemites and the people as they raised the question of the person of Jesus in terms of:

1. the hidden Messiah (the Jerusalemites: vv. 26-27)
2. the miracle-working Messiah (many of the people: v. 31)
3. the Messiah who gives living water (some of the people: vv. 37-41a)
4. the Davidic Messiah (some of the people: vv. 41b-42).

---

[79] The use of Mic 5:2 as a prophecy about the birthplace of the Messiah is of uncertain origin (Jewish or Christian?), but is here presumed for the story of Jesus. See Lindars, *John*, 303.

[80] For detail on the history of Jesus' origins, see R. E. Brown, *The Birth of the Messiah: A Commentary on the Infancy Narratives in Matthew and Luke* (2d ed.; New York: Doubleday, 1993) 513-16.

All these attempts to understand Jesus fall short of the mark. But by now the characters in the story: "the Jews," the Jerusalemites, and "the people," are well instructed by the word of Jesus. "The Jews" have been instructed at length in John 5, especially in 5:19-47, and in the latter part of the discourse on the true bread from heaven (6:41-59). "The people," concluding from the multiplication of the loaves and fishes that Jesus is the prophet, the one who is to come, and that he should be king (6:14-15), have had that understanding of Jesus corrected through Jesus' discourse at Capernaum (vv. 22-40). The Jerusalemites have been told they are mistaken in their belief that they know where he comes from (7:28a). He is the Sent One of the God whom they do not know (vv. 28b-29). The opponents of Jesus are not without guilt. Through the section of the Gospel that ran from Cana to Cana (2:1—4:54), the reader learned that belief in Jesus meant to receive him (see 1:12) by accepting his word (see 2:1-12; 3:25-36; 4:39-42, 46-54). "The Jews," the Jerusalemites, and "the people" have all been addressed by the word of Jesus, but they are refusing to accept that word. As Jesus is being judged by the characters in the story and found wanting to such an extent that they plan to kill him (7:1, 19, 25, 30, 32), the reader is judging the characters in the story and finding them wanting as they refuse to accept the word of Jesus. "The Jews" have queried Jesus' teaching authority (vv. 15-24), arranged his arrest, and discussed his origins and destiny (vv. 32-36), but they have not entered the debate about Jesus' messianic role. The Jerusalemites suspect that the only explanation possible for the lack of action against Jesus is the secret knowledge of the authorities that Jesus is the Messiah (see v. 16).

There has been a considerable passage of time between the original sending of the *hypēretai* to arrest Jesus (v. 32), and their return to the chief priests and the Pharisees (v. 45). They were sent out "about the middle of the feast" (v. 14), and they now return "on the last day of the feast" (v. 37). These indications are accepted by the reader as they stand. The officers of the Temple have heard Jesus' proclamation of himself as the source of living water (vv. 37-38) and have attended the discussion between Jesus and the people that followed, on the last day of the feast (vv. 40-44). The narrative (especially v. 46) presupposes that the officers have been at hand over the intervening days, listening to what Jesus said. They return to their masters empty-handed, and are asked to explain why (v. 45).[81]

The officials recognize the uniqueness and the authority of the word of Jesus in their answer: *oudepote elalēsen houtōs anthrōpos*. Unable to see beyond "this man," they are nevertheless rendered powerless by his word, and they are accused of being led astray. The narrative has come full cycle.

---

[81] The arrangement of the narrative is not "artificial" (Brown, *John*, 1:325). It makes good sense, as Schnackenburg, *St John*, 2:159, appreciates.

It began with some of the people suggesting that Jesus was leading the people astray (v. 12: *planai ton ochlon*), but they were afraid to speak openly about him for fear of the Jews (vv. 12-13). Now, at the end of the debates over Jesus' messianic status, "the Jews" openly proclaim: "Are you led astray, you also?" (v. 47: *mē kai hymeis peplanēsthe?*). Through these words, Jesus is publicly accused of being a *planos* whose teaching is *planē*, a deceiver of the people, a term used in rabbinic Judaism to speak of a pseudo-messiah.[82] Not one of the authorities (*mē tis ek tōn archontōn . . . ē ek tōn Pharisaiōn*) has fallen to the subtleties of this man's word. "The Jews" have never entered into discussion over the messianic possibilities of Jesus' life and words. This has happened only with "the people" and the Jerusalemites. Now some of the officials who come from the entourage of the Jewish leadership are falling victims to Jesus' deception, joining the ignorant and accursed ones, that part of the people who do not know the Law (vv. 47-49).[83] The reader knows wherein the truth lies. Those accused by the authorities as ignorant and accursed have in fact accepted the word of Jesus and have knowledge of the truth. By contrast, the authorities who have excluded themselves from all discussion over Jesus as the Messiah are the ignorant and accursed. The members of the Johannine community, expelled from the synagogue because of their acceptance of Jesus as the Christ (see 9:22; 12:42; 16:2), recognize the irony.[84]

"The Jews" have made their judgment (vv. 45-49), but Nicodemus, already known to the reader from 3:1-21, here described as "one of them" (*heis ōn ex autōn*), who speaks of "our Law" (*ho nomos hēmōn*), begs to differ (vv. 50-51). The arrogance of v. 48 (*not one* of the Pharisees has fallen to his trickery) is being challenged. The person of Jesus again creates a *schisma*. The issue is no longer over Jesus as the Messiah, but over the correctness of the procedure that is being used against Jesus. "The Jews" have already made a judgment, and they claim that they judge according to their firm knowledge of the Law. Nicodemus questions the very basis of their judgment in asking whether they have correctly applied the Law without hearing from Jesus exactly what he does (v. 51). Nicodemus appears in the narrative as a defender of the Law, but which aspect of the Law? The reader is aware that Jesus has not abolished the Law; he has brought it to its fulfillment. The gift of the Law to Moses has been perfected in the fullness of the gift of the truth that came through Jesus Christ (7:17-19; see 1:16-17).

There are now two defenders of Jesus. The officers (*hypēretai*) claim that

---

[82] See Pancaro, *Law*, 101–5.

[83] See ibid., 103–5. On the ʿ*am hāʾāreṣ* see, among many, Schnackenburg, *St John*, 2:160.

[84] See especially Pancaro, *Law*, 101–5; Martyn, *History and Theology*, 90–100.

no one has ever spoken as Jesus speaks; they display an initial openness to
the word of Jesus (v. 46). Nicodemus takes this further as he questions
"the Jews'" rejection of Jesus by asking why they do not "hear him" (*ean
mē akousē prōton par' autou*) and come to know what he does (*gnō ti poiei*).
No legal precept in the Old Testament or in rabbinic Judaism demands
that the accused be heard and that the accuser come to know what he
does.[85] Nicodemus enunciates a new understanding of the Law here: no
judgment can be pronounced against Jesus unless his word first be heard
in faith and his signs and works be recognized for what they are: the
action of God in his Son.[86] Nicodemus challenges "the Jews" by informing them that the only ones able to make a right judgment of Jesus are
those who believe in him. As Jesus has taught in his earlier encounter with
"the Jews" (see vv. 17-19), only a proper understanding of who Jesus is
enables a person to do the will of God (v. 17) and to live according to the
Law (v. 19). "The Jews" have never entered into dialogue with Jesus, but
one of them, Nicodemus, who earlier in the story was baffled by these
principles (see 3:1-11), now advocates a new understanding of God's
design for his people; it is found in the words and deeds of Jesus (v. 51).[87]

"The Jews" may appear to have control of the situation, but their own
ranks are split by the presence of Jesus. The irony of the narrative is that
those who condemn Jesus on the basis of the Law have missed the point of
the Law. Because Jesus is the Sent One of God and thus makes God known,
the Law is being perfected in him. "The Jews" are not prepared to move
away from what they can determine and control, and thus they attempt to
escape from Nicodemus's accusations by heaping abuse on him (v. 52), as
they heaped abuse on the officers (vv. 47-48). Full of their knowledge, they
are not led astray by him (v. 48). They regard the "crowd who do not know
the Law" (v. 49), the guards (v. 47), and Nicodemus (v. 52) as falling for his
false teaching. Ironically, "the Jews" claim that false teachers and their fol-
lowers must fall under the curse of the Law. The reader is aware that "the
Jews" are the ones refusing to do the will of God (v. 17) and no longer

---

[85] See Pancaro, *Law*, 138–43. Both aspects, hearing what he has to say for himself and thus
coming to know what he does (v. 51), must be taken into account. Against, for example,
Bauer, *Johannesevangelium*, 115, who lists Deut 1:16-17; 17:4; Josephus, *Antiquities* 6.6.3; *War*
1.209. Many commentators give these and similar texts (see Exod 23:1; Josephus *Antiquities*
14:167; *ExodR* 21:3), but they do not respond exactly to Nicodemus's objection.

[86] For this understanding of *akouein* and *ginōskein ti poiein* in the Fourth Gospel, see Pancaro, *Law*, 149–56.

[87] See ibid., 156: "Jesus no longer appears as a violator of the Law, but as the one who ful-
fils it (cf. Jn 7:21-23). *Jn brings this home at 7,51 by having the Law of the Jews establish conditions for the judgement of Jesus which can be met only by those who believe on him.*" See idem,
"The Metamorphosis of a Legal Principle in the Fourth Gospel. A Closer Look at 7,51," *Bib* 53
(1972) 340–61; Léon-Dufour, *Lecture*, 2:243–46.

practicing the Law (v. 19). In a final attempt to demolish the accusations of Nicodemus, "the Jews" join some of the people, who thought that Jesus could not be the Messiah because he came from Galilee (v. 52; see vv. 27 and 41). The reader knows that he did not come from Galilee, and that there were prophets from Galilee (v. 52).[88] But Jesus is not just a prophet, and Jesus is not from Galilee.

At a feast during which the priests professed their faith in YHWH as the only true God, "the Jews" have refused to accept God as the source of Jesus' authority (vv. 14-24). At a feast during which water was poured in ritual prayer, asking for the living waters of the autumn rains, Jesus has proclaimed that he is the river of living water (vv. 37-39). At a feast during which the gift of living water was associated with the promise of the coming Messiah, authoritatively teaching the Law, Jesus' messianic credentials have been discussed (vv. 25-31, 40-44). But the discussion has moved around traditional Jewish messianic expectations: the hidden Messiah (vv. 26-27), the Messiah as a miracle worker (v. 31), the Messiah who gives living water (v. 41a), and the Davidic Messiah (vv. 41b-42). Jesus' interlocutors have also refused to accept that there is any possible further understanding of the Law. They have condemned Jesus as a deceiver (*planos*), rather than accept that in and through him the will of God is made known. But the reader has also encountered signs of hope. As well as rejection (vv. 30, 32, 44, 37-49), there has been indecision (vv. 25-26, 35-36, 41-44) and the beginnings of belief (vv. 31, 41a).

Jesus as the Light of the World: 8:12-30

8:12-20   Jesus' two encounters with "the Jews" on the occasion of the feast of Tabernacles have been dominated by "the Jews'" inability to move beyond the Law (7:14-24, 45-52). Jesus now responds to the claim that Moses and the Law are sufficient for a correct understanding of God's dealings with the world (*palin oun autois elalēsen ho Iēsous*).[89] The only interlocutors mentioned in 8:12-30 are the Pharisees (v. 13) and "the Jews" (v. 22), who represent an audience that rejects the claim that Jesus is the Messiah (7:32, 47-49), and has decided to kill him (5:18; 7:1, 19, 25). Jesus announces, *egō eimi to phōs tou kosmou* (v. 12a), within the context of a feast where the Temple became the light of all Jerusalem (see *Sukkah* 5:3).

---

[88] Westcott, *St John*, 125, lists Jonah, Hosea, Nahum, and perhaps Elijah, Elisha, and Amos from Galilee. Some early readings (P[66] and P[75]) have *ho prophētēs*, and this is accepted by J. Mehlmann, "Propheta a Moyse promissus in Io 7,52 citatus," *VD* 44 (1966) 79-88, and Schnackenburg, *St John*, 2:161. But it is probably an assimilation of v. 40.

[89] The expression *palin* is used regularly in the Fourth Gospel to link one section of the narrative to another (see, so far, 1:35; 4:3; 4:46, 54; 6:15). See K. Tsuchido, "Tradition and Redaction in John 8:12-30," *Bulletin of the Japanese Biblical Institute* 6 (1980) 59-60.

The link with Tabernacles must not be lost from view. The reader has seen that "the Jews" are not prepared to move beyond Moses (7:14-24, 47-49), and Nicodemus's attempt to show them that the Mosaic tradition can be properly understood only by those who hear Jesus and see his deeds (7:51) has led only to abuse and rejection of his criticism (7:52). Jesus claims to be the perfection of the Law.[90] Basing themselves on Ps 119:105 and Prov 6:23 (see also Wis 18:4; Sir 24:27; Bar 4:2), the rabbis spoke of the Law as a lamp or a light (*Test Levi* 14:4; *ExodR* 36:3).[91] What was promised by the Law as a lamp to guide the steps of Israel (see Ps 119:105) is now Jesus, the light of the world. Within the present context of discussion, doubt, and *schisma*, Jesus indicates that the presence of the light is also a call to decision. The light of Jesus carries with it a chance for darkness or light, for death or life. This double possibility is presented in 8:12b: one can escape from darkness to light by following Jesus (see 1:11-12; 3:19).[92]

The two affirmations of v. 12 form the program for the rest of chap. 8. On the one hand Jesus personifies the liturgy of the feast of Tabernacles, perfecting the Law as the light of the world (v. 12a); on the other hand, such a revelation of God brings judgment (v. 12b). The acceptance or refusal of the revelation of the Father by Jesus is at the heart of every discussion that follows.[93] An issue of law emerges immediately. According to the legal demands of Num 35:30 and Deut 17:6, Jesus' witness to himself as the "light of the world" (v. 12a) is invalid (*ouk estin alēthēs*), if one accepts that Jesus' words are *martyria* in a forensic sense. But Jesus is not a defendant searching out witnesses to state his case, as in 5:31. In chap. 5 Jesus accepted the situation of a trial, during which the accused became the accuser and the accusers became the accused. Here there is no trace of a trial, but the Pharisees attempt to understand and control Jesus by means of their legal tradition. Within the setting of Tabernacles, Jesus personifies both the light of the Temple and the light of the Law. His claim in v. 12 is an aggressive affirmation of that truth. To quibble over its truthfulness on the basis of Torah and the legal tradition that depends on it is to miss the

---

[90] Talbert, *Reading John*, 153, also claims that Jesus' words raise the eschatological hopes, evoked at Tabernacles, associated with the end-time return of the pillar of fire (see Exod 13:21; 14:24; 40:38).

[91] See Str-B 2:521–22, 552–53. For a review of the possible links between the Law and Jesus as "the light" in Jewish literature, see Lindars, *John*, 313–15. Brown, *John*, 1:340, lists the Qumran parallels. For possible wisdom background, see Scott, *Sophia*, 119–21.

[92] See Blank, *Krisis*, 184–86.

[93] There is considerable scholarly discussion over the division of chap. 8. For a documented survey of the discussion, see Moloney, *Son of Man*, 125–27. I am reading the narrative in two parts: vv. 12-30 and vv. 31-59. Some come to belief (vv. 12-30) and some do not (vv. 31-59). Verse 12b is acted out.

point. The Pharisees attack the value of his *martyria*. But Jesus is claiming to be the unique revelation of God to the world (v. 12).[94] What once the Law was to Israel, now Jesus is to the world. The words of Jesus in v. 12 are not *martyria* but *phaneron*.[95] Jesus claims that he perfects the gift of the Law as the light of Israel. He is the light of the world. To judge Jesus' claims as forensic *martyria*, open to the judgment of Torah, is to miss the point.

Because of his origin and his destiny (v. 14), Jesus' witness cannot be controlled by the traditional norms.[96] He has already argued this case with the Pharisees (see 7:32-36), but they have not accepted his claims. Once again there is a conflict between the vertical plane represented by Jesus' origins with and return to the Father, and the horizontal plane of the Pharisees, attempting to control and condemn Jesus by means of the Mosaic Law. He insists that the Pharisees' inability to transcend what they can see, touch, measure, and control is the reason for their failure. They are judging *kata tēn sarka* (v. 15a). This is a repetition of Jesus' earlier accusation of "the Jews," whom he accused of judging *kat' opsin* (7:24). There has been progress in the narrative. Jesus has now pointed to himself as the light of the world (v. 12), and this use of *sarx* has links with the *sarx* of Jesus (see 1:14). The Pharisees are unable to go beyond mere external experience because they stop at the "fleshly" Jesus.

In contrast to the Pharisees, who are making superficial judgments about the truthfulness of Jesus' words, Jesus judges no one on the basis of his own authority (vv. 15b-16).[97] He will have no part of the superficial judgment of others, exemplified by the judgment of the Pharisees (v. 15b). The basis of Jesus' judgment is never his own authority; it flows from the union that he has with the one who sent him (v. 16; see 5:22-23a).[98] Jesus, the one sent by the Father, makes God known (v. 16b; see v. 12a), and a *krisis alēthinē* flows from his presence among women and men, as they accept or refuse this revelation (vv. 15b-16a; see v. 12b). The judgment flowing from the acceptance or refusal of the revelation that takes place in

[94] On this, see de la Potterie, *La vérité*, 1:83–87; Schnackenburg, *St John*, 2:225–38.

[95] The noun *phaneron* never appears in the Fourth Gospel. I am using it here, in contrast to the forensic use of *martyria* on the lips of the Pharisees, in the light of the use of *phaneroō* (see especially 7:4, 10).

[96] A number of scholars have argued that vv. 14c-16 interrupt the flow of the narrative. For a discussion, defending the present state of the text, see Pancaro, *Law*, 264–65. Pancaro rightly points out that the themes of *martyria* and *krisis* are closely related.

[97] It is necessary to link v. 15b to v. 16. Jesus' claim to judge nobody looks back to the superficial judgment of the Pharisees. He judges nobody in this way (v. 15b). But he does judge as a result of his unity with the Father (v. 16).

[98] There is, therefore, no contradiction between vv. 15b and 16 (see also 3:17; 5:27). See Brown, *John*, 1:345.

Jesus (v. 12a: *to phōs tou kosmou*) has no trace of falsity; it is authentic, judgment as it should be (*alēthinē*).[99]

Jesus' description of what is written in the Law in v. 17 contrasts with the uniqueness of Jesus' witness.[100] Jesus accepts that the Law of "the Jews" demands the witness of two men for true testimony (v. 17; see Deut 17:6; 19:15; *Ketubot* 2:9); he is not prepared to quibble over that. But such legislation does not apply to Jesus.[101] Any discussion concerning Jesus' witness and his judgment must take due account of his origin with the Father (v. 18). To stop short at the historical Jesus (*kata tēn sarka*) and to attempt to apply the niceties of the Law to him is to miss the point. The Law has been superseded by a completely new reality: the presence of God in the person and message of the one he sent.[102] A knowledge of God has come through the Law, but Jesus cannot be understood, much less judged, by such "knowledge." "All supposed 'knowledge' about God and salvation becomes shattering ignorance where there is no faith in him who possesses the true knowledge of God and reveals the way to salvation."[103] The point at issue here is not so much the vindication of the testimony of Jesus before his questioners, but rather the aggressive affirmation of the origin of Jesus that, in turn, puts the validity of his witness outside the reach of the questioning of the Law.[104] The reader recalls Nicodemus's insistence that the only way to judge Jesus properly is to hear what he has to say and to see what he does (7:51).

The all-pervading question of Jesus' origins renders pointless the problem posed by the Pharisees in v. 13, and thus they return to the dialogue gasping with puzzlement in their further question of v. 19. They are locked within their own world. Unable to move outside their own legal system, they take it for granted that he is speaking of two witnesses, himself and his Father. Thus they ask: "*Where* is your Father?" The question of

---

[99] Some ancient witnesses (P66, Sinaiticus, etc.) have *alēthēs*. This is probably the result of assimilation to vv. 13, 14, and 17. The reading *alēthinēs* is well supported (P75, Vaticanus, Bezae, Regius, Freer Gospels).

[100] Some critics read v. 17 as a statement of a legal principle that Jesus then shows to be fulfilled in the "two witnesses" of himself and his Father in v. 18. I am reading vv. 17-18 as an indication that the prescription of the law (v. 17) does not apply to the uniqueness of Jesus' revelation (v. 18). See Schnackenburg, *St John*, 2:194.

[101] This is the significance of the separation created between Jesus and the "Jews" by his description of the Law as "*your* Law."

[102] The expression *egō eimi ho martyrōn* should be linked with Isa 43:10; it is a claim to be the authentic revelation of God. See Moloney, *Son of Man*, 129–30.

[103] Schnackenburg, *St John*, 2:195.

[104] For a forensic interpretation of vv. 17-18 (Jesus and the Father are two witnesses), see Pancaro, *Law*, 275–78; J. H. Neyrey, "Jesus the Judge: Forensic Process in John 8,21-59," *Bib* 68 (1987) 512–15.

place is something with which they can cope. They avoid the crucial question: "Who is your Father?"[105] Jesus condemns them because of their total ignorance. The verb "to know" is used four times, twice negatively and twice positively, to drive home the importance of a true recognition of Jesus. But because of their close-minded limitations, they have fallen into a terrible ignorance. They are ignorant of who Jesus is and who his Father is. The implication is that to know one is to know the other. The reader waits to see how the Pharisees will react to this claim of Jesus' oneness with the Father, in which knowledge of Jesus would lead to knowledge of the Father (v. 19). For a human being to claim such intimacy with God that knowledge of the man produces knowledge of God is nothing short of blasphemy, parallel to Jesus' claim in 5:17: "My Father is working, and I am working still." The reaction of "the Jews" to that claim was a decision that Jesus must die (5:18). The reader expects a parallel reaction from the Pharisees, faced by such an audacious claim. Surprisingly, nothing happens. The author, anxious to keep the reader's attention focused on the Jewish feast and its location in the Temple, reminds the reader that all these things took place in the treasury, in the Temple.[106] But no one arrested him: "The hour had not yet come" (v. 20). The *oupō* again informs the reader that the hour had "not yet" come (see 7:30), but this assures the reader that there will be a moment in the future when it will come. *How* it will happen and *when* it will happen remain to be discovered.

8:21-30   Resuming the dialogue by means of *palin* in v. 21,[107] characters now openly debate the issue that has lurked close to the surface throughout vv. 12-20: Jesus' origin and destiny. For the third time (see 7:33-34; 8:14), Jesus tells his opponents he is going to a destiny that is beyond their reach.[108] Here there is a threat added to Jesus' words. He continues to tell his opponents that he is going away and they will not be able to go where he is going, and adds that they will seek him, but die in their

---

[105] See Westcott, *St John*, 129. It is unlikely that the issue of Jesus' illegitimacy lurks behind the question, as is suggested by Hoskyns, *Fourth Gospel*, 332–33, following Cyril of Alexandria.

[106] The "treasury" was situated between the court of the women and the inner court (see Schnackenburg, *St John*, 2:196). A location is maintained close to the lights blazing in the court of the women (see *Sukkah* 5:2).

[107] Despite many commentators, vv. 12-20 and vv. 21-30 are closely linked. See Léon-Dufour, *Lecture*, 2:258–59.

[108] I use the expression "opponents," because in 7:33-34 and in 8:14 he is speaking to the Pharisees. Strictly speaking, he is still speaking to the Pharisees in 8:21, as the *autois* must look back to "the Pharisees" of v. 13. However, in v. 22 it is "the Jews" who are puzzled by these words. As throughout chaps. 7–8, "the Jews" and the Pharisees are the same group. See Tsuchido, "Tradition and Redaction," 60.

sins. The verb *zēteō* has been used earlier to inform the reader that Jesus' opponents would seek him but would not find him (7:34, 36). It has also been used regularly to tell the reader that "the Jews" sought to kill Jesus (see 5:18; 7:1, 19, 20, 25, 30). Jesus now reverses the process. A going away of Jesus will produce the death of those who are seeking him. The reader finds an interplay of possibilities. The "going away" of Jesus will be through the violent intervention of "the Jews," but the reader also knows that this going away is part of "the hour of Jesus," the design of God that will lead Jesus back to where he came from. "The Jews" are informed that his going away to a destiny, beyond their grasp, will lead to their death.[109] It may not be the same as the physical death of Jesus, but it will be the spiritual death that flows from a rejection of the revelation of God in and through Jesus (see 5:24). The play upon the theme of death and killing continues into the apparently pointless query of "the Jews," who wonder if he will kill himself (v. 22). At one level this is nonsense. Jesus is not on a suicide mission (see Gen 9:5; 2 Sam 17:23; Josephus, *War* 3.375). Yet the reader knows that "the Jews" are seeking to kill him (see 5:18; 7:7, 19, 25), and that Jesus will do whatever the Father wishes him to do (see 4:34). In some sense, there is a death willed by Jesus that will take him back to the Father, to a place where "the Jews" can never come. The key to this subtle play upon the misunderstanding of "the Jews" is again expressed in terms of Jesus' origins (v. 23). Recalling his discussion with Nicodemus (3:12-15), Jesus tells them that they fail to understand because they (*hymeis*) are *ek tōn katō*, while he (*egō*) is *ek tōn anō*.[110] This is the gulf that must be overcome if "the Jews" wish to be saved from their sins. As has often been apparent during the celebration of the feast of Tabernacles, the discussion moves along planes that never meet. Jesus explains himself and his action in terms of the link between himself and "above"; his opponents can respond only in terms of the horizontal, human traditions of "below."

Despite the conflict preceding this encounter, caused by the clash that necessarily follows from the division between "above" and "below," there is still hope for "the Jews." "The procession of the Jews along the road of sin which leads to death is imposed upon them by no categorical necessity."[111] Jesus continues to discuss with them, as he proceeds to tell them how they could overcome the gulf between above and below. Recalling the threat of v. 21, that they would die in their sins (v. 24a), he sounds a note of hope. He tells them how they may avoid this death: "You will die in

---

[109] On the misunderstanding, see Leroy, *Rätsel und Missverständnis*, 59–63.

[110] The use of the pronouns accentuates the distance between Jesus and "the Jews."

[111] Hoskyns, *Fourth Gospel*, 334.

your sins *ean gar mē pisteusēte hoti egō eimi.*" Bultmann rightly comments: "The division between what is above and what is below need not be absolute. For the Revealer who comes down from above enables man to ascend the heights. The division is only made final by unbelief."[112] A note of hope has entered the narrative. Jesus instructs "the Jews" on the way to avoid spiritual death. However, he makes demands. He asks that they believe in him as *egō eimi*. There has been much discussion over the origin and the meaning of the absolute use of the expression *egō eimi* in the Fourth Gospel,[113] and its use in this context. It has its roots in Deutero-Isaiah (see especially Isa 43:10; 45:18; see also 41:4; 43:13; 46:4; 48:12), where YHWH is revealed as the unique God of Israel, over against all other gods. So it is in the Fourth Gospel: Jesus reveals his *unique* claim to divinity, his union with the Father, by use of this formula.[114] By belief in Jesus as the revelation of the Father "the Jews" are to bridge the gulf between "below" and "above" that is leading them to death in their sin.[115]

The "who are you?" of v. 25a is not a rejection of Jesus but an honest question which indicates that many of the pretensions of "the Jews" seem to be, at least temporarily, laid aside. They are asking one of the crucial questions of the narrative, but they have taken a long time to come to this point. If only they had listened to what Jesus has said to them from their first encounter in 2:13-22 down to the present scene, there would be no need for this question. The reader senses that their question is coming too late. Only now, after Jesus' revelation of himself as *egō eimi*, do "the Jews" ask a question that Jesus has been answering throughout the story. Jesus' response to "the Jews" is a rhetorical question,[116] reflecting "a mood of

[112] Bultmann, *John*, 348.

[113] See F. J. Moloney, "Johannine Theology," *NJBC*, 1423-24. Fuller bibliographical references are given there.

[114] See especially H. Zimmermann, "Das absolute *egō eimi* als neutestamentliche Offenbarungsformel," *BZ* 4 (1960) 54-69, 266-76. See p. 270: "Wenn also Jesus das *egō eimi* ausspricht, offenbart er zunächst nicht sich, sondern den Vater (s. Joh 8:24f)." See also J. Riedl, "Wenn ihr den Menschensohn erhöht habt, werdet ihr erkennen (Joh 8,28)," in *Jesus und der Menschensohn: Für Anton Vögtle*, ed. R. Pesch and R. Schnackenburg (Freiburg: Herder, 1975) 364-66; Tsuchido, "Tradition and Redaction," 64-66. Against E. D. Freed, "*Egō eimi* in John VIII.28 in the Light of Its Context and Jewish Messianic Belief," *JTS* 33 (1982) 163-66, who argues that *egō eimi* was a pre-Johannine title for the Messiah that "the Jews" refuse to recognize in Jesus.

[115] See Schnackenburg, *St John*, 2:200. Against Bultmann, *John*, 348-49, who draws vv. 24 and 28 together by eliminating vv. 26-27 as a fragment clumsily inserted (see pp. 350-51), arguing that v. 24 means "unless you believe that I am the Son of Man."

[116] The text at this point is notoriously obscure. Are we dealing with a question or a statement? Is *tēn archēn* an accusative noun or to be read adverbially? Are we to read *hoti* or *ho ti*? For the above reading, see Moloney, *Son of Man*, 133-34.

yearning impatience."[117] Throughout the encounters between Jesus and "the Jews" in chaps. 7–8, "the Jews" have not been able to reach beyond what they can see, touch, and control. Their measure is always the Mosaic tradition. In vv. 23-24 Jesus has described the gap that must be bridged if "the Jews" are to be saved from their sins, but their question of v. 25a displays puzzlement. In the face of such obtuseness Jesus now asks: "What is the point of talking to you."[118]

Despite Jesus' exasperation, hope endures. There are many dire judgments Jesus could bring against them on account of their hardheadedness: "I have much to say about you and much to judge" (v. 26a). But (*alla*) this must not be his way.[119] Jesus has not come to do the things that *he* might regard as opportune or even appropriate. The truth lies in the one who sent him, and Jesus comes to declare to the world what he has heard from him (v. 26b). Jesus' mission, to do the will of the one who sent him (see 4:34), will not be swayed by the fickleness and ignorance of his audience. Jesus can only proclaim that which is *alēthēs*; he can only do the will of the one who sent him. The narrator's comment in v. 27 directs the reader toward the Father who sent Jesus. Jesus is concerned with "the Jews'" reaction not to himself but to the Father who sent him. This is the point that "the Jews" cannot grasp. Their question "who are you?" (v. 25a) can be understood only in terms of the Father, but they did not understand that he spoke to them of the Father (v. 27). The narrator reminds the reader of the tragedy of the situation. "The Jews," whose priests each morning during the celebration of Tabernacles swore their allegiance to the one true God (see *Sukkah* 5:4), are not able to understand that Jesus is speaking to them about that God, his Father. Jesus makes a final attempt to convince his audience (vv. 28-29). He directs his words to "the Jews," telling them of a future time when *they* will lift up the Son of Man.

Throughout the story, Jesus has continued to claim that he makes God known and that anyone who believes in him will come to eternal life. Both the dark and the bright side of the story coalesce in v. 28.[120] "The Jews" are told they will see to it that the Son of Man is lifted up. The reader

---

[117] R. H. Strachan, *The Fourth Gospel: Its Significance and Environment* (3d ed.; London: SCM Press, 1941) 209. See also van den Bussche, *Jean*, 310; Schnackenburg, *St John*, 2:200. For a rejection of this interpretation, see E. L. Miller, "The Christology of John 8:25," *TZ* 36 (1980) 257–65. Miller proposes a high christological self-revelation (p. 263: "I am the One at the Beginning, which is what I keep telling you"). See also Brodie, *John*, 327–28. They do not relate this satisfactorily, however, to v. 26.

[118] Reading *tēn archēn hoti kai lalō hymin* as "Why am I speaking to you at all?"

[119] The contrast between v. 26a and v. 26b is created by the use of *alla*. See Barrett, *St John*, 284.

[120] For a more detailed study of 8:28-29, see Moloney, *Son of Man*, 135–41.

is aware that this refers to the future event of the crucifixion of Jesus (see 3:13-14). However, in the elevated Son of Man, a "lifting up" that "the Jews" will execute, the revelation of God will take place.[121] Then they will know that there is a oneness between Jesus and the Father. "The Jews" have already been told that the only way they could be freed from their sins was to believe Jesus' claim: *egō eimi* (v. 24). They will eventually be called on to make this act of faith, and the use of the double-meaning *hypsoō* and the title "the Son of Man" indicate—at least for the reader— Jesus' death by crucifixion (see 3:14). The promise of v. 28a is about neither salvation nor condemnation, but rather about the possibility of both, offered to Jews of all times.[122] The linking of the term *egō eimi* with the lifting up of Jesus is further explained in v. 28b: Jesus' claim to be the revelation of God in his lifting up flows from the fact that he depends totally on the Father.[123] Recalling 5:19-30, the reader is reminded that what Jesus does and says is ultimately the action and the word of the Father. As such it is authentic revelation, and a further spelling out of what Jesus claimed in v. 12: Jesus is the light of the world who will bring the light of life to all who follow him (see also 3:16-21, 31-36).

This hopeful encounter with "the Jews," where Jesus continues his attempts to convince them of his claim to be the revelation of God his Father, concludes with a final affirmation of the validity of Jesus' revelation. Its validity flows not only because Jesus has spoken what he heard from the Father (v. 28b), but also because the Father remains constantly with him (v. 29).[124] It is because of the continual presence of the Father "with" Jesus that he can claim "I am." The Father did not leave Jesus to work out his task alone; the Father was with him (v. 29ab). *Because of this,* all the Son does is pleasing to the Father, as it is in perfect concurrence with his will (v. 29c). It can be no other way. In perfect oneness of purpose and action, the Father who sent Jesus is always delighted with the never-failing response of his Son. Without any further detail, the narrator

---

[121] See Riedl, "Wenn ihr den Menschensohn," 360–61; J. E. Morgan-Wynne, "The Cross and the Revelation of Jesus as *egō eimi* in the Fourth Gospel (John 8.28)," in *Studia Biblica 1978 II: Papers on the Gospels: Sixth International Congress on Biblical Studies. Oxford 3-7 April 1978,* ed. E. A. Livingstone (JSNTSup 2; Sheffield: JSOT Press, 1980) 219–20.

[122] See Léon-Dufour, *Lecture,* 2:274–75; Schnackenburg, *St John,* 2:202–3; Riedl, "Wenn ihr den Menschensohn," 362–70. For Bultmann, *John,* 349–50, these words indicate that it is "too late."

[123] As Bernard, *St John,* 2:303, rightly points out, the *hoti* applies to "I am he" and "I do nothing on my own accord." "The Jews" will come to know both truths.

[124] After the present tense *met' emou estin,* one expects a perfect tense. Instead one finds the aorist *aphēken.* This could be a reference to the incarnation. God is present with the Word before (see 1:1-2) and after the incarnation (1:14). See Moloney, *Son of Man,* 139, and Morgan-Wynne, "Cross," 221–23.

simply informs the reader that these words of Jesus (*tauta autou lalountos*) brought many (*polloi*) of "the Jews" to belief in him (*episteusan eis auton*). A Christian community exists because this was true.

During the celebration of Tabernacles Jesus has pointed to himself as the light of the world, perfecting and rendering universal the celebration of the Temple as the light of all Jerusalem (v. 12). The discussion that followed this revelation ultimately turns upon God as the Father of Jesus. The obtuseness and resistance from the Pharisees (vv. 12-20) and "the Jews" (vv. 21-30) are created by their determination to judge everything according to their Law (see v. 17). They are controlled by the things of "below," but Jesus and his Father can be understood only by one who is open to things "from above" (see v. 23). Thus they know neither Jesus nor his Father (see v. 19). Throughout the story of the celebration of the feast of Tabernacles, Jesus insists that only acceptance of God as the Father of Jesus will solve the mystery of Jesus, the source of living water (7:37-38) and the light of the world (8:12). But "they did not understand that he spoke to them of the Father" (v. 27). As each day the priests proclaim their allegiance to the one true God, turning their backs on the rising sun, they are now running the danger of turning their backs on the source of living water (7:37-38), the light of the world (8:12), the one sent by God (8:16, 18, 26, 29).

Jesus fulfills, universalizes, and transcends all the symbols and expectations of Tabernacles because of his union with God (8:28-29). In an important prolepsis, Jesus has told "the Jews" that they are to look forward to an event some time in the future, when they will lift up the Son of Man; then they will recognize his oneness with God (vv. 28-29). Surprisingly, many of "the Jews" accept him (v. 30: *polloi episteusan eis auton*).[125] But "many" does not mean "all." The reader is aware that the threat of death (see 7:1, 11, 19, 25) and the violence that has surrounded Jesus' presence at the feast of Tabernacles (see 7:30, 32, 44; 8:20) has not disappeared.

Jesus and "the Jews": 8:31-59
A mutual hostility marks the final encounter between Jesus and "the Jews" within the Temple precincts. For clarity, I divide vv. 31-59 into three sections, but 8:31-59 is marked by a unity created by the relentless increase in hostility between the only protagonists in the story, Jesus and "the Jews," and by reference to Abraham (see vv. 33, 37, 39, 40, 52, 53, 56, 57, 58).[126]

---

[125] The use of the expression *pisteuein eis* is sometimes claimed as an indication of correct Johannine faith, while *pisteuein en* or *pisteuein* followed by the dative is regarded as a limited expression of faith. This distinction must not be applied too rigidly but determined from context.

[126] This unity makes it difficult to divide the encounter into neat literary sections. On this,

8:31-38   Jesus continues to speak to "the Jews" (v. 31: *elegen oun ho Iēsous*), but the narrative demands that the many who came to believe in him in v. 30 (*polloi episteusan eis auton*), and the group, now described as "the Jews who had believed in him" (v. 31: *tous pepisteukotas autǭ Ioudaious*), cannot be the same. The change in the tense of the verb, from aorist (v. 30) to perfect (v. 31), and the change in syntax, from *pisteuein eis* (v. 30) to *pisteuein* followed by the dative (v. 31), inform the reader that an ongoing section of "the Jews" have the beginnings of a belief in Jesus, but still have some way to go. The reader associates the group referred to in 8:31 with "the Jews" described in 2:23-24: "Many believed in his name when they saw the signs that he did, but Jesus did not trust himself to them."[127] The many who believed in Jesus (aorist tense) in v. 30, because of his promise in vv. 28-29, have departed from the scene. Among those who remain are a group from "the Jews" who have come to a partial faith in Jesus, and who still remain there (perfect tense). Jesus now attempts to draw them into authentic belief.[128]

"The Jews" of v. 31 are exhorted to persist, to go on living (*ean hymeis meinēte*), in the word of Jesus. The use of *ean* with the aorist subjunctive indicates a desire on the part of Jesus that an action already initiated be brought to its impending fruition.[129] There is a dynamic in the journey of faith from a partial to a full faith. By committing themselves to that jour-

---

see C. H. Dodd, "Behind a Johannine Dialogue," in *More New Testament Studies* (Manchester: Manchester University Press, 1968) 41–42; R. Robert, "Étude littéraire de Jean VIII, 21-59," *RevThom* 89 (1989) 71–84; Schenke, "Joh 7–10," 185–87; J. O. Tuñí Vancells, *La verdad os hará libres Jn 8,32: Liberación y libertad del creyente en el cuarto evangelio* (Barcelona: Herder, 1973) 104–24. My own divisions (see also *UBSGNT*; Lindars, *John*, 323, 327, 331; Brodie, *John*, 340–41) are offered as approximations. I find oversubtle the work of Neyrey, "Jesus the Judge," 509–42. He traces a legal process that starts in vv. 12-20 (Jesus questioned), vv. 21-30 (Jesus judges), followed by four tests for believers (vv. 31-37, 38-40, 41-47, 48-55), and a final test (vv. 58-59). This process both highlights the experience of Johannine Christians and challenges pseudo-believers.

[127] Here *pisteuein eis* is used in a context that reflects a limited faith. See Moloney, *Belief*, 104–6.

[128] The problem of "the Jews" who believe in vv. 30-31, and then attempt to murder Jesus in v. 59, is the source of much debate. In a celebrated study, Dodd ("Behind a Johannine Dialogue," 42–47) claims that the "believing Jews" of vv. 30-31 are the same, and that they are Judaizing Christians. For my separation of the believers in v. 30 and v. 31, see Westcott, *St John*, 133; Lightfoot, *St John*, 192; Brodie, *John*, 328–29. Brown, *John*, 1:354–55, explains the difficulty as a gloss using "the Jews" as the inhabitants of Jerusalem. For a survey, see J. Swetnam, "The Meaning of *pepisteukotas* in John 8,31," *Bib* 61 (1980) 106–7. Swetnam (pp. 107-9) suggests that the verb is pluperfect in meaning: "the Jews" once believed, but no longer do so. G. Segalla, "Un appello alla perseveranza nella fede in Gv 8,31-32?" *Bib* 62 (1981) 387–89, responds to Swetnam, suggesting a position close to my own.

[129] See BDF, 188–90, paras. 371–72.

ney, by "remaining" in the word of Jesus that they are struggling to grasp, they can be regarded as *mathētai* of Jesus. The reader learns from these words of Jesus that the disciple is still at the school of Jesus. "It is not immediate assent but steadiness of faith that gives character to genuine discipleship."[130] A commitment to this journey into true faith will lead "the Jews" into *tēn alētheian* (v. 32a). The reader knows that Jesus Christ is the fullness of a gift that is the truth (see 1:14, 17). "The Jews" are being asked to go on accepting the revelation of God in and through the word of Jesus, to arrive at the knowledge of God, made possible through the revelation that takes place uniquely in Jesus (see 1:18).[131] This knowledge will produce freedom (v. 32b). Freedom flows from the acceptance of Jesus as the revelation of God: light (see 1:9; 3:21; 8:12), eternal life (see 1:4; 3:15, 36; 5:24, 25; 6:27, 33, 40, 47, 51, 54, 68), the true bread from heaven (6:27, 33, 35, 50-51, 57-58), living water (4:14; 7:37-38), salvation (see 3:17; 4:42).[132] To believe in the revelation of God that takes place through Jesus Christ gives one power to become a child of God (see 1:12-13). Freedom is given to the children of a good father. Judaism taught that study of the Law made a person free (see *ExodR* 12:2; *Sifre Lev* 11; *Sifre Num* 115:5, 1-3; *Pirke Abot* 3:5; 6:2), and *Targum Neophiti* on Gen 15:11 even promises delivery of the wicked "in the merits of their father Abram."[133] This promise is now transcended. "The Jews" are being promised by the Son of God that through acceptance of his revelation of God (*hē alētheia*), they will become children of God. It is as children of God that they will be set free (*eleutherōsei hymas*).[134]

But "the Jews" claim freedom as *sperma Abraam* (v. 33). The conflict

---

[130] Bultmann, *John*, 434.

[131] For *hē alētheia* as the revelation of God in Jesus, see de la Potterie, *La vérité*, 1:23–36; D. Atal, "'Die Wahrheit wird euch freimachen' (Joh 8,32)," in *Biblische Randbemerkungen: Schülerfestschrift für Rudolf Schnackenburg zum 60. Geburtstag*, ed. H. Merklein and J. Lange (Würzburg: Echter Verlag, 1974) 283–99. For a diachronic and synchronic study of 8:32 and its context, see de la Potterie, *La vérité*, 2:789–866. See also Vancells, *La verdad*, 125–64.

[132] See Becker, *Johannesevangelium*, 1:303: "Wahrheit ist Selbstoffenbarung Jesu als alleiniger Gottesoffenbarung, heilvoller Erschlossenheit göttlicher Wirklichkeit im Wort Jesu." See also B. C. Lategan, "The truth that sets man free: John 8:31-36," *Neot* 2 (1968) 71–74. Against Bultmann, *John*, 434: "God's *alētheia* thus is God's reality, which alone is reality because it is life and gives life."

[133] See S. Sabugal, "... 'Y la Verdad os hará libres' (Jn 8,32 a la luz de TPI Gen 15,11)," *Aug* 14 (1974) 177–81. Sabugal points forward to "the Jews'" confidence because of their Abrahamic paternity (see v. 33) as an indication that there is a misunderstanding of "freedom" in the context.

[134] For this understanding of v. 32, see the exhaustive exegesis of de la Potterie, *La vérité*, 2:844–66. For the link between the Law and freedom, see 2:811–14. Stoic and gnostic parallels can be found for v. 32. For this material, and an evaluation of its relevance for v. 32, see ibid., 2:792–805.

that follows (vv. 34-47) presupposes that the revelation of Jesus promised in vv. 31-32 would give "the Jews" the freedom that is power to become *tekna theou* (1:12), but they are unable to look beyond what they can understand and control. They insist that they have never been slaves to anyone because they are *sperma Abraam* (v. 33a).[135] The reader is aware that the claim to a perennial freedom from slavery is not true.[136] "The Jews" question Jesus' right and ability to tell them he has a way that will lead them into freedom (v. 33b). The clash between the horizontal and vertical perspectives reemerges. Jesus' words, "Amen, amen, I say to you" (v. 34), link what is to follow with what has gone before. "The Jews" claim freedom because they are *sperma Abraam* (v. 33), but Jesus responds that physical descent is not the measure of freedom or slavery (v. 34). The conditions for sinfulness lie in what people *do: pas ho poiōn tēn hamartian*, not in their bloodline. Anyone who deliberately sins becomes the slave of sin.[137] There are two possible categories of people in a home: slaves and sons. "The Jews" claim to be sons, but are they? A slave has no permanent position in a household, while a son does. The reader here meets language that, in the immediately previous context, was associated with the word of Jesus. "The Jews" who had the beginnings of belief had been urged: *meinēte en tǭ logǭ tǭ emǭ*. Such a "remaining" or "abiding" in the word of Jesus produces true freedom (v. 32). Slaves do not remain in the household, while sons remain forever (v. 35).[138] Are Jesus' listeners able to accept his recommendation that they remain in his word (v. 31), or are they to be judged as slaves, because they do evil things (v. 34)? Is their presence in the household temporary, or is it *eis ton aiōna* (v. 35)?

There is a shift in the meaning of *ho huios* as it is used in v. 35 and repeated in v. 36.[139] Jesus' earlier words about abiding in the household

---

[135] On the importance of the Jewish claim to be the physical descendants of Abraham, see J. Jeremias, *Jerusalem in the Time of Jesus: An Investigation into Economic and Social Conditions during the New Testament Period* (London: SCM Press, 1969) 271–302.

[136] See Bauer, *Johannesevangelium*, 125. This freedom, however, may refer to their spiritual freedom, no matter what their political situation. See, for example, D. A. Carson, *The Gospel According to John* (Grand Rapids: Eerdmans, 1991) 349.

[137] See Schnackenburg, *St John*, 2:208. Some witnesses (Sinaitic Syriac, Bezae, Clement of Alexandria) omit *tēs hamartias*. Bauer, *Johannesevangelium*, 125, Dodd, "Behind a Johannine Dialogue," 49 n. 1; and Vancells, *La verdad*, 169 n. 28, point out that this makes better sense, but for those reasons it should be retained. See Léon-Dufour, *Lecture*, 2:284–85.

[138] The link is created by the use of *meneō* in v. 31 and v. 35, *douleuō* in v. 33 and *doulos* in vv. 34-35, and *sperma* in v. 33 and the allied *huios* in vv. 34-35.

[139] Dodd, *Historical Tradition*, 381–83, and others (especially B. Lindars, "Slave and Son in John 8:31-36," in *The New Testament Age: Essays in Honor of Bo Reicke*, ed. W. C. Weinrich [Macon: Mercer University Press, 1984] 270–86) argue that vv. 35-36 originally formed a parable about slaves and sons.

speak of the son in a general sense (v. 35). Then he speaks of the Christian who becomes a child of God through accepting Jesus, through belief in his name (see 1:12). Jesus tells his listeners how the freedom of the children of God is possible (v. 36). It is Jesus, the Son of God, who sets people free, in a genuine freedom that will last *eis ton aiōna* (v. 36; see v. 35).[140] Jesus knows (*oida*) that, at the level of bloodline, "the Jews" can claim physical descent from Abraham. They are indeed *sperma Abraam*, but is the physical issue the determining one (v. 37)? Jesus makes known, by means of his word, what he knows from his oneness with the Father (v. 38: *ha egō heōraka para tǭ patri lalō*),[141] but "the Jews" are unable to "make space" for the word of Jesus (v. 37c). The verb *chōreō* means "to make space," and it involves an active opening up of the recipient so that something or someone might enter (see especially Mark 2:2, but also Matt 19:11-12). There is no receptivity, no openness, to the word of Jesus among "the Jews."[142] Jesus indicates that he is aware of the plot of "the Jews" who seek to kill him (v. 37b; see 5:18; 7:1). They may claim to be *sperma Abraam*, but they are not his children. If they were, they would never seek to rid themselves of the Son of God.

Everyone in the story, Jesus, "the Jews," and the reader, knows that such a plot exists (5:16-18; 7:30, 44; 8:20). They seek to kill the Son of God, and thus show themselves to be the children of another father (v. 38). Jesus makes known the Father whom he has seen through the words that he speaks (v. 38a); "the Jews" make known another father, whom they have heard, by the deeds they do (v. 38b). Upon reading Jesus' accusation of "the Jews'" being children of another father because of what they do (v. 38: *poieite*), the reader recalls the earlier, more general charge: *pas ho poiōn tēn hamartian doulos estin tēs hamartias* (v. 34). There has been a rapid, dramatic change of atmosphere from v. 31. There the reader found Jesus addressing "the Jews" who had the beginnings of belief. In v. 38 the reader finds Jesus accusing them of belonging to another father because of their

---

[140] Some manuscripts (e.g., Sinaiticus, Freer Gospels) omit "the son continues for ever." This is almost certainly the result of homoioteleuton. See Barrett, *St John*, 346.

[141] There is considerable textual disturbance in v. 38. The main difficulty is the addition of possessive adjectives to "*my* Father . . . *your* father." This is probably an attempt to clarify. The distinction is already made clear by the use of *egō . . . hymeis*. The other major variant is the repetition of *heōrakate* in v. 38b, instead of *ēkousate*. This is also most probably a scribal error, creating a parallel between vv. 38a and 38b.

[142] See Hoskyns, *Fourth Gospel*, 341. Against Bauer, *Johannesevangelium*, 125, who decides against "sich verbreiten" in favor of "Fortschritte machen." See the discussion of *chōrein* in Bernard, *St John*, 2:309.

deeds and their refusal to make space for the word of Jesus. Who might that father be? Obviously, it cannot be the Father of Jesus.[143]

8:39-47   Who is the Father of Jesus, and who is the father of "the Jews"? "The Jews" lay claim to their physical roots: *ho patēr hēmōn Abraam estin* (v. 39). The reader knows the story of Abraham, and his place in the hierarchy of Jewish patriarchs. The fame that surrounded this figure has its roots in his openness to the word of God. He was a man of faith who, from his setting out from Ur of the Chaldees (see Gen 12:1-9) to risking the life of his only son (see Gen 22:1-17), "made space" for the word of God as it came to him. If "the Jews" were the genuine children of Abraham (v. 39b: *tekna tou Abraam*, in contrast to *sperma Abraam* in vv. 33 and 37), they would behave as he had (v. 39), but they do not.[144] They have rejected the revelation of the word of God in their rejection of Jesus. They seek to kill the one who makes known the truth that comes from God,[145] and in doing so have lost their claim to be children of Abraham. Abraham welcomed the heavenly messengers (see Gen 18:1-8); in rejecting a man who brings a message from God, "the Jews" do not behave as Abraham did (v. 40).[146] Therefore their paternity must lie elsewhere (v. 41a), as Jesus has hinted earlier (v. 38). To be a child of God, one must accept the word of God. To refuse his word is to choose another father (see vv. 37-38, repeated in vv. 39-41a).

"The Jews" launch into an *ad hominem* attack on Jesus. Whatever may have been "the Jews'" knowledge of Jesus' origins,[147] they accuse him of birth in fornication, while they are children of the one God (v. 41b). This charge is based in the Old Testament use of the imagery of fornication to speak of spiritual infidelity to or apostasy from God (see, for example, Hos 1:2; 2:46; 4:15; Ezek 16:15, 33-34; see also *NumR* 2:17-26).[148] They

---

[143] Jesus is not telling "the Jews" at this stage that they are the children of the devil. A question has been raised: If they slay the Son of God, then whose children are they? It will be answered later (see v. 44). See Brown, *John*, 1:356.

[144] Bernard, *St John*, 2:310, follows Vaticanus in reading the imperative *poieite*: "If you are Abraham's children, do Abraham's works." See also, Westcott, *St John*, 135; Lagrange, *Saint Jean*, 245–46. This reading is also found in P⁶⁶. See the discussion in Barrett, *St John*, 347.

[145] Too much should not be read into *anthrōpos*. It simply means "the one" (*tis*). See BDF 158, para. 301 (2).

[146] Talbert, *Reading John*, 156. Talbert cites *Pirke Abot* 5:19 as a rabbinic distinction between people who act like Abraham and others who act like Balaam. See also *Pirke Abot* 5:29.

[147] For a discussion of the charge of illegitimacy, see J. P. Meier, *A Marginal Jew: Rethinking the Historical Jesus* (ABRL; New York: Doubleday, 1991) 222–29, 245–52. It is hard to be sure whether "the Jews" in 8:41 are speaking out of this background.

[148] See Westcott, *St John*, 136.

have moved logically from their claim to be children of Abraham (v. 39) to a claim to have one Father: *hena patera echomen ton theon* (v. 41c). Because of the covenant forged between YHWH and his people, "the Jews" regard themselves as God's children (see Exod 4:22; Deut 14:1; 32:6; Jer 3:4, 19; 31:9; Isa 63:16; 64:7). The early morning ceremony of the feast of Tabernacles forms the background to this strongly worded claim. "The Jews"—disassociating themselves from their unfaithful "fathers"—join in the priests' claim at the morning ritual: "Our eyes are turned toward the Lord" (*Sukkah* 5:4). The reader knows that God is the Father of Jesus (see especially 5:19-30). He is not the master of his own destiny; he has come from God (see 1:1-18), to do not his own will but the will of the one who sent him (4:34). Another note is added as "the Jews" are told that if they were really the children of God, then they would love Jesus, who proceeded and came forth from God as his sent one (v. 42).[149] In 3:35 the narrator informed the reader that the Father loved the Son, and that is the basis for what is now claimed in 8:42: children of the same father love one another. The anger and mounting violence of the narrative show that Jesus and "the Jews" cannot be children of the same Father.

Jesus poses a rhetorical question (v. 43a), asking why there is no understanding of what he says (*lalian tēn emēn*), and no grasping and obeying of his message (*logon ton emon*).[150] The instruction the reader received through the stories assembled along the journey from Cana to Cana can be sensed as Jesus accuses the Jews: *ou dynasthe akouein ton logon ton emon* (v. 43b). This has already been said in v. 37: "because my word finds no space in you," but there is an intensification of what was said earlier. "The Jews" are not capable (*ou dynasthe*) of hearing the word of Jesus because of their origins: their father is the devil (v. 44a).[151] "The Jews" speak and act in accordance with their origins: "Your will is to do your father's desires" (v. 44b). The root motivation for the pattern of being and behaving is the same for both Jesus and "the Jews." They behave in a particular way because of their respective origins. The difference between them lies in

---

[149] A series of terms stresses Jesus' dependence upon God: *exēlthon, hēchō, apesteilen.* As Schnackenburg, *St John,* 2:212, points out, all these verbs refer to the event of Jesus' coming into the world. The verb *hēchō* was familiar to the religious language of the time, used for the saving appearance of a deity. On this, see Barrett, *St John,* 348.

[150] The noun *lalia* is used to speak of Jesus' audible word. Bultmann, *John,* 316 n. 7, and Schnackenburg, *St John,* 2:491 n. 101, suggest that this expression is taking account of current language associated with revealer figures. Unable to understand his spoken word, "the Jews" cannot grasp and obey ("hear") Jesus' *logos.* See Barrett, *St John,* 348.

[151] This may mean "you are of the father of the devil," which has traces of gnostic doctrine. See, for this reading, Westcott, *St John,* 137. For this possible background and early Christian reflection on the idea, see Bauer, *Johannesevangelium,* 127–29; Bultmann, *John,* 318–20. The dualism is moral, not metaphysical. See, among many, Schnackenburg, *St John,* 2:214–15.

their *different* origins. Jesus is "from God," while "the Jews" are from the devil.[152] The description of the devil that follows is based on the actions of the devil "from the beginning" (v. 44b: *ap' archēs*). By means of lies and deceit, he robbed Adam of YHWH's original promise of immortality. He is thus a liar and a murderer (Gen 3:1-24; see also Wis 2:24). His deceits also led to the first murder, Cain's slaying of Abel (see Gen 4:1-15).[153] In the beginning the devil was against God, deceiving and murdering human-kind (contrast John 1:1). The devil is a liar, and all that flows from him is deceit. Everything about the devil is opposed to Jesus: "he has nothing to do with the truth (v. 44c: *en tē alētheią ouk estēken*) because there is no truth in him (*hoti ouk estin alētheia en autǭ*)." Jesus reveals the truth as he tells the story of God (1:18; see 1:14, 17; 8:32, 40), while the devil is the denial of all truth. It was the devil's role at the beginning of all human his-tory, instituting a situation of lies, deceit, and death, that made him "the father of lies" (v. 44d). There are two powers at the beginning of the human story: God who is true and the devil who is the father of lies. Jesus speaks the truth (v. 45: *tēn alētheian legō*). The word of Jesus is the revela-tion of the truth in the human story, reflecting his origins in God, his Father.[154] But "the Jews," reflecting their origins in one who of his very nature speaks a lie (v. 44d: *hotan lalę to pseudos, ek tōn idiōn lalei*), do not believe in his word (v. 45). The revelation of *truth* among the children of one who is the father of *lies* leads inevitably to rejection and denial. A *pseudos* cannot accept a word that reveals *alētheia*. "The Jews" fail the test of faith, known to the reader from the Cana to Cana journey (2:1—4:54). The logic of Jesus' argument is inescapable. "The Jews" must be children of the liar, as they will not accept the revelation of the truth.[155] The devil enters the story of Jesus for the first time.

Jesus closes this discussion with an accusation formed by two rhetorical

---

[152] Jesus' words in vv. 44-47 are the most negative things said against "the Jews" in the New Testament. See Becker, *Johannes*, 1:304. But "the Jews" are never the Jewish people in the Fourth Gospel. The term reflects a christological polemic that has led to a breakdown between the Johannine community and the (local?) synagogue. See E. Grässer, "Die Juden als Teufelsöhne in Joh 8,37-47," in *Der Alte Bund im Neuen* (WUNT 35; Tübingen: J. C. B. Mohr [Paul Siebeck], 1985) 154–67; F. Porsch, "'Ihr hat den Teufel zum Vater' (Joh 8,44)," *BK* 44 (1989) 50–57. This has not been appreciated by G. Reim, "Joh 8.44—Gotteskinder/Teufels-kinder: Wie antijudaistisch ist 'Die wohl antijudaistische Äusserung des NT'?" *NTS* 30 (1984) 619–24, who attempts to link the passage with Cain and Abel speculation, via a remanaging of the text.

[153] Lindars, *John*, 329; Léon-Dufour, *Lecture*, 2:291. Brown, *John*, 1:358, argues for the Cain and Abel story as background to this passage. This is rejected by Schnackenburg, *St John*, 2:211, 409 n. 102.

[154] Lindars, *John*, 330, rightly points to the father-son concept as "central to the whole argument."

[155] Against Bultmann's interpretation of *alētheia* as God's reality and *pseudos* as the will that creates its own reality (*John*, 321).

questions (v. 46), answering the second in v. 47. Jesus challenges "the Jews," children of the father of all lies, to convict him of sin (v. 46a). Such a conviction is not possible. The liar is in no position to convict the one who speaks the truth. That they are liars is at the heart of Jesus' second question. Jesus accuses "the Jews" that it is against their very nature as children of the devil to be able to accept the word of truth. They belong to untruth. It is clear to the reader that "the Jews" should answer Jesus' question, "Why do you not believe me?" with the words, "Because we cannot." Jesus has already said this in an earlier question: "Why do you not understand what I say?" (v. 43a). He answered it in v. 43b: *hoti ou dynasthe.* Jesus' response to the question of the unbelief of "the Jews" restates a basic truth (v. 47). In the Johannine view of things, two classes of people are involved in this discussion: those who are "of God" (*ek tou theou*), and those who are "not of God" (*tou theou ouk este*). "The Jews" belong to the latter group. For the reader Jesus is the revelation of God, and the person who is "of God" will hear it. Such "hearing," which will lead to life, is impossible for "the Jews" because of their origins in the father of all lies and the father of death (v. 44). The discussion of the two fathers has come full circle since "the Jews" claimed Abraham in v. 39.

8:48-59.   The final encounter between Jesus and "the Jews" in the Temple is a genuine dialogue, during which two points of view clash. "The Jews" interrogate (vv. 48, 53, 57), affirm their point of view (v. 52), and react (v. 59a). Jesus answers their questions (vv. 49, 54-55), affirms his point of view (vv. 50-51, 56, 58), and reacts (v. 59b). The reader is called to make a decision as two sides of an argument are presented. "The Jews" defend themselves against Jesus' charge that they are the sons of the devil by counterattack. They charge that Jesus is a Samaritan, a member of a mixed and apostate race,[156] that he has a demon and therefore is insane (v. 48; see 7:20). They are quite certain about this claim, as they preface their accusation with the words *ou kalōs legomen.* They are setting their word (*legomen*), which they are not prepared to question, against the word of Jesus (see v. 45: *alētheian legō*), which has accused them of having the devil as their father. Jesus responds by returning to the issue at the center of the debate: his Father. His words to "the Jews" flow from his union with the Father whom he seeks to honor (*timō*), just as they seek to dishonor (*atimazete*) Jesus (v. 49).[157]

---

[156] Bauer, *Johannesevangelium*, 130–31, points out that the association of being Samaritan and being possessed could come from the Jewish belief that Samaritan prophets were possessed by demons.

[157] The contrast between Jesus and "the Jews" is highlighted by the emphatic use of *egō . . . hymeis*. See Westcott, *St John*, 138.

The reader recalls that judgment flows from the acceptance or refusal of Jesus (see 3:16-21, 36; 5:27), and that to honor the Father one must honor the Son (see 5:23). Jesus does not seek to establish his own fame (*doxa*), but as the Sent One of the Father, such fame will come in the Father's time and in the Father's way. There is one who seeks the glory of Jesus (*ho zētōn*), and this figure also judges (*krinōn*). But "the Jews" are seeking (*zētein*) to kill Jesus (see 5:18; 7:1), having already judged *kat' opsin* (7:24) and *kata tēn sarka* (8:15) that Jesus' claims are only worthy of death (see 7:25; 8:20). Two parties are "searching" and "judging": "the Jews" and the Father of Jesus. There is a certain ambiguity about the judging role of the Father of Jesus. It has earlier been said that the Father does not judge (see 3:17; 5:22), but it has been made equally clear that judgment has been given to the Son by the Father (5:22, 27, 30; 8:16). The reader now learns that it is not the Son who judges but the Father (8:50). There is no real contradiction, as judgment in the Fourth Gospel flows from the acceptance or refusal of the revelation of God that comes in and through the light brought by the Son: "This is the judgment, that the light has come into the world, and people loved darkness rather than light" (3:19). The judgment that flows from the acceptance or refusal of the *doxa* of Jesus may not be the result of God's direct action, but behind such judgment lies the one who sent Jesus, the one seeking the glory of Jesus: God. God can, therefore, still be presented as *ho krinōn* (v. 50).

The word of Jesus, the revelation of God, therefore,[158] is the decisive factor. Jesus does not seek his own glory, but a *doxa* there will be, as he makes God known. Everlasting life flows from the keeping of the word of Jesus, holding on to it, carrying out its demands, and thus living by it (v. 51). Jesus' response to "the Jews'" rejection of his person (v. 48) is to affirm again the central function of the revelation of God that takes place in and through him, leading to either life or death (vv. 50-51). "The Jews," however, will not be moved, and they respond according to their usual rubric: they lay claim to their ancestry in Abraham and the prophets (vv. 52-53). Their misunderstanding of the words of Jesus is rooted in an inability to accept the inbreak *from above*. Their response to Jesus is conditioned by their determination to be satisfied by what comes *from below*: their human heritage.[159] The reader recognizes this in the familiar "we know" (*nyn egnōkamen*). Now "the Jews" *know* that their charge of demon possession (see v. 48) is true because the very words of Jesus condemn him. The reader is aware that there is no openness to the words of Jesus. In a way

---

[158] I use "therefore" to indicate the link between what has preceded and what follows. This is implied in the expression *amēn amēn legō hymin*.

[159] See Leroy, *Rätsel und Missverständnis*, 76–82.

that recalls the Samaritan woman's inability to accept that Jesus could be greater than Jacob (see 4:11-12), "the Jews" ask: "Are you greater than our Father Abraham . . . the prophets?" (v. 53). They died; how can Jesus offer eternal life? The undisclosed, but thinly disguised presupposition behind the question of "the Jews" is: Jesus is not greater than Abraham or the prophets.

The reader knows that Jesus died, but the death of Jesus cannot be compared with that of Abraham and the prophets (see 3:14; 8:28). "The Jews" are not only refusing to accept and keep the word of Jesus, *they are not listening to his word*. Jesus does not seek his own *doxa*; this depends entirely on the Father (v. 54; see v. 50). An intervention of the Father will establish the *doxa* of Jesus.[160] The enigma is that "the Jews" lay claim to the one true God as their father (see also v. 41),[161] but such a claim is untrue. They are liars, as their father was the father of all lies (see v. 44). They cannot dishonor (see v. 49) and seek to kill (see 5:18; 7:1) the Son of God and claim that his Father is also their one true God. Once the reader has entered into the logic of the storyteller, this point becomes obvious. "The Jews" claim one true God, but they do not know this God because they refuse to acknowledge his Son and to accept his word. Over against this the reader meets the knowledge and revelation of the Son. For Jesus not to accept his knowledge of his Father and his preparedness to keep the word of the Father would mean that he would join "the Jews" in their lies (v. 55). The history of salvation has pointed toward this appearance of the Son of God, keeping the word of God and making it known. Abraham may be at the source of the physical origins of "the Jews," but he is separated from them radically by the fact that he accepted God's designs through history, while they do not (v. 56). His own faith, as it is recorded in the stories from Genesis, was an example of that, and he looked forward to the accomplishment of God's plans. Early Jewish tradition held that Abraham had been privileged with a disclosure of the secrets of the ages to come, especially the messianic age (see *Targum Onkelos* on Gen 17:16-17; *GenR* 44:22, 28; *4 Ezra* 3:14; *Test Levi* 18:14; *2 Baruch* 4:4; *Apocalypse of Abraham* 31:1-3; *Tanḥ Bereshit* 6:20; *b. Sanhedrin* 108b), and this further claim to fame probably lies behind these words of Jesus.[162] The problem does not lie with Abra-

---

[160] Against Bernard, *St John*, 2:319, who limits the meaning of *doxa* to "honor" here. Hints of Jesus' future glorification are also involved. See Brown, *John*, 1:366; Schnackenburg, *St John*, 2:220–21; Carson, *John*, 356.

[161] Reading *theos hēmōn* in v. 54. Not only does this make better grammatical sense (see Lagrange, *Saint Jean*, 253), but it points to the falsity of "the Jews'" claims. They must not associate the God of Jesus with their god, who is, after v. 44, the devil.

[162] See, for example, Schnackenburg, *St John*, 2:221–23; Perkins, "The Gospel according to John," *NJBC*, 967. There is little need to claim that Jesus speaks of a heavenly Abraham seeing

ham, but with Jesus. He teaches that "the work of salvation . . . was actually complete in Jesus."[163] "The Jews," despite their claims to physical generation from their father Abraham, are separated from him by a huge gulf: he rejoiced in the coming of Jesus (v. 56),[164] while "the Jews" seek to kill Jesus.

While Jesus speaks to "the Jews" of the history of salvation and its culminating point in the revelation of the Father now taking place in his Son, "the Jews" can only query how a man less than fifty years old could claim to have seen Abraham (v. 57).[165] "The Jews" have not listened to the words of Jesus. He did not say that he had seen Abraham, but that Abraham had seen the day of Jesus. Abraham had been blessed with a sight of the fullness of God's revelation in the human story of Jesus. As in vv. 52-53, "the Jews" show that they are not only unable to keep the word of Jesus; they are unwilling to listen. Summing up all that has been said through this discussion of the respective places of Abraham and Jesus in God's story, Jesus closes the discussion by speaking in a way incomprehensible to "the Jews." Jesus is able to call upon his having existed as the *logos*, turned in loving union toward God before the beginning of time (1:1: *en archē ēn ho logos, kai ho logos ēn pros ton theon*). Abraham, for all his greatness, belongs to the sequence of events that mark time. There was a time when he belonged to a narrative. His story is finished; he has come and gone. "The Jews" are only able to call upon the memory of his story.[166] This is not the case with Jesus. As he speaks to them from within the story time of the events of the feast of Tabernacles, he transcends story time in an analepsis that reaches behind the days of Abraham, behind any time, to proclaim that before the time of Abraham, he was already in existence (see 1:1).[167] The reader has had access to this information, provided by the prologue (see 1:1-5); but "the Jews" have not. The use of the *egō eimi* here

---

him in his ministry. See S. Cavaletti, "La visione messianica di Abramo (Giov. 8,58)," *BibOr* 3 (1961) 179–81; Lindars, *John*, 334–35.

[163] Barrett, *St John*, 352.

[164] There may be a link between the "rejoicing" of Abraham here and his joy in Gen 17:17. See Hoskyns, *Fourth Gospel*, 347–48.

[165] The mention of fifty years indicates the common view of the end of a man's working life (see Num 4:2-3, 39; 8:24-25), but M. J. Edwards, "'Not Yet Fifty Years Old': John 8:57," *NTS* 40 (1994) 449–54, has pointed out that the book of *Jubilees* uses "fifty years" to measure eras since the creation. As Jesus' opponents apply this measure, his reply in 8:58 mocks them. He is superior to every span of time.

[166] See Leroy, *Rätsel und Missverständnis*, 84-88.

[167] Lindars, *John*, 336, points to the unifying use of *egō eimi* in John 8: "'I am the light of the world' (verse 12) becomes 'I am (he),' i.e. the light and all other predicates which denote salvation (verses 24 and 28); and this in its turn becomes the simple 'I am' of the present verse, denoting timeless pre-existence."

does not carry its christological significance as the revealer of the one true God within the human story.[168] It is a use of the present tense of the verb "to be" reaching outside all time, recalling the use of the imperfect of the verb "to be" that highlighted the early part of the prologue (1:1-4). But biblical tradition lies behind the expression (see Isa 43:11-13; 46:4; 48:12; Ps 90:2). Jesus can thus speak a word that offers true freedom (see vv. 31-32) and a life that overcomes death (see v. 51). C. K. Barrett has written of 1:1, "If this be not true the book is blasphemous."[169] Because "the Jews" have not read the prologue, which was directed only to the reader, and because they are totally conditioned by their own cultural, social, and religious criteria, they are unable to accept that such words are true. They necessarily judge Jesus as a blasphemer, and take up stones to slay him (v. 59a). The reader knows that Jesus will not be slain by stoning. This cannot be the end, as he will be glorified by means of a "lifting up" (see 3:14: *hypsōthēnai dei*; 8:28: *hypsōsēte*). Jesus hides himself (v. 59b: *ekrybē*), and the reader recalls that his arrival in the Temple was in secret (7:10: *en kryptō*) as the feast of Tabernacles opened. A major section of the narrative is closed by this return to the theme of secrecy, as Jesus leaves the Temple for the first time since 7:10 (8:59b).

CONCLUSION

The story of Jesus' presence at the feast of Tabernacles makes christological claims that correspond with major celebrations of the feast.[170]

- Jesus is the revealer of the one and only God. He makes God known with a unique authority, over against all other false gods, and all forms of idolatry (see *Sukkah* 5:4; see John 7:14-24; 8:39-59).
- Jesus is the Messiah who cannot be explained in terms of Israel's traditional messianic expectations (see Zech 14:16-19; see John 7:25-31). Israel's messianic hopes are not nullified, but transcended and transformed.
- Jesus is the Messiah who is unacceptable to the Pharisees ("the Jews"), who claim to know everything that is to be known about the

[168] There are no metaphysical claims here, e.g., "the timeless being of Deity" (Bernard, *St John*, 2:322; Brodie, *John*, 336). For E. D. Freed, "Who or What Was before Abraham in John 8:58?" *JSNT* 17 (1983) 52–59, Jesus' words point to the Jewish belief in the preexistence of the Messiah. Jesus is that Messiah, "hidden to Jewish understanding" (p. 57).

[169] Barrett, *St John*, 156.

[170] See also Vancells, *La verdad*, 120–23. Vancells also adds the regular appearance of *egō eimi* (8:24, 28, 58) as a repetition of the twofold use of *ʾānnâ YHWH* in Ps 118:25 (see pp. 120–21).

destiny of the Messiah in 7:32-36. They display no openness to Jesus' transformation of traditional messianic expectation.

- Jesus is the personification and the universalization of the celebration of the gift of living water at the feast of Tabernacles (see *Sukkah* 4:9-10; see John 7:37). Jesus is now the source of living water. The messianic hopes attached to such a gift are also transformed and transcended (see 7:38-52).

- Jesus is the personification and the universalization of the celebration of the light of the Temple and of the city of Jerusalem at the feast of Tabernacles (see *Sukkah* 5:2-4; see John 8:12). Judgment flows from the acceptance or refusal of the revelation of the one true God in and through Jesus (see 8:12b-59).

- The morning celebration of Israel's allegiance to its traditional God is at stake (see *Sukkah* 5:4). "They did not understand that he spoke to them of the Father" (John 8:27). The attempt to kill Jesus shows that "the Jews" are not children of Abraham or of the one true God, but children of the devil (see 8:37, 59; see also 5:23).

As with the story of the celebration of the Passover, the Jewish feast is the setting for Jesus' claims: "If anyone thirst, let him come to me and drink" (7:37); "I am the light of the world" (8:12).[171] What had been done in the Jewish Temple on the feast of Tabernacles was but a sign and a shadow of the perfection of the gift of God in the person of Jesus Christ (1:16-17), the Son of the one true God (7:14-24), the Messiah who could not be contained within Jewish national and religious expectations (7:25-31, 32-36), the perfection of the gift of the Law as living water (7:37-39), and the light of the world (8:12). The Christians of the Johannine community had not lost contact with the celebration of the feast of Tabernacles, the *zikkarōn* of God's liberating, nourishing, and caring presence to his people. In their unconditional commitment to the word of Jesus (see 2:1—4:54), they could claim: "We are the Lord's, and our eyes are turned to the Lord" (*Sukkah* 5:4). In Jesus Christ Tabernacle traditions have become enfleshed, not destroyed. The Johannine community belonged to the Mosaic tradition, but it was a tradition now perfected in the fullness of the gift of Jesus Christ (1:17). A serious problem for a community that had its roots in Judaism, but that had been forced away from those roots because of its faith in Jesus as the Christ, has been faced and resolved, at least theologically.[172] The real reader, the Johannine commu-

---

[171] John 6 presents Jesus as the bread from heaven and John 7 presents him as the living water. *EcclR* 1:8 tells of the rabbinic belief that the latter redeemer would bring down the manna and that the latter redeemer would bring up water.

[172] Problems remained, however (see, for example, 6:60-71).

nity, and the implied reader are at one as the story indicates that those who would use the Mosaic tradition to understand Jesus have no claim to be children of Abraham or children of God. They are children of the devil, a murderer from the beginning of time and the father of all lies. It is "the Jews" who have lost their way and who are ultimately shown to have no claim to be the rightful heirs to Abraham. Jesus has incarnated all that was celebrated throughout the Jewish feast.

Chapter Four

Jesus and Tabernacles, 2
John 9:1–10:21

¶ JOHN 9:1–10:21, which opens and closes with reference to the man born blind, is marked by a temporal, spatial, and thematic unity.[1] A man born blind comes to sight and faith in the Son of Man while Jewish leaders move toward blindness (9:1-38).[2] The Jewish leaders are then condemned as blind, thieves, robbers, strangers, and hirelings who do not care for their sheep, unlike the Good Shepherd (9:39–10:13). The encounter climaxes with a presentation of Jesus as the Good Shepherd (10:14-18) and a further *schisma* among "the Jews" (vv. 19-21).

---

[1] The unity of John 9:1–10:21 is a matter of some controversy. Some would see 10:1-21 as an intrusion, others would trace its insertion to a later stage in the development of the Johannine tradition, and others would regard it as essential to the argument of 9:1-41. Many rearrangements of the material have been suggested. For a survey, see R. Schnackenburg, "Die Hirtenrede Joh 10,1-18," in *Das Johannesevangelium; Ergänzende Auslegungen und Exkurse* (HTKNT IV/4; Freiburg: Herder, 1984) 131–43; P.-R. Tragan, *La parabole du "pasteur" et ses explications: Jean 10:1-18. La genèse, les milieux littéraires* (Studia Anselmiana 67; Rome: Edizioni Anselmiana, 1980) 55–175.

[2] The alternation between "the Jews" (see 9:18, 22; 10:19) and "the Pharisees" (see 9:13, 15, 16, 40) as major protagonists in 9:1–10:21 again (as in chaps. 7–8) allows the reader to take for granted that they represent the same group, opposed to Jesus. See H. Thyen, "Johannes 10 im Kontext des vierten Evangeliums," in *The Shepherd Discourse of John 10 and Its Context*, ed. J. Beutler and R. T. Fortna (SNTSMS 67; Cambridge: Cambridge University Press, 1991) 123. For Martyn, *History and Theology,* 31 n. 29, "the Pharisees" represent a reading back into the story of Jesus the experience of the Johannine Christians before the *Bet Din* in Jamnia.

THE SHAPE OF THE NARRATIVE

There have been various attempts to show where tradition and redaction combine to form the narrative of the man born blind,[3] but it is universally admitted that, whatever the sources for the present text, "we have here Johannine dramatic skill at its best."[4] Recalling "the ancient maxim that no more than two active characters shall normally appear on stage at one time, and that scenes are often divided by adherence to this rule,"[5] Martyn suggests a sevenfold division, which I develop into eight scenes, including 10:1-21, as follows:[6]

    I.   *9:1-5:* Jesus and the disciples.
    II. *9:6-7:* Jesus and the man born blind.
    III. *9:8-12:* The blind man and his neighbors.
    IV. *9:13-17:* The blind man and the Pharisees.
    V. *9:18-23:* The Pharisees and the blind man's parents.
    VI. *9:24-34:* The Pharisees and the blind man.
    VII. *9:35-38:* Jesus and the blind man.
    VIII. *9:39—10:21:* Jesus and the Pharisees.[7]

The first scene (9:1-5) opens and the final scene (9:39—10:21) closes with reference to the man born blind.[8]

The story of the man born blind and Jesus' discourse on shepherds continue Jesus' words and actions during the feast of Tabernacles (7:2, 37):[9]

1. Jesus proclaims *that* he is the light of the world (9:5; see 8:12), and the journey of the man born blind into the man who confesses his faith in the Son of Man whom he sees and hears (see 9:34-35) shows *how* this is true.
2. The water of Siloam, which effects the cure of the once blind man, is

---

[3] For a survey, see Painter, *Quest*, 308–18.

[4] Brown, *John*, 1:376.

[5] Martyn, *History and Theology*, 26.

[6] Martyn describes vv. 1-7 as "Jesus, his disciples and the blind man" (*History and Theology*, 26), but this introduces three active characters. I will thus further divide vv. 1-7 into vv. 1-5 and 6-7.

[7] On 9:39-41 as an introduction to 10:1-21, see Dodd, *Interpretation*, 358.

[8] Studies of 9:1-41 often link vv. 1-5 (Jesus and the disciples) with vv. 39-41 (Jesus and the Pharisees) as opening and closing units. See M. Gourgues, "L'aveugle-né (Jn 9). Du miracle au signe: typologie des réactions à l'égard du Fils de l'homme," *NRT* 104 (1982) 381–83. The larger unit (9:1—10:21) opens and closes with a reference, in the third person, to the blind man (9:1; 10:21).

[9] See especially S. Sabugal, *La curación del ciego de nacimiento (Jn 9,1-41): Análisis exegético y teológico* (BEB 2; Madrid: Biblia y Fe, 1977) 17–27.

interpreted as "the Sent One" (9:7). The reader is shown *how* Jesus is life-giving water (see 7:37-38).

3. Jesus announces that he is the Good Shepherd who lays down his life for his sheep (vv. 14-18). The Good Shepherd tells *how* he will exercise his messianic role.

In several of Jesus' discussions with "the people," the reader has met suggestions of a messianic hope that Jesus is not prepared to accept: the hidden Messiah (see 7:27-29), the miracle-working Messiah (see 7:31), the Messiah who gives living water (see 7:37-38, 41a), and the Davidic Messiah (see 7:41b-42). In 10:14 Jesus will repeat a claim he has already made in v. 11: "I am the Good Shepherd." But he goes on to explain the way in which he will shepherd his flock: "I lay down my life for my sheep" (v. 15b). The overall impression created by the narrative is that Jesus is unwilling to accept the messianic expectations of "the people," but he speaks of himself as the Good Shepherd who lays down his life for his sheep. Is there any Jewish background for the idea that the Messiah would be a shepherd?[10]

It is widely acknowledged that there is no direct citation from the Old Testament in 10:1-18.[11] Yet a long-standing biblical tradition presents the unfaithful leaders of Israel as bad shepherds who consign their flock to wolves (see Jer 23:1-8; Ezekiel 34; 22:27; Zeph 3:3; Zech 10:2-3; 11:4-17). This theme is continued in other Jewish literature that is pre-Christian or contemporaneous with the Fourth Gospel (*1 Enoch* 89:12-27, 42-44, 59-70, 74-76; 90:22-25; *Test Gad* 1:2-4). Throughout the Old Testament, God is repeatedly spoken of as the shepherd of his people,[12] and at the time when the Exile caused many to doubt, God was presented as the future shepherd of his people (see Jer 31:10; 13:17; 23:3; Isa 40:11; 49:9-10). Ezek 34:11-16 speaks of God's future gathering of his flock as the good shepherd. This image is continued into the later writings (see Zeph 3:19; Mic 2:12; 4:6-7; Qoh 12:11; Sir 18:13). As the monarchy disappeared prophets spoke of a future Davidic figure who would be shepherd to the people (see Mic 5:3; Jer 3:15; 23:4-6; Ezek 34:23-24; 37:24; Zech 13:7-9).[13] The notion appears of "one shepherd" who will form "one flock."

---

[10] For what follows, see especially Beutler, "Der alttestamentlich," 23–32; Manns, *L'Evangile*, 227–33; and A. Reinhartz, *The Word in the World: The Cosmological Tale in the Fourth Gospel* (SBLMS 45; Atlanta: Scholars Press, 1992) 105–31.

[11] For themes that emerge from the possible targumic interpretations of the Old Testament (Ezekiel 34; Isaiah 42, 53; Micah 2:12; Exodus 15; Canticles 1; Jeremiah 33; Zechariah 8) which may be behind John 10, see Manns, *L'Evangile*, 227–33.

[12] The texts are too numerous to cite. For a full list and some detailed comments, see B. Willmes, *Die sogenannte Hirtenallegorie Ez 34: Studien zum Bild des Hirten im Alten Testament* (BBET 19; Frankfurt: Peter Lang, 1984) 279–311.

[13] See ibid., 342–50.

I will set up over them one shepherd, my servant David, and he shall feed them and be their shepherd. And I the Lord will be their God, and my servant David shall be prince among them (Ezek 34:23-24; see 37:24).

The image continues and strengthens in other Jewish literature (see LXX Ps 2:9; *Psalms of Solomon* 17:24, 40; CD 13:7-9; *2 Baruch* 77:13-17), and doubtless forms the background for Jesus' words in John 10:1-18.

READING THE NARRATIVE

The reader follows Jesus, who is forced out of (*kai exēlthen*) the Temple by the violence of "the Jews" (8:59). In 9:1 Jesus is "passing by" (*kai paragōn*). The temporal setting is still the feast of Tabernacles (see 7:2),[14] and the location is still the city of Jerusalem (see 7:10, 14). No change in time is indicated until 10:22.[15] The shape of 9:1—10:21, determined by the presence of two active characters playing a role in successive themes, is not complex. I will read the story to 9:38, and only then discuss the more complex issue of the shape of 9:39—10:21.

I. JESUS AND THE DISCIPLES: 9:1-5

Jesus sees a man who has never experienced sight or light.[16] Working from a biblical principle that God cannot be credited with the evil that happens to people (see Exod 20:5; Num 14:18; Deut 5:9; Tob 3:3-4), the disciples pose a logical question. A child born with an ailment suffered either because of the sins of parents or because of sin committed while still in the womb.[17] The disciples ask who is responsible. Jesus' answer cuts across all accepted explanations. Jesus' practice of transcending a discussion by shifting its point of reference is by now commonplace. While the disciples wonder about human responsibility for suffering, and address Jesus as "Rabbi" (see 1:38, 49; 3:2; 4:31; 6:25), Jesus tells them that this situation

---

[14] Many would disagree. See, for example, Lindars, *John*, 341; Becker, *Johannes*, 1:311. For Westcott, *St John*, 143, all the events of John 9–10 take place on the feast of the Dedication (see 10:22).

[15] Many see no significance in the change of time in v. 22, as vv. 26b-28 presuppose vv. 14-18. Talbert, *Reading John*, 164–65, argues for 10:1—11:54 as a unit. Kysar, *John's Story*, 51–55, reads 10:1-42 as "sheep, shepherds and gates." Westcott, *St John*, 143, reads 9:1—10:39 as a unit dedicated to "the new spiritual Temple," focused on Dedication.

[16] For the importance of this, see Barrett, *St John*, 356.

[17] For rabbinic reflection on prenatal sin, see Str-B 2:527–29.

exists *hina phanerōthę̄ ta erga tou theou en autǭ* (v. 3).[18] God is to reveal his works in what follows. God will enter dramatically into the experience of the blind man.

What this will mean is further spelled out for the reader in vv. 4-5 through words of Jesus that set the theme for all that is to follow.[19] Jesus' point of view is firmly established. The reader is aware that Jesus does not perform his works on his own authority (see, for example, 3:11-21, 31-36; 5:19-30). Jesus now includes the disciples in his work: "We must work the works of him who sent me" (v. 4a).[20] The disciples are being associated with the task of Jesus to work the works of the one who sent Jesus. Jesus is the revelation of God in the human story (see 1:18), and now his disciples are formally associated with him in that task (v. 4). But the revelation of God, which has already been described for the reader as the light (1:4-9) and identified with the person of Jesus (8:12), is conditioned by the arrival of the darkness, the "night" that would follow from the absence of Jesus in the human story, and bring an end to the light of the "day." In that situation, no one is able to make God known (v. 4). It is tempting to associate the day with the presence of the historical Jesus, and the night to the time after his departure. However, Jesus' association of his disciples with the task of working the works of God makes this reading impossible. The presence of the light in the world, doing the works of the Father, will not be limited to the historical life of Jesus; it will continue into the presence of Jesus in his associates, the disciples. This is a first, yet firm, indication of the future association of the disciples of Jesus with his mission, an association that would continue the presence of the light of Jesus in the world. Jesus has already announced that he is the light of the world in 8:12. That announcement, within the context of the Jewish feast of Tabernacles, continuing what was said of the Logos in 1:4-9, returns in 9:5.[21] The disciples of Jesus continue the works of Jesus (v. 4), but it is the presence of Jesus in the world that brings light into the world (v. 5).[22]

---

[18] It is just possible that *hina phanerōthę̄* is imperative: "Let the works of God be displayed in him!" See Beasley-Murray, *John*, 151. This interpretation eases this hard word of Jesus, but loses the contact between 9:3 and 11:4.

[19] On this, see Blank, *Krisis*, 252–54.

[20] I am reading the plural *hēmas dei*, following P⁶⁶, P⁷⁵, the first hand of Sinaiticus, Vaticanus, Regius, Freer Gospels, Sinaitic Syriac, Bohairic Coptic, Georgian, Origen, Jerome, Nonnus, and Cyril, rather than the (to be expected) singular *eme dei*. A change from plural to singular by the copyists is more likely. The plural reading is "unquestionably right" (Lindars, *John*, 342).

[21] The *egō eimi* formula is missing here. Schnackenburg (*St John*, 2:242) points out that the sign itself performs the function of the *egō eimi*.

[22] Westcott, *St John*, 144–45; Lindars, *John*, 343.

II. Jesus and the Man Born Blind: 9:6-7

Jesus adapts a traditional practice of placing spittle on the eyes of a person afflicted with sight problems.[23] He forms mud from the dust of the earth and places it on the man's eyes. The smearing on the man's eyes creates a situation where Jesus can order the man: "Go, wash in the Pool of Siloam (which means the Sent One)" (v. 7a). The man born blind responds unquestioningly to the word of Jesus and sees. Radical obedience is demonstrated by the use of four verbs: he went, he washed, he came back, seeing (v. 7b: *apēlthen oun kai enipsato kai ēlthen blepōn*). This is not the first time that the reader has encountered a miraculous consequence to an acceptance of the word of Jesus (see 2:1-12; 4:46-54; 5:2-9a).

The context of the feast of Tabernacles makes the waters of the pool of Siloam particularly important. It is not the contact with the waters of Siloam that effects the cure of the man who comes to the light for the first time, but contact with the Sent One. This identification is made through a sleight of hand,[24] which serves the narrator's purpose. Jesus' claim to be the living water (7:37) and the light of the world (8:12) has now been put to the test. Jesus, the light of the world (9:5), the Sent One (9:7; see 3:17, 34; 5:36), has restored sight to a man who had never seen the light. The first two scenes of the drama function as promise (vv. 1-5) and fulfillment (vv. 6-7).[25]

III. The Blind Man and His Neighbors: 9:8-12

The cured man's neighbors and acquaintances are divided. The action of Jesus, the light of the world and the Sent One, does not lead to the praise of God, but to *schisma*: Is this the man? (v. 8). Some say it is the same person, but others claim that he is only a look-alike (vv. 9-10a). In a way similar to Jesus' own self-identification (see 4:26; 6:20; 8:58), the cured man

---

[23] See Mark 8:23; Pliny, *Natural History* 28.7; Tacitus *Histories* 4.81; Suetonius, *Life of Caesar* 8.7.2-3; Dio Cassius 66.8. For rabbinic parallels, see Str-B 2:15-17.

[24] The word "Siloam" means literally a discharge (of waters), and thus does not mean "the Sent One" (*ho hermēneuetai apestalmenos*), although consonants of the verb "to send" (Hebrew *šālaḥ*) are in the name. "Siloam" is close enough for popular etymology to make the link. Such an individualizing and messianic interpretation may have even been current. See K. Müller, "Joh 9,7 und das jüdische Verständnis des Siloh-Spruches," *BZ* 13 (1969) 251–56; G. Reim, "Joh 9—Tradition und zeitgenössische messianische Diskussion," *BZ* 22 (1978) 245–53, especially 250–52; Manns, *L'Evangile*, 196–203.

[25] See J. Staley, "Stumbling in the Dark, Reaching for the Light: Reading Characters in John 5 and 9," *Sem* 53 (1991) 64–65.

must speak for himself: "I am the man" (v. 9b: *egō eimi*). The cured man is ignorant of the reason for transformation that his contact with the light of the world and the living water has worked in him.[26] When interrogated about how he was given his sight (v. 10), he can only tell the facts of the miracle, the clay, the anointing, the command, the obedience, and the sight (v. 11). For the first time the question of "how" the man received his sight is asked. The answer to that question will always remain the same (see vv. 10, 15, 16, 19, 21, 26). The man once blind can only identify "who" healed him as "the man called Jesus" (v. 11: *ho anthrōpos ho lego-menos Iēsous*).[27] When asked of Jesus' present location, the cured man says, for the first time: *ouk oida* (v. 12). Jesus has disappeared from the scene, even though he is at the center of the discussion. The reader sympathizes with the healed man but, knowing of the real origins of Jesus (see 1:1-5), has a growing awareness of the irony of the situation.[28] The man is unable to recognize that he has been given the light through the intervention of the Sent One of God, but he admits his ignorance: "I do not know."

IV. THE BLIND MAN AND THE PHARISEES: 9:13-17

The neighbors and acquaintances bridge the scene, as they take the man to the Pharisees (v. 13). The reader learns, by means of a laconic comment from the narrator, that the day on which Jesus made the clay was a Sabbath (v. 14).[29] The Pharisees ask "how" the miracle occurred, and the cured man reports (v. 15). The Pharisees thus learn of Jesus' offense against Sabbath legislation: he made clay. There is no question concerning the miracle, but neither is there a question that Jesus broke the Law (see *Shabbat* 7:2; 8:1).[30] At this stage of the Pharisees' response to the gift of the light, they

---

[26] See M. W. G. Stibbe, *John* (Readings: A New Biblical Commentary; Sheffield: JSOT Press, 1993), 111. A number of commentators regard the man's answer as the first sign of his representing Jesus as he creates schism around himself. Most critics, however, sense the Johannine Christians, rather than Jesus, behind the experience of the man. See, for example, D. Rensberger, *Johannine Faith and the Liberating Community* (Philadelphia: Westminster Press, 1988) 42.

[27] For Manns, *L'Evangile*, 203–7, this is already messianic, evoking a Jewish messianic use of *geber* and *ʾîš*.

[28] Against J. W. Holleran, "Seeing the Light: A Narrative Reading of John 9," *ETL* 49 (1993) 364, who regards the reader's ignorance as equal to that of the man.

[29] On the effect of this delay in announcing that it was a Sabbath, see Staley, "Stumbling in the Dark," 65–66.

[30] See Thomas, "The Fourth Gospel," 172–73. Holleran, "Seeing the Light," 21–22, regards this as the only important indication of time. For Staley, "Stumbling in the Dark," 66–67, the ex-blind man's careful use of language to report the miracle did not provide material for this accusation. The cured man shows adroitness, and the Pharisees show malice.

fasten upon the external rite of the making of clay. They do not raise the question of the person of Jesus because they are concerned only with the preservation of their legal tradition (see 5:16-18).[31]

Jesus' action produces a discussion that leads to a further *schisma*. Some of the Pharisees claim that Jesus cannot be from God. Here is a man who does not keep the Sabbath (v. 16a).[32] But others (*alloi*) point to Jesus' signs as an indication that he could not be a sinner (v. 16b).[33] The Pharisees begin to debate who Jesus is and where he is from. On the occasion of the earlier conflict between Jesus and "the Jews" over his Sabbath authority, Jesus reduced his questioners to silence as he explained that it flowed from his relationship with God (see 5:19-30). The Pharisees have seemingly forgotten this earlier discussion, but the reader has not. Jesus' origins "from God" have been denied by some of the Pharisees (v. 16a), while others are more open on the question (v. 16b). At this stage of the story, the Pharisees are able to accept the fact that a miracle has taken place. But there is a *schisma* over the origins and the sanctity of the man who worked the miracle, and the Pharisees return to the cured man and ask him to give them an assessment of the person who opened his eyes. As he had earlier spoken of "the man called Jesus," he now confesses: "He is a prophet" (v. 17).

V. The Pharisees and the Blind Man's Parents: 9:18-23

The reader follows the cured man's progress (see vv. 5, 7, 11, 17) as the Pharisees move in the opposite direction. "The Jews did not believe (*ouk episteusan*) that he had been blind and had received his sight" (v. 18a). Belief is beyond them; they must have the facts. Attempting to prove that the man was not *born* blind, they summon the people who bore him (v. 18b). As the cured man moves toward the light, "the Jews" move away from it by denying that the light of the world (v. 5) ever gave sight to a man born blind (v. 7). The discussion between "the Jews" and the parents does not resolve their problem; it does nothing to lead "the Jews" toward the light (vv. 19-21). The parents are subjected to a subtle abuse; they are suspected of lying. The interrogation of "the Jews" presupposes that the

[31] As there is an apparently indiscriminate use of "the Jews" and "the Pharisees" (see 9:13, 15, 16 [Pharisees], 18, 22, 24, 26, 28, 34 ["the Jews"], 40 [Pharisees]; 10:19 ["the Jews"]), they continue to represent one group.

[32] This nonappreciation of Jesus is implied by the unusual word order: *ouk estin houtos para theou ho anthrōpos*.

[33] They refer to "signs," and look back to the miracle of John 5. See Schnackenburg, *St John*, 2:248.

man was never born blind, and the parents should not claim that such was the case (v. 19a). "The Jews" are not prepared to accept that there is anything more to this question than the issue of "how": "How then does he now see?" (v. 19b). The parents can only affirm the fact of his being blind at birth (v. 20), then they withdraw from the discussion (v. 21). The fact of the miracle has now been told (vv. 6-7) and re-told three times (vv. 11, 15, 20-21). But true faith in Jesus will not result from a simple telling of the facts. This question hinges on the identity of Jesus, the light of the world (v. 5), the Sent One of God (v. 7).

The parents were afraid of "the Jews." A decision had already been made that anyone who confessed that Jesus was the Christ was to be put out of the synagogue (v. 22: *aposynagōgos genētai*). For this reason they avoid the christological debate with "the Jews" and send the Pharisees back to their son (v. 23). The narrator is working on at least two levels here.[34] At the level of the story, we read of the threat to both the parents and their son. If the parents make claims for Jesus, their place in the synagogue is at stake. The parents are not prepared to take that risk. It remains to be seen if the man born blind will bow to the pressure of this threat to his place within the synagogue. However, the Johannine Christians had lived through this experience, and had forged their Christology within a context of conflict and hostility. "The Jews" rejected Jesus' claims and thus rejected all those who accepted them.[35] It is probably not only the parents of the man born blind who have decided that they do not wish to be involved in a debate about the christological status of Jesus of Nazareth. Subsequent generations have experienced a similar faintness of heart.[36]

VI. THE PHARISEES AND THE BLIND MAN: 9:24-34

The man born blind is summoned a second time. Whereas the man had earlier said that he did not "know" the whereabouts of Jesus (v. 12), and in

---

[34] While scholarship is correct in seeing the Johannine narrative as a "two-level drama" (see Martyn, *History and Theology*, 30), reflecting the story of Jesus and the story of the church, Reinhartz, *Word in the World*, 1-6, 16-47, has pointed out that there is a third level to the drama, a cosmological tale: "the meta-tale which provides the overarching temporal, geographical, theological and narrative framework of the other two tales" (p. 5).

[35] As Lindars, *John*, 347, rightly says: "John speaks of the cost of discipleship in terms of the conditions with which his readers were familiar."

[36] R. E. Brown, *The Community of the Beloved Disciple: The Life, Loves, and Hates of an Individual Church in New Testament Times* (London: Geoffrey Chapman, 1979) 71–73, has suggested that there were "crypto-Christians" who recognized the truth about Jesus but did not have the courage to confess their belief. They remained within the security of the Mosaic traditions.

many ways remained in darkness, "the Jews" have no such humility or
hesitation. Using an oath formula employed before taking testimony or a
confession of guilt (see Josh 7:19; 2 Chr 30:6-9; Jer 13:16; 1 Esdras 9:8; *Sanhedrin* 6:2), they command the man to give praise (*doxan*) to God. But it is
to a God of their own making, not the God of Jesus Christ, because they
"know" (*hēmeis oidamen*) that Jesus is a sinner (v. 24).[37] The blind man is
not prepared to accept the "knowledge" of "the Jews." He simply does not
know (*ouk oida*) whether Jesus is a sinner, but he is aware of the miracle.
Can this be the work of a sinner? He again poses the question asked by
some of the Pharisees before they closed their minds to the possible action
of God in and through Jesus (see v. 16). While the man, in his ignorance,
moves toward the light, "the Jews," in their knowledge, move toward the
darkness. But the man born blind continues to base his defense of Jesus on
the fact of the miracle, and thus "the Jews" again ask for information
about what happened (v. 26). The issue of "how" rather than "who" is still
occupying them. The man wonders why they want to hear it again. They
have resisted "listening" (*ouk ēkousate*) up to this point, but now they
wish to hear the story once more. Perhaps they are interested in becoming
disciples of Jesus? The reader, who has followed the gradual movement of
"the Jews" away from Jesus, senses that the cured man's question is not
without its irony. He is not mocking "the Jews."[38] They want to hear the
story of the deeds of Jesus. This is part of the process in becoming a disciple of Jesus (see 2:11), even though true discipleship will have to go further
than faith in his miracles (see 2:23-25).

But "the Jews," accusing the man of being a disciple of "that fellow,"
proudly claim to be disciples of Moses (v. 28). Such discipleship is based on
the certain knowledge (*hēmeis oidamen*) that God has spoken through
Moses (v. 29a). However, "the Jews" do not know the origins of Jesus: "We
do not know (*ouk oidamen*) where he comes from" (v. 29b). The reader is
aware that this confession of total allegiance to Moses and the Mosaic revelation of God (see Exod 33:11; Num 12:2-8), over against a rejection of
"that fellow Jesus" on the basis of their ignorance of his origins, explains
the failure of "the Jews" to accept Jesus. "The Jews" are locked into adhesion to the former gift of God that came through the mediation of Moses.
They reject the perfection of God's gift, the perfect telling of the story of
God (see 1:17-18), because they refuse to accept that Jesus is "from God."
Thus they return to the fact of the miracle (v. 30). There is a principle at
stake, "known" (*oidamen*) by both "the Jews" and the man who was born

[37] There may be a subtle irony here, as the reader suspects that the man born blind will
eventually give glory to God in his witness to Jesus. On this possibility, see Pancaro, *Law*,
20-21.

[38] See Holleran, "Seeing the Light," 373-74. Against Staley, "Stumbling in the Dark," 68.

blind.[39] They should be working out of this common principle: God listens to people who do his will, not to sinners (v. 31). It is obvious from the "how" of the events that the "who" of Jesus must be explained in terms of a close relationship to God. Both "the Jews" and the man born blind should know this. At this point they are at one; both parties "know" (*oidamen*). Both the man born blind and "the Jews" have their knowledge from the Mosaic tradition. The man admits his lack of knowledge concerning Jesus (see vv. 12, 25), while "the Jews" aggressively assert their self-sufficient knowledge (see vv. 24, 29).[40] The reader is aware that the nonknowing man born blind is moving toward the light while the all-knowing "Jews" are moving into darkness. Here, the cured man reminds them, they are at one: God listens to a worshiper of God who does his will (v. 31). The miracle has no precedent. Never before in the recorded story of God's people, from the creation to the events that are happening around them, has a person who was born blind been given sight (v. 32).[41] There must be a very special relationship between the person who does such things and God who makes such a new creation possible (see v. 1: *typhlon ek genetēs*).

Something new has entered the human story. The man born blind, who at first stated that "the man called Jesus" had worked the cure (v. 11), and progressed from there to tell the Pharisees he thought Jesus was "a prophet" (v. 17), now draws a conclusion concerning Jesus. The possibility of this conclusion has been with the reader since the Pharisees first divided over the person of Jesus: "This man is not from God" (v. 16a). The man born blind has come to the opposite conclusion: "If this man were not from God (*para theou*) he could do nothing" (v. 33). The cured man has not come to perfect faith, as he explains the origins of Jesus on the basis of the miracle (v. 33b). There is still a shadow of doubt in the words *ei mē ēn houtos para theou* (v. 33a), but he has come a long way since telling his neighbors that "the man called Jesus" had cured him (see v. 11). There is no hesitation in the reaction of "the Jews" who accuse the man of being born in utter sin (v. 34a; see Ps 51:5). In his sin and ignorance he is behaving outrageously and unacceptably, questioning the knowledge of "the Jews," attempting to teach them that their understanding of God and the

---

[39] Haenchen, *John*, 2:40, describes this use of *oidamen*: "It is generally acknowledged."

[40] It is not Judaism that is failing to recognize Jesus, but "the Jews." See Pancaro, *Law*, 16–30.

[41] This is true of the biblical record. See Brown, *John*, 1:375. G. Reim, "Johannesevangelium und Synagogengottesdienst—eine Beobachtung," *BZ* 27 (1983) 101, sets these words within a synagogue reading, beginning with Gen 1:1, passing through the great prophetic texts (reflected in John 9). Something new and unheard of is happening with the gift of sight to a man born blind.

one to whom he has spoken may be wrong (v. 34b). Because of this they cast him out from their midst (v. 34c: *kai exebalon auton exō*).[42]

VII. JESUS AND THE BLIND MAN: 9:35-38

Jesus, hearing that the man had been cast out, finds him and asks: "Do you believe in the Son of Man?" (v. 35). The reader, who is following the journey of the man born blind from darkness to light, realizes that he has come to a crisis point. Jesus asks for a commitment of faith. The reader is well informed about the Son of Man (see 1:51; 3:13-14; 5:27; 6:27, 53, 62), a figure who makes God known in the human story. His presence among us is critical, revealing God and bringing judgment, but the consummation of his revealing role is yet to come. It is with this in mind that the reader awaits the response of the man born blind to Jesus' question: "Do you believe in the Son of Man?"[43]

Jesus' question puzzles the man born blind, and he responds with a question of his own. He does not know enough (see vv. 12, 25, 36) to be able to make a decision, and thus he turns to Jesus, initially calling him *kyrie* ("sir"), seeking further information. The man is confident Jesus will be able to inform him who the Son of Man is, so that he might believe in him (v. 36). Jesus' response to the man born blind is solemn, and satisfying. Employing terms that confirm the reader's understanding and knowledge of the Son of Man, Jesus responds: *kai heōrakas auton kai ho lalōn meta sou ekeinos estin*. This is the one: the person you are seeing, the one speaking to you.[44] It is impossible for anyone to *see* God or come to the knowledge of God (see 1:18; 5:37), but Jesus reveals what he has *seen* (see 1:34; 3:11, 22; 8:38). He *speaks* what he has *seen* with his Father (6:46; 8:38). Those who believe in Jesus will *see* (see 1:50-51), while those who *refuse to see* are condemned (see 3:36; 5:37-38; 6:36). The supreme revelation of God will take place when the believer *looks upon* the Son of Man (see 3:13-15). Jesus is challenging the man to accept that God is made known in the Son of Man. Similarly, when Jesus *speaks*, the reader has no doubt that he makes God known. The use of the verb *laleō* on the lips of Jesus carries with it the assurance of being the revelation of God (see 8:12, 20). Jesus *speaks* of what he knows from the Father (see 3:11, 34; 8:25-26,

---

[42] Once again the lived experience of members of the Johannine community, however local that experience might have been, lies behind this expulsion. See D. Rensberger, *Johannine Faith and Liberating Community* (Philadelphia: Westminster Press, 1988) 26–27; Beck, "Narrative Function," 152–53.

[43] For a study of the use of "the Son of Man" in 9:35, see Moloney, *Son of Man*, 149–59.

[44] There is a close parallel between 9:37: *ho lalōn meta sou ekeinos estin*, and Jesus' revelation to the Samaritan woman in 4:26: *egō eimi ho lalōn soi*.

38), and he *speaks* with an unquestionable authority (see 7:17, 18, 26, 46). His word gives life, peace, and joy (see 6:63), but also condemns those who refuse to listen (see 8:40). Jesus can say to the Samaritan woman that the one who reveals God in a unique way, the *egō eimi, speaks* to her (see 4:26).[45]

The man born blind is being asked if he is prepared to go a step further in his journey to sight. Is he prepared to accept that in Jesus, the man standing before him, whom he can see and hear, he will find the revelation of God?[46] The man responds: *pisteuō, kyrie* (v. 38a). While the man's question used *kyrie* as a title of respect (v. 36: "sir"), the expression now has its full christological meaning: "I believe, Lord," as the man bows down before Jesus in an act of worship and acceptance of Jesus (v. 38b: *kai proskynēsen autǭ*). Doubted by his friends and neighbors (vv. 8-12), abandoned by his parents (vv. 18-23), questioned, insulted, and cast out by "the Jews" (vv. 13-17, 24-34), he has stumbled from belief in Jesus as "a man" (v. 12), to "a prophet" (v. 17), to a suggestion that he must be "from God" (v. 33), finally to prostrate himself in belief before him as the one who makes God known, the Son of Man, the Sent One of God, the light of the world.[47]

VIII. Jesus and the Pharisees: 9:39–10:21

The Shape of John 9:39–10:21
There is no break between 9:41 and 10:1,[48] but there is some debate concerning the place of 9:39 in the narrative. Some would read it as the conclusion of 9:1-39,[49] while others read it as an affirmation from Jesus that opens the shepherd discourse.[50] It is difficult to accept that Jesus'

---

[45] See Moloney, *Son of Man*, 154–55.

[46] See Beasley-Murray, *John*, 159. Against M. Müller, "Have You Faith in the Son of Man? (John 9.35)," *NTS* 37 (1991) 291–94, who claims that "Son of Man" is a circumlocution for "me."

[47] Some scholars regard vv. 38-39a as an addition. This is based on some manuscript evidence, that only here in the Fourth Gospel is *proskynein* used, and that *ephē* is rare (elsewhere only at 1:23). See C. L. Porter, "John 9,38,39a: A Liturgical Addition to the Text," *NTS* 13 (1966–67) 387–94. On both external and internal ground such skepticism is unwarranted.

[48] See J. L. de Villiers, "The Shepherd and his Flock," *Neot* 2 (1968) 90–91; Busse, "Open Questions," 8–9; Thyen, "Johannes 10," 123. Beutler and Fortna regard the unity of John 9–10 as "one of the most important results of the two-year study" (*Shepherd Discourse*, 3).

[49] See Thyen, "Johannes 10," 123; Léon-Dufour, *Lecture*, 2:348–51; Kysar, *John's Story*, 50-51.

[50] See U. Busse, "Open Questions in John 10," in *The Shepherd Discourse of John 10 and Its Content*, ed. J. Beutler and R. T. Fortna (SNTSMS 67; Cambridge: University Press, 1991), 8. Menken, *Numerical*, 193–97, claims that it both closes 9:1-39 and serves as a starting point for what follows.

encounter with the man born blind continues into v. 39, as his words create a response from "some of the Pharisees" in v. 40. It is on the basis of vv. 39-41 that the discourse of 10:1-21 unfolds. The narrative demands that the positive response of the man born blind (9:35-38) be matched by a response from "the Jews." This response is triggered by 9:39 and the arrogant reply from "some of the Pharisees" in v. 40. Jesus' final words in v. 41 on the blindness of "the Jews" lead directly into the discourse of 10:1-21. In v. 6 the narrator interrupts words of Jesus to comment on the inability of the Pharisees to understand what Jesus is saying to them, and vv. 19-21 report the *schisma* that results from the teaching of Jesus. Jesus' use of the *egō eimi* with a predicate in v. 14, followed by his further description of what he means when he claims to be the Good Shepherd, may indicate another turning point, but this is complicated by the fact that Jesus has already claimed *egō eimi ho poimēn ho kalos* in v. 11.[51] But the contrast between Jesus and his care for his flock, and others who are called thieves, robbers (see vv. 8, 10), and hirelings (vv. 12-13), ceases at v. 13. Jesus' self-identification as the Good Shepherd in v. 11 is part of the polemic. He is good while others are wicked. In vv. 14-18 contrasts disappear. Jesus' words describe the identity and mission of the Good Shepherd (vv. 14-16), based in the relationship that he has with the Father (vv. 17-18). On these grounds I read 9:39—10:21 in five stages:

(a) *9:39-41:* Introduction: Jesus, the light who brings judgment, is questioned by the Pharisees, and he condemns them for their blind arrogance and subsequent guilt.

(b) *10:1-6:* Jesus tells a parable about entering the sheepfold, and the Pharisees cannot understand.

(c) *10:7-13:* Jesus contrasts himself, the door, and the Good Shepherd, with others who are thieves, robbers, and hirelings.

(d) *10:14-18:* Jesus is the Good Shepherd who, because of a union of love and freedom with the Father, lays down his life for his sheep.

(e) *10:19-21*: Conclusion: There is a *schisma* among "the Jews."

Reading John 9:39—10:21
Introduction: 9:39-41.   The reader is aware that Jesus did not come into the world to judge (see 3:17; 5:24; 8:15), but all judgment has been given to him (5:27). Jesus now announces that he has come into the world *eis krima*. Jesus is the light of the world (8:12; 9:5), the revelation of God in the human story, and his judgment is "the judicial decision which consists

---

[51] Many commentators divide the discourse at v. 11. See, for example, Brown, *John*, 1:395; Léon-Dufour, *Lecture*, 2:392; Schnackenburg, *St John*, 2:294; R. Kysar, "Johannine Metaphor—Meaning and Function: A Literary Case Study of John 10:1-8 [*sic.*]," *Sem* 53 (1991) 86-88.

in the separation of those who are willing to believe from those who are unwilling to do so."[52] As a commentary on the story of the journey to sight of the man born blind and "the Jews'" journey into blindness, Jesus describes the judgment that he brings as the blind come to sight and those seeing move toward blindness. The man's insistence that he did not know (*ouk oida*; see vv. 12, 25, 26) and his search for the Son of Man, that he might believe (v. 36), contrasts with "the Jews'" arrogant affirmations of their knowledge (*oidamen*; see vv. 24, 29, 31), which leads to their decision that Jesus is a sinner, a person whose origins are not known (see vv. 24, 29). They are content in the knowledge that God has spoken to Moses, and in their self-sufficiency they have become blind. They have refused to accept Jesus as the light of the world (9:5) and the Sent One of God (9:7), and the reader accepts Jesus' indication that they have brought judgment on themselves (v. 39). But they continue their arrogance by questioning whether Jesus dares to say that they are blind (v. 40).[53] Jesus' response closes this discussion and opens the shepherd discourse of 10:1-21. If they had been prepared to admit their need for light, they would now have no guilt, but because they claim all knowledge (v. 41: *blepomen*), there is no room for the revelation of the light that comes through Jesus, and thus they fall under judgment.

The Parable on Entering the Sheepfold: 10:1-6.   The double "amen" of 10:1 links Jesus' words to his statement to the Pharisees in 9:41. The reader does not raise problems concerning "the gate"; it refers to the gate of a sheepfold. The background for Jesus' words is the widespread use of the image of the shepherd to speak both positively and negatively of Israel's leaders. There are two ways in which one enters the sheepfold, depending on whether one wants to shepherd or to harm the sheep. One might enter the fold by subterfuge (v. 1), or through the doorway of the fold (v. 2). Anyone who approaches the sheep by subterfuge is a thief and a robber (*kleptēs estin kai lēstēs*). The person who enters through the door is the shepherd (*poimēn estin tōn probatōn*). Another figure is introduced into the parable: the gatekeeper (*ho thyrōros*), but he is a minor figure, called for by the pastoral realities behind the parable.[54] He has no hesitation in allowing the shepherd to enter (v. 3a), just as the sheep have no hesitation in responding to the voice of the one who leads and nourishes them. Each sheep has its familiar name and responds immediately to the voice of the one calling

---

[52] BAGD, 451, s.v. *krima*, para. 7.

[53] "The Jews" and "the Pharisees" continue to be identified, as throughout this narrative. On the irony of this question, see Stibbe, *John*, 110–11.

[54] He is a subshepherd of some sort. See Léon-Dufour, *Lecture*, 2:360 n. 69. Symbolic interpretations are not necessary.

it by that name (v. 3b).[55] Once the sheep have been called by name, assembled, and taken out of the fold to frequent their pasture, the shepherd walks ahead of them, and they gladly follow the shepherd, whose voice is familiar to them (v. 4).[56] The opposite happens in the case of a stranger (*allotrios*), whose voice the sheep do not know. Sheep will not follow a stranger, and they flee in their panic (v. 5). A contrast between those who care for the sheep and those who do not has been established for the reader.

There is no subtle allegory here for the reader.[57] The words of Jesus, after 9:1-38, linked by 9:39-41 and the double "amen" of 10:1, have their obvious application: Jesus leads his sheep with care and nourishes them, healing (9:6-7) and seeking out (v. 36) the man born blind. "The Jews" have dealt with both the man born blind and Jesus with mounting arrogance. They have cast out the man born blind (v. 34) and decided that Jesus is a sinner (v. 24). The expression "robber" (*lēstēs*) applied to "the Jews" perhaps hints to the reader that those who pretend to lead the sheep are in fact intent on their own false messianic choices.[58] The reader's identification of characters in the story with the shepherd and thieves, robbers, and strangers is confirmed by the narrator's comment in v. 6. Jesus is speaking to "the Jews" by means of a *paroimia*, but they did not understand "what it was that he was saying to them" (*tina ēn ha elalei autois*). Jesus' words of vv. 1-5 have the form of a parable, but function more as a similitude, and there has been some discussion over the uniquely Johannine use of the expression.[59] Both the more Synoptic *parabolē* and the Johannine *paroimia*

---

[55] J. A. T. Robinson, "The Parable of the Shepherd," *ZNW* 46 (1955) 233–40 (followed by, e.g., Dodd, Brown, Lindars, Talbert), claims that vv. 1-5 are the result of a fusion of two parables. Verses 1-3a are a challenge to the doorkeepers of Israel, while vv. 3b-5 present the shepherd. Against this, among many, see Painter, *Quest*, 346–49.

[56] Num 27:17 is close to vv. 3-4, and Barrett, among others, suggests that a messianic interpretation is being given to this Old Testament passage (*St John*, 369). This is not necessary, as both Numbers and the Johannine passage reflect pastoral practice.

[57] Allegorical readings of vv. 1-5 are myriad. Most interpret the passage in an ecclesiological sense, with Christ the shepherd creating a new community (Temple, etc.) over against bankrupt Judaism. See, from different perspectives, I. de la Potterie, "Le Bon Pasteur," in *Populus Dei: Studi in onore del Cardinale Alfredo Ottaviani per il cinquantesimo del sacerdozio, 19 marzo, 1966* (2 vols.; Rome: LAS, 1969) 2:936–43; and Becker, *Johannes*, 1:326–28. I am interpreting 10:1-18 as predominantly christological.

[58] On *lēstēs* in this sense, see M. Hengel, *The Zealots: Investigations into the Jewish Freedom Movement in the Period from Herod I until 70 A.D.* (Edinburgh: T. & T. Clark, 1989) 24–46; K. H. Rengstorf, "*lēstēs*," *TDNT* 4:257–62; T. Rajak, *Josephus: The Historian and His Society* (Philadelphia: Fortress Press, 1984) 78–103. See A. J. Simonis, *Die Hirtenrede im Johannesevangelium: Versuch einer Analyse von Johannes 10,1-18 nach Entstehung Hintergrund und Inhalt* (AnBib 29; Rome: Biblical Institute Press, 1967) 127–42.

[59] For a survey, see Reinhartz, *Word in the World*, 50–70.

translate the Hebrew *māšāl* in the LXX. The major themes of vv. 1-5, shepherd, door, thieves, and robbers, reappear in vv. 7-18, as the author plays on expressions from the parable in the more direct instruction of the reader. The *paroima*, therefore, is an image field that is approached from all angles.[60]

The sheep who belong to the fold of the shepherd have been described as those who know the voice of the shepherd and follow him. The reader knows that the criterion for true belief in Jesus, the Sent One of God, is to listen to his voice (see 2:1—4:54). The image of the sheep following the shepherd whose voice they recognize is building on information supplied earlier in the narrative. But "the Jews" do not understand what Jesus is saying to them (v. 6b). They do not belong to his flock as they do not recognize his voice, and they do not follow him. They are now blind (9:41), thieves, robbers (10:1), and strangers (v. 5).[61]

The Contrast between the Good Shepherd and Others: 10:7-13.   Jesus again (*palin*) speaks to "the Jews," linking what follows with the preceding parable through the double "amen" (v. 7a). In another "I am" saying with a predicate, Jesus affirms that he is "the door of the sheep" (v. 7b: *egō eimi hē thyra tōn probatōn*).[62] Jesus, identified with a shepherd in vv. 1-5, now presents himself as "the door." The reader looks back to the parable and recalls that the door was the criterion for right access to the sheep (see vv. 1-2). Jesus is now explaining the parable of vv. 1-5 in stages. In the parable, right access to the sheep was through the door. Jesus now claims to be that door, and he will continue to do so throughout vv. 7-10.[63] He will, however, subsequently develop the image of himself as the shepherd (v. 11),

---

[60] See K. Berger, *Formgeschichte des Neuen Testaments* (Heidelberg: Quelle & Meyer, 1984) 38–40.

[61] See de la Potterie, "Le Bon Pasteur," 2:940–43; Léon-Dufour, *Lecture*, 2:361-63. This reversal of the experience of the man born blind (9:34) through the narrator's comment in 10:6 is a further indication of the unity of 9:1—10:21.

[62] There is ancient textual evidence (P⁷⁵, Sahidic Coptic) for the reading "I am the shepherd (*hē poimēn*) of the sheep," rather than "I am the door (*hē thyra*) of the sheep." This reading would make excellent sense of the passage, and for that reason must be rejected. See Brown, *John*, 1:386. But see Tragan, *La Parabole*, 182–90; and Busse, "Open Questions," 9–10. For the suggestion (first made by C. C. Torrey) that the confusion is the result of a mistranslation of an original Aramaic expression, see M. Black, *An Aramaic Approach to the Gospels and Acts* (3d ed.; Oxford: Clarendon Press, 1967) 259 n. 1.

[63] There is a pastoral practice in the Near East, which has no literary support, where the shepherd is the door. The shepherd lies down across the door, thus acting as both shepherd and door. On this, see E. F. Bishop, "The Door of the Sheep—John x.7-9," *ExpT* 71 (1959–60) 307–9. It is used, without documentation, by W. Barclay, *The Gospel of John* (2d ed.; 2 vols.; Daily Study Bible; Edinburgh: Saint Andrew Press, 1975) 2:58–59. See also L. Morris, *The Gospel According to John* (NICNT; Grand Rapids: Eerdmans, 1971) 507 n. 30.

claiming to be *ho poimēn ho kalos*, over against thieves, robbers, and hirelings. This reflection will continue throughout vv. 11-13. Once two of the major images from vv. 1-5 (the door [vv. 1-3; see vv. 7-10] and the shepherd [vv. 2-4; see vv. 12-13]) have been exploited, contrasted with the third major image (thieves and robbers [vv. 1 and 5; see vv. 7-13]), Jesus will conclude his words with a description of the Good Shepherd (vv. 14-18).[64]

The reader is focused on Jesus' polemical response to "the Jews" that began in 9:40-41. His use of *egō eimi* lays claim to uniqueness. *Only* Jesus is the door of the sheep. It is *only* through him that one can have access to the sheep or through which the sheep can pass to good pasture (v. 7).[65] Those who came before Jesus are described as thieves (*kleptai*) and robbers (*lēstai*). But who are *pantes hosoi ēlthon pro emou* of v. 8: the righteous ones of the Old Testament?[66] The reader's understanding of these words of Jesus are determined by their context and by his spiraling exposition of the parable of vv. 1-5. In terms of the story, "the Jews" came "before" Jesus. The dispute with the man born blind informed the reader of the certainty of "the Jews": they knew that God had spoken through Moses (9:29a), they rejected Jesus as a sinner: they did not know where he came from (9:29b). The people who "came before" Jesus are the religious leaders of Israel, who have a traditional right to be called shepherds of the people.[67] The immediate narrative context of the feast of Tabernacles determines the meaning of "all who came before me." The claims of "the Jews" to be the leaders of the people are false. They are thieves and robbers, the purveyors of a messianic hope of their own making. The sheep have not listened to them. As "the Jews" moved toward darkness and blindness (9:39-41), the man born blind increasingly ignored their leadership and their insistence on the authority of their interpretation of the

---

[64] Although I differ in my application of their approach, I am following J. Schneider, "Zur Komposition von Joh. 10," *ConNT* 11 (1947) 220–25, and others, in reading vv. 1-5 as a parable and vv. 7-18 as an exposition of elements provided by vv. 1-5. This does not exclude development and the introduction of new ideas, as O. Kiefer, *Die Hirtenrede* (SBS 23; Stuttgart: Katholisches Bibelwerk, 1967) 39–40; de Villiers, "Shepherd," 91–93; and Kysar, "Johannine Metaphor," 96–101, have pointed out.

[65] I am associating *both* meanings of "the door." The expression *hē thyra tōn probatōn* can mean either the door *to* the sheep or the door *that is used by* the sheep.

[66] There is considerable textual uncertainty here. Codex Bezae omits *pantes*. P[45], P[75], the original hand of Sinaiticus, Old Latin, Vulgate, Sinaitic Syriac, and the Peshitta omit *pro emou*. Koridethi has the order *pro emou ēlthon*. It is difficult to decide, but the scribes have softened an attack on the righteous of the Old Testament. Thus *pantes hosoi ēlthon pro emou* is the *lectio difficilior* and should be accepted.

[67] See Westcott, *St John*, 153; Kiefer, *Die Hirtenrede*, 52–56; Simonis, *Die Hirtenrede*, 108–14; Brown, *John*, 1:393–94.

Mosaic tradition (9:24-33). This led him out of their company (9:34), into the company of Jesus and the light of authentic faith in the revelation of God that takes place in Jesus, the Son of Man (9:35-38). The present "leaders" are thieves and robbers because of a rigid commitment to their own messianic expectations.

Jesus returns to the image of v. 7, explaining what it means to be the door of the sheep: Jesus is the mediator who will provide all that the sheep need for life. Although there is a rich background from the ancient world, both Greek and Jewish, for the image of "the door,"[68] basing himself on the experience of ancient pastoral life, Jesus contrasts two ways in which people might "come" to the sheep. The thief comes only to steal, kill, and destroy. There is nothing creative about the approach of those who have come before Jesus, claiming to be shepherds but who are in fact thieves and robbers. But Jesus has come that the sheep may find pasture (see Ezek 34:14), thus have life, and have it abundantly (see Ezek 34:25-31). The image of Jesus as the door makes sense in this context. Jesus has now shown that the sheep, who need both the protection of a sheepfold and access to good pastures, find both in him. He is the one *through whom* both are possible. Those who *enter* (v. 9: *eiselthē*) are saved; those who *go out* (v. 9: *exeleusetai*) find pasture. Because Jesus is the door, offering both salvation and pasture, he provides the sheep with abundant life (v. 10). It is through him (v. 9: *di' emou*) that others have life (see 1:3-4, 17).

The reader does not miss the polemic involved in Jesus' claim to be *ho poimēn ho kalos* (v. 11). The contrast continues between Jesus as the door who came to give salvation and good pasture, and the thieves and robbers who came before him. The door of v. 2 has been rendered christological in vv. 7-10; the shepherd of v. 2 is made christological in vv. 11-13. However, there is a difference. While the function of the image of "the door" was to point to Jesus as the unique mediator of all that is good, to life and salvation, the image of "the shepherd" links Jesus with a tradition of a messianic shepherd of the people of God. The uniqueness of Jesus' role as the Good Shepherd is presented to the reader in v. 11: "the Good Shepherd lays down his life for the sheep." The positioning of the adjective after the noun stresses that Jesus is the Good Shepherd, in contrast to a bad shepherd.[69] A good shepherd lays down his life for the sheep, and this self-gift

---

[68] For a survey of the rich background that may lie behind Jesus' claim to be "the door," see Barrett, *St John*, 372. For links between "the door" and "the shepherd" in the wisdom traditions, see Scott, *Sophia*, 121–23. There is no need to discover messianic overtones in the Johannine use of the expression, on the basis of Ps 118:20. See, for example, J. Jeremias, "*thyra*," *TDNT* 3 (1965) 179–80. Barrett rightly reads "door" as: "The single means of access to all that is good is Jesus" (*St John*, 373).

[69] Barrett, *St John*, 373, suggests that *kalos* may be parallel to *alēthinos* here.

of the shepherd unto death for his sheep finds no parallel in the Old Testament texts that speak of the messianic shepherd. There are possible links with various Old Testament traditions (see, for example, Isa 53:12; Zech 13:7),[70] but the reader is struck by Jesus' self-revelation as a shepherd who lays down his life for his sheep (*tēn psychēn autou tithēsin hyper tōn probatōn*). Although it is possible to interpret these words as "to risk one's life," too much of the story points toward a violent end to Jesus' life (see 2:20-22; 3:13-14; 5:16-18; 6:27, 51, 53-54; 7:30; 8:20). Jesus will not fit the model of the expected Davidic shepherd-messiah. He may be the Messiah, but he will exercise this messiahship by giving himself freely unto death for his sheep. The reader knows of the crucifixion; only in the Johannine story is the story of the cross linked with the self-gift of the messianic Good Shepherd.[71]

In direct contrast to the performance of the Good Shepherd, the hireling is described (v. 12). Jewish tradition had already presented the false leaders of Israel as those who did not perform their God-given tasks for the people, and who left them prey to wolves (see Jer 23:1-8; Ezekiel 34; 22:27; Zeph 3:3; Zech 10:2-3; 11:4-17; *1 Enoch* 89:12-27, 42-44, 59-70, 74-76; 90:22-25; *Test Gad* 1:2-4). The context remains a debate between Jesus, the Good Shepherd, and "the Jews." The experience of the man born blind proves Jesus' case. "The Jews" have expelled the man from their midst (9:34), and Jesus has sought him out (9:35).

Although the major influence on the use of the symbols of the hireling and the wolf comes from Jewish traditions about good and bad shepherds, the flight of Jewish leadership to Jamnia prior to the destruction of Jerusalem in A.D. 70 and subsequent events form part of the background. Under the leadership of Johanan ben Zakkai, some managed to escape besieged Jerusalem to establish postwar Judaism at Jamnia. The Pharisees in John 9:1—10:21 represent postwar Judaism, "the Jews" who have shown that they were more anxious to preserve their own lives while the people of Jerusalem, the sheep of the flock, were snatched and scattered.[72] In a final word of condemnation, Jesus stresses the negative nature of the relationship between the hireling and the sheep (v. 13).[73] The Good Shepherd

[70] On possible Isaian background, see A. Feuillet, "Deux références évangéliques cachées au Serviteur martyrisé," *NRT* 106 (1984) 556–61.

[71] See Lightfoot, *St John*, 207–8.

[72] It is these literary possibilities that link the conflict between Jesus and "the Jews" with the pain of the separation between the Johannine community and its Jewish neighbors (see 9:22). It is more than the "retrospective glance" suggested by Schnelle, *Antidocetic Christology*, 31. *Yadayim* 4:6–7 represents Johannan ben Zakkai as a Sadducee debating against the Pharisees over what is clean and unclean. The post-70 Johannine expressions "the Jews" and "the Pharisees" are more clearly defined than they were in pre-70 Judaism.

[73] Many manuscripts add *ho de misthōtos pheugei* to the beginning of v. 13. It was added to

gives his life for his sheep, and the hireling is interested only in his personal gain. The hireling's flight flows from his character and his relationship with the sheep. He cares for himself and his personal gain, not for the sheep. The reader links the hireling with "the Jews" who have repeatedly refused to accept Jesus' claim that he is from God, that he will return to God, and that he makes God known. Nothing that Jesus says or does shakes "the Jews" from their unflinching adhesion to the former gift, which came through Moses. Their self-interest blocks them from accepting the fullness of the gift that comes through Jesus Christ (see 1:16-17).

Jesus, the Messianic Good Shepherd: 10:14-18.   From v. 14 on, conflicts are left behind.[74] Through the conflict in vv. 7-13 Jesus has spoken of himself as the door (vv. 7-10) and the Good Shepherd (vv. 11-13). But there is a quality to Jesus' shepherding that reaches beyond anything expected of a shepherd. Indeed, the reader knows that it reaches beyond the expected Davidic shepherd-Messiah: he lays down his life for his sheep (v. 11b). Thus, while v. 14 repeats what has been said of the shepherd in vv. 2-4 and of the Good Shepherd in v. 11, it leads the reader into climactic words from Jesus. There is a spiraling play on the use of the verb *ginōskein*. Jesus is the Good Shepherd who *knows* his sheep, and his sheep *know* him (v. 14), but behind the mutuality of the Good Shepherd and his sheep there is a more basic mutuality between the Father and Jesus: as the Father *knows* Jesus, so also does Jesus *know* the Father.[75] Through the use of *kathōs . . . kagō*, an intimate link is made between the way the Father knows the Son and the way the Son knows the Father.[76] The mutuality created by this knowledge can be seen in the self-gift of the Good Shepherd. There is a logical link between the mutual knowledge and Jesus' laying down of his life for his sheep (v. 15). The expected Davidic shepherd-Messiah has been eclipsed by Jesus, the shepherd-Messiah who lays down his life for his sheep. The roots of the uniqueness of Jesus' messiahship lie in the issue that separates Jesus and "the Jews": his oneness with God (see esp. 5:16-18).

The theme of unity flows into v. 16, but another tension-creating prolepsis enters the narrative. Jesus has an audience: "the Jews," and he tells them of sheep who are not "of this fold" (*ek tēs aulēs tautēs*). "The *aulē* is

---

improve the meaning, but should be omitted, as in P[45], P[66], P[75], Sinaiticus, Vaticanus, Claromontanus, Freer Gospels, Koridethi, and others.

[74] This feature of 10:1-21 is seldom noticed by the commentators, but see Bultmann, *John,* 380; Kiefer, *Die Hirtenrede,* 60–61; Tragan, *La Parabole,* 207–8, 216–17.

[75] The importance of "knowledge" has led Bultmann to argue that the shepherd imagery is gnostic, not biblical (*John,* 367–70). See, however, Schnackenburg, *St John,* 2:298.

[76] On this, see O. de Dinechin, "*Kathōs*: La similitude dans l'évangile de saint Jean," *RSR* 58 (1970) 195–236. On 10:15, see pp. 198–207.

Israel and it contains some who are Christ's own sheep and some (the unbelieving Jews) who are not."[77] In close association with Jesus' promise that the Good Shepherd will lay down his life for his sheep, he tells "the Jews" that he will bring others into this fold, so that there will be one shepherd, one fold.[78] The idea of one shepherd leading one people of God comes from the biblical tradition (see Mic 5:3-5; Jer 3:15; 23:4-6; Ezek 34:23-24) and continues to be used in later Jewish literature (see Psalms of Solomon 17:24, 40; CD 13:7-9; *2 Baruch* 77:13-17). But there is newness in Jesus' linking his self-gift with the gathering of others into the one fold under the one shepherd. Jesus does not abandon the traditional image of the messianic Good Shepherd, but he expands it in a way unknown to the Jewish tradition. Jesus is the Good Shepherd who lays down his life for his sheep because of the union between himself and the Father (v. 15). The world outside Israel will be drawn into the fold of Jesus through his willing gift of himself unto death (v. 16).

The Father's love for Jesus is shown in Jesus' laying down his life so that he might take it up again (v. 17). "What is being said here is that in his sacrifice the Father's love for him is truly present, and that this sacrifice is therefore a revelation of the Father's love."[79] Many themes come together in this dense presentation of Jesus' messianic status and role. Crucial to them all, however, is the relationship between the Father and the Son (see vv. 15, 17-18). The death of Jesus has been prominent in Jesus' revelation of himself as the Good Shepherd (see vv. 11, 15), but his death leads to his taking life up again (v. 17b). The reader thus recognizes Jesus' claim to being loved by his Father because of his willingness both to give himself in love for his sheep and to have life again as a consequence of that death.[80] Jesus will die violently at the hands of "the Jews," but will take up his life again because the Father loves him. How can death be the action of the Good Shepherd (v. 14)? How is it that he is loved by the Father as he lays down his life out of love for his sheep (v. 15)? How can this death lead to a gathering of others who are not yet of his fold (v. 16)? What does it mean to say that God's love is shown in a free giving of one's life, only to take it up again (v. 17)?[81] The reader accepts *that* this will happen, but is

---

[77] Barrett, *St John*, 376. Against Brown, *John*, 1:396, who argues for "the existing Church" at the time of the Evangelist.

[78] For Jewish material which indicates that the Messiah would gather the people, see O. Hofius, "Die Sammlung der Heiden zur Herde Israels (Joh 10:16; 11:51f.)," *ZNW* 58 (1967) 289–91; Manns, *L'Evangile*, 231–33.

[79] Bultmann, *John*, 384. See also Hoskyns, *Fourth Gospel*, 379.

[80] Reading *hina* as weak, not stressing purpose ("so that I might"), but consequence. See Barrett, *St John*, 377.

[81] Unlike most New Testament authors, who refer to the resurrection of Jesus as the action

encouraged to read on to discover *how* it will take place in subsequent events.[82]

In a statement that repeats more aggressively what has already been said, Jesus closes his discourse by speaking of his authority (*exousia*). The reader knows the story that lies ahead will report the suffering, death, and resurrection of Jesus. However, these events will not fall upon Jesus like some terrible accident, or merely as the result of the ill will of those who hate and persecute him. It is on the basis of Jesus' decision, through the exercising of his authority, that he will lay down his life and he will take it up again. No one (*oudeis*) takes it from him. But the final words of the Good Shepherd (see vv. 11, 14) look back to the Father. Jesus' transformation of the traditional messianic expectation of a Davidic shepherd-Messiah, gathering one flock under one shepherd by means of the unconditional gift of himself unto death, only to take up his life again, is a charge received from the Father (v. 18c). Jesus' self-revelation as the messianic Good Shepherd has come full circle. It began with his teaching on the union of knowledge that exists between the Father and the Son (v. 15), and it closes with his admission/that whatever he does is the fulfillment of the command (*tēn entolēn*) of the Father (v. 18).

The Response of "the Jews": Schisma: 10:19-21.   As often during the feast of Tabernacles (see 7:12, 25-27, 31, 40-41; 9:16), Jesus' words produce a *schisma* among "the Jews" (v. 19). On the one hand many of them, the majority (*polloi ex autōn*), totally reject his word, judging him to be possessed by a demon and thus insane. Demon possession and insanity are one and the same thing (see 7:20; 8:48). By dismissing Jesus in this way, they are able to regard his words as worthless: "it is not worthwhile listening to him."[83] But not all "the Jews" reject the word of Jesus. Another group, a minority (*alloi*), are still open to its possibilities. The events that led to this discussion—the miracle of the man born blind and the subse-

---

of God, the author of the Fourth Gospel presents Jesus as responsible for his resurrection. See Brown, *John*, 1:399. He takes up his life. Indeed, in v. 18 Jesus states that he has the authority (*exousia*) to take it up again. See Bernard, *St John*, 2:365. But Schnackenburg, *St John*, 2:301–2, insists rightly on the Johannine idea of the union of the life-sacrifice and subsequent resurrection as lying "within the Father's mandate" (p. 301).

[82] On the role of prolepsis in 10:1-21, see Stibbe, *John*, 115–16. Kysar, "Johannine Metaphor," 94–96, follows J. L. Staley, *The Print's First Kiss: A Rhetorical Investigation of the Implied Reader in the Fourth Gospel* (SBLDS 82; Atlanta: Scholars Press, 1988) 105–7, in suggesting that the reader risks taking the wrong side, and is propelled on in the narrative to keep up with the author. I disagree. On arrival at John 10, there is a close bond between the reader and the author.

[83] Schnackenburg, *St John*, 2:303.

quent "trials" of both the man and Jesus in absentia—are recalled. Two things indicate that Jesus might not be possessed: He does not speak as if he were possessed, and he has cured the blind man.

The reader senses that the final scene (9:1—10:21) of Jesus' presence in Jerusalem for the feast of Tabernacles (7:1—10:21) has come to an end. It closes as it began, with reference to a man born blind (see 9:1-5; 10:21). Some of "the Jews," recalling words of the blind man (see 9:31-33), suggest that a demon could not be responsible for the miracle (v. 21). Many of "the Jews" flatly reject the word of Jesus (v. 20), while others remain open to both his words (v. 21a) and his deeds (v. 21b). The question of who Jesus is still remains with a section of the audience, and thus the story of Jesus' encounter with "the Jews" has not come to an end. Some are still prepared to listen to him (v. 21), even though "many" have decided that both Jesus and the words he speaks are worthless (v. 20).

CONCLUSION

Throughout 7:1—10:21, elements central to the Jewish celebration of the feast of Tabernacles have been present to the story. Jesus is the living water (7:37-38), the light of the world (8:12; 9:5), the Son, the Sent One, and consequently the revealer of the one true God (7:14-24; 8:39-59; 9:7). Throughout the celebration of the feast the question of Jesus' messianic status has been raised (7:25-31, 40-44). Separated from the Temple because of the anger and violence of "the Jews" (see 8:59), Jesus' actions and words bring these Tabernacle themes to a climax in 9:39—10:21.[84] Jesus, because he is the Sent One, transforms the waters of Siloam (see 9:7) and gives light to a man who has never seen. But the physical miracle is only the beginning of a longer journey of faith that leads from his understanding of Jesus as "the man called Jesus" (v. 11) to his falling before the Son of Man whom he sees and hears, confessing, "Lord, I believe" (v. 38). "The Jews" who turned toward the Holy of Holies each day to celebrate their unswerving loyalty to the one true God, but who have rejected Jesus' claims to be the revelation of the Father, are now condemned because of their gradual movement into blindness and darkness. Jesus condemns them as blind (vv. 39-41), and draws a comparison between his role as the door of the sheep and the Good Shepherd and their performance as thieves and robbers, strangers and hirelings (10:1-13).

---

[84] Against U. Schnelle, *Antidocetic Christology*, 115–16. Schnelle sees the two miracle stories in chaps. 9 and 11 as forming a "compositionally closed unit," and agrees with Schnackenburg (see *St John*, 2:238) that "the festival framework as a compositional device recedes dramatically" (p. 116).

But what of the messianic question, so urgently associated with Tabernacles (see 7:25-31, 40-44)? Jesus transcends all suggested messianic expectations by speaking of his relationship with God, his Father, and of the mystery of his origins and his destiny. Only at the end of the events reported from the feast of Tabernacles does Jesus describe himself as the Good Shepherd, a messianic figure with its roots in the Jewish tradition, but the traditional image is transcended (10:14-18).[85] His shepherding flows from his knowledge and love of the Father, reciprocated by the knowledge and love that the Father has for him. Accepting the charge that the Father has given him, he will lay down his life for his sheep, but he will take it up again. It is the relationship between Jesus and the Father that explains his person and mission, but this is precisely the element that "the Jews" will not accept. They know that God spoke to Moses. They do not even know where this man came from (9:29). Many of them consider Jesus' words worthless, the words of one possessed (10:20).

The reader knows that the only way to true belief in God is to accept the word of Jesus (2:1—4:54). But this leads to a question about Israel's traditional experience of the presence of God through the *zikkārôn* of the feasts. The reader has followed Jesus through the celebration of Sabbath (5:1-47), Passover (6:1-71), and Tabernacles (7:1—10:21) as Jesus claims to transform the signs and shadows of what was done, only for Israel, in the Temple. In a document that appeared about the same time as the Fourth Gospel, written explicitly to address the problems of the loss of Jerusalem and its Temple, the author of *2 Baruch* reports:

> The whole people answered and they said to me:
> ". . . For the shepherds of Israel have perished, and the lamps which gave light are extinguished, and the fountains from which we used to drink have withheld their streams. Now we have been left in the darkness and in the thick forest and in the aridness of the desert."
> And I answered and said to them:
> "Shepherds and lanterns and fountains came from the Law and when we go away, the Law will abide. If you, therefore, look upon the Law and are intent upon wisdom, then the lamp will not be wanting and the shepherd will not give way and the fountain will not dry up" (*2 Baruch* 77:11, 13-16).[86]

As postwar Judaism and the Johannine form of postwar Christianity struggle to establish their identity, both look to their Jewish heritage. The

---

[85] See Léon-Dufour, *Lecture*, 2:382: "Jésus parle le langage d'Israël, mais sa nouveauté troue la page."

[86] Translation from A. J. F. Klijn, "2 (Syriac Apocalypse of) Baruch," in *The Old Testament Pseudepigrapha*, ed. J. H. Charlesworth (2 vols.; London: Darton, Longman & Todd, 1983-85) 1:647. On the dating of *2 Baruch*, see 1:616-17.

author of *2 Baruch* looks to the Law for the never-failing presence of shepherd, light, and water. These symbols, linked intimately to the feast of Tabernacles, are not abandoned by the author of John. The Johannine story of Jesus' presence at the feast of Tabernacles tells the members of a Christian community that they also have access to living water, to light, and to the shepherd. However, Jesus is living water for *any one who thirsts* (7:37), the light *of the world* (8:12; 9:5), and the Good Shepherd who lays down his life for his sheep, *to gather into one, the sheep who, as yet, do not belong to this fold* (10:15-16). The signs and shadows of the celebration of Tabernacles in the Temple have become flesh in the person of Jesus, the Sent One of the Father. What was done in the Temple for a former people of God is now available to "anyone," to "the world," to other sheep who are not of this fold. "The Jews" insist they know that God has spoken to Moses, and are thus in agreement with the author of *2 Baruch* on the need to hold fast to the Law. The Law and the nation are essential to their evolving self-identity.[87] But the Johannine Christians respond that God is speaking to them, through Jesus Christ. Gone are national boundaries, and gone is the centrality of the former gift of the Law. Something new is happening, as the former gift has been perfected in Jesus Christ (see 1:16-17).

---

[87] See G. W. E. Nickelsburg, *Jewish Literature Between the Bible and the Mishnah: A Historical and Literary Introduction* (Philadelphia: Fortress Press, 1981) 280–87.

Chapter Five

Jesus and Dedication
John 10:22-42

¶ THE READER LEARNS: "It was the feast of the Dedication in Jerusalem" (10:22). This was a relatively recent celebration in Israel, instituted to commemorate the rededication of the Temple, after Judas Maccabeus's successful campaign to take possession of Jerusalem in 164 B.C.[1] In 175 B.C. Antiochus IV ascended the throne in Syria. He planned to extend his kingdom into Egypt, but to do this he wished to consolidate his control over the outlying areas of his present rule (see 1 Macc 1:41). The most recalcitrant portion of this united front that he hoped to establish was the Jews, and he found support among corrupt segments of the Jewish aristocracy and priesthood. He deposed the rightful high priest, Onias III, and "sold" the high priesthood to Onias's brother Joshua, who changed his name to the Greek "Jason." A gymnasium, the hallmark of Greek civilization, was built in Jerusalem (1 Macc 1:11-13). Jews, hiding their circumcision as they participated naked in the events of the gymnasium, disowned the sign of the covenant. Antiochus, now calling himself "Epiphanes" ("the manifest god") decreed that the nation must worship the Greek god, Zeus Olympios. All this was done so that the people "should forget the law and change all the ordinances" (1 Macc 1:49; see vv.

---

[1] See O. S. Rankin, *The Origins of the Festival of Hanukkah: The Jewish New-Age Festival* (Edinburgh: T. & T. Clark, 1930); E. Nodet, "La Dédicace, les Maccabées et le Messie," *RB* 93 (1986) 321–75; Yee, *Jewish Feasts*, 83–86.

41-50). Persecution became widespread and opposition to the decrees of the Emperor led to death (1 Macc 1:60-64; see 1:56-58). On the 25th of Kislev in 167 B.C., a sacrifice to Zeus was offered in the Temple on a pagan altar. This altar, built over the altar of holocausts, was called "the desolating sacrilege" (1 Macc 1:59; see Dan 11:31).

These events led to a revolt initiated by a Jewish priest, Mattathias, and finally brought to a conclusion by his son, Judas Maccabeus. Through a remarkable series of events and fortunate coincidences, Judas had the better of the forces of Antiochus and eventually defeated them in 164 B.C. (1 Macc 2:1—4:35). The first task that Judas attended to was the purification of the Temple. "The desolating sacrilege" was torn down, and a new altar of holocausts was erected. The Temple area was rebuilt and refurbished. Lamps were set up to illuminate the sacred ground once again, marking the restoration of Temple order (1 Macc 4:46-51; see 2 Macc 10:1-4). The Temple was rededicated on the 25th Kislev, 164 B.C., three years after its defilement. The feast of the Dedication was the yearly celebration of this event. The accounts of the celebration in 1 Macc 4:52-59 and 2 Macc 10:5-8 reveal similarities between the feast of the Dedication and the feast of Tabernacles. In fact, 2 Macc 1:9 refers to Dedication as "the feast of the booths in the month of Kislev" (see also 2 Macc 10:6). As with Tabernacles (see Lev 23:42-43) the feast was celebrated so that Israel might remember God's protection during its wanderings in the wilderness.[2] But while Tabernacles recalled YHWH's care for his people during the Exodus, Dedication recalled his ongoing care for them in the restoration of the Temple, where God dwelled among his people. The Temple was the visible evidence of God's presence. Another element in the celebration of Dedication separating it from Tabernacles was the memory of the apostasy among the Jews that had led to the desecration of the Temple. Division among the people and the apostasy of some of the more powerful from the Jewish nation had led to the original desecration. They had blasphemed the Holy One of Israel and lead others into idolatry. "The feast of the Dedication . . . summoned the people to remain steadfast to the law of their God and, by doing so, proclaim, 'Never again!'"[3] It is against this background that Jesus' presence in the Temple on the feast of the Dedication is acted out (John 10:22-42).[4]

---

[2] See Nodet, "La Dédicace," 523–37.

[3] Yee, *Jewish Feasts*, 88. See Nodet, "La Dédicace," 337–40.

[4] The majority of commentators do not make this link. See, for example, Barrett, *St John*, 379.

THE SHAPE OF THE NARRATIVE

Following the action and the characters, the narrative unfolds as follows:

I.   *Verses 22-23:* Setting—it is winter time, at the feast of the Dedication, and Jesus is in the Temple.

II. *Verse 24:* "The Jews" enter the story, and raise the question of the Messiah.

III. *Verses 25-30:* Jesus responds in words that provide the *raison d'être* of Jesus' messianic status.

IV. *Verses 31-39:* Jesus points to his works as proof of his oneness with the Father (vv. 32, 34-35, 37-38), while "the Jews" attempt to stone him (vv. 31, 33), charge him with blasphemy (vv. 33, 36), and seek to arrest him (v. 39).

V.   *Verses 40-42:* Jesus leaves Jerusalem and its Temple, ending his presence initiated in v. 22 (v. 40). "Many" (*polloi*) search for Jesus, recalling that everything John the Baptist said about him was true (vv. 41-42).

READING THE NARRATIVE

The reader follows the change of time and place,[5] as Jesus walks in the portico of Solomon, some three months after the celebration of the feast of Tabernacles (vv. 22-23).[6] But the audience is still "the Jews," who gather around Jesus (v. 24).[7] The question raised by "the Jews" continues an issue that has dominated the feast of Tabernacles: Is Jesus the Messiah? (v. 24). The question asked, however, is ironic: "How long will you keep us in sus-

---

[5] These indications must be taken seriously. See U. Busse, "Open Questions," 6–9.

[6] According to Josephus (*War* 5.184–185; *Antiquities* 15.396–401; 20.220–21) the portico was on the eastern side of the Temple. On the wisdom of walking in this location in midwinter, see Brown, *John*, 1:405. J. C. VanderKam, "John 10 and the Feast of the Dedication," in *Of Scribes and Scrolls: Studies on the Hebrew Bible, Intertestamental Judaism, and Christian Origins Presented to John Strugnell on the Occasion of His Sixtieth Birthday*, ed. H. W. Attridge, J. J. Collins, and T. H. Tobin (College Theology Society Resources in Religion 5; Lanham: University Press of America, 1990) 205–6, regards the mention of Solomon's portico as a reference to the only part of the Temple of Solomon still standing at the time of Jesus. It is soon to be replaced by the temple of Jesus' body (see 2:19–22).

[7] Commentators sometimes remark that the "gathering" of "the Jews" around Jesus (*ekyklōsan*) is threatening.

pense? . . . tell us plainly" (v. 24).[8] The reader has followed a debate over the Messiah since 7:25. In 10:14-18 Jesus has presented himself as the Good Shepherd, a Messiah beyond the traditional messianic expectations of Israel. Three months later, as "the Jews" ask how much longer they must wait (10:24), they appear to have forgotten they have already been told plainly (*parrēsią*) that Jesus is the Christ. "The Jews" continue to refuse to listen to the word of Jesus because he has not told them what they want to hear. They continue to judge *kat' opsin* (7:24), *kata tēn sarka* (8:15). Jesus thus replies: "I have told you and you do not believe" (10:25a). Not only the words of Jesus tell of his messianic status, but also his works. His words make God known, and his works are done in the name of the Father. What Jesus says and does tells the story of God (see 1:18). Jesus' words and deeds reveal the Good Shepherd who both calls his sheep and gives himself for them (10:14-18). "The Jews" are unable to believe, because they will not accept his word and are unable to hear him as he speaks to them. As Jesus used the imagery of the messianic Good Shepherd (10:14-18) in speaking to "the Jews" during the feast of Tabernacles, he now returns to that image.[9] They do not belong to his sheep, and thus they are unable to accept his word, unable to believe that he is the Messiah. In an application of the image of the parable to the people in the story, consequences are drawn. The reader recalls that the sheep hear the voice of the Good Shepherd (v. 16), but "the Jews" do not (v. 26). "Allegory and application merge."[10]

This deliberate recalling of the image of the shepherd's own sheep, hearing (*akousousin*) his voice, following (*akolouthousin*) him so that he might give them eternal life (*zōēn aiōnion*) that they may never be lost (*ou mē apolōntai eis ton aiōna*), conjures up for the reader a series of terms that have been gathering around the identity of the authentic believer throughout the unfolding narrative (see *akouein,* 1:41; 3:8, 29; 4:42; 5:24, 28; 6:45; 8:38-43, 47; 10:3, 16; *zōē aiōnios,* 3:15, 16, 36; 4:14, 36; 5:24, 39; 6:27, 40, 47, 54, 68; *akolouthein,* 1:37, 44; 8:12; 10:4, 5; *apolymi,* 3:16; 6:12, 27, 39; 10:10).[11] This rich evocation of themes from across the narrative so

---

[8] The expression *tēn psychēn hēmōn aireis* is obscure. It may contain a hint of anger. Barrett, *St John,* 380, suggests that it may mean: "How much longer will you annoy/vex us."

[9] This use of shepherd imagery has led scholars to argue that the narrative is confused, and that vv. 26b-29 (30) are out of place.

[10] Lindars, *John,* 368.

[11] There is a close link between 10:25-29 and 6:31-59. U. von Wahlde, "Literary Structure and Theological Argument in Three Discourses with the Jews in the Fourth Gospel," *JBL 103* (1984) 575–84, and Stibbe, *John,* 117, also see links with 8:13-59. Stibbe uses these links as an indication that 10:22-39 is a summary of John 5–10.

far and their association with the image of Jesus as the Good Shepherd (10:14-18) inform the reader that belief in Jesus as the Messiah *in his terms* will bring life (vv. 27-28). But the opposite will also be true: refusal of such belief, because of an unwillingness to work *beyond the limitations of their terms,* will lead "the Jews" into death.

Those who hear the voice of Jesus cannot be snatched away from their attachment to him (v. 28c). Earlier Jesus spoke of wolves who snatched the sheep from the hireling (see v. 12), but now his argument goes beyond the *Christology* of that imagery into its *theology.* The sheep cannot be snatched away, not only as a result of their belonging to Jesus, but because the life that the believer receives from attachment to Jesus is a gift of the Father. In a situation where the Father of Jesus ensures a life-giving attachment to Jesus, no power can snatch away the believer who rests, ultimately, in the hand of God himself. No power is greater than God, and thus the believer's union with God is assured, as the Father of Jesus is greater than all other powers (v. 29).[12] As Israel celebrated God's presence at the feast of the Dedication, Jesus is telling "the Jews" that there is another way God is present to them, there is another way they can be sure they are in the Father's hand: belief in the word of Jesus.[13] Within the context of the feast of the Dedication "the Jews" pride themselves in their reconsecrated Temple, the physical evidence of their belonging to God and, in some way, of God's belonging to them. But Jesus insists that faith in his word ties the believer not only to Jesus but to God, the Father of Jesus.

The affirmation of 10:30 confirms what the reader already knows: "I and the Father are one." There is no longer any need to look to the physical building on the Temple Mount to know of God's presence to his people. Jesus, who stands before "the Jews" in the portico of Solomon in the Temple, points to himself and claims that he is the visible presence of God among them. The argument over Jesus' messianic claims comes to a conclusion. No Messiah in the Jewish expectation would claim to replace the Temple itself, but that is what Jesus does in 10:30. The claims of the prologue are being acted out in the story of Jesus: "The Word became flesh and dwelled among us. We have seen his glory, the glory of the only begotten Son who is turned in loving union toward the Father" (1:14). The author is not primarily interested in metaphysics, but in a oneness of pur-

---

[12] Reading, with the RSV, "My Father, who has given them to me, is greater than all." There are five well attested variants for the first part of v. 29. For the discussion, see J. N. Birsdall, "John x.29," *JTS* 11 (1960) 342–44; J. Whittaker, "A Hellenistic Context for John 10,29," *VC* 24 (1970) 241–60.

[13] The theme of God's care for his people links Dedication to Tabernacles. See 2 Macc 10:6.

pose, created by a union of love and obedience.[14] The setting of these words of Jesus within the feast of the Dedication determines the reader's understanding that the union between God and the Temple which was seen as God's presence to his people, is perfected in Jesus because of his oneness with the Father.

Although the feast of the Dedication was the most recent and least important of the feasts in John 5-10,[15] Jesus' claim in 10:30 forms the bedrock for the argument developed throughout chaps. 5-10. Because of the oneness that exists between Jesus and the Father (10:30), Jesus can claim the Sabbath privilege of giving life and judging (see 5:19-30); of being the bread of life, perfecting the promise of the nourishing revelation of God to his people in the gift of the manna of the Law celebrated at the Passover (see 6:44-50); of being the water of life and the light of the world (7:37-39; 8:12; 9:5); the Messiah who perfects Israel's messianic hopes celebrated at Tabernacles (10:1-21). But another memory is associated with the feast of the Dedication. Israel had lost its Temple because leading Jews betrayed YHWH and his people. Will "the Jews" stand by their resolve never again to betray their God? "The Jews" take up stones against Jesus (v. 31), repeating the profanations of Antiochus IV and his representatives. They are attempting to rid Israel of the visible presence of God in their midst.

The encounter between Jesus and "the Jews" on the feast of the Dedication was initiated by a question from "the Jews" (see v. 24). This is now reversed, as Jesus asks them a question: "I have shown you many good works from the Father; for which of these do you stone me?" (v. 32). For which particular revelation of the *doxa* of God (see 2:1-11; 4:46-54; 5:1-9a; 6:1-15; 9:1-7) have "the Jews" chosen to eliminate him? "The Jews" show they will not recognize the truth of Jesus' accusing question. Once again they fall back on a superficial interpretation of the Law, claiming they are not stoning him for any *ergon kalon*, but for blasphemy. Jesus' blasphemy lies in his claim, as a man, to being divine (v. 33).[16] "The Jews" continue to

---

[14] Barrett, *St John*, 382. See also Brown, *John*, 1:408. There is, nevertheless, a glimpse of "the metaphysical depths contained in the relationship between Jesus and the Father" (Schnackenburg, *St John*, 2:308). See especially Bühner, *Der Gesandte und sein Weg*, 209-35. For a survey of possible understandings of *hen esmen*, see Carson, *John*, 394-95. For the importance of this verse in later trinitarian debate, see T. E. Pollard, "The Exegesis of John X, 30 in the Early Trinitarian Controversies," *NTS* 3 (1956-57) 334-39.

[15] Nodet, "La Dédicace," 321-75, would challenge this for the time of Jesus and the Fourth Gospel (see pp. 321-23). He presents good evidence to show that Dedication was a major celebration that waned once hopes of a military messianic victory disappeared.

[16] The charge *poieis seauton theon*, without an article before *theon*, is virtually adjectival. See Lindars, *John*, 372. This makes a comfortable passage to Jesus' use of *theioi este* in v. 34.

pay no heed to Jesus' claims, as they celebrate the feast of the Dedication, remembering the reconsecration of a temple built in stone by human beings. They betray their God as they attempt to eliminate the one who now dwells among them in the flesh of his only begotten Son (see 1:14; 8:30). Their understanding of Jesus as a blasphemer is deeply ironic.

Jesus' response (vv. 34-38) is a more developed restatement of what he has already said in v. 30. If it is correct that Jesus and the Father are one, and of this the reader is quite certain, then a charge of blasphemy against Jesus is a serious betrayal of the God of Israel. The claim that the Son of God offends God is thus an accusation of those who wish to stone him. Jesus follows the Jewish technique of arguing from the minor to the major (*qal waḥōmer*).[17] With a reference to "your Law" (*en tō̢ nomō̢ hymōn*), meaning the whole of the Scriptures, Jesus cites Ps 82:6: "I said, you are gods."[18] If in the Scriptures, which always remain in force,[19] the people of God could be called "gods" (v. 35: minor), how much more can the one whom God has consecrated and sent call himself "the Son of God" (v. 36: major).[20] "The Jews" are condemned by their own Scriptures. Jesus claims that he offends nothing from the authentic tradition of Israel but perfects all that God had promised as he consecrated (*hēgiasen*) and sent the Son of God into the world (v. 36).

What is implied by the claim that God consecrated (*hēgiasen*) the one he sent into the world? The reader is familiar with the notion of Jesus as the Son, the Sent One, but not as one consecrated by God. Most scholars, paying little attention to the context of the feast of the Dedication, argue that the expression has no sacral significance, and that it simply means "to set apart for his purposes."[21] But Dedication remembered the consecration of the altar of holocausts that replaced "the desolating sacrilege" of Antiochus IV.[22] Jesus' presence to the world as the one sent by the Father, and

---

[17] On this, see Manns, *L'Evangile*, 313–14.

[18] On the use of the psalm (which he claims comes from Old Greek Ps 81:6), see Schuchard, *Scripture Within Scripture*, 59–70. It is widely accepted that *nomos* here means the Scriptures as such. Some witnesses (P[45], first hand of Sinaiticus, Bezae, etc.) omit *hymōn*. It does seem strange that a Jew (Jesus) would speak to Jews of "your Law." However, Jesus' words show the gulf between "the Jews'" understanding of God and his own.

[19] For this meaning of *ou dynatai lythēnai*, see Lindars, *John*, 375.

[20] There is difficulty over the meaning of what Bauer calls "die elastische Art des antiken Begriffs *theos*" (*Johannesevangelium*, 147). The original psalm may regard as "gods": Israel's judges, the people of Israel, angelic powers, or the gods of the nations. For the rabbis, the Law was given to angels/gods. I am reading that the people addressed, human beings, can be called "gods." See the discussion in Brown, *John*, 1:409–11.

[21] Barrett, *St John*, 385.

[22] VanderKam, "John 10," 211–14, sees Antiochus's claim to be "God Manifest" behind the presentation of Jesus' parallel but justified claim to oneness with God. This identification

the visible presence of God in the world, brings to perfection what was only a sign and a shadow in Judas's act of consecration in 164 B.C. God is no longer present in the consecrated stone altar, but in the flesh and blood of the consecrated and sent Son of God (v. 36).[23]

Jesus is the living presence of the Son of God among them (v. 36b), and his works reflect his Father. If "the Jews" wish to show their loyalty to their God, the Father of Jesus, then they are to accept all that Jesus says and does. If Jesus were not doing the works of his Father, then "the Jews" would be right in not believing him, but this case is not feasible after all "the Jews" have seen and heard (v. 37). How serious, then, is the situation of "the Jews" who stand accused of not accepting the visible presence of God in the works of Jesus. They celebrate their allegiance to the God of Israel present in the Temple, but they are not prepared to accept that God, visible in the works of Jesus. Jesus summons them to accept the truth that the God of Israel, once present to his people in the Temple, is now present to them in the works of his Son (v. 38). He closes his words to "the Jews" on the feast of the Dedication, and the whole of the section dedicated to the Jewish feasts, by restating v. 30. There is only one way to God, and that is through his Son. There is only one place where the Father may be found and understood, and that is in the story of his Son. Jesus speaks to his unbelieving listeners, exhorting them to accept the revelation of God in his works. If they do this they may come to understand (*hina gnōte kai ginōskēte*)[24] the truth of v. 30, that Jesus and the Father are one: "The Father is in me and I am in the Father" (v. 38).

"Again they tried to arrest him, but he escaped from their hands" (v. 39). The autumn feast of Tabernacles produced a *schisma* and a glimmer of hope for "the Jews." Some of them still saw the possibility that Jesus may have been the messianic miracle worker (10:21). Now, in the middle of winter, as Jesus points to himself as the place where "the Jews" can find the abiding presence of God among them, such hopes disappear. "The Jews" attempt to stone him (vv. 31, 33) and to arrest him (v. 39). But because the events of the story are determined by God, the plans of "the Jews" cannot as yet be realized. The reader knows that the hour has not yet come (see 2:4; 7:30; 8:20). *For the moment*, "he escaped from their hands" (v. 39).

---

also lies behind "the Jews'" accusation that Jesus, like Antiochus (see 2 Macc 9:28), is a blasphemer (see John 10:33, 36).

[23] See especially Brown, *John*, 1:411. Brown entitles his study of 10:22-39, "Jesus is consecrated in place of the temple altar" (1:401). See also VanderKam, "John 10," 206-7.

[24] As Barrett, *St John*, 386, notes: "The aorist subjunctive denotes the beginning of knowledge at a point in time—'that you may perceive.'" Some good witnesses (P[45], P[66], P[75], Vaticanus, etc.) read *kai pisteuēte*, which is the easier reading, and thus should be rejected.

The story of Jesus' presence at the Jewish feasts has come to an end, and the narrator must clear the stage to prepare for the next phase of the story. He does this through a brief report, the "bridge passage" of vv. 40-42, which serves a number of purposes for the author. It brings to a close Jesus' presence in Jerusalem for the feasts of the Jews, and keeps alive the story of the response to Jesus, as others come to believe in him as the fulfillment of the prophecies of John the Baptist. But it also looks back to the beginning of the story. The narrator makes explicit mention of the other side of the Jordan, the place where John baptized (v. 40). The reader recalls the "first day" of the narrative. As that day concluded, the narrator told the reader: "This took place in Bethany beyond the Jordan, where John was baptizing" (1:28). In a sense Jesus' ministry is at an end. His life has come full circle, and the deliberate recalling of the "first day" suggests that the "last day" is at hand.[25] Jesus leaves the scene of the action, crossing the Jordan to the place where John first baptized. He remains there. The action and the words of Jesus come to a temporary halt in this new location (v. 40; see 1:28; 3:26).[26]

An undetermined "many" (*polloi*) seek him out. The possibility that Jesus might be the Messiah again emerges. Reflecting the story of John the Baptist recorded in the Johannine Gospel, these people point out that John did no sign.[27] However, his prophecies about this man have come true. John pointed to Jesus as the Lamb of God who takes away the sin of the world (1:29, 36), a person filled with the Spirit (1:32) who baptizes with the Spirit (1:33). He is the bridegroom who has the bride (3:29), and if the Baptist is not the Christ (1:20, 25; see 3:28), the inference is that Jesus is the Christ. Thus many believed in him there (10:42). Hope once again returns to the reader as "many" come to believe that Jesus is the fulfillment of the prophecies of John the Baptist, a man sent by God (see 1:6-8). While most have rejected him, still "many" come to faith in him. "For the moment in a place still echoing with the cry of John the Baptist's witness and still bright with the light of his lamp (v[erse] 35), Jesus pauses and is greeted by faith. The darkness has not yet come."[28]

---

[25] See Thyen, "Johannes 10," 123–24.

[26] See F. F. Segovia, "The Journey(s) of the Word of God: A Reading of the Plot of the Fourth Gospel," *Sem* 53 (1991) 39–40.

[27] This is consistent with all the traditions concerning John the Baptist. See E. Bammel, "John Did No Miracles: John 10:41," in *Miracles: Cambridge Studies in Their Philosophy and History* (London: Mowbrays, 1965) 197–202.

[28] Brown, *John*, 1:415.

CONCLUSION

On a Sabbath Jesus insisted that he was working as his Father was working still, exercising the powers of giving life and judging, given to him by the Father (chap. 5). At Passover Jesus claimed to be the true bread from heaven (chap. 6). At Tabernacles Jesus declared that he was the living water and the light of the world, and the story of the man born blind showed that his claims were true. Jesus is the authentic revelation of the one true God, the messianic Good Shepherd who freely lays down his life for his sheep, that they may have a life which no one can take from them (7:1–10:21). Jesus personifies, fulfills, and perfects the signs and shadows of the Jewish feasts, the celebration of the *zikkārôn* of God's action among his people. There is no longer any need to look to the signs and shadows. They have been enfleshed in the person of Jesus Christ. The claims made for Jesus from 5:1 to 10:21 are true because Jesus and the Father are one (10:30). It is because Jesus is the living presence of God among his people, the perfection of everything Israel thought of their Temple, that he can claim to be Lord of the Sabbath, the true bread from heaven, the light of the world, the living water, the revelation of the one true God and the messianic Good Shepherd.

There is a closeness between the Johannine community and the implied reader emerging from the text at 10:42. Embodied in the incarnate Son of God the reader finds the perfection of what was done in the Jewish Temple in signs and shadows. The Johannine story has conveyed the author's point of view with force. There have been two gifts from God. The former gift, which came through Moses, has been an essential part of God's dealings with the human story. This gift, however, has now been perfected and fulfilled in the gift that comes through Jesus Christ, the fullness of a gift that is the truth (see 1:16-17). To seek the gift of God in the feasts of "the Jews" (see 5:1, 9b; 6:4; 7:2; 10:22) is to look in the wrong place. The Johannine Gospel instructs its readers of all times and in all places that Jesus Christ makes real what were signs and shadows. There is no attempt to denigrate the established and cherished ways of remembering and rendering present God's saving action among his people. The account of Jesus' presence at the great feasts of Israel—Sabbath, Passover, Tabernacles, and Dedication—affirms that the former order has been perfected, not destroyed.

The crucial difference between the two orders is the person of Jesus Christ. The conflict between "the Jews" and Jesus, as it is reported in these narratives, is not a conflict between Jesus and Israel, God's chosen people. It is a conflict between Jesus and some from Israel who had decided once and for all that Jesus was not the Christ, and that anyone who confessed he was must be put out of the synagogue (see 9:22). As Jesus and "the Jews" are on a collision course, so also are "the Jews" and the Johannine Christians. But the latter are proud to look back on their Jewish heritage, to see in their former festive celebrations of the God of Israel signs and shadows of the presence of Jesus among them, judge and life-giver, the true bread from heaven, the giver of living water, the light of the world, the messianic Good Shepherd, sent by God to lay down his life freely for his own, the true presence of Israel's one and only God, the living Temple of God in their midst.

"The one Word is revealed in the witness of the Old Testament and the Word made flesh. There is a continuity of salvation history. But the coming of the Word made flesh has fulfilled the witness of the Old Testament and abolished its significance as a closed system."[29] The tragedy is that "the Jews" have decided that Jesus, the Son of God, is a blasphemer, and that he must die. In their inability to move beyond their closed system, they reject the incarnate Word of God, and thus frustrate God's saving purpose. The reader justifiably suspects that the remaining part of the narrative will devote its attention to the enigma of a God who reveals his own glory and glorifies his Son through his death.

[29] J. Painter, *John: Witness and Theologian* (London: SPCK, 1975) 32.

Chapter Six

A Resurrection
That Will Lead to Death
John 11:1-54

THE READER AWAITS the clash between Jesus and "the Jews" that intensified as Jesus celebrated the Jewish feasts (chaps. 5-10). Death and
resurrection are in the air. Whatever the history behind the development of the traditions surrounding the story of Jesus' raising of Lazarus,[1]
"the miracle has been made to serve the purposes of Johannine theology."[2]

THE SHAPE OF THE NARRATIVE

A focus upon the characters involved, their response to Jesus, the passing
of time, and the sequence of events, suggests the following shape for 11:1-
54:

---

[1] For surveys, see A. Marchadour, *Lazare: Histoire d'un récit. Récits d'une histoire* (LD 132;
Paris: Cerf, 1988) 33–63; J. Kremer, *Lazarus: Die Geschichte einer Auferstehung. Text, Wirkungsgeschichte und Botschaft von Joh 11:1-46* (Stuttgart: Katholisches Bibelwerk, 1985) 82–109; B.
Byrne, *Lazarus: A Contemporary Reading of John 11:1-46* (Zacchaeus Studies: New Testament;
Collegeville: Liturgical Press, 1991) 69–83. Many (though not all) hold that there was an original Lazarus-Jesus story that grew with the successive addition of Mary, then Martha, and
then "the Jews." As these characters became the foreground, Lazarus became the background
for the story. Kerygmatic and christological elements were added as the tradition grew. But
see Dodd, *Historical Tradition*, 232; Culpepper, *Anatomy*, 73; and Marchadour, *Lazare*, 54–63,
who point to the thoroughly Johannine nature of the passage.

[2] Brown, *John*, 1:430.

I. *Verses 1-6:* Introduction. In these verses, set at "the place where John had first baptized" (see 10:40; 11:6), the reader meets Lazarus, Mary, Martha, Jesus, and the disciples of Jesus. The only characters not introduced who play a role in the story of the raising of Lazarus are "the Jews." But the presence of "many" in 10:41-42 indicates that there are others with Jesus "in the place where he was" (11:6). Major themes are introduced: illness and death (vv. 1, 4); Mary will later do something significant for Jesus (v. 2); a sense of familiarity (v. 3) and affection (v. 5). Most importantly, however, the reader learns that the glory of God and the glorification of the Son of God will result from this illness that is not unto death (v. 4).

II. *Verses 7-16:* Two decisions are made. Jesus decides to go to Judea, and he motivates his decision (vv. 7-15). Thomas, in the name of the disciples, decides that they should go up with Jesus, even if they must die with him (v. 16).

III. *Verses 17-27:* Jesus' encounter with Martha. Jesus reveals himself as the resurrection and the life (see vv. 25-26), but *he is misunderstood* by Martha as a miracle worker (vv. 21-22), and in terms of the Jewish Messiah (v. 27).

IV. *Verses 28-37:* Jesus' encounter with Mary and "the Jews." Mary responds to the voice of Jesus, surpassing the misunderstanding of her sister (vv. 28-32). Jesus reveals his profound emotion as Mary's tears join those of "the Jews" (see vv. 33-35) who regard him as a failed miracle worker (vv. 36-37).[3]

V. *Verses 38-44:* The miracle. At the tomb (v. 38), in the face of further misunderstanding (see vv. 39-40), Jesus calls Lazarus forth from the grave so that the doubting, incredulous, and misunderstanding characters in the story might believe that he is the Sent One of God (see vv. 40, 42).

VI. *Verses 45-54:* The decision of "the Jews." The leaders of "the Jews" decide that Jesus must die (vv. 47-50), and the narrator explains further the implications of that death (vv. 51-52). Jesus and his disciples go to Ephraim (vv. 53-54).

---

[3] Brown, *John*, 1:427–28, points out that "the Jews" in this section of the Gospel seem to represent the ordinary people, not the hostile Jewish authorities. Brown uses this as an indication that chaps. 11–12 were added to an original account of the ministry, which concluded at 10:40-42. Against this, see Schnelle, *Antidocetic Christology*, 125. S. M. Schneiders, "Death in the Community of Eternal Life: History, Theology and Spirituality in John 11," *Int* 41 (1987) 45, is correct in claiming that "the Jews" "serve to lace the story tightly into its Gospel context."

READING THE NARRATIVE

I. Introduction: Verses 1-6

Three new characters are introduced to the reader: Lazarus, Mary, and Martha, of Bethany.[4] Jesus is at another place called Bethany, where John the Baptist first baptized (10:30; see 1:28). The reader distinguishes between the two Bethanys, as the author names this Bethany as the village of Mary and Martha (v. 1). The name "Mary" is listed before that of her sister in v. 1, and the reader is told that Mary anointed the Lord with ointment and wiped his feet with her hair (v. 2ab). The participles are in the aorist tense (*aleipsasa, ekmaxasa*). What can this mean? A gap has been created in the narrative,[5] as the reader seeks further information about a woman named Mary and an anointing of Jesus.[6] There is more to it, as Lazarus, the brother of Mary, was ill (v. 2c). The reader waits for answers; suspense is a feature of this story.

The two sisters are able to communicate directly with Jesus, addressing him as *kyrie*, about the illness of their brother, naming him as *hon phileis*.[7] This message leads to Jesus' words to his disciples that set the theme for both the account of the resurrection of Lazarus and for the second half of the Gospel. The reported illness does not have the *ultimate purpose* of leading Lazarus to his death (*ouk estin pros thanaton*).[8] The disciples are informed that two consequences will flow from the events surrounding the illness of Lazarus. The story is to be the means by which (*di' autēs*) the glory of God will shine forth and the Son of God will be glorified.[9] This is a hint to the reader that Jesus will work a miracle to heal Lazarus, and thus the *doxa* will be seen, as it was at Cana (see 2:11). Jesus promises that Lazarus's illness will be the means by which the *doxa* will be seen, and the reader justifiably looks forward to a miracle. But what of the glorification

---

[4] The meaning of the name "Lazarus" (a shortened form of "God helps") is not explained and is not symbolic.

[5] On the function of "gaps" (also called "blanks," or "places of indeterminacy") in a narrative, see W. Iser, *The Act of Reading: A Theory of Aesthetic Response* (London: Routledge & Kegan Paul, 1978) 182–87 and passim.

[6] For most commentators (e.g., Bernard, *St John*, 2:372–73; Brown, *John*, 1:423; Schnackenburg, *St John*, 2:322; Lindars, *John*, 386–87), this is an added parenthesis.

[7] This expression and the various other indications of affection between Jesus and Lazarus have led some scholars to suggest that Lazarus was the Beloved Disciple. Most recently, see M. W. G. Stibbe, *John as Storyteller: Narrative Criticism and the Fourth Gospel* (SNTSMS 73; Cambridge: University Press, 1992) 77–82. For a survey, see Kremer, *Lazarus*, 55 n. 50.

[8] For this meaning of *pros*, see BAGD, 710, s.v. *pros*, para. III (3c).

[9] Few commentators notice the importance of the *di' autēs*. See, for example, Brown, *John*, 1:423: "Presumably through the sickness." For this use of *dia* as "the circumstances in which one finds oneself because of something," see BDF, 119, para. 223 (3).

of the Son of God?[10] On two earlier occasions, during the celebration of the feast of Tabernacles, the future glorification of Jesus was mentioned. The narrator told the reader that the Spirit had not yet been given, because Jesus had not yet been glorified (7:39). Later, as "the Jews" pressed him to make himself known, Jesus pointed to his Father as the one who would glorify him (8:52-54).

The reader searches for solutions, but Jesus' words about his hour (see 2:4; 7:7-8, 30; 8:20) and his being "lifted up" (see 3:14; 8:28) suggest that his glorification will be linked to his death. The events surrounding Lazarus will set in motion the glorification of the Son of God (v. 4). Because of Jesus' love for Martha, her sister, and Lazarus (v. 5), he stays where he is for two further days (v. 6). This is strange; out of love, Jesus does not go to his loved ones when they need him.[11] Here, as in other places in the Gospel (see 2:1-12; 4:46-54; 7:2-14), Jesus' actions cannot be measured by human standards. He responds to criteria greater than those expected by the reader.[12] His love for the family will be evidenced through deeds that will show forth the *doxa tou theou*.

II. Two Decisions: Verses 7-16

Jesus summons the disciples to go once again with him into Judea (v. 7).[13] After the forced flight at the threat of violence, recorded in 10:39-40, the disciples question the wisdom of such a journey. Addressing Jesus as "Rabbi," an indication that they have not come to authentic belief in Jesus (see its use in 1:38, 49; 3:2, 26; 4:31; 6:25; 9:2), the disciples recall the very recent attempts that "the Jews" had made to stone him (v. 8; see 8:59; 10:31). There is a close temporal and logical link between the violence that closed Jesus' presence in Jerusalem for the feast of Tabernacles and his summons to go into Judea created by the double use of "again" (*palin*) in vv. 6-7. Jesus' response to the disciples transcends the prudence that recent events should impose. Recalling the images of light and darkness, day and night, sight and blindness, so prominent during Jesus' presence in Jerusalem for Tabernacles (7:1—10:21), Jesus indicates the critical nature of

---

[10] Only in 5:25, here, and in 11:25 does Jesus speak of himself as Son of God. Some early manuscripts (P[66], P[45]) omit or substitute "of God."

[11] Some (e.g., Segalla, *Giovanni*, 323; Lindars, *John*, 388; Kremer, *Lazarus*, 58) regard v. 5 as a redactional conclusion to vv. 1-4, unconnected with v. 6. Thus v. 6 flows more naturally from v. 4. But vv. 5-6 are logically linked by *oun* (v. 6); see Lagrange, *Saint Jean*, 297.

[12] See C. H. Giblin, "Suggestion, Negative Response, and Positive Action in St John's Gospel (John 2.1-11; 4.46-54; 7.2-14; 11.1-44)," *NTS* 26 (1979–80) 208-10.

[13] A further stage in the narrative is also indicated by the pleonastic *epeita meta touto*. On this, see Barrett, *St John*, 391.

his journey to Judea (11:9-10). This use of the symbol of walking in the light, which looks back to the Jewish feasts for its christological meaning, but points forward to the promised clash between light and darkness (see 1:5), links chap. 11 with what has gone before and points forward to what is yet to come.

Jesus has already instructed his disciples to walk in the light that the day provided by Jesus, the light of the world, creates (see 9:4-5). The same imagery is used in his discussions with "the Jews" during the feast of Tabernacles (see 8:12, 24). The disciples are invited to join him, not stumbling but walking in the light (v. 9).[14] Whatever may happen in the story that is yet to be told, Jesus is the light. Using the Jewish calculation of twelve hours for the light of day and twelve hours for the darkness of night,[15] the disciples are told of the need to walk in the light of the world (v. 9). Because of the lack of a full appropriation of the light that Jesus brings, the disciples might stumble because they have no light in them (v. 10).[16] The reader follows the progress of the disciples closely. Will these words of Jesus, the light of the world (see 8:12; 9:5; 11:9), enable them to recognize the victory of light over darkness?

Returning to the matter at hand, Jesus informs his disciples that their friend Lazarus (*Lazaros ho philos hēmōn*) has fallen asleep, and that he is going to Bethany to wake Lazarus from that sleep (v. 11).[17] The reader is accustomed to Jesus' knowledge of facts about which he had been provided no information (see 1:47-49; 2:24-25; 4:16-18; 6:64), but the disciples take his words at their face value. If Lazarus is asleep, there is every chance that he will recover (v. 12).[18] The narrator tells the reader that the disciples are wrong in their understanding of the words of Jesus: it is death that Jesus means, not sleep in the usual sense of that word (v. 13). As always, the reader is able to look on from outside the experience of the characters in the story; the reader, but not the disciples, is aware that Jesus

[14] On the rhetorical structure of this "parable," see Lindars, *John*, 389; G. Rochais, *Les récits de résurrection des morts dans le Nouveau Testament* (SNTSMS 40; Cambridge: Cambridge University Press, 1981) 138-39; Byrne, *Lazarus*, 43-44.

[15] Some commentators link the twelve hours with the hour of Jesus that has not yet come. See, for example, Becker, *Johannes*, 2:366-67; Rochais, *Les récits*, 139. But see Kremer, *Lazarus*, 60, for the case against this identification.

[16] The Jewish notion of the eye being the seat of the light is invoked in v. 10. See, among many, Schnackenburg, *St John*, 2:325-26.

[17] On the traditionally Christian background for sleeping language for death, see Westcott, *St John*, 166; Bauer, *Johannesevangelium*, 149. There are no known parallels between waking from sleep and resurrection. Rochais, *Les récits*, 139-40, links it with the Greek versions of Job 14:12-15.

[18] It is often pointed out that the disciples use the verb *sōzein*, which means both physical recovery and spiritual salvation.

is going to Bethany to raise Lazarus from the sleep of death. But the disciples are given a chance to catch up with the reader. Jesus tells them plainly, "Lazarus is dead" (v. 14), and rejoices for the sake of the disciples, so that they might come to believe (*chairō d' hymas hina pisteusēte*). From the first indication in the story that Lazarus has died and that Jesus' journey to Bethany is to wake him from that sleep (vv. 10-13), the reader knows that the raising of Lazarus is not for Lazarus.[19] The use of the aorist tense (*hina pisteusēte*) links Jesus' hopes with the possibility that the disciples might come to faith as a result of the event that is about to take place. The motivation for Jesus' decision to go to Bethany is a response to God that leads him into danger so that others might come to true faith.

Thomas recognizes the risk involved and encourages his fellow disciples to join Jesus' journey, that they might die with him (v. 16), but the reader knows that Thomas misunderstands. Jesus has not asked his disciples to follow him on a suicidal journey. He has informed them that he rejoices in the events taking place, so that through them the disciples might come to belief. This does not play any part in Thomas's words. Thomas, recognizing that Jesus is leading them back into the violence of Judea, recommends that the disciples not abandon their Master in his moment of danger, but join him, even if it might cost them their lives.[20] While these words reinforce the reader's suspicions that the journey to Judea will lead to death, the reader knows that Jesus seeks belief (v. 15), not death (v. 16), from his disciples.[21] The motivations for the two decisions to go to Bethany are at cross-purposes. Misunderstanding among the disciples intensifies.

III. JESUS AND MARTHA: VERSES 17-27

Jesus arrives in Bethany to find that Lazarus has been in the tomb for four days (v. 17). Lazarus's entombed body is in a state of advanced decay.[22] Bethany is close to Jerusalem, about two miles (v. 18: fifteen stadia). This information makes the journey of "the Jews" from Jerusalem to console

---

[19] On the lack of interest in the person of Lazarus, see Léon-Dufour, *Lecture*, 2:404–5. However, Marchadour, *Lazare*, 126–27, rightly points out that he is the empty hole that drives the narrative, as it is gradually filled. See also M. W. G. Stibbe, "A Tomb with a View: John 11.1-44 in Narrative-Critical Perspective," *NTS* 40 (1994) 42–43.

[20] It is grammatically possible that Thomas is referring to death with Lazarus. Lagrange, *Saint Jean*, 299, regards this suggestion as "fantasy."

[21] Against those who see the words of Thomas as an invitation to all disciples of Jesus. See, for example, Lightfoot, *St John*, 220–21; Beasley-Murray, *John*, 189; Brodie, *John*, 392.

[22] There is a widely cited Jewish opinion that the soul was near the body for three days, but by the fourth day all hope of resuscitation was gone. See Str-B 2:544.

the two sisters on the loss of their brother (v. 19) a genuine possibility.[23] Only "the Jews" are described as mourning; nothing is said of the sisters' emotional state. The *place* of Jesus' passion and death is now nearby. The increasing hostility of chaps. 5–10, the presence, however innocent, of "the Jews," and the turn toward the theme of death in vv. 2, 4, 8, and 16, lead the reader to wonder if the *time* of Jesus' death is near at hand.[24]

Although the initial message to Jesus, announcing that Lazarus was ill, came from *both* sisters (see v. 3), once they hear that Jesus has arrived, only Martha moves into action, as she goes out to meet Jesus (*erchetai hypēntēsen autǭ*). Mary is described as stationary, seated (*ekathezeto*) in the house (v. 20). The two women will respond to Jesus in different ways.[25] The words of Martha to Jesus, repeating the earlier salutation *kyrie* (see vv. 3, 21), are a confession of faith that Jesus' presence would have healed Lazarus of his fatal illness (v. 21). She gives her reason for such faith: whatever Jesus might ask of God—even now—will happen (v. 22). The reader is by now suspicious of such an understanding of Jesus (see 2:23-25; 1:49-51; 3:1-11; 4:25-26; 6:25-27; 7:31). In 9:11, 17, 25-32, 35-38, the man born blind moved beyond the limitations of a miracle faith. Both Nicodemus (see 3:2) and the man born blind (see 9:31-33) had expressed their belief that Jesus had special access to God, and was able to work miracles because of this authority.[26] Martha repeats their understanding of Jesus as a rabbi from God who does wonderful signs because God is with him (see 3:2; 9:31-32).[27]

Jesus *corrects her misunderstanding* by informing her that Lazarus will rise (v. 23). The reader recalls that Jesus has already informed his disciples that Lazarus is asleep, and that Jesus was going to Bethany "to awake him

---

[23] The verb *paramytheisthai*, used here to describe the actions of "the Jews," is rare in the New Testament (see v. 31; 1 Thess 2:11; 5:14). It is a word of wide meaning (see LSJ, 1318, s.v.), but there is no cause for suspecting the genuineness of the care shown to the bereaved family, or to read the use of this verb as describing non-Christian concern over death. See Barrett, *St John*, 394. For details on the importance of offering consolation, see Str-B 4:592–607.

[24] While it is true that "the Jews" in 11:8, 19, 31, 33, 36, 45, 54 do not play the negative role that has marked their appearance in the story thus far (Kremer, *Lazarus*, 64), the reader comes to John 11 with that negative response in mind. See Stibbe, "Tomb," 47–48.

[25] This is often noticed (e.g., Bultmann, *John*, 401 n. 4), but scholars generally give all the credit to Martha, and portray Mary as behaving as one would expect from a person grieving. On the basis of Job 2:8, 13; Ezek 8:14, mourning is assumed.

[26] Schnackenburg, *St John*, 2:329, notes rightly that the idea "is in accord with Jewish piety."

[27] Against, for example, Westcott, *St John*, 168; Bultmann, *John*, 401–2; and Marchadour, *Lazare*, 119, who regard Martha's words in v. 22 as already a satisfactory expression of Johannine faith.

out of his sleep" (v. 11). Martha was not present at that earlier conversation, held on the other side of the Jordan (see 10:40), but she does not allow Jesus any space to explain what he means; she knows (v. 24a: *oida hoti*). She tells Jesus that she accepts a current Jewish understanding of a final resurrection (v. 24). Belief in "the last day" seems to have its roots in the Old Testament (see Isa 2:2; Mic 4:1), and the idea of a final resurrection was a constituent part of Pharisaic Judaism (see Dan 12:1-3; 2 Macc 7:22-24; 12:44; Acts 23:8; Josephus, *War* 2:163; *Sanhedrin* 10:1; *Soṭa* 9:15; *Berakot* 5:2; see also Mark 12:18-27 and parallels).[28] This is the faith expressed by Martha. *She tells Jesus* what resurrection means. Jesus must wrest the initiative from the energetic Martha. His words transcend traditional eschatological expectation, and center on his person as the resurrection and the life (v. 25).[29] In an *egō eimi* statement, Jesus points to the essential nature of belief in him as the only way to resurrection and life (vv. 25-26). This self-revelation of Jesus to Martha has been made clear for the reader in 5:19-30.[30] Here, as there, Jesus states that faith in him brings life both now and hereafter.

Commentators have differed in their understanding of the possible meanings (physical or spiritual?) of "life" in the expression "and whoever lives" (v. 26a: *kai pas ho zōn*).[31] The blending of realized and traditional eschatology, familiar to the reader from 5:24-29 (see also 6:40, 54), returns. People die physically (11:25b), but faith in Jesus ensures a life that transcends death. Thus Jesus insists that faith in him produces a spiritual life both now and hereafter. Jesus' words claim: the believer, even if he or she dies physically, will live spiritually (v. 25). The believer who is alive spiritually will never die spiritually (v. 26).[32] Jesus *is* resurrection and life, and thus the believer on this side of death *lives* in the spirit (see 3:6; 5:24-25), and the one who believes in him now *will live* on the other side of

---

[28] For a full-scale discussion, see H. C. Cavallin, "Leben nach dem Tod im Spätjudentum und frühen Christentum," in *ANRW* 19.1 (1979) 240–345.

[29] The words *kai hē zōē* are missing from some good witnesses (P[45], Old Latin [Vercellensis], Sinaitic Syriac, Cyprian, and in some of Origen's texts). Brown, *John*, 1:425, claims that omission is harder to explain than addition. Barrett, *St John*, 396, suspects that the shorter text may be original, but "makes little difference to the sense." This is hardly the case, given the play on *zōē* in vv. 25b-26. On this, see Dodd, *Interpretation*, 364–65; Stimpfle, *Blinde sehen*, 109.

[30] See Barrett, *St John*, 395–96; J. H. Neyrey, *An Ideology of Revolt: John's Christology in a Social Science Perspective* (Philadelphia: Fortress Press, 1992) 81–92. For Neyrey, chap. 11 demonstrates the claims of 5:21-29, and makes Jesus equal to God.

[31] For a summary of the discussion, see Beasley-Murray, *John*, 190–91.

[32] Brown, *John*, 1:425.

physical death (see 5:28-29; 6:40, 54).[33] Jesus bluntly asks Mary: *pisteueis touto?*

The context of a discussion between Martha and Jesus, where two people who have contrasting ideas about the true meaning of resurrection, determines the interpretation of Martha's response. She has expressed her confidence in Jesus as miracle worker (v. 21) and then attempted to tell him the meaning of resurrection (v. 24). She now claims that she has believed for some time (v. 27a: *egō pepisteuka*). The use of the personal pronoun and perfect tense of the verb must be given full weight, indicating Martha's expression of *her long-held convictions*. In the past she (*egō*) came to believe (*pepisteuka*) in Jesus, and she still retains that faith.[34] This suggests to the reader that Jesus' self-revelation of vv. 25-26 has not changed her understanding of Jesus. Martha's confession makes no use of the words of Jesus (vv. 25-26). She states her faith in an expression of first-century Jewish messianic expectation: the Christ (*ho christos*), the Son of God (*ho huios tou theou*), the one who is coming into the world (*ho eis ton kosmon erchomenos*) (v. 27b). All these expressions have been used earlier in the Gospel in a way that fell short of true Johannine faith. The first disciples (see 1:41) and Nathanael (see 1:49) called Jesus "the Christ" and "the Son of God." They were corrected by the words of Jesus that promised the sight of greater things (1:50-51).[35] After the miracle of the loaves and fishes, the crowds confessed that Jesus was the one who was coming into the world (see 6:14), but they also were corrected by Jesus' stern warning that they should not work for a food that perishes (see 6:25-27).[36] Martha has a limited faith, matching that of Nicodemus (see 3:1-11) and the Samaritan woman (see 4:25-26), who earlier used Jewish messianic expressions to voice their faith in Jesus.

No character in the story as it is reported in 11:1-27 has shown true faith in Jesus: neither the disciples (v. 16) nor Martha (vv. 21, 24, 27).[37] But Jesus

[33] The question of physical life and death was important in the Johannine community. See Stimpfle, *Blinde sehen*, 111–16; Schneiders, "Death in the Community," 46–52. See also Stibbe, "Tomb," 50–54; J. P. Martin, "History and Eschatology in the Lazarus Narrative," *SJT* 17 (1964) 332–43; B. McNeil, "The Raising of Lazarus," *DRev* 92 (1974) 269–75; C. F. D. Moule, "The Meaning of 'Life' in the Gospel and the Epistles of John: A Study in the Story of Lazarus, John 11:1-44," *Theology* 78 (1975) 114–25.

[34] I am giving the perfect tense its full value (see 8:31, where the perfect tense is also used in this way). On this, see BDF, 175–76, para. 340. See also Stimpfle, *Blinde sehen*, 119. This is generally explained away by commentators who claim that this is a characteristic use of *pisteuein* in the Fourth Gospel (see Barrett, *St John*, 396). The *pepisteuka* of 11:27 is a genuine perfect tense, indicating a coming to faith that *preceded* the words of Jesus in vv. 25-26.

[35] On this, see Moloney, *Belief*, 67–75.

[36] Brown, *John*, 1:425, sees the problem of the parallel between 6:14 and 11:27, but suggests that Martha expresses a different expectation.

[37] My reading does not represent the common opinion among scholars. Schnackenburg,

will not renounce his mission to make God known to them (see 1:18). The reader knows, on the authority of the word of Jesus, that the glory of God will result from the miracle and that the Son of God will be glorified by means of it (see v. 4). Jesus has instructed his disciples that the miracle at Bethany will take place "so that you may believe" (v. 15). Jesus' self-revelation (vv. 25-27) will continue so that the promise of v. 4 will be fulfilled.

IV. JESUS AND MARY: VERSES 28-37

The narrator links Martha's return to her sister with her partial confession of faith in v. 27 (v. 28a: *kai touto eipousa*), as she summons Mary by quietly telling her: *ho didaskalos parestin* (v. 28b). The reader now finds Martha calling Jesus "the Teacher." This continues her limited faith in the word and person of Jesus (see 1:38; 3:2).[38] Martha passes from one series of limited expressions of faith (vv. 21-22, 24, 27) to another (v. 28). She reports Jesus' presence "quietly" (*lathrą*),[39] and informs her sister that the Teacher is calling her (v. 28b: *kai phōnei se*).[40] Without exception, every reference

---

St John, 2:328; and Lindars, *John,* 396, regard Martha's words as the theological climax of the chapter, and Bultmann, *John,* 404, sees them as an expression of genuine faith. For R. E. Brown, "Roles of Women in the Fourth Gospel," *TS* 36 (1975) 693-94, Martha replaces Peter as the one who makes the supreme confession of faith. So also S. M. Schneiders, "Women in the Fourth Gospel and the Role of Women in the Contemporary Church," *BTB* 12 (1982) 41. For Scott, *Sophia,* 199-206, Martha's confession is "both fully Johannine and . . . consistent with the pattern of the revelation of Jesus as Sophia incarnate" (p. 206). Kremer, *Lazarus,* 70, presents a consensus of scholarship: "Auf dem Höhepunkt und am Schluss des Gesprächs zwischen Marta und Jesus kommt diesem kurzen Credo ein besonderes Gewicht zu." The list could go on. See, for example, Barrett, Beasley-Murray, Becker, Brodie, Carson, Gnilka, Haenchen, Lagrange, Marchadour, Marsh, Rochais, Schneiders, Schnelle, Segalla, Stibbe, van Tilborg. Scholars discuss its origins as a primitive creed (see Barrett, *St John,* 397) and even suggest that it was a baptismal confession (see G. Bornkamm, "Das Bekenntnis im Hebräerbrief," in *Studien zu Antike und Urchristentum: Gesammelte Aufsätze Band II* [BEvT 28; Munich: Kaiser, 1959] 191-92 n. 8). But what came first, the Johannine context, or the creedal use of Martha's words in the Christian church? Verses 21-27 must be interpreted within their Johannine narrative context, as does Lee, *Symbolic Narratives,* 205-6.

[38] On these uses of *didaskalos* as imperfect confessions of faith, see Moloney, *Belief,* 67-68, 108-9. It is, of course, the Greek for "Rabbi," which has always been used to address Jesus in contexts of limited faith: see 1:38, 49; 3:2; 4:31; 6:25; 9:2; 11:8. Barrett, *St John,* 397, admits: "The description is surprising after the exalted terms of Martha's confession of faith (v. 27)."

[39] Brown, *John,* 1:425, suggests that this is a "cautious whispering" to keep Jesus' presence a secret from "the Jews." Kremer, *Lazarus,* 71, links it with the Johannine church's exclusion from the synagogue. The detail also indicates the weakening of Martha's role in the narrative.

[40] Martha is also reported as "calling" her sister (*ephōnēsen*), but it is the *phōnē* of Jesus that is decisive.

to the *phōnē* of Jesus in the story to this point is a call to the fullness of life with him (see 3:8, 29; 5:25, 28; 10:3, 4, 16, 27). Jesus condemns "the Jews" who never hear the voice of the Sent One (see 5:37). There is a heavy concentration on the voice of the shepherd in 10:1-18 (see vv. 3, 4, 16, 17). In Jesus' description of the shepherd, which the reader has just left behind, the only place where Jesus uses the verb *phōneō* to speak of his own activity has appeared: "The sheep hear his voice (*tēs phōnēs autou*), and he calls (*phōnei*) his own sheep by name and leads them out" (10:3). Mary is one of the Lord's own sheep, and he is summoning her. In stark contrast with her sister, who refused to allow Jesus to take the initiative from her (see vv. 21-22, 24, 27), Mary is called forth by the word of Jesus.[41]

The reader is already aware, from the information provided in v. 2, that Mary will be the special sister.[42] Every carefully etched detail of v. 29 continues to enhance the author's portrait of Mary. *This* woman (v. 29a: *ekeinē*), when she hears of his call (v. 29b: *hōs ēkousen*), responds immediately (v. 29c: *ēgerthē tachy kai ērcheto pros auton*). The reader has become accustomed to the use of the verb *akouein* in descriptions of a positive response to the word of Jesus (see 1:37, 40; 3:8, 29, 32; 4:42, 47; 5:24, 25, 28, 30; 6:45; 7:40, 51; 8:47). Again this verb has been used four times, in the immediate context, of the sheep responding to the voice of the Good Shepherd (10:3, 16, 20, 27).[43] The narrator paints in some geographical detail, so that the motion of the characters in the narrative can make sense. Jesus has not yet arrived in the village, but is still at the place where Martha met him (v. 30). This necessitates movement from Mary (v. 29), and enables the narrator to introduce "the Jews" who were with her in the house, comforting her (v. 31a). Nothing is said about the emotional state of Mary. It is only "the Jews" who offer consolation (see vv. 19, 31). The focus of the narrative changes briefly, as Mary's actions (see v. 29) are reported through the eyes of "the Jews." Their interpretation of Mary's immediate rising and exit is that she is going to the tomb to weep there, so

---

[41] The following positive interpretation is again at variance with commentary on this passage. I disagree with the remarks of Brown, *John*, 1:435: "This scene does not advance the action; vs. 34 could easily follow vs. 27, and no one would know the difference." Rochais, *Les récits*, 143, regards vv. 28-31 "versets de remplissage." Scott, *Sophia*, 206, comments that "Mary's role . . . is almost insignificant in comparison with that of her sister." I regard this widespread opinion as a misunderstanding of the author's narrative strategy. What of v. 2 and 12:1-8? Schneiders, "Women," 41-42; and Culpepper, *Anatomy*, 140-42, present Mary as a model disciple, but look ahead to 12:1-8 and tend to ignore 11:28-37.

[42] Historical studies of this passage disregard v. 2. See Schnackenburg, *St John*, 2:333: "Mary thus gives the impression of being nothing but a complaining woman." On v. 2 as a gloss, see ibid., 2:322.

[43] The same verb has been used against those who do not listen to the voice of Jesus (see 5:37; 6:60; 8:38, 43, 47).

they follow her (v. 31b). The reader knows that Mary is responding to the call of Jesus, which transcends human concerns. There is a clash of worlds: that which flows from the presence of Jesus (see v. 28: *ho didaskalos parestin*),[44] and that which flows from accepted religious, cultural, and historical custom (see v. 31c: *doxantes hoti hypagei eis to mnēmeion hina klausę ekei*).[45]

The focus returns to Mary, who comes to the place where Jesus was. On arrival, a further contrast between herself and Martha appears. In v. 21 the narrator reported: "Martha said to Jesus. . . ." Mary's encounter with Jesus begins with two verbs. When she saw Jesus (v. 32b: *idousa auton*) she fell at his feet (v. 32c: *epesen autou pros tous podas*). Her attitude is highlighted by receptivity and respect for the person of Jesus.[46] The reader recalls that on only one other occasion did Jesus' presence provoke such a reaction. When the man born blind heard that the Son of Man was the one whom he could see, and who was speaking to him (9:37), he confessed his faith (v. 38a: *pisteuō kyrie*) and fell to the ground before Jesus (v. 38b: *prosekynēsen autǭ*).[47] By means of participial constructions (11:32a: *idousa auton . . . epesen . . . legousa autǭ*), the narrator stresses that from her position at the feet of Jesus, Mary repeats *part* of the words of Martha (v. 32b; see v. 22). The words of Mary addressed to Jesus omit the motivation that Martha gave for her confidence in Jesus' ability to heal Lazarus from his fatal illness: "whatever you ask from God, God will give you" (v. 22).[48] Martha's request paralleled other expressions of faith in the Gospel that accepted Jesus as a messianic miracle worker, but no such misunderstanding lies behind Mary's trust in Jesus' presence. The context gives the words of Mary a different meaning. She has responded to the call of the Good Shepherd (see vv. 28-29) and, in the midst of misunderstanding from "the Jews" (v. 31), has placed herself in a position of total trust in him (v. 32a). Her words indicate her belief that the presence of Jesus would have saved Lazarus (v. 32b). Jesus is accepted, unconditionally, as the resurrection and the life (see vv. 25-26). Only Mary accepts the significance of Jesus'

---

[44] Barrett, *St John*, 397, notes the relationship between this verb and the noun *parousia*.

[45] Some manuscripts (e.g., P[66], Alexandrinus, Koridethi) read *legontes* rather than *doxazontes*. The sense of an inner expression of common opinion must be maintained, on both textual and narrative grounds. As Schnackenburg, *St John*, 2:334, correctly notes: "She is *expected* to give way to her grief and 'weep' at the tomb" (emphasis mine).

[46] It is not, as Byrne, *Lazarus*, 56, comments, "extremity of emotion." Equally unacceptable is Brodie's judgment that Martha rises above the bitterness, while Mary sinks into unrestrained mourning (*John*, 386).

[47] The verbs are not the same, but the action is. The reader also recalls the use of the verb *proskyneō* in the discussion of true worship in 4:20-24.

[48] Byrne, *Lazarus*, 56, misses the point when he describes Mary's words as "a poor, truncated piece compared with Martha's."

revelation of himself as *egō eimi* (see v. 26). It is Mary who makes a confession of faith with these words, not Martha. The repetition of the words of Martha by Mary do not show that she is in some way a weaker "shadow" of her more powerful sister.[49] Mary is the character in the story reflecting true faith (see vv. 29, 32), while Martha has fallen short of such faith (see vv. 21-22, 24, 27).

Jesus is strangely moved as Mary *adds her tears to the tears of "the Jews" who have come out with her* (v. 33). Up to this point of the story Mary's attention has been totally focused on her response to Jesus. The death of Lazarus should not be at center stage—but even Mary succumbs! Jesus has informed the disciples that the problem of Lazarus's death will be solved (see v. 11). The reader knows that Jesus is about to perform an action that will show forth the glory of God, through which the Son of God will be glorified (see vv. 4, 11). The miracle is an attempt, on the part of Jesus, to bring his disciples (v. 15) and Martha (vv. 25-26) to true faith. Even more importantly, it is a parable of Jesus' self-revelation as the resurrection and the life (see vv. 25-26). It is not compassion—or lack of it—that creates Jesus' emotion. Jesus is moved to anger in spirit and is troubled (v. 33b: *enebrimēsato tǭ pneumati kai etaraxen heauton*). Some important variations in the textual tradition and much scholarly debate have been created by the use of the verb *embrimasthai*. The verb is associated with anger, and in its Johannine form its force is accentuated with the addition of a prefix.[50] The debate hinges around the seemingly impossible portrait of Jesus' anger when faced with the loss of Lazarus, which has produced the tears of Mary and "the Jews."[51] The emerging reader, however, aware that the end of Jesus' public ministry is close at hand, joins Jesus' frustrated and angry disappointment (*enebrimēsato*) and deep, shuddering, internal emotion (*etaraxen*).[52] Mary, who earlier has shown every sign of moving in the

---

[49] An expression used by Bauer, *Johannesevangelium*, 157, citing Wellhausen.

[50] The basic meaning of the verb is to express anger outwardly, for example, with a snort or the like. But this is internalized here by the addition of *en pneumati*. On the verb, see LSJ, 330, s.v. *brimazō*; 540, s.v. *embrimaomai*, and the survey of its use in classical literature in B. Lindars, "Rebuking the Spirit: A New Analysis of the Lazarus Story of John 11," *NTS* 38 (1992) 92–96.

[51] It is not possible to offer a history of this discussion here. For surveys, see Barrett, *St John*, 398–400; Brown, *John*, 1:425–26. For earlier discussions, see Lagrange, *Saint Jean*, 303–5. Attempts have been made to lessen the idea of anger, to the extent that P[45], P[66], and Codex Bezae offer a softer reading, adding "as if" before the verb. Black, *Aramaic Approach*, 240–43, suggests that the two Greek words translate one Aramaic expression meaning "to be strongly moved."

[52] Commentators point out rightly that the expressions *tǭ pneumati* of v. 33 and the *en heautoi* of v. 38 are parallel. There is no reference to anger "in the Spirit," but a deep, internal, and spiritual experience.

world of Jesus rather than that of "the Jews" (see v. 31), is now reported as having joined "the Jews" in their tears (v. 33a).

The events of Bethany must not be regarded as an end in themselves.[53] Only one character in the story has moved toward Jesus, heard his voice, shown her receptivity and commitment to who he is, and trusted in the power of his presence: Mary, the one who will anoint Jesus (see vv. 2, 29, 32). However, she is now reported as weeping with "the Jews." Till now, nothing has been said of the tears or mourning of Mary.[54] She was not reported as crying earlier in the narrative. It was "the Jews" who were in the house, mourning (see vv. 19, 31). Now, after a demonstration of authentic faith (vv. 28-32), she is described as in tears (v. 33). But more dramatically for the reader: she is in tears, *along with "the Jews"* who came out to Jesus with her (v. 33a). This is the crucial issue. Will no one come to true belief? Mary, who earlier responded to the voice of Jesus, rather than to the expectations of "the Jews" that she would go to weep at the tomb (v. 31), is now with "the Jews," overcome by tears at the loss of her brother (v. 33a). Has she, along with "the Jews," made the death of Lazarus the center of attention, and thus lost Jesus? This is a reversal of her earlier response to Jesus (vv. 28-32).

Jesus comes to the end of his ministry, angry (or perhaps "severely disappointed" is a better English rendition)[55] that even Mary, the one who shows signs of belief in who he is (the Good Shepherd, see vv. 28-29) and what he comes to bring (resurrection and life, see vv. 25-26, 32), is at risk.[56] The human event of the death of Lazarus, and the expected emotional response of tears and mourning shown by "the Jews" (see vv. 19, 31) threaten the incipient, but authentic, faith of Mary. Thus Jesus is deeply moved by a justifiable anger and emotion. But Jesus must proceed with the mission that has been entrusted to him. He must wake Lazarus from his sleep (see v. 11), glorify God, and through this event experience his

[53] See W. Wuellner, "Putting Life Back into the Lazarus Story and Its Reading: The Narrative Rhetoric of John 11 as the Narration of Faith," *Sem* 53 (1991) 114–32.

[54] Mary's remaining seated in the house (see v. 20) does not indicate her taking up a traditional position of mourning. It is inaccurate to claim: "Marie de bout en bout est marquée par une série cumulative de notions funèbres" (Marchadour, *Lazare*, 124).

[55] Westcott, *St John*, 170, points out that "indignation" is part of the general notion implied by the verb.

[56] There is no need to resort to a softening of the context, suggesting that Jesus is moved by his sympathy for the sufferers. Barrett, *St John*, 398, rightly dismisses any suggestions that Jesus is angry with the hypocrisy of the tears of "the Jews." It is the *association* of Mary with "the Jews" that creates the problem. Recently, Lindars, "Rebuking the Spirit," 97–104, has claimed that John's source (parallel to Synoptic exorcisms: see Mark 1:43; 9:25-29) originally had Jesus rebuking the spirit. In John, not demons but death is overcome. In accommodating the source to its present context, John's use of *embrimasthai* is conditioned by *tarassō*, and thus comes to mean emotionally moved.

own glorification (v. 4).[57] Thus he asks to be led to the tomb of Lazarus, and "they" invite him to "come and see." It is Mary and "the Jews" (v. 33) who comprise the "they" (v. 34).[58] They respectfully (*kyrie*) invite Jesus to proceed to the tomb, to see the situation of a person who has been enclosed there for four days (see v. 17).[59] Once again, it is this association of the one who had best responded to the call of the Good Shepherd with "the Jews" that leads to Jesus' tears (v. 35). The emotion of v. 33b continues in the tears described in v. 35, and the remarks of "the Jews" in v. 36 continue to reflect misunderstanding.[60] Jesus is not weeping because of the death of Lazarus, the disappointment of Martha, or the tears of Mary. The deliberate use of another verb to speak of the weeping of Jesus (*dakryō*, rather than the *klaiō* used of Mary and "the Jews" in vv. 31 and 33) informs the reader that his weeping cannot be associated with the mourning that has created his emotional response.[61] Jesus' love for Lazarus (v. 36; see v. 3) is not the point of his tears. He is weeping because of the danger that his unconditional gift of himself in love as the Good Shepherd (see 10:11, 14-15), the resurrection and the life who offers life here and hereafter to all who would believe in him (11:25-26), will never be understood or accepted. While Mary moved toward Jesus, responding to his voice (vv. 28-29) and trusting in him as the resurrection and the life (see v. 32), there was hope that one of the characters had come to believe. But once she joined "the Jews" in their sorrowing and tears, Jesus' promises seem to have been forgotten. In this clash of worlds, the world of Jesus—totally determined by his response to his Father—seems to have been lost, and

[57] Barrett, *St John*, 399, also associates the forthcoming miracle and his imminent passion with the anger of Jesus, but in a way that parallels his brusque reply to his mother in 2:4, and other situations where a miracle is forced upon him. Byrne, *Lazarus*, 58–60, interprets Jesus' emotion as the result of his being torn between feeling for those in sorrow, and his need to go to his own death by means of the miracle he is about to perform. See also Brown, *John*, 1:435, who suggests that Jesus is angry in the face of the presence of Satan. I sense in these interpretations a psychologizing of the Johannine Jesus that cannot be traced elsewhere in the Gospel.

[58] Against Westcott, *St John*, 171, and Bernard, *St John*, 2:394, who guess that "they" must refer to Martha and Mary.

[59] The expression used in v. 34, "come and see," recalls Jesus' provocative use of those words in 1:39. Lightfoot, *St John*, 233, makes much of this, drawing a contrast between the invitation of Jesus and the invitation of human beings. The repetition is probably coincidental.

[60] Many commentators remark that at least in v. 36 "the Jews" interpret the actions of Jesus correctly. See, for example, Bernard, *St John*, 2:394; Barrett, *St John*, 400; Schnelle, *Antidocetic Christology*, 131.

[61] This is the only place in the New Testament where the verb *dakryō* appears. The noun *dakryon* appears in Heb 5:7 (significantly in the famous passage on Jesus' loud cries and tears).

Jesus weeps in his frustration and disappointment (v. 35). This, however, has not altered his response to his task to make visible the glory of God and to go through his own glorification. He asks: "Where have you laid him?" (v. 34a). The reader, still aware that Jesus will wake Lazarus from his sleep (see v. 11), waits for the miracle.

"The Jews'" misunderstanding comes to its climax in v. 37. Looking back to the miracle of the man born blind (9:1-7), some of "the Jews" join Martha's understanding of Jesus as a miracle worker (see 11:21-22). Here Mary is not associated with them. Only "the Jews" who recall that Jesus had shown he was able to work significant miracles are mentioned. Why is it he could not prevent the death of Lazarus? Jesus has every reason for profound emotion as "the Jews" continue to ignore who he is and the promises he is making as his public ministry draws to a close. They, like Martha, are unprepared to move away from their own criteria for judging the person and mission of Jesus. The reader is aware that in this attempt to assess Jesus as a miracle worker "the Jews"—as always in John—are wrong. They have not moved from the messianic expectations expressed during the feast of Tabernacles, when some of the people asked: "When the Christ appears, will he do more signs than this man has done?" (7:31). However, even that incorrect assessment of Jesus is now in crisis: he has not been able to cure the illness of Lazarus.

But what of Mary? For the moment, she disappears from the action, swallowed up in the human emotions surrounding the death of her brother. Will the early promise of her authentic belief in Jesus, the Good Shepherd who was calling her (see vv. 28-29), and her trust in his authority as the resurrection and the life (see v. 32), come to nothing? One sign that she has not fallen completely into the world imposed by "the Jews" is that she is no longer with them in their understanding of Jesus as a failed miracle worker in v. 37. The reader, who has known from the beginning of the story of the events at Bethany that she is the one who anointed Jesus and wiped his feet with her hair (see v. 2), is aware that this cannot be the end of her story.

V. The Miracle: Verses 38-44

Again moved to anger by the ongoing inability of "the Jews" to understand him (v. 38a; see vv. 36-37), Jesus "came to the tomb" (v. 36b: *erchetai eis to mnēmeion*). In the earlier episodes Jesus has delayed (v. 6), asked for belief (vv. 16, 27), and shown anger and emotion (vv. 33, 35, 38a). He asked to be shown the place where Lazarus was buried. Mary and "the Jews" offered to take him to the place that he might see it (v. 34). Now the reader finds that Jesus is not *shown* to the tomb; he *went* there. He is the master of the situation. Jesus moves decisively to fulfill God's design (see v. 4), which involves waking Lazarus from sleep (see v. 11). A series of initiatives from Jesus will dominate the brief account of Jesus' presence at the tomb (vv. 38-44). The imperative mood will be used four times (vv. 39, 43, 44 [twice]). Only in his communication with the Father does Jesus show an attitude of dependence (see vv. 41-42). The tomb is described: "it was a cave, and a stone lay on it" (v. 38b).[62] Jesus orders: "Take away the stone" (v. 39a).[63] Martha, the sister of the dead man, reappears and objects to Jesus' command (v. 39b). She tells Jesus how things are in her world: as Lazarus has been dead four days there will be an odor. Does Martha believe that Jesus is the resurrection and the life, and that whoever lives and believes in him will never die (see vv. 25-26)? Martha has never expressed such faith. She has always believed that Jesus is *her* expected Messiah (see v. 27). She informs "the resurrection and the life" (see v. 25) that a body shut up in a tomb for four days will be badly decomposed.[64] Martha's first words in the Fourth Gospel proclaimed her faith in Jesus as a miracle worker (vv. 21-22); her parting words tell Jesus that he has no authority over a person who has been dead for four days (v. 39).

Jesus no longer attempts to free her from her prison, but looks back to his earlier words and speaks of the sight of the glory of God. Martha is told that if she would believe in the word of Jesus (v. 40: *ouk eipon soi hoti ean pisteusēs*), she would see the *doxa tou theou*. The guiding, caring, saving presence of God would be visible to her through the events that she is about to witness—if only she would believe.[65] The verb is in the singular; it is the faith of Martha that is in question. Jesus' earlier words to the disciples promised that the illness of Lazarus was not unto death, but for the *doxa* of God and for the glorification of the Son of God (see v. 4). What is

---

[62] The general term *mnēmeion* is further described as a cave (*spēlaion*). This type of burial place was widespread in first-century Palestine.

[63] Kremer, *Lazarus*, 75, points out that Mary Magdalene will find the stone of Jesus' tomb already removed. See also Byrne, *Lazarus*, 63.

[64] See also Byrne, *Lazarus*, 62. A. Loisy, *Le quatrième évangile* (Paris: Emile Nourry, 1921) 352–53; and Bultmann, *John*, 407 n. 7, point to the contradiction, but most scholars struggle to combine v. 27 with this answer to Jesus' command in v. 39. See, for example, Lindars, *John*, 399–400; Rochais, *Les récits*, 144; Kremer, *Lazarus*, 75. Some simply ignore the contradiction. See, for example, Barrett, *St John*, 402; Beasley-Murray, *John*, 194. Others (e.g., Bultmann, *John*, 407 n. 7; M. Wilcox, "The 'Prayer' of Jesus in John XI.41b-42," *NTS* 24 [1977–78] 128–29) put it down to confusion in the sources.

[65] For this meaning of *doxa tou theou*, see Moloney, *Belief*, 55–57. All the bystanders will see the events, but only the believer will see the *doxa*. See Lightfoot, *St John*, 224. Generally, scholars read v. 40 not as a recommendation to greater faith but as a promise (see, for example, Kremer, *Lazarus*, 76).

needed is true belief, and Martha's words in v. 39 have shown Jesus that she still has some way to go in her journey of faith (v. 40a). As the experience of the disciples at Cana has shown, the eyes of faith see already, in the wonderful actions of Jesus, the revelation of the *doxa* (see 2:11).[66] There can be no resisting the command of Jesus (see v. 39a). Martha's attempt to stop the action (v. 39b) is ignored, and the stone is taken away (v. 41a).

Jesus' attitude changes as he prays so that he can be heard by all the people who are at the tomb: Martha, Mary, "the Jews," and the disciples, who may not have been in the action but have not been dismissed from it (see v. 16). There must be no doubt about the source of all that Jesus does. Adopting a position of prayer by lifting his eyes (v. 41b), Jesus expresses his gratitude and absolute trust in the communion between himself and his Father (vv. 41c-42a).[67] Jesus is turned in loving union toward his Father. It is on the basis of this union that he is able to tell the story of God, whom no one has ever seen (see 1:18). Jesus has never swerved from this oneness and his unconditional response to the Father (see 4:34; 5:19-30, 36-37, 43; 6:27, 37-38, 40, 45, 46, 57, 65; 8:18-19, 28, 38, 49, 54; 10:10, 15-18, 25, 29-30, 32, 37-38). The reader is well schooled in this truth, but what of the people gathered around the tomb? The story thus far of Martha, "the Jews," and even Mary (11:33) indicates that they still have much to learn. Thus Jesus prays loudly, announcing to the gathering his thanks to the Father for having heard him (v. 41c). The prayer is a proclamation to the group gathered at the now-opened tomb that the actions which will take place come from Jesus' oneness with the Father. "He is no magician, no *theios anēr*, who works by his own power and seeks his own *doxa*."[68] More, his actions indicate to the believer that Jesus is the Sent One of the Father.[69] The reader is aware of an approaching climax. The moment has come for Jesus to perform a deed which will show forth the glory of God, through which he will himself be glorified (see vv. 4, 40). It will provide a chance for the disciples (see vv. 15, 42), for "the Jews" (v. 42), and for both Martha (see vv. 26-27, 39, 42) and Mary (see vv. 33,

---

[66] See Kremer, *Lazarus*, 36–38; Schnelle, *Antidocetic Christology*, 134.

[67] Is this a prayer? The question is raised by Wilcox, "'Prayer' of Jesus," 130–32, who concludes that it has its origins in a pre-Johannine use of LXX Ps 117:21. For G. Reim, *Studien zum alttestamentlichen Hintergrund des Johannesevangeliums* (SNTSMS 22; Cambridge: Cambridge University Press, 1974) 219, Jesus' prayer of thanksgiving is a possible allusion to the prayer of Elijah in 1 Kgs 18:36-37.

[68] Bultmann, *John*, 408.

[69] There is a great distance between this prayer and Martha's belief that anything Jesus asks of God, even now God would do (see v. 22). Jesus' prayer is expressed in terms of a relationship between himself as the Son and the Sent One of the Father (vv. 41-42). This complements the *egō eimi* statement of v. 25, but transcends Mary's belief in Jesus as Messiah, Davidic Son of God, the one who is to come of v. 27.

42) to believe that God is made known through the words and actions of his Sent One, Jesus.

Jesus' crying out with a loud voice (*phōnē megalē*), into the emptiness of a dead man's tomb (v. 43b), is linked with his prayer (vv. 41-42): "When he had said this" (v. 43a). What is about to happen flows from the proclamation of Jesus' prayer to his Father: it is so that the people at the tomb might come to believe that Jesus is the Sent One of the Father (see v. 42b). Dramatically using his name, Jesus calls forth the dead man: *Lazare, deuro exō* (v. 43c). Jesus, the resurrection and the life (see v. 25), has total command over the dead Lazarus (see v. 26).[70] He comes forth from the cave, still tightly bound in the clothing of death (v. 44a).[71] The detailed report of the binding of his hands and feet with bandages and the cloth wrapping his face are a striking pictorial image for the reader, but this is, after all, the way a man who has been raised from the dead would have to come forth.[72] However, the reader also wonders why the clothing of death is described in such detail. Another gap has been created in the narrative that will not be filled until the reader arrives at the tomb of Jesus (see 19:40-41 [*mnēmeion kainon*]; 20:5-7).[73] The account of the miracle closes with Jesus' final double imperative (v. 44b: *lysate auton . . . aphete auton*). He orders the bystanders to unbind Lazarus from the clothing of death with which they had, only four days before, honored and respected his dead body.[74] He must be freed from the trappings of death to be free to go his way (*hypagein*), to return to normal life. The resurrection and the life (v. 25), the Sent One of the Father (v. 42), has intervened, making visible the action of God in the lives of all of them, not only Lazarus (see vv. 4, 40). The physical transformation of the dead body of Lazarus to the risen Lazarus is not the main point of the story. Jesus' action has revealed the *doxa tou theou* (see vv. 4, 40) so that the disciples might believe (see vv. 15, 42), so that Martha and Mary might believe (vv. 26, 40, 42), so that Mary and "the Jews" might believe (vv. 33, 42). The greater transformation would be acceptance on the part of all who witnessed the miracle that

[70] It is often rightly said that the miracle is a parabolic repetition of Jesus' self-revelation in vv. 25-27. See, for example, Dodd, *Interpretation*, 366–67; Byrne, *Lazarus*, 65.

[71] On two occasions the *phōnē* of Jesus is met by a positive response (see vv. 28-29, 43-44). See 5:25, 28 for Jesus' promise of the voice of the Son summoning the dead from their tombs.

[72] There is no need to raise the problem of how a man so bound could walk, as do Hoskyns, *Fourth Gospel*, 475; and Bultmann, *John*, 409. They suggest that we have a "miracle within a miracle" (Hoskyns). For the patristic discussion, see Bauer, *Johannesevangelium*, 154.

[73] See Byrne, *Lazarus*, 64–65; W. E. Reiser, "The Case of the Tidy Tomb: The Place of the Napkins of John 11:44 and 20:7," *HeyJ* 14 (1973) 47–57; B. Osborne, "A Folded Napkin in an Empty Tomb: John 11:44 and 20:7 Again," *HeyJ* 14 (1973) 437–40.

[74] It is often rightly remarked that the cloths are a sign that Lazarus will eventually die a definitive death.

Jesus was the Son of the Father, the Sent One of God (see v. 42).[75] A remarkable sign has shown the glory of God (v. 4c),[76] but the reader has yet to discover how the miracle of the raising of Lazarus will be the means by which
the Son of God will be glorified (v. 4d: *hina doxasthę̄ ho huios tou theou d'*
autēs).

VI. THE DECISION OF "THE JEWS": VERSES 45-54

Many of "the Jews" believe because of the miracle (v. 45), but some inform
their leaders what Jesus had done (v. 46). Those who believe are associated
with Mary. They had gone to Mary (see vv. 19), and had followed her when
she responded to the call of Jesus (v. 31).[77] Jesus has expressed angry emotion on account of their unbelief (see vv. 33, 38), but has performed a
great sign so that Mary and "the Jews" (among others) might come to
believe that he is the Sent One of the Father (see v. 42). Some of "the Jews"
come to faith. Throughout the growing conflict between Jesus and "the
Jews" heated discussions have regularly produced a remnant who believed
in him (see 7:31; 8:30; 10:42). The author singles out the name of Mary,
even though "the Jews" were originally reported as going to *both* Martha
and Mary (see v. 19). There must be some reason for the continued interest in the person of Mary. Some of "the Jews" return to the Pharisees (see
7:49) to report the deeds of Jesus.[78] Nothing is said of his words, his self-
revelation as the resurrection and the life (vv. 25-27), or his prayer that
they might come to faith in him as the Sent One of the Father (v. 42). They
have gone no further than Martha (see vv. 21-22) and report to the Pharisees that Jesus is a wonderful miracle worker (v. 46; contrast vv. 36-37).[79]
Faced with this difficulty, rightly understood as a rabble-rousing threat to
their established authority, the chief priests and the Pharisees gather the
council (*synedrion*).[80] The misunderstanding of some of "the Jews" con-

---

[75] See Kremer, *Lazarus*, 80; Schnelle, *Antidocetic Christology*, 134–35.

[76] The obvious omission of any domestic sequels keeps the reader's attention focused on
the significance of the events at a deeper level. See Marchadour, *Lazare*, 128–29.

[77] I read *hoi elthontes pros Mariam* as a recollection of their earlier approach to join Martha
and Mary (v. 19).

[78] There is no need for "the Pharisees" to be regarded as an official body, which would be
historically incorrect. On this, see Barrett, *St John*, 405.

[79] There is no malice in this report. Bauer, *Johannesevangelium*, 155; Bultmann, *John*,
409–10; and Haenchen, *John*, 2:74, regard the action of the Jews as a denunciation.

[80] The Sanhedrin, the governing council and chief court of the Jewish nation, is meant. For
the historical difficulties, which must again be resolved by recourse to the Johannine understanding of "the Jews," see W. Grundmann, "The Decision of the Supreme Court to Put Jesus
to Death (John 11:47-57) in Its Context: Tradition and Redaction in the Gospel of John," in

tinues: he is a worker of miracles who is attracting the people (v. 47a), and something must be done to bring his activities to an end, or else "every one" (*pantes*) will believe in him (vv. 47b-48a).[81]

The delicate balance of power between Rome and the local religious and political authorities at the time of Jesus[82] lies behind the Sanhedrin's conclusion that such popular messianic, miracle-working figures will create difficulties if left at liberty. No doubt, the terrible destruction of the Jewish War of 65–70 is reflected in the words of the leaders of "the Jews": "The Romans will come and destroy both our holy place and our nation" (v. 48).[83] Caiaphas, the high priest remembered as holding office in the year that Jesus was crucified, speaks up (v. 49ab).[84] Accusing his fellow leaders of an inability to think and plan correctly (vv. 49c-50a), he takes a position that is, ironically, opportunist yet full of meaning for the reader.[85] Many attempts have been made to trace a Jewish tradition that may have provided Caiaphas with the suggestion that the life may be sacrificed so

---

Jesus and the Politics of His Day, ed. E. Bammel and C. F. D. Moule (Cambridge: Cambridge University Press, 1984) 297–98.

[81] As Barrett, *St John*, 405, points out, a question is posed: "What are we doing?" (*ti poioumen?*). This gives the following *hoti* the meaning of "for," or "because." Bauer, *Johannesevangelium*, 155, suggests that the question ironically expects the answer, "Nothing!" Against many (e.g., Schnackenburg, *St John*, 2:347), who make the question a future: "What are we to do?"

[82] See W. Grimm, "Die Preisgabe eines Menschen zur Rettung des Volkes: Priesterliche Tradition bei Johannes und Josephus," in *Josephus-Studien: Untersuchungen zu Josephus, dem Antiken Judentum und dem Neuen Testament. Otto Michel zum 70. Geburtstag gewidmet*, ed. O. Betz, K. Haacker, and M. Hengel (Göttingen: Vandenhoeck & Ruprecht, 1974) 135. It is regularly pointed out that this scene replaces the Synoptic trial before the Jewish authorities.

[83] The use of *ho topos* refers to the Temple (see 4:20; Matt 24:15; Acts 6:13; 21:28), so intimately associated with the existence of Israel as a nation. See L. Cilia, *La morte di Gesù e l'unità degli uomini (Gv 11,47-53; 12,32): Contributo allo studio della soteriologia giovannea* (Bologna: Private publication, 1992) 21–31. Irony is present and will increase in the words of Caiaphas that follow. J. A. T. Robinson, *The Priority of John* (London: SCM Press, 1985) 70, 227, misses this. He regards these words as indicating that the Temple was still standing when the Fourth Gospel was written. But, ironically, the exact opposite is the case. For some, the leaders are concerned not about destruction, but about the loss of their authority as the Romans "take away" (*arousin*) their power base. See especially E. Bammel, "'Ex illa itaque die consilium fecerunt . . .' (John 11:53)," in *The Trial of Jesus: Cambridge Studies in Honour of C. F. D. Moule*, ed. E. Bammel (SBT 2/13; London: SCM Press, 1970) 20–26.

[84] The high priest was elected for life, not for a year. Thus, as Barrett, *St John*, 406, comments: "Caiaphas was high priest in that memorable year of our Lord's passion." This interpretation goes back to Origen (see Lagrange, *Saint Jean*, 314). Against this, see Becker, *Johannes*, 368-69, Bammel, "Ex illa," 38–39, and the discussion in Beasley-Murray, *John*, 197–98.

[85] See P. Duke, *Irony in the Fourth Gospel* (Atlanta: John Knox, 1985) 87–89. Grimm, "Die Preisgabe," 134–41, shows that such opportunism is well represented in Josephus's portrait of the priests.

that the rest of the nation might be saved (v. 50bc).[86] The rest of the Sanhedrin might well lack understanding on that question (vv. 49c-50a). But
there was a recent tradition that a good person might lay down his or her
life for the nation and effect God's blessing on them all.[87] The Maccabean
martyrs had been an example of this, and a tradition of a good person
dying for the nation was strong in first-century Israel. Ironically, Caiaphas
speaks of the value of ridding themselves of Jesus, a troublemaker, so that
the nation might profit.[88] But he is speaking in a way that recalls the tradition of the courageous and self-sacrificing martyrs for the nation, whose
death gave life to God's chosen people.[89]

Understanding the high priest as a spokesman for God, the narrator tells
the reader that the deeper meaning of Caiaphas's words are prophetic.
Caiaphas did not know what he was saying, but his being high priest led
him to prophesy unknowingly that Jesus would die for the nation (v. 51).[90]
But the benefits of Jesus' death cannot be limited to the people of Israel, as
were the deaths of the Maccabean martyrs.[91] The narrator reminds the

[86] Texts such as 2 Sam 20:22; Jonah 1:12-15; GenR 90:9; SamR 32:3; QohR 9:18,2 are cited.
See Bauer, Johannesevangelium, 156; and especially Bammel, "Ex illa," 26–32. M. Barker,
"John 11.50," in Trial of Jesus, 41–46, attempts to link Caiaphas's words with current mes-
sianic expectation. All the parallels are either too late or deal with genuine malefactors.

[87] For this suggestion, see Grimm, "Die Preisgabe," 140–41. The following generalizations
are based upon the so-called Maccabean literature (some of which may be as recent as A.D. 40
[4 Maccabees]). On the antiquity and importance of the cult to these martyrs, see E. Bam-
mell, "Zum jüdischen Märtyrerkult," in Judaica: Kleine Schriften I (WUNT 37; Tübingen:
J. C. B. Mohr [Paul Siebeck] 1986) 79–85.

[88] There is a textual difficulty in v. 50. Does Caiaphas say that it is expedient "for you"
(hymin: e.g., P[45], P[66], Vaticanus, Bezae, and some Vulgate manuscripts) or "for us" (hēmin:
e.g., Alexandrinus, Koridethi, Freer Gospels, Paris, Leningrad)? The pronoun is omitted by
Sinaiticus. The slightly superior external evidence and Caiaphas's assuming a superior position (shown in his contemptuous hymeis in v. 49) support hymin as the correct reading.

[89] Two words are used for Israel as a nation: laos, which applies to the chosen people, and
ethnos, which relates to its civic situation. See Bauer, Johannesevangelium, 156; Lagrange,
Saint Jean, 315. See J. Painter, "The Church and Israel in the Gospel of John: A Response," NTS
25 (1978–79) 103–12, who rightly argues that the two words represent traditional Israel. He
disagrees with S. Pancaro, "'People of God' in St John's Gospel," NTS 16 (1969–70) 114–29;
idem, "The Relationship of the Church to Israel in the Gospel of John," NTS 21 (1974–75) ✓
396–405, who claims that laos points toward the new Israel, the church. There is a development, but it is focused on the use of ethnos in vv. 51-52, rather than on laos.

[90] For the high priest as a prophet, see C. H. Dodd, "The Prophecy of Caiaphas: John 11:47-
53," in More New Testament Studies (Manchester: Manchester University Press, 1968) 63–66; P.
Schäfer, Die Vorstellung vom Heiligen Geist in der rabbinischen Literatur (SANT 28; Munich:
Kösel, 1972) 135–39; see also Josephus, War 1:68–69; Antiquities 6:115–16; 13:282-83, 299;
Philo, De Specialibus Legibus 4:191–92.

[91] Barrett, St John, 407, points out correctly (and gives Old Testament and Jewish parallels)
that Jesus' words could simply mean the gathering of dispersed Israelites. See also J. Beutler,
"Two Ways of Gathering: The Plot to Kill Jesus in John 11.47-53," NTS 40 (1994) 403–4. Léon-

reader that Jesus will die for Israel, but not only for that nation; his death will gather into one the children of God who are scattered abroad (v. 52; see 10:15-16). It will mark the beginnings of another nation (*ethnos*), a new community.[92] The *meaning* of the death of Jesus is explained to the reader in this comment from the narrator. Many hints given during the course of the story are now coming to a head. The hour of Jesus must be at hand (see 2:5; 7:20; 8:30). He will be lifted up, as Moses lifted up the serpent in the wilderness, so that all who believe in him might have life (see 3:14). Even those who lift him up might come to believe in Jesus as *egō eimi* (8:28). The death of Jesus will lead to the glorification of the Son of God (see v. 4). But there is more to the death of Jesus than *his* hour, *his* lifting up, and *his* glorification. The death of Jesus is not *for himself* but for others. He gives his life for his sheep (see 6:51c; 10:15), and in giving his life he gathers sheep of other folds (see 10:16), the children of God who are scattered abroad (11:52).

As yet there is little evidence that such a "gathering" is taking place. Some of the disciples (see 2:11; 6:68-69) and some of "the Jews" (see 7:31; 8:30; 10:42; 11:45) have believed in him, but the reader is aware that the motivations and the depth of this faith may leave a lot to be desired. It is with little opposition that "the Jews" take counsel, based on the words of Caiaphas, on the best way to put Jesus to death (v. 53). The story of the events surrounding the illness, death, and resurrection of Lazarus of Bethany close as they began: Jesus must depart to another place because he is unable to go about openly among "the Jews." His life is in danger (v. 54a; see 10:40; 11:5-8). He retires to a village close to the edge of the wilderness, still in the company of his disciples (v. 54b). But while his earlier stay in the remote village from which he came to Bethany was marked by many people who came to him there (see 10:41), at Ephraim he is alone with his disciples (11:54).

CONCLUSION

The die is cast. The reader is aware that the stay at the edge of the desert is but a brief pause in the narrative, as Jesus moves resolutely toward

---

Dufour, *Lecture*, 2:431–32 (and also Brown, *John*, 1:439) notices a subtle irony between the gathering of the synagogue (v. 47) and Jesus' gathering of the dispersed (v. 52). See also Beutler, "Two Ways," 399–402.

[92] The expression *ethnos* has now been given a broader—all embracing—meaning. Painter, "Church and Israel," 112, is too restrictive, only allowing the images of John 10 and 15 as ecclesial. As Brown, *John*, 1:443, strongly contends, v. 52 argues not only for the universality of salvation but also for its communitarian nature. John may not mention "the church," but the dispersed children of God are to be gathered and formed into one (*synagagē eis hen*).

violence, informing his disciples, Martha, Mary, and "the Jews" that he will be glorified by means of it (see v. 4), that he is the resurrection and the life (vv. 25-26), and that his deeds show forth the glory of God for them to believe that he is the Sent One of the Father (vv. 40, 42). The reader has also been told that Jesus' death would gather into one the children of God who are scattered abroad (vv. 51-52). Hence with mixed feelings the reader looks forward to violent events that will be the perfection of the hour: Jesus' lifting up, his glorification, the revelation of the glory of God, and the gathering of many.

But there is one figure at Bethany whose story has only been partly told. Of the two women in the story, Mary made a promising response to Jesus' call (see vv. 28-32), only to be swept up into the emotion created by Lazarus's death, joining "the Jews" in their tears (see v. 33). Has the miracle of Lazarus done anything for her belief in Jesus? What of the anointing, mentioned by the narrator in v. 2? The reader has been reminded of her role when told of "the Jews" who came to faith in Jesus. They were those who had gone to Mary (see v. 45). Although the initial report of "the Jews'" going to mourn over Lazarus told the reader that they went to *both* Martha and Mary (see v. 19), as "the Jews" come to faith, *only* Mary is mentioned (v. 45). The reader looks forward to a fuller report of the events mentioned in v. 2, in the hope that this woman, who began so well in her response to Jesus, might have a fitting conclusion to her story.

Chapter Seven

The Hour Has Come
John 11:55—12:50

¶ THE READER WAITS with Jesus and his disciples at Ephraim, after the resurrection of Lazarus (11:38-44), and the subsequent planning of the "the Jews" to put him to death (11:53-54). Jesus has told his disciples that the Son of God would be glorified by means of the resurrection of Lazarus (11:4), and the unresolved question of an anointing remains in the background (11:2).

THE SHAPE OF THE NARRATIVE

The characters, time, space, and argument of 11:55—12:50 shape the narrative as follows:

 I. *11:55-57:* Introduction. The main characters, the time, and the major themes are introduced: "the Jews" (vv. 55-56), the chief priests and the Pharisees (v. 57), and Jesus (vv. 56-57); the time is the Passover (v. 55), marked by superficiality (vv. 55-56), and the threat to the life of Jesus (v. 57).
 II. *12:1-8:* The anointing of Jesus. Mary fulfills the prolepsis of 11:2: she anoints the feet of Jesus and wipes them with her hair, as Judas complains.
 III. *12:9-19:* The entry of Jesus into Jerusalem. Jesus' entry is framed by passages that refer to Lazarus.[1]

---

[1] This frame is missed by those who read 12:1-11 as the anointing.

(a) *12:9-11:* Jesus and Lazarus. "The Jews" decide to eliminate Jesus *and* Lazarus. The narrator comments: "Many of the Jews were going away and believing in Jesus" (v. 11).

(b) *12:12-16:* The entry into Jerusalem. Jesus enters Jerusalem, and his disciples do not—as yet—understand the full meaning of the events. But "when Jesus was glorified, they remembered" (v. 16).

(c) *12:17-19:* Jesus and Lazarus. Because of Lazarus, Jesus attracts the crowds. The Pharisees complain: "The world has gone after him" (v. 19).

IV. *12:20-36:* The coming of the Greeks and the arrival of the hour. Greeks ask to see Jesus (vv. 20-22). His response is a discourse on the arrival of "the hour," broken only by a voice from heaven (v. 28b) and misunderstanding (vv. 29, 34). Jesus leaves the scene (v. 36b).

V. *12:37-50:* A double conclusion to the public ministry. The narrator reflects on the failure of "the Jews" to accept Jesus (vv. 37-43), and Jesus summarizes the significance of his public ministry with words situated in neither time nor place (vv. 44-50).

READING THE NARRATIVE

I. INTRODUCTION: 11:55-57

Solemnly introducing the feast (*ēn de engys to pascha tōn Ioudaiōn*), the narrator takes the reader away from the fringes of the desert (see 11:54) to the crowds (*polloi . . . ek tēs chōras*) who go up to Jerusalem and are bustling about in order to fulfill ritual purifications in preparation for the celebration of the feast (see Num 9:6-13; 2 Chr 30:15-19; Josephus, *War* 1.229; 6:290; *Pesaḥim* 9:1).[2] As the narrative moves toward the arrest and slaying of Jesus by the leaders of "the Jews" (see 11:53), the crowds are seeing to their ritual lustrations in preparation for the celebration of "the feast of the Jews." The irony is intensified as the narrator reports that the crowds were seeking Jesus (v. 56a: *ezētoun oun ton Iēsoun*). The verb *zēteō* marks "the Jews'" attempts to arrest and kill Jesus (see 5:18; 7:1, 19-20, 25, 30; 8:37, 40; 10:39).

Jesus has become a matter for discussion (v. 56b: *ti dokei hymin?*). The crowd suggests that he will probably not come to this particular feast. The chief priests and the Pharisees had given orders: whoever knows where

---

[2] The technical term for purification, *agnizein,* is used (see also Acts 21:24, 26; 24:18). See F. Hauck, "*agnos ktl.,*" *TDNT* 1:123.

Jesus is should let them know, so that they might arrest him (v. 57).[3] As the Passover approaches (v. 55), Jesus is away from the scene, with his disciples at the fringe of the desert (v. 54). "The Jews" have made public their decision that Jesus must die for the nation (vv. 50, 57), and the chattering crowds go about their lustrations (vv. 55-56).

II. THE ANOINTING OF JESUS: 12:1-8

Six days before the feast of the Passover,[4] Jesus returns to Bethany. The narrator reminds the reader that Lazarus, the person whom Jesus had raised from the dead, lived in Bethany (v. 1b).[5] Not only does Jesus return to the village, but he shares a meal with the family of Lazarus (v. 2a).[6] Martha, earlier the leading figure of the events of Bethany (see 11:17-27), now serves (v. 2b). The reader senses that Martha's previous arrogance (see 11:21-24, 27, 39) has been transformed,[7] but the narrator focuses the reader's attention on Lazarus: "Lazarus was one of those at table with him" (12:2c). Mary becomes the main protagonist in events that fill the gap created by the prolepsis of 11:2: she anoints Jesus' feet and she wipes his feet with her hair (12:3). The narrator describes the actions of Mary, anointing his feet and wiping them with her hair, repeating the verbs used as aorist participles in 11:2. Now the deed is done (*ēleipsen . . . exemaxen*). Although a parallel scene is reported in the Synoptic tradition (see Mark 14:3-9; Matt 26:6-13; Luke 7:36-50), its use here is entirely determined by its Johannine context.[8] The choice of the feet, rather than the more usual anointing of the head, both fulfills the prolepsis of 11:2 and indicates the uniqueness of the event. It is not a royal anointing, nor a welcome for an honored guest. A part of the body is anointed, followed by an extravagant wiping with the hair. What does it mean? This question will be answered

---

[3] The historically unlikely combination of "the chief priests and the Pharisees" is used by the narrator to indicate the leaders of "the Jews." See 7:32, 45; 11:47. On the Johannine nature of this combination, see K. Tsuchido, "Tradition and Redaction in John 12.1-43," *NTS* 30 (1984) 610.

[4] There is no need to trace symbolism in these six days.

[5] The reference to the resurrection of Lazarus is somewhat heavy-handed, and has led to both textual variants and suggestions that it is a gloss. See Barrett, *St John*, 410–11.

[6] The verb *epoiēsan* has no subject, but the reader supposes, from the context, that the family at Bethany (Lazarus and his sisters) provides the meal. See Becker, *Johannes*, 2:373.

[7] Scott, *Sophia*, 212–14, reads this remark as a pointer to the continued response of the perfect disciple to the revelation of Jesus as Sophia incarnate.

[8] For the discussion, see Moloney, *Son of Man*, 164–66.

by Jesus in v. 7.[9] The abundance of affection is accentuated by the remark from the narrator that the house was filled with the fragrance of the ointment.

Some scholars, following a rabbinic tradition and Clement of Alexandria, understand this remark as the Johannine version of Mark 14:9: the spreading of the odor is a symbol of the spread of the message of the gospel throughout the gentile world.[10] Loisy takes this further, understanding the whole incident as a symbol of the gentile church receiving the gospel message at the feet of Jesus.[11] The gesture is one of affection and dedication, and the spreading of the odor is a striking way to tell the reader of its extravagance. It is also a final moment of contrast between Martha and Mary. Martha objected that an evil odor would come from the tomb of the deceased Lazarus (11:39), but Mary's loving gesture fills the house with fragrance (12:3).[12] Judas Iscariot, already known as a disciple who will betray Jesus (see 6:60, 71), is introduced (v. 4a),[13] reminding the reader of Judas's status (v. 4b). The passion of Jesus is at hand. Judas objects to the extravagance. Such a wasteful spreading about of the *nardos pistikēs* has no place in the ministry of a man like Jesus, or of his disciples.[14] Such a precious possession could have been sold for a large amount of money (300 denarii),[15] and the proceeds given to the poor (v. 5). Such activity may have been part of the mission of the historical Jesus, but it plays no role in his activity and teaching in the Fourth Gospel.[16] The reader, already warned of the treachery of Judas, is aware that social concern cannot be the real motive for his objection. The narra-

---

[9] On the uniqueness of the gesture, see B. Prete, "'I poveri' nel racconto giovanneo dell'unzione di Betania (Giov. 12,1-18)," in *Evangelizare Pauperibus: Atti della XXIV Settimana Biblica Associazione Biblica Italiana* (Brescia: Paideia, 1978) 435. Lindars, *John*, 416–17, suggests that this is a gesture of humility that points forward to the footwashing of chap. 13.

[10] See *EcclesR* 7:1; *SongR* 1:22; Ignatius, *Ephesians* 17:1; Clement of Alexandria, *Paedagogus* 2:8 (PG 8:466–90). On this, see Bauer, *Johannesevangelium*, 159; Hoskyns, *Fourth Gospel*, 415; Strachan, *Fourth Gospel*, 248.

[11] Loisy, *Quatrième évangile*, 362–63. See also Brodie, *John*, 407, who extends the idea to a message that fills the whole of creation (see Eph 1:23).

[12] Suggested by Lee, *Symbolic Narratives*, 222 n. 2.

[13] Via Judas, the reader links Mary's gesture with Jesus' death. See Tsuchido, "Tradition and Redaction," 610–11.

[14] On the ointment, mentioned by both Mark (14:3) and John, see Moloney, *Son of Man*, 164. Its description indicates its costliness.

[15] A denarius was a day's wage.

[16] A recent study, R. J. Karris, *Jesus and the Marginalized in John's Gospel* (Zacchaeus Studies: New Testament; Collegeville: Liturgical Press, 1990), strains to find evidence to the contrary. Prete, "I poveri," 439–44, makes a link between the archetypal selfishness of Judas and the continual presence of the poor.

tor informs further: Judas is not interested in the poor. He is a thief, and has taken from the money box that he is supposed to administer (v. 6). While Mary shows her extravagant love and dedication, Judas, who will betray Jesus unto death, objects because of his self-interest. Who has rightly appreciated the presence of Jesus: Mary or Judas?

The anointing is explained in the notoriously difficult words of Jesus in v. 7. They close the episode and show that Mary, who earlier had promisingly responded to the call of the Good Shepherd (10:28-32), concludes her role in the Gospel by being the first to understand the significance of the death of Jesus. There has been considerable discussion over the sense of *hina . . . tērēsē auto*. The Greek should be translated: "So that she might keep it for the preparation of my burial."[17] Is Mary to keep some of the ointment for the anointing of Jesus after his death?[18] If so, what grounds did Judas have for complaint if the ointment had not already been used (see v. 5)? A major break should be made after *aphes autēn*. Jesus commands: "Leave her alone." He then begins a new sentence: "The purpose was that (*hina*) she might keep this for the day of preparation for my burial."[19] The day of Jesus' presence in Bethany, at table with Lazarus (see v. 2), is the day of preparation for the burial of Jesus. The passion is at hand, and Mary's action is preparation for the death of Jesus. "The reader is invited to see in Mary's action a symbolic embalming of His body for burial, as though he were already dead."[20] For the first time in the narrative, Jesus' proximate death is recognized, and Mary has symbolized the singular significance of that death by the anointing of his body, and wiping it with her hair.

The words of Jesus that close the episode enhance this reading (v. 8).[21] Human history produces poor people (see Deut 15:11) who will always be among us. However, a once-and-for-all event has cut across that story and entered it for a brief time: the inbreak of the Logos (see 1:14). Jesus, the

---

[17] The word *entaphismos* does not mean "burial" but "laying out for burial." See LSJ, 575, s.v.

[18] See Bauer, *Johannesevangelium*, 159; Westcott, *St John*, 178. In Mark 14:3 the jar is broken, but this is not mentioned in John.

[19] See Brown, *John*, 1:449. For a full discussion of the difficulties and possibilities for v. 7, see J. A. Kleist, "A Note on the Greek Text of St. John 12,7," *Classical Journal* 21 (1925) 46–48; W. Kühne, "Eine kritische Studie zu Joh. 12,7," *Theologische Studien und Kritiken* 98–99 (1926) 476–77.

[20] Lightfoot, *St John*, 236. Against those who see the anointing as royal. See, for example, J. E. Bruns, "A Note on Jn 12,3," *CBQ* 28 (1966) 219–22; Barrett, *St John*, 409.

[21] Against those who see the verse as having little to do with the context, or regard it as an addition. For a survey, see R. Holst, "The One Anointing of Jesus: Another Application of the Form-Critical Method," *JBL* 95 (1976) 444–46. It is omitted by Bezae and the Sinaitic Syriac. P[75] has a shorter text. The verse must be regarded as original.

Sent One of the Father (see, most recently, 11:42) and the presence of the one "from above" (see 3:13; 6:62; 8:23), meets little recognition from the characters. He is with them for a very short period (see 7:32-36; 8:12-14; 9:4-5), and only Mary commits herself unconditionally to his presence. She first appeared in the story responding to Jesus' presence with trust (see 11:29-32). However, the grief created by the loss of her brother engulfed her, and she faltered as she joined "the Jews" in their mourning and tears (v. 33). Jesus raised her brother, to show the believer the glory of God (v. 40), and so that the bystanders might come to believe that Jesus is the Sent One of the Father (see v. 42). The miracle has brought one of those bystanders to an unconditional commitment of faith. In a proleptic anticipation of the glorification of the Son (see 11:4), highlighted by Judas's selfish rejection of her gesture (12:4-6), she anoints his body for death (11:2; 12:3). She has returned to her acceptance of Jesus as the Good Shepherd who lays down his life for his sheep (see 10:14-15, 18; 11:28-32; 12:3, 7-8). The final events of Jesus' public ministry are surrounded with superficiality (see 11:16, 21-22, 24, 27, 39, 55-56) and the threat of a violent death (see 11:57; 12:4-6, 8), but the luminous presence and symbolic action of Mary (see 11:2, 28-32, 45; 12:3, 7-8) point the reader toward a more positive understanding of the violent events that lie ahead.

III. JESUS' ENTRY INTO JERUSALEM: 12:9-19

The Decision to Kill Both Jesus and Lazarus: 12:9-11
"A great crowd of the Jews" came to know that Jesus was at Bethany, and thus they went out to the village (v. 9a). The motivation for this short journey, however, was not only to see the miracle worker; they were curious to see Lazarus as well (v. 9b). The plan to kill Jesus is already in place (see 11:57), but now the chief priests are faced with Jesus' increased popularity because of the raising of Lazarus.[22] They decide that it is opportune also to rid themselves of Lazarus, living evidence that Jesus is a miracle worker (v. 10). The crucial expression in the narrator's bland report is "also" (*hina kai ton Lazaron apokteinōsin*). The narrator concludes his brief report of these events, and the danger of their consequences for Lazarus, by commenting: "On account of him many of the Jews were going away and believing in Jesus" (v. 11). Jesus is being widely recognized as a miracle worker (see 11:47-48).[23] However, the reader senses the development of

---

[22] The author continues to use unlikely combinations (here, "Pharisees" and "chief priests") to speak of opposition to Jesus.

[23] This is still a limited faith. See Becker, *Johannes*, 2:375. Against, for example, Lindars, *John*, 420; and Carson, *John*, 431, who see this as leaving Judaism to become disciples.

another theme. In 10:15-16 and in 11:50-52 the reader was informed that
the death of Jesus would lead to a "gathering." Now, as the plot to kill Jesus
intensifies, many of the Jews are going away and believing in him (12:11).

The Entry of Jesus into Jerusalem: 12:12-16
On the following day the crowd in Jerusalem for the celebration of the
feast receives news that Jesus is coming into the city. The different
"crowds" (ho ochlos) that appear in vv. 9-19 (see vv. 9, 12, 17) have a place
in the deliberate design of the author. There has been a crowd of "the
Jews" in Bethany, many of whom come to believe in Jesus because of the
miracle (see v. 11). Another crowd is still in the city of Jerusalem, described
in 11:55-56, performing their rituals in preparation for Passover, wondering whether Jesus would come to the celebration. Now they hear that he is
coming to Jerusalem (v. 12b). It is from the superficial background of lustrations and chatter that they go out to meet Jesus.[24] They take palm
branches and sing his praises with an adaptation of Ps 118:25-26 (v. 13).
Both the palm branches (ta baïa) and the use of the psalm reflect the
superficiality of the crowd in the city. The only use of ta baïa in the LXX is
in 1 Macc 13:51, where the Jews enter and take possession of Jerusalem
after Simon had conquered the Jerusalem citadel in 142 B.C. Palm fronds
also appear on coins from 140 B.C. to A.D. 70, bearing the inscription "For
the redemption of Zion." The use of palm fronds is closely associated with
Maccabean nationalism.[25] Only the Fourth Gospel has the crowd welcoming Jesus into the city with ta baïa in their hands. The people in the crowd
are welcoming *their* expected national, political Messiah. The gesture is
further interpreted in this direction by the words that the crowd adds to
Psalm 118: kai ho basileus tou Israēl.[26] Like the crowds by the side of the
lake in 6:14-15, they wished to make Jesus *their* king.

Earlier in the story, Jesus had fled before an attempt to make him king
(see 6:14-15). Now as the end is approaching, he does not flee but enters
the city on an ass (v. 14).[27] In doing so, he faces their acclamations, cor-

---

[24] On the issue of the relationship between this account and the Synoptic tradition (see
Mark 11:1-11; Matt 21:1-11; Luke 19:29-38), see the summary in Brown, *John*, 1:459-61. As
always, there is little consensus, ranging from Marcan dependence to a separate Johannine
tradition.

[25] See especially W. R. Farmer, "The Palm Branches in John 12,13," *JTS* 3 (1952) 62–66. See
also H. St. J. Hart, "Judea and Rome: The Official Commentary," *JTS* 3 (1952) 172–98, and
plates I–III, for evidence of the Roman use of the palm in coins used to commemorate *Judea
Capta*.

[26] The acclamation "Hosanna" (see Ps 118:25) is a petition: "give salvation," but the reader
understands it as an acclamation. See Carson, *John*, 423.

[27] The adversative nature of his actions is indicated by the use of de (heurōn de ho Iēsous).

recting them in the light of the prophecy of Zechariah (v. 15; see Zech 9:9).[28] That Jesus does not deny or flee from this royal acclamation (see John 1:49; 6:14-15) makes the reader aware that the story has taken a dramatic turn. Jesus faces the faulty acclamations and sets about correcting them. Jesus is not the royal king welcomed by the crowds (v. 13), but he is a king (v. 15b: *idou ho basileus sou erchetai*) who comes into the city seated (see v. 14a: *ekathisen ep' auto*)—not "riding" or "mounted"—on an ass rather than a war chariot (v. 15c).[29] A king he is, but not the king expected by the crowds who welcome him into Jerusalem with palm fronds and a royal acclamation.[30] This impression is heightened by the prolepsis that the narrator introduces in a reflection on the response of the disciples. They did not understand this "at first" (*to prōton*). As bystanders in the "story time" of the events as they were happening, the disciples are unable to understand (v. 16a). Jesus is being welcomed as the king of Israel, but he challenges that welcome. The narrator informs the reader that later (*all' hote*), they came to recognize that the words from Zechariah, about a messiah who rides an ass into Jerusalem had been written about Jesus, and it had happened to him (v. 16c). What made the difference? They eventually come to a right understanding of these events—and also of the true meaning of the prophecy of Zechariah—after the glorification of Jesus (v. 16b). The reader is lured further into the narrative. Jesus is not king of Israel in the way expected by the crowd, but the Messiah prophesied by Zechariah. The fulfillment of the prophecy is linked to the moment of Jesus' glorification, which will take place some time in the future, when something will be *done* to Jesus.

The Gathering of the Crowd to Meet the Miracle Worker: 12:17-19

The narrator recalls "the Jews" who had mourned with Martha and Mary (see 11:19, 31), who had gone to the tomb, witnessed the resurrection of Lazarus (see vv. 42-44), and come to faith in Jesus as a miracle worker (see v. 45). They are "the crowd who had been with him when he called Lazarus

---

[28] The quotation is very loose, perhaps influenced by Isa 44:2; Isa 40:9; Zeph 3:16; or Gen 49:11. On this, see Barrett, *St John*, 418–19; and especially M. J. J. Menken, "Die Redaktion des Zitates aus Sach 9,9 in Joh 12,15," *ZNW* 80 (1989) 193–209.

[29] See Schuchard, *Scripture Within Scripture*, 71–84. The Zechariah passage conveys the idea of the Messiah who comes on a donkey rather than a war chariot (see Lindars, *John*, 424). Brown, *John*, 1:462–63, rightly rejecting the humility theme, suggests that the real point of the passage is its reference to the context of Zeph 3:9-10, which tells of a *universal* king, as does the context of Zech 9:9 (see 9:11).

[30] Against Barrett, *St John*, 416, who sees the entry as a proclamation that Jesus is the messianic king.

out of the tomb" (12:17).[31] They gave testimony (*emartyrei*) to the fact of the miracle. The imperfect tense of the verb indicates that they made it part of their ongoing conversations about Jesus.[32] The narrator looks back to a moment before the entry of Jesus into Jerusalem, informing the reader that the story of Lazarus's raising was the motive for the people's going out to meet Jesus. While there is no ill will in the crowds, there is no progress in faith. The crowds involved in vv. 9-19 are attracted to Jesus because of their interest in him as a miracle worker (see v. 9: the crowd who went out to see Lazarus as well as Jesus; v. 17: the crowd who had been at the miracle; vv. 12, 18: the crowd who had welcomed him into Jerusalem). These "crowds" are not motivated by a genuine understanding of Jesus as the Sent One of the Father (see 11:42). The kingly welcome that they afforded him (see vv. 12-13) is a public statement of their hope that Jesus will respond to their royal messianic expectations.

However limited the faith of the crowds might be, the Pharisees have every reason to be concerned (v. 19). The political problems with the Romans remain (see 11:47-48). Whatever actions the leaders of "the Jews" may have taken in asking that Jesus' whereabouts be made known so that they might arrest him (see 11:57) are fruitless (12:19b: *ouk ōpheleite ouden*). Advancing on the comment made by the narrator in v. 11, that many Jews were going to Jesus, they now complain: "The world has gone after him" (v. 19c). As they lament the dangerous gathering of more and more people around Jesus, the words of Jesus (see 10:15-16), of Caiaphas (11:50), and of the narrator (11:52) are being fulfilled. But an essential element in the "gathering" is that the Good Shepherd lay down his life (10:15), that one man should die (11:50-52). The reader knows that if "the world" is attracted to Jesus, the hour of his violent death (see 7:30; 8:20) must also be at hand.

IV. THE HOUR HAS COME: 12:20-36

Among the large crowds who went up to worship were some Greeks (*ēsan de Hellēnes tines*). Their presence in Jerusalem for the Passover (see 11:55; 12:1; see Josephus, *War* 6:427; 7:45) makes them Greeks by birth, "God-fearers" who admired and lived Judaism as best they could from within

---

[31] Taking the more difficult reading *hote*, along with the majority of witnesses (e.g., Sinaiticus, Vaticanus, Alexandrinus, Freer Gospels, Koridethi), rather than the smoother, but less strongly witnessed *hoti* (e.g., P66, Bezae, Claromontanus). This reading links the crowd with those who had been at the resurrection of Lazarus.

[32] See Brown, *John*, 1:458.

their limitations.[33] Their desire to see Jesus (see vv. 21-22) is proof that, ironically, the words of the Pharisees are true: "The world has gone after him" (v. 19). These people need intermediaries familiar with their world so that they might attain their desires. Because they are Greek (v. 21a: *oun*), they go to a disciple with a Greek name, Philip, who came from Bethsaida in Galilee, a town on the northern periphery of Israel, close to the gentile Decapolis. There is more to the request "to see Jesus" (v. 22b: *thelomen ton Iēsoun idein*) than simple curiosity. Although many places in the Fourth Gospel use the verb *eidon* for the everyday experience of seeing, the reader is familiar with the use of the verbs "to see" (*horaō* and its substitute *eidon*) within contexts that are associated with the affirmation, the acceptance, or the refusal of Jesus' role as the revealer (see 1:18, 33, 34, 39, 50, 51; 3:3, 11, 32, 36; 4:45; 5:37; 6:2, 36, 46; 8:38, 57; 9:37; 11:32, 40).[34] In the immediate context of this request, Jesus has informed the man born blind, who was searching for the Son of Man to believe in him, that he was the one he could see (9:37: *heōrakas auton*). He has told Martha that she would see (*opsḗ*) the glory of God, if only she would believe (11:40). The Greeks are presented to the reader as desiring such sight. The gentile nature of the seekers is accentuated as Philip goes to another disciple with a Greek name, Andrew, who—the reader recalls—comes from the same town as Philip (see 1:44; see also their association in 6:7-8).[35] Together they speak to Jesus (v. 22).

The scene has been set. The advent of the Greeks is the event that triggers Jesus' explanation of the hour of his glorification (vv. 23-36). The discourse, broken by words from heaven (see v. 28bc) and from the crowd (see vv. 29, 34), unfolds in the following manner:[36]

1. (a) A first revelation (vv. 23-28a): the hour of the glorification of the Son of Man, with an explanation given by a heavenly voice (v. 28b).

    (b) The crowd misunderstands this revelation (v. 29), and the misunderstanding leads to further explanation from Jesus (v. 30).

---

[33] For a full discussion, see H. B. Kossen, "Who were the Greeks of John XII 20?" in *Studies in John: Presented to Dr. J. N. Sevenster on the Occasion of His Seventieth Birthday* (NovTSup 24; Leiden: E. J. Brill, 1970) 97–110.

[34] This is particularly the case for *horaō*. *Eidon* is generally used for everyday events. However, *idein* is used in 12:21 as a substitute second aorist for *horaō*. See BDF, 54, para. 101. For J. Beutler, "Greeks Come to See Jesus (John 20,20f)," *Bib* 71 (1990) 333–47 (especially 342–45), this request is linked to LXX Isa 52:15, and forms part of a wide-ranging use of Isaian servant material across John 12:20-50.

[35] They are the only two disciples whose names are known only in their Greek form.

[36] Many commentators suggest a threefold division: vv. 23-26, 27-30, 31-36a. I am following the suggestions of I. de la Potterie, "L'exaltation du Fils de l'homme (Jn. 12,31-36)," *Greg* 49 (1968) 461-62.

2. (a) A second revelation (vv. 31-33): the judgment of the world and the lifting up of Jesus (vv. 31-32), with an explanation provided by the narrator (v. 33).
   (b) The crowd misunderstands this revelation (v. 34), and the misunderstanding leads to further explanation from Jesus (vv. 35-36a).
3. The narrator reports Jesus' final departure from the scene: Jesus hid himself from them (v. 36b).

The Hour of the Son of Man: 12:23-30

The theme of "gathering," which has been emerging since 10:15-16 (see 11:50-52; 12:11, 19), is dramatically developed as the request of the Greeks reaches Jesus. The hour has come (v. 23a)! The tension created by the hour that had not yet come (see 2:4; 7:6, 8, 30; 8:20) is resolved. The hour can be put off no longer, because the world is coming to Jesus (see vv. 20-22). The gathering at the hour of Jesus is also the glorification of the Son of Man (v. 23b). The hour has come and is still present: the verb is in the perfect tense (*elēlythen*). The events of Lazarus are to lead to the glorification of the Son (see 11:4), and Jesus announces that it is taking place now. But it is spoken of as the glorification of "the Son of Man." The reader recalls the association of "the Son of Man" with a "lifting up" (see 3:14; 8:28), with the self-gift of Jesus as the revelation of God (see 6:27, 51c-53). There can be no mistaking the message: Jesus is about to be slain, but the hour of his death is his lifting up, his glorification, his self-gift for the life of the world, the moment of gathering.[37]

The image of the single grain of wheat that will remain alone unless it falls into the ground and dies is eloquent and applies to Jesus. Death produces fruit. The theme of "gathering" forms the background (see 10:15-16; 11:50-51; 12:11, 19). However, it has further ramifications. The image of the seed that must die to be fruitful is eloquent, even though—the reader senses—it does not entirely correspond to the hour of Jesus. The seed must "fall into the earth" (*pesōn eis tēn gēn*) to bear much fruit, but the death of Jesus has been described as a "lifting up" (see 3:14: *hypsōthēnai dei*; see also 8:28). Jesus' use of the image of falling into the earth to speak of the fruitfulness of death also instructs the bystanders: those who wish to come to eternal life must, like him, be prepared to lay down their lives in self-gift (v. 25). But there is more to this self-gift than generosity. The disciple of Jesus is called to reverse the attitude of Jesus' opponents who are unable to accept the revelation of the Father in and through Jesus. They are clinging with closed fists to what is theirs: they love their life (v. 25a:

---

[37] For a detailed study of "the Son of Man" in 12:23, see Moloney, *Son of Man*, 176-81.

ho philōn tēn psychēn autou).[38] They make an absolute of what this world can offer (v. 25b: *en tǭ kosmǭ toutǭ*). This can only lead to its loss. The one who is prepared to let go, to hate this life (*ho misōn tēn psychēn autou*), has eternal life (*zēn aiōnion*): a totally satisfying life both now and hereafter.[39] The disciple must be where Jesus is—and there self-gift in love is crucial. The follower (*ean . . . emoi akoloutheitō*) is the servant *(ean emoi . . . diakonǭ)*, and must be where the Master is (v. 26ab).[40] But there is more to the relationship between Jesus and the disciple than a master and a servant, a follower who imitates his leader (v. 25) and who is where his master is (v. 26a). Jesus points to the Father and informs his listeners that service of Jesus, looking beyond the absolutes of this world, being where he is, falling into the ground in a loving "letting go" of the absolutes imposed by "this world" so that fruit might be produced, will lead to the servant being honored by the Father (v. 26c). All known paradigms of servants and masters are shattered as the reader is informed that any one who follows Jesus and serves him by being where he is, falling into the ground to bear fruit, will be honored by the Father.[41]

Having briefly associated others with his mission of fruitful loss of self unto death, Jesus turns back to his own situation.[42] In a passage that has connection with Synoptic Gethsemane traditions (see especially Mark 14:34), Jesus speaks of the terror that he feels as the hour is now with him (v. 27a).[43] The use of *nyn*, "*Now* is my soul troubled," links this anguish with the "hour" of v. 23: it has come.[44] Jesus asks his Father to bring him safely through this hour (v. 27b). Jesus' life has been a continual response

---

[38] On *psychē* in the sense of a person's human experience of life in 12:25 (as in 10:15—but not in 12:27), see Brown, *John*, 1:467.

[39] See W. A. Beardslee, "Saving One's Life by Losing It," *JAAR* 47 (1979) 57–72.

[40] This does not only mean suffering, although that is the main point of the immediate context. There is a hint here, which will be developed later in the Gospel (especially in chap. 17), of the disciples' eventually being swept into the oneness that unites the Father and the Son (see 17:24-26).

[41] For Léon-Dufour, *Lecture*, 2:465–66, behind Jesus' words lies a community coming to grips with the physical reality of death by martyrdom that forms part of following Jesus to the cross. These words were no doubt eloquent in a community suffering exclusion and death because of their faith in Jesus (see 9:22; 12:42; 16:2).

[42] Against G. C. Nicholson, *Death as Departure: The Johannine Descent-Ascent Schema* (SBLDS 63; Chico: Scholars Press, 1983) 124, who considers vv. 20-26 as directed to the disciples and vv. 27-36a as directed to the crowd.

[43] As Schnackenburg, *St John*, 2:387, comments rightly, "Even in John, the cross has not lost its human darkness." See also W. Thüsing, *Die Erhöhung und Verherrlichung Jesu im Johannesevangelium* (3d ed.; NTAbh XXI/1–2; Münster: Aschendorff, 1979) 78–82.

[44] On the link between this use of *tarassō*, Psalms 42/43, and Gethsemane traditions, see Thüsing, *Erhöhung*, 79–88; and J. Beutler, "Psalm 42/43 im Johannesevangelium," *NTS* 25 (1978–79) 34–38. For Nicholson, *Death as Departure*, 127–29, Jesus' emotion is created by concern over the future steadfastness of the disciples.

to the will of his Father, bringing to perfection the task that the Father gave him to do (see 4:34). The hour has now come (v. 23), and Jesus has no doubt that his Father will lead him through it.[45] There is no surprise in Jesus' statement of confidence in the Father, as the purpose of Jesus' presence has been determined by the hour that is now with him (v. 27c). Jesus goes into the hour with determination, trust, and full awareness, because the Father stands behind his actions, and everything that Jesus does is for the Father. Paralleling his appeal to the Father to bring him safely through the hour, Jesus now asks that the name of the Father be glorified (v. 28a).[46] However central Jesus is to the story, the reader does not lose contact with the never-failing and directing presence of God: the Father leads Jesus safely through the hour (v. 27b) . . . the Father's name is to be glorified (v. 28a).

Jesus' prayer is met by "the Father's answer."[47] A voice from heaven speaks of the glorification of the name of God as both past and future. These words inform the reader of the critical nature of the present discourse, interpreting all that has happened in the story so far, and all that is yet to take place. Throughout the ministry, the words and deeds of Jesus have glorified the name of God (v. 28c: *edoxasa*). Those who have believed have seen the revelation of the *doxa* (see 2:4; 9:3; 11:40).[48] The hour has come (v. 23), but the voice from heaven assures Jesus (and the reader) that what is yet to come will also glorify the name of God (v. 28c: *palin doxasō*).[49] Both the word of Jesus (v. 23) and the word from heaven (v. 28c)

---

[45] For this interpretation of v. 27b as a statement rather than a question, respecting that the hour has already come, see Westcott, *John*, 182, and the earlier discussion summarized by Lagrange, *Saint Jean*, 332–33. It is further developed in X. Léon-Dufour, "Père, fais-moi passer sain et sauf à travers cette heure! (Jean 12,27)," in *Neues Testament und Geschichte: Historisches Geschehen und Deutung im Neuen Testament: Oscar Cullmann zum 70. Geburtstag*, ed. H. Baltensweiler and Bo Reicke (Tübingen: J. C. B. Mohr [Paul Siebeck], 1972) 156–65.

[46] As Léon-Dufour, *Lecture*, 2:466, translates: "*Père assure-moi le salut dès cette heure!* Mais oui! c'est pour cela que je suis venu jusqu'à cette heure. *Père glorifie ton nom!*" (emphasis mine, to show the parallel).

[47] Schnackenburg, *St John*, 2:387. It is sometimes suggested that this is a *bat qôl*, a divine communication that replaced the prophetic word. See Bauer, *Johannesevangelium*, 163. This hardly fits the context of the communication between the Father and the Son.

[48] The strategic placing of the references to the *doxa* at the first and the last of Jesus' signs (see 2:11 and 11:40) indicates to the reader that the whole of the ministry has been a revelation of the *doxa*.

[49] See Schnackenburg, *St John*, 2:388. I am limiting the revelation of the glory of God (to be distinguished from the future glory of the exalted Jesus) to the cross. See also Blank, *Krisis*, 276–80; Dodd, *Interpretation*, 372–79; Lindars, *John*, 432. Against, for example, Thüsing, *Erhöhung*, 193–98, who links the aorist tense with Jesus' life and the hour of the cross, and the future tense with the glorification of the exalted Christ. Also against a number of commentators, who extend the future glory to the future preaching of the gospel. See, for example,

are misunderstood. The people in the crowd wonder about the nature of the noise they have heard. Some suggest that it was a natural phenomenon, thunder, while others say that an angel has spoken to him (v. 29).[50] The secret of Jesus can be understood only by those prepared to accept that he is from God (see 1:1-5), and that his story is determined by his origins and his union with God (see 1:18; 3:13; 6:62; 8:23). But "the crowd" wonders about the *origins* of the sound. The crowd belongs to those who love—rather than hate—the allure of this world (see v. 25). Because this is the case, Jesus tells the people in the crowd that the voice from heaven came for them. Recalling his prayer for the people standing at the tomb of Lazarus (see 11:42), Jesus points out that he has no need for assurance from above, but the crowd is still in need of something so that they might come to believe in Jesus. The voice from above is for their sake (*d' hymas*), not for Jesus (*ou di' eme*). The only explanation for the hour of the glorification of the Son of Man (v. 23), the falling of the grain into the earth so that it might bear fruit (v. 24), must come from above (v. 30).

The Judgment of the World and the Lifting Up of Jesus: 12:31-36a

A second moment of revelation opens as Jesus announces the judgment of the world (*nyn krisis estin tou kosmou*). There is a close link between "the hour" associated with the glorification of the Son of Man (v. 23) and the "now" of the judgment of the world (v. 31). The moment of judgment is associated with the glorification of the Son of Man—and it is *now*. The revelation of God, perfected in Jesus, places the world in a situation of judgment. This understanding of the presence of Jesus as bringing *krisis* has been made clear to the reader on several occasions (see 3:19; 5:22, 24, 27, 30; 8:16). The coming of Jesus necessarily brings a judgment, and the hour of the glorification of the Son of Man is the culminating moment of judgment for the prince of this world.[51] The expression *ho kosmos* in this Gospel can have several meanings, as the reader knows from the threefold use of this word in 1:10.[52] In itself, the world is neutral. It can decide to be part of the loving revelation of God and thus be saved (see 1:29; 3:16-17; 4:42; 6:33, 51; 8:12; 9:5; 10:36), or it can become an end unto itself (see

---

Westcott, *St John*, 182; and especially Nicholson, *Death as Departure*, 129–30. The use of *palin* indicates to the reader that the same glory continues to shine, both in the past works of Jesus and in his future glorification. *Both* moments belong to the historical appearance of the Son and show the unfailing union between Father and Son (see 1:18).

[50] On the background to voices that sound like thunder, or a revelation that may come from angels, see Schnackenburg, *St John*, 2:389–90. The basis of the failure lies in the crowd's attempt to understand the noise as a mediation. See Lagrange, *Saint Jean*, 334.

[51] See Blank, *Krisis*, 281–86.

[52] On this, see Moloney, *Belief in the Word*, 37–38.

7:7; 8:23), slave to the ruler of *this* world (*ho archōn tou kosmou toutou*). The hour of the Son of Man marks the casting out (*ekblēthēsetai exō*) of this ruler.

Throughout the story so far, the reader has followed the refusal of "the Jews" and their leaders to accept Jesus. They are not prepared to question the absolutes of their own culture, history, and religion. They have made "*this* world" an absolute. They will not accept that there is *another* world, and that Jesus, who comes from above (see 3:13; 6:62; 8:23), makes it known (see 1:18). A single force is in question here, a prince of evil drawing "the world" into the prison of *this world,* which it thinks it can control and understand.[53] But there is more to it in the Johannine story. The *archōn tou kosmou toutou* has very real representatives. The only *archontes* that the reader has met in the story have been the leaders of "the Jews" (see 3:1; 7:26, 48). The authorities cast out the man born blind (9:34: *exebalon auton exō*) because he dared to suggest that the man who had cured him might be "from God" (9:33: *para theou*). Jesus has attempted to explain the voice from above as a message to "the Jews" that he can only be understood in terms of his relationship with God (see 12:30). They are not prepared to let go of "the world" that they know and control (v. 29). Jesus now announces that the hour of the glorification of the Son of Man is the judgment of *this world,* and that the judgment of the *archontes* is being reversed. In mythic terms, Jesus can say that the ruler of this world is now cast out: he is judged. The struggle between the light and the darkness is *now* (see vv. 23, 27, 31), and the darkness does not overcome the light (see 1:5).[54] But this struggle is not a mythic gnostic battle, going on in the heavens. It takes place in the events of the story of Jesus, and supremely in the story of his being lifted up, and thus glorified. In the story of Jesus, and in the story of the Johannine community, "the Jews" are unwilling to accept that in Jesus the freedom that comes from acceptance of the revelation of God (see 1:3c-4; 8:31-32) breaks into this world. This inability to accept God's offer of freedom in Jesus makes them slaves to the *archōn tou kosmou toutou,* but the time of this ascendency has come to an end.

In close parallel with his earlier words on the glorification of the Son of Man, Jesus announces that when he is lifted up from the earth (*ean hypsōthō ek tēs gēs*) he will draw everyone to himself (v. 32).[55] The reader is instructed on a death that will bring many sheep into one fold (10:15-16),

---

[53] On the development of the Christian notion of a ruler or prince of this world, see Schnackenburg, *St John,* 2:391.

[54] See Blank, *Krisis,* 281-86.

[55] The neuter plural *panta,* indicating that the elevated Jesus would draw all reality, is found in P[66], first hand of Sinaiticus, Old Latin, Bezae, and some of the versions. However, this variant may indicate only humanity in general. See Brown, *John,* 1:468.

a death for the nation, and not only for the nation but for the children of God who are scattered abroad (11:50-52). Many Jews are going to him (12:11), and the Pharisees have complained that the world is going after him (12:19). The arrival of the Greeks led Jesus to affirm the ironic truth of the statement of the Pharisees. His hour of glorification and fruitful dying has come (vv. 23-24). In his being raised from the ground, a physical "lifting up" and a moment of exaltation, he will draw everyone to himself (v. 32).[56] The narrator explains what is meant by the "lifting up" of Jesus from the earth: "He said this to show by what death he was to die" (v. 33). The reader now knows that the hour of Jesus, the glorification of the Son of Man, the lifting up, and the gathering are all associated with the event of the crucifixion: a death by a lifting up on a stake, as Moses lifted up the serpent in the wilderness (see 3:14). But the crowd will not be moved.[57] Correctly associating Jesus' parallel statements about the hour of the Son of Man (v. 23), and interpreting the "lifting up" as a reference to death by crucifixion, the crowd questions everything that Jesus has said, in the light of their Law (v. 34a). "The Jews" are not prepared to listen to Jesus, because they "know" that God has spoken through Moses (see also 9:24, 29, 31). Instead of opening themselves to the revelation of God in and

---

[56] The lifting up "from the earth" means crucifixion. It does not look to some future journey of Jesus into the heavens, taking the believers with him as, among others, Nicholson, *Death as Departure*, 132–36, would maintain. The reader takes the narrator's comment in v. 33 as meaning what it says: "lifting up" = "the death by which Jesus was to die." See especially Thüsing, *Erhöhung*, 3–12; and Cilia, *La morte*, 99–107. In 8:28 "the Jews" were told that they would be responsible for the lifting up (*hotan hypsōsēte*). The lifting up must refer to something that "the Jews" do to Jesus. See J. Riedl, "Wenn ihr den Menschensohn erhöht habt, werdet ihr erkennen (Joh 8,28)," in *Jesus und der Menschensohn: Für Anton Vögtle*, ed. R. Pesch and R. Schnackenburg (Freiburg: Herder, 1975) 360–62. The reader also recalls the parallel drawn between Moses' lifting up of the serpent and the lifting up of the Son of Man in 3:14. There is no suggestion of the serpent ascending into heaven. Nicholson, *Death as Departure*, 98–103 (on 3:14) and 136–38 (on 12:33) insists that the Evangelist wants the reader to look *beyond* the cross, and not *at* the cross. I disagree. On this unresolved debate concerning the extension of the hour and the glorification of Jesus, see Moloney, *Son of Man*, 61–64, and the discussion there. The reader is being prepared to look at the cross to see the revelation of God in the hour = the glorification = the lifting up = the death of the Son of Man. On the cross as revelation, see J. T. Forestell, *The Word of the Cross: Salvation as Revelation in the Fourth Gospel* (AnBib 57; Rome: Biblical Institute Press, 1974) 58–102. Certainly, *through* the hour of the cross the Son will be glorified in his return to the Father. The reader is yet to meet this idea of Jesus' going from one place to another (see 13:1), and is thus totally focused on Jesus' oncoming death in 12:20-36. There are two separate issues that must not be confused: (1) the revelation of the glory of God (the glorification of the Son of Man [12:23], the lifting up [v. 32], the way in which Jesus is to die [v. 33]) = *on* the cross, and (2) the glorification of Jesus as Son of the Father (see 7:39; 11:4) = *through* the cross.

[57] See Schnackenburg, *St John*, 2:381. Schnackenburg points out that "the crowd" now represents "the Jews."

through Jesus, the fullness of the gift of truth who perfects the gift of Moses (see 1:17), they become more arrogant in their rejection of him. Their Law tells them that the Messiah remains for ever (see LXX Ps 88:37).[58] "How can *you* say (*legeis sy*) the Son of Man must be lifted up? Who is *this* (*houtos*) Son of Man?" (John 12:34b). The use of the pronoun *sy* and the relative pronoun *houtos* make their arrogance clear to the reader. No Jewish Messiah can possibly be lifted up.[59]

Jesus' final attempt to overcome the increasingly arrogant misunderstanding of his revelation runs close to being a warning.[60] Recalling his earlier words, as he revealed himself as the light of the world (see 8:12), he insists on the unique moment that is now theirs. "The Jews" have the light with them for only a short while (v. 35a; see also 7:33; 9:4; 11:9). They should walk in this light, because those who walk in the darkness lose their way (see 9:4; 11:10), and do not know where they are going (v. 35b).[61] In a final clarification of what it means to "walk in the light," Jesus commands "the Jews" that they are to "believe in the light." This is the only way to life and light (v. 36a). The reader recalls Jesus' earlier revelation (8:12a), associated with a promise, "the one who follows me will not walk in darkness" (8:12b), which quickly became a warning: "I told you that you would die in your sins, for you will die in your sins unless you believe that I am he" (8:24). On that same occasion Jesus explained to "the Jews" why they find it so difficult to walk in his light: "You are from below, I am from above; you are of this world, I am not of this world" (8:23). The situation has not changed. The raising of Lazarus (11:38-44) and his entry into Jerusalem (12:9-19) have not made serious inroads into the world of "the Jews." Some have marveled at his authority as a miracle worker (see

[58] Scholars debate just what Scripture is referred to in v. 34. For the many possibilities, see Bauer, *Johannesevangelium*, 164. Barrett, *St John*, 427, settles for the common messianic teaching of the Scriptures. For a documented discussion, see Moloney, *Son of Man*, 182–83. Beutler, "Greeks Come," 337–42, argues for LXX Isa 52:13—53:12 as background to John 12:23, 32, 34. For the choice of LXX Ps 88:37, see W. C. van Unnik, "The Quotation from the Old Testament in John 12,34," *NovT* 3 (1959) 174–79.

[59] See Bultmann, *John*, 354–56; Lindars, *John*, 434–35. Behind this question lies the synagogue seeking their answers in their Mosaic tradition and the Johannine community claiming that Jesus is something more than the Jewish Messiah. This has been shown in 12:9-19. He is the Son of Man who draws all to himself by being lifted up (see 12:23, 32). The underlying debate is deeply christological. See Tsuchido, "Tradition and Redaction," 609–19; and M. de Jonge, "Jewish Expectations about the Messiah according to the Fourth Gospel," *NTS* 19 (1972–73) 246–70.

[60] Yet, as Léon-Dufour, *Lecture*, 2:481, rightly points out, this appeal at the close of Jesus' ministry leaves options open. But a warning bell still sounds. Segalla, *Giovanni*, 351, calls vv. 35-36a "un monito-invito."

[61] It is often pointed out that the symbol of light and walking are found in Judaism and at Qumran. For a summary, see Barrett, *St John*, 429.

11:21, 37, 45, 47; 12:9-11, 12, 17). Locked in their prison of "this world" (see 12:15, 31) and "our Law" (see 12:34) there is little chance that "the Jews" will believe in the light that is to be found in Jesus (see 1:4-5; 8:12; 9:5; 11:9-10).

Jesus' Final Departure: 12:36b

"When Jesus had said this, he departed and hid himself from them" (v. 36b). This departure is marked by a deliberate and active hiding (*ekrybē ap' autōn*) on the part of Jesus. On other occasions Jesus has separated himself from his opponents (see 3:22-25; 4:43-44; 7:1; 8:59; 10:40-42; 11:54), but on each of these occasions the reader was informed of the place where Jesus went and of the identity of the people who went with him. Now, as the ministry closes, he disappears, alone, hiding himself from the Jews in some unnamed place. A light that is hidden can no longer direct the steps of the one walking.[62]

IV. Two Reflections on the Ministry of Jesus: 12:37-50

In 1:11 the reader was told that Jesus came to his own, but they refused him. This has proved to be true in the story of 1:19–12:36. Why did this happen? The narrator answers the question (vv. 37-43), and then the voice of Jesus is heard again. He calls out (v. 44: *ekraxen*) from an unknown time and place, proclaiming the unique revelation of God that takes place in him, and the judgment that flows from this revelation (vv. 44-50).[63] There is nothing awkward or out of place in the author's arrangement of the conclusion to the story of the public ministry of Jesus.[64]

---

[62] See Dodd, *Interpretation*, 380; Stibbe, *John*, 137. For a condemnatory understanding of Jesus' departure, see R. Mörchen, "'Weggehen.' Beobachtungen zu Joh 12,36b," *BZ* 28 (1984) 240–42.

[63] As Stibbe, *John*, 137, remarks, "the two principal voices in John's story assert themselves."

[64] Against the many attempts to find a better location for vv. 44-50, or to show they have been added to the Gospel as an explanatory gloss. For the discussion, see Moloney, *Son of Man*, 163–64; Schnackenburg, *St John*, 2:411–12, 530 nn. 1–6. D. M. Smith, "The Setting and Shape of a Johannine Narrative Source," in *Johannine Christianity: Essays on Its Setting, Sources, and Theology* (Edinburgh: T. & T. Clark, 1984) 90–93, suggests that vv. 37-40 were part of a source that linked the seemingly contradictory Christologies of an impressive messianic claimant (ministry) and Jesus rejected and crucified (passion account). C. A. Evans, "Obduracy and the Lord's Servant: Some Observations on the Use of the Old Testament in the Fourth Gospel," in *Early Jewish and Christian Exegesis: Studies in Memory of William Hugh Brownlee*, ed. C. A. Evans and W. F. Stinespring (Scholars Press Homage Series; Atlanta: Scholars Press, 1987) 232–36, suggested that 12:38-41 formed part of a larger midrash of Isa 52:7–53:17, at work in John 12:1-43. But in a later work, Evans, *To See and Not Perceive: Isaiah 6.9-10*

The Unfaith of "the Jews": 12:37-43

The many "signs" that Jesus had done before "the Jews" have not led them to faith (v. 37).[65] The reader knows that belief in Jesus on the basis of his signs is only the beginning of faith (see 2:1-11; 9:1-38; 11:15, 42), and some promising starts (see 2:23; 7:31; 8:30; 10:42; 11:45, 48; 12:11) have come to nothing (see 2:24-25; 7:35; 8:31-33; 11:46; 12:12-15, 34). The failure is part of God's plan (12:38-41). Citing texts from Isaiah in a unique way (Isa 53:1; 6:10),[66] the narrator repeats the tradition of the earliest church (for Isa 53:1, see Rom 10:16; and for Isa 6:9-10, see Mark 4:11-12; 8:17-18; Matt 13:13-15; Luke 8:10; 19:42; Acts 28:26-27; Rom 11:8, 10). There are no apologies for the action of God, as foretold by the prophet. The narrator states that these things happened so that the prophecy of Isaiah would be fulfilled (v. 38a: *hina . . . plērōthȩ̄*).[67] After the citation of Isa 53:1, asking who has believed in the revelation of God (v. 38b),[68] the divine necessity of the unbelief of "the Jews" is again stated. In order to fulfill the scriptures *it was impossible for them to believe* (v. 39: *ouk ēdynanto pisteuein*). The Johannine use of the Isaian passage, which omits the reference to hearing, insists that God was responsible for their blindness and their hardness of heart, lest they should turn to Jesus for healing (v. 40).[69] This version of the "divine hardening" tradition is sharper than anything else in the New Testament. Still reflecting the earliest traditions of Christianity, the narrator tells the reader that Isaiah was able to see the glory of Jesus and speak of it with authority. From the link of Isaiah's vision of Isa 6:1-5 with the sight of the glory of God,[70] it is only a short step to claim that Isaiah saw Jesus, the *doxa tou theou* as he existed before

---

in Early Jewish and Christian Interpretation (JSOTSup 64; Sheffield: JSOT Press, 1989) 134, agrees with Smith.

[65] There is no need to remark on the paucity of *sēmeia* in the Fourth Gospel. "*tosauto sēmeia* do not refer simply to the signs narrated in the gospel, but to the entire miracle activity of Jesus" (Forestell, *Word of the Cross*, 69). Brown, *John* 1:485, suggests that Deut 29:2-4 lies behind this statement.

[66] The citation from Isa 53:1 is close to the LXX, while that of Isa 6:10 seems to be a loose citation of the Hebrew, reworked by the author. On this, see R. Schnackenburg, "Joh 12,39-41: Zur christologischen Schriftauslegung das vierten Evangeliums," in *Neues Testament und Geschichte*, 169–71; and Schuchard, *Scripture Within Scripture*, 85–106.

[67] On the absolute nature of this statement, in which the *hina* must be given its full telic force, see Bernard, *St John*, 2:449. Both the *fact* of the failure (v. 39) and the *reason* for the failure (v. 40) fulfill Scripture. See Lindars, *John*, 439.

[68] In the words of Isaiah, "our message" looks to the teaching of Jesus, while "the arm of the Lord" refers to his deeds.

[69] The shift to the first person in v. 40e refers to Jesus.

[70] This was done by the targum on Isa 6:1, 5.

all time (see John 1:1-2).[71] Isaiah, like Abraham and all the prophets of old, was able to speak of having seen the Christ (see 8:56).

But at no stage in the story so far has it appeared that the failure of "the Jews" was a divine necessity, so that the Scriptures might be fulfilled.[72] Indeed, Jesus continued to appeal to them even as he disappeared from the scene (see 12:35-36a). If "the Jews" failed, it is because they made a decision against Jesus.[73] Thus, having provided the reader with what had become an official response to a most disturbing fact of history, the narrator now offers a more personal explanation.[74] Almost negating his use of the theory of the "divine hardening," the narrator tells the reader that some of the *archontes* did come to belief in Jesus (v. 42a).[75] The problem was not that the revelation of God in Jesus failed, but that those called to belief in him failed. Reflecting the situation of the Johannine community, cast out of the synagogue because of their faith in Jesus, the narrator

---

[71] See Lagrange, *Saint Jean*, 343; Bauer, *Johannesevangelium*, 165; Schnackenburg, "Joh 12:37-41," 174–76. With most critics, I am reading *hoti* ("because") rather than *hote* ("when"). For the evidence, see Lindars, *John*, 439.

[72] Against the majority of commentators who try to show that vv. 38-41 follow the continual rejection of Jesus by "the Jews" throughout the narrative. See especially Becker, *Johannes*, 408–12; Schnackenburg, "Joh 12,37-41," 176–77; Schuchard, *Scripture Within Scripture*, 98–106. *Never* in the narrative is the impression created that God caused "the Jews" to reject Jesus. J. M. Lieu, "Blindness in the Johannine Tradition," *NTS* 34 (1988) 83–95, faces this difficulty. On the basis of John 9, 12:39-43, and 1 John 2:11, she suggests that blindness and unbelief were linked in the Johannine tradition. This suggestion partially explains why Isa 6:9-10 was taken from the tradition, even though it hardly fits the context. B. Hollenbach, "Lest they should turn and be forgiven: Irony," *BT* 34 (1983) 317–20, sees the difficulty and suggests that Isaiah 6 is being used ironically: "the last thing they want is to see."

[73] For the seriousness of this problem, and the many attempts to resolve it, see Blank, *Krisis*, 301–3. Blank suggests that the devil is the subject of the verbs "make blind" and "harden" in v. 40 (see pp. 303–5). This, however, only shifts the problem. The rejection of Jesus through his ministry is not reported as motivated by the devil. The discussion of 8:39-47 ("your father the devil") is about origins, but it does not take freedom away from "the Jews" (see especially 8:34).

[74] This use of Isaiah and the theory of "divine hardening" indicates the continuity between the older traditions and Johannine reflection upon them. On this continuity, see B. Lindars, *New Testament Apologetic: The Doctrinal Significance of the Old Testament Quotations* (London: SCM Press, 1961) 161; Schnackenburg, "Joh 12,39-41," 168–69. In 12:37-43, it appears to me, the tradition is recorded and reworked (vv. 38-41), and then left to one side. This is one of the places in the Fourth Gospel where the author's respect for the tradition creates an *aporia*. In vv. 42-43 the narrator gives a more satisfactory Johannine answer to the problem posed in v. 37.

[75] On vv. 42-43 as a "correction," see Léon-Dufour, *Lecture*, 2:491. Haenchen, *John*, 2:101, calls v. 42 "a consoling message." Verses 42-43 are something of a correction of vv. 37-41, but hardly a consoling message.

points to the weakness of some leaders of "the Jews" who did not have the courage of their convictions. They refused to confess their faith (*ouk hōmologoun*) because they were afraid they would be cast out of the synagogue by the Pharisees (see 9:22).

Unlike the man born blind—who was a Jew (see 9:34b)—"the Jews" were too concerned with the things of "this world" (see 12:25-26) to commit themselves unconditionally to the revelation of God in the person of Jesus. In a concluding statement, playing on the twofold meaning of the Greek word *doxa* (see also 5:41-44; 7:18; 8:50-54), the narrator provides the reader with a key to the failure of "the Jews" that corresponds *exactly* with what has happened throughout 1:19—12:36. "The Jews" have never been able to let go of all they could control, manipulate, and understand: their messianic expectations (see 1:19-51; 3:2-5; 4:19, 25-26; 6:14-15; 7:25-31, 40-44; 12:34), the Law of Moses (5:16-18; 7:45-52; 9:28-29; 10:31-39; 12:34), and their "knowledge" (see 3:2; 4:25; 7:27; 9:24, 29; 11:22, 24). They have attempted to approach and understand Jesus' revelation as *ta epigeia*, and thus have never been able to grasp *ta epourania* (see 3:12). There is a chasm between the world of "the Jews" who are *ek tōn katō* and Jesus who is *ek tōn anō* (see 8:23). Even in their belief (see 12:42), they cannot let go of this world. They love the esteem, the honor, the praise, and the respect of human beings and "this world" (*tēn doxan tōn anthrōpōn*) so much that they are prepared to sacrifice the presence of the revelation of God into the world (*tēn doxan tou theou*) (v. 43; see 1:14; 2:11; 11:4, 40). In this double meaning of *doxa*—human esteem and the revelation of God—the reader finds the key for a correct understanding of the conflict between Jesus and "the Jews" that has developed during the public ministry of Jesus. There is an inevitable clash between "the Jews," who will not sacrifice the *horizontal* dimension of all that this world can offer, and the *vertical* inbreak of God, who sends his Son from above so that the world might be saved (see 3:16-17).

Jesus "Cries Out" His Final Message: 12:44-50

There can be no limitation of time and space for Jesus' final words (see v. 36b). The passage has been constructed by the author as a concluding summary, a gathering of words of Jesus from across the story of his ministry.[76] Jesus can be understood only in terms of the Father who sent him. Thus the final words of Jesus are a commentary on the closing remarks of

---

[76] Dodd, *Interpretation*, 382, entitles vv. 44-50 the kerygma of Jesus. On the Johannine nature of vv. 44-50, see Schnackenburg, *St John*, 2:419–21. For van den Bussche, *Jean*, 364; Panimolle, *Lettura Pastorale*, 3:143; Stibbe, *John*, 139; and Brodie, *John*, 420–21, 12:44-50 forms an inclusion with 1:1-18.

the narrator on the failure of "the Jews": Jesus makes known the *doxa* of God (see v. 43). In six sentences, the word *egō* is used four times (vv. 46, 47, 49, 50), but the "I" of Jesus is subordinated to the Father and to Jesus' role as the Sent One, making the Father known.

Jesus is the unique revelation of *the Father who sent him* (v. 44; see 3:15-16; 5:36-38; 6:29, 35, 40; 7:38; 8:19, 24, 42, 45-46), and thus to see Jesus is to see the *one who sent him* (v. 45; see 1:18; 6:40; 8:19; 10:30, 38). Out of this close relationship with the Father Jesus can claim to bring *light into the world*, so that those who believe in him can emerge from the darkness and walk permanently in the light (v. 46; see 1:4-5; 8:12; 9:5, 39; 11:9-10; 12:35-36).[77] The world judges itself as it accepts or refuses the light of the world, the revelation *of the Father*, and thus Jesus does not actively judge. He has come to save the world, but the world, free to reject his saving presence, has done so,[78] and is thus judged (v. 47; see 3:16-17, 34; 5:24; 8:15, 31). For a brief moment, the mission from the Father is laid aside, and, recalling the crucial importance of "belief in the word" (see 2:1—4:54), Jesus speaks of his word standing in judgment over against all who would reject it.[79] This judgment is acted out both now and hereafter (v. 48; see 3:18; 5:24, 29, 44-45; 7:51; 8:40).[80] But Jesus' dependence on the Father, even in this, is immediately recalled. The word of Jesus is not his own. He does not work out of his own authority, but speaks *what the Father has commanded him to say*. It is with absolute confidence that Jesus can claim that this word brings eternal life. Jesus has spoken *the word of the Father*

---

[77] Lindars, *John*, 440, points out that the idea of walking in the light (see 3:21; 8:12; 12:35) has been replaced by "remain in the light" to indicate the abiding effect of a decision for or against Jesus.

[78] Some manuscripts omit the negative, and others change the verb from "keep" to "believe." "Does not keep" must be retained.

[79] The verb *athetein* is used only here in the Fourth Gospel. It has the meaning of a deliberate and considered rejection. See BAGD, 21, s.v. para. 1b. See Blank, *Krisis*, 308–10.

[80] Brown, *John*, 1:491–93, points to the link between the many echoes of Deuteronomy in the idea of God's punishing those who do not listen to the words of his messenger (vv. 47-48; see, e.g., Deut 18:18-19; 31:19, 26) and in the transmission of the commandment of God so that the children of God might have life (vv. 49-50; see, e.g., Deut 8:3; 32:45-47). See also M.-E. Boismard, "Les citations targumiques dans le quatrième évangile," *RB* 66 (1959) 376–78; M. J. O'Connell, "The Concept of Commandment in the Old Testament," *TS* 21 (1960) 398–401. In an overly complex suggestion (given the large number of Johannine parallels to vv. 44-50), P. Borgen, "The Use of Tradition in John 12.44-50," *NTS* 26 (1979-80) 18–35, argues that on the basis of a traditional Jesus logion in vv. 44-45, fragments of legal and eschatological terminology, other words from the Gospel, terminology on agency, and the influence of the Old Testament, the Evangelist has developed the passage to present Jesus as the divine agent whose words replace the role of Moses and the Torah. For Stibbe, *John*, 140, reference to "the last day" in v. 48 is "a flash forward to the conclusion of the real world and real time." It creates a proleptic sense of ending.

with uncompromising trust and obedience (vv. 49-50; see 4:34; 5:22, 30, 39; 6:38; 7:16-17; 8:26, 28, 38; 10:18).

These words of Jesus recall two earlier moments at the beginning of his ministry. His dialogue with Nicodemus became a monologue (see 3:11-21), and John the Baptist's final witness to Jesus was followed by a reflection from the narrator (3:31-36). These two mini-discourses made the same point: Jesus is the unique revelation of God. Life or death, light or darkness flows from the acceptance or refusal of this revelation.[81] Thus the ministry of Jesus has opened and closed with affirmations of Jesus' role as the revelation of the *doxa tou theou*, and of the consequences of this truth. As the curtain falls on Jesus' public presence to "the Jews" (v. 36b), the reader of the story has been informed of the roots of the emerging *krisis*: "the Jews" loved the *doxa tōn anthrōpōn* rather than the *doxa tou theou* (see v. 43), but Jesus did not falter in bringing to perfection the task his Father gave him, making known the *doxa tou theou*.[82] This information has been provided by both the narrator (vv. 42-43) and most authoritatively by the voice of Jesus (vv. 44-50).

CONCLUSION

A number of features indicate to the reader that 11:1—12:36 forms a unit.[83] Jesus has made a decisive journey to Bethany (see 11:1, 7, 17; 12:1) and then to Jerusalem (see 11:55-57; 12:12-15) on the occasion of the feast of the Passover (see 11:55; 12:1, 12, 20). From the outset, the reader has been informed that Jesus' journey will be for the glory of God, so that the Son of God might be glorified (see 11:4; see v. 40). In Jerusalem, as "the world" desires to see him, the hour of Jesus' glorification is announced (12:19-20, 23, 31-32). The same characters are actively involved with Jesus throughout: Lazarus (11:1-2, 5, 14, 17, 43-44; 12:1, 9-11, 16-19), Martha (11:1, 3, 18, 20-28, 39, 42; 12:2), Mary (11:1-3, 20, 28-33, 42; 12:1-8), the disciples (11:1-16, 42; 12:4-6, 16, 21-22), and "the Jews" (11:8, 19, 31, 33, 36-37, 42, 45-46, 47-50, 54, 55-57; 12:9-11, 12-13, 17-19, 29, 34). Characters, place, and time combine to form a unified story across John 11–12.[84]

---

[81] On the relationship between 3:11-21, 31-36, and 12:44-50, see W. Loader, "The Central Structure of Johannine Theology," *NTS* 30 (1984) 188–216; idem, *The Christology of the Fourth Gospel* (BBET 23; Frankfurt: Peter Lang, 1989) 20–34; Ashton, *Understanding*, 541–45.

[82] This is the point of the *de* in v. 44, coming hard on the narrator's description of the unfaith of "the Jews" in v. 43.

[83] Segovia, "The Journey(s)," 44, misses this. Using the criterion of motion, he divides this material into 11:1-54 (journey to Bethany), 11:55—12:10 (second journey to Bethany), and 12:12—17:26 (final journey to Jerusalem). See his structure on pp. 50–51.

[84] See also M. de Merode, "L'accueil triomphal de Jésus selon *Jean*, 11–12," *RTL* 13 (1982) 49–62.

Through the interplay of Jesus, Lazarus, Martha, Mary, and "the Jews," within the spatial and temporal context of Jesus' movement to Jerusalem at the time of Passover, the reader is informed that this Passover will be marked by the death of Jesus. But this violent end is announced as the moment of the glory of God (11:4), the glorification of Jesus (12:23, 31), and the hour of his being lifted up from the earth (12:32). But the death of Jesus is not *for himself*. Jesus will lay down his life *for others*. In the midst of increasing misunderstanding (see 11:8, 12, 16, 21-22, 24, 27, 33, 39, 47, 55; 12:9, 13, 29, 34) and mounting violence (see 11:8, 16, 47-50, 54, 57; 12:10-11), the theme of "gathering" has emerged (10:15-16; 11:50-52; 12:9, 19, 20, 32). But the enigma remains: "He said this to show by what death he was to die" (v. 33). The reader knows that this is not the story of a brave man who was condemned to death, crucified, but raised from the dead. The Johannine story of this man, as it has been told thus far, indicates that ahead of the reader lies an account of a death that is also the drawing of *pantas* around the lifted up and glorified Son of Man (12:23, 32). The reader is involved as one of the *pantas*! The rest of the story will tell of the destiny of *both* Jesus *and* the reader.[85]

---

[85] For the unity between chaps. 11 and 12 and their close relationship with the story yet to come, see C. H. Giblin, "The Tripartite Narrative Structure of John's Gospel," *Bib* 71 (1990) 449-68.

Chapter Eight

Looking Back

❡ THE READER LEARNS who Jesus is and what he does in the prologue (1:1-18), but the characters in the story have not read the prologue. Over the first days of Jesus' public appearance, John the Baptist fulfills the promise of the prologue (see 1:6-8, 15) by giving witness to Jesus as the Lamb of God who takes away the sin of the world (see vv. 29, 35) and as the Son of God (v. 34), within a context of people from Jerusalem who are looking for a Messiah (vv. 19-28). The Baptist directs disciples to Jesus as "the Lamb of God," (v. 35) and they follow him, believing that they have found their Messiah (see vv. 38, 41, 45, 49). Jesus promises the future sight of something greater than the expected Messiah: the revelation of the heavenly in the Son of Man (vv. 50-51). The reader wonders: If something more than the messianic faith expressed in 1:35-49 is required for the sight of "greater things" in the Son of Man (vv. 50-51), what is the nature of belief?

Concluding the first days, and recalling the revelation of the *doxa* of God at Sinai (see John 2:1; Exod 19:11, 16; John 2:11), the reader sets out on a journey with Jesus and a series of characters from Cana to Cana (John 2:1—4:54). Set within the frame of the two Cana miracles, where a Jewish woman (2:5) and a gentile official (4:50) commit themselves to the word of Jesus, bringing others to believe in Jesus (2:1-12; 4:46-54), the author has assembled a series of narratives within Jewish (2:13—3:36) and non-Jewish (4:1-42) settings. "The Jews" in the Temple refuse the word of Jesus (2:13-22), and the narrator reflects on a faith based on Jesus' signs (2:23-

25). Nicodemus is prepared to accept that Jesus is a teacher from God because of his signs, and Jesus attempts to lead him beyond that limited faith (3:1-21). John the Baptist witnesses to Jesus as the friend of the bridegroom who stands and hears his voice (3:22-36). Characters from Judaism have told a story of no faith ("the Jews"), partial faith (Nicodemus), and authentic belief in the word of Jesus (John the Baptist).

The Samaritan woman moves from a rejection of the word of Jesus (4:1-15) to a suspicion that he might be the expected Messiah (4:16-30). Jesus comments to his disciples on the task which he must perform, the fruits of which they will enjoy (4:31-38); and the Samaritan villagers believe, having heard the word of Jesus, that he is the Savior of the world (4:39-42). People from outside the world of Israel have journeyed from no faith (the Samaritan woman) to partial faith (the Samaritan woman) to an authentic belief in the word of Jesus (the Samaritan villagers). But if the word of Jesus is the revelation of God, and acceptance of that word is the criterion of true faith in God, what of Israel's traditional place of encounter with YHWH in the celebration of its feasts? So much depends on the right celebration of Israel's traditional feasts: "If you will succeed in keeping the Sabbath, the Holy One, blessed be He, will give you three festivals, Passover, Pentecost, and Tabernacles" (*Mekilta* on Exod 16:25). Emerging from 1:1—4:54, the reader meets a comment from the narrator: "After this there was a feast of the Jews" (5:1). The story of Jesus' ministry that follows is set within the feasts of Sabbath (chap. 5; see 5:9), Passover (chap. 6; see 6:4), Tabernacles (7:1—10:21; see 7:2, 14, 37), and Dedication (10:22-42; see 10:22). The narrative moves from one feast of "the Jews" to another, following the chronological order of the feasts over any one year. The problem raised for the reader of 1:1—4:54 is being faced.

The celebration of the Sabbath is essential to the events and words of Jesus in John 5. A miracle worked on a Sabbath creates difficulties (vv. 1-13). After an encounter between Jesus and the cured man, which suggests that Jesus cannot be limited to expected Sabbath behavior (v. 14), a trial opens (vv. 15-16) and a verdict is given: Jesus must die (vv. 17-18). Jesus' defense of his Sabbath activity as the Son of the Father who can exercise the Sabbath function of life-giver and judge depends entirely on the Jewish understanding of YHWH as the only one who can give life and who judges on the Sabbath (vv. 19-30). But it is not enough for Jesus to affirm he is the Son of the Father and does everything the Father teaches him to do (vv. 19 and 30). He must face the normal processes of a trial and bring other witnesses (vv. 31-32). John the Baptist (vv. 33-35), the works of Jesus, the Sent One of the Father (v. 36), and the Father himself (vv. 37-40) bear witness to his Sabbath authority. The inability of "the Jews" to see and accept these witnesses leads to an ironic change in the direction of the trial: the judges become the accused. Their search for human esteem cannot match Jesus' authority as the revelation of the glory of the one and only Sabbath God; they stand condemned, unable to believe the words of Jesus (vv. 41-47). Life and freedom come from acceptance of the word of Jesus (v. 24), the Son of the Father, Lord of the Sabbath, life-giver, and judge (vv. 19 and 30).

Jesus comes to the other side of the Sea of Galilee on the occasion of the celebration of the Passover (6:1-4). Philip and Andrew play a role in the discussion leading up to the multiplication of loaves and fishes (vv. 5-10) to feed a multitude. The disciples gather the fragments of the loaves, that they might not be lost (vv. 12-13). But the crowds decide that Jesus fulfills their messianic hopes, and they wish to make him king (vv. 14-15). Jesus, the disciples, and the crowd separate, but on a stormy sea the disciples experience Jesus' self-revelation as *egō eimi* (vv. 16-21). Jesus, the disciples, and the crowd gather again at Capernaum (see vv. 22-24), where Jesus asks them to look beyond the bread given to their ancestors in the wilderness (vv. 32-33) who have died (vv. 49, 58). He is the true bread from heaven that will endure forever (vv. 27, 47-48) and will give life to the world (vv. 33, 50-51ab). He will give himself unto death (v. 51c), as the revelation of God that will provide eternal life (vv. 40, 46-47, 53-54, 58). The nourishing, saving presence of the God of Israel is still present to his people. The reader is told that only in Jesus is the true bread from heaven to be found. The bread from heaven is Jesus' broken flesh and shed blood for the life of the world (see vv. 51c-58). It is yet to be given, but the fragments of the meal beside the lake have been gathered, so that they might not perish (vv. 12-13), and Jesus has told the crowd not to labor for a food that perishes (v. 27). The story of the fragments, associated with the demand that one eat the flesh and drink the blood of the Son of Man (see vv. 53-54), reminds the reader of the Christian celebration of the Lord's Table. But among the disciples who have accepted Jesus' self-revelation as *egō eimi* (see vv. 16-21) the word and presence of Jesus produce rejection (vv. 60-66), a confession of faith (vv. 67-69), and a reminder of the perennial possibility of failure (vv. 70-71).

At the feast of Tabernacles in Jerusalem (see 7:2) "the Jews" object to Jesus' authority and his oneness with God, whom he continues to call "Father" (see 7:14-24; 8:39-59). The reader is aware that they are turning their backs on the one who makes known the one true God (see *Sukkah* 5:4). As the people wonder about the coming Messiah, Jesus refuses to conform to Israel's traditional messianic expectation (see 7:25-31). Jesus is unacceptable to the Pharisees, who claim to know everything that is to be known about the destiny of the Messiah (7:32-36). They display no openness to Jesus' transformation of traditional messianic expectation. He is the personification and the universalization of the celebration of the gift of living water at the feast of Tabernacles (see *Sukkah* 4:9-10), the source of living water (John 7:37-38), no matter how firmly the former tradition is reaffirmed by those who oppose Jesus (7:37-52). Jesus is the personification and the universalization of the celebration of the light of the Temple and of the city of Jerusalem at the feast of Tabernacles (8:12; see *Sukkah* 5:2-4), but this theme leads to the double possibility of light and darkness, life and death, a judgment that flows from the acceptance or refusal of the revelation of the one true God in and through Jesus (8:12-59). Some accept his revelation (vv. 12-30), while others move from an initial belief to a desire to execute him for blasphemy (vv. 31-59). Israel's allegiance to their traditional God is at stake. "They did not understand that he spoke to them of the Father" (8:27). The claim that their eyes were "turned toward the Lord" (see *Sukkah* 5:4) is a lie, and the attempt to kill Jesus shows that "the Jews" are not children of Abraham or of the one true God, but children of the devil (8:39-57). This accusation inevitably arouses disbelief and anger, but the reader knows that these reactions flow from "the Jews'" inability to abandon their superficial understanding of the ways of God (*kat' opsin*, 7:24; *kata tēn sarka*, 8:15).

Separated from the Temple because of the violence of "the Jews" (see 8:59), the reader discovers that Jesus' actions and words bring Tabernacle themes to a climax in 9:1—10:21. Jesus, because he is the Sent One (see 9:7), gives light to a man who has never seen. But the physical miracle is only the beginning of a longer journey of faith that leads from his understanding of Jesus as "the man called Jesus" (v. 11) to his falling before the Son of Man whom he sees and hears, confessing, "Lord, I believe" (v. 38). The reader finds that Jesus not only *claims* to be the light of the world (8:12; 9:5), but his actions and his presence to a man once without light who now sees *show* that he is the light of the world. Furthermore, part of this miracle story proved the truth of Jesus' claim to be the living water (7:37). During a feast that was marked by the daily procession to the waters of Siloam to gather water for the ritual lustrations, Jesus is presented as the living water. An aside from the author makes clear to the reader that the man is not cured by the magic of the water, but because of his contact with the real meaning of Siloam: the Sent One (9:7). The living water carried up to the Temple has been perfected in the person of Jesus, who creates sight and true belief in a person who was born blind. Throughout the journey of the man from blindness to sight, "the Jews," who turned toward the Holy of Holies each day to celebrate their unswerving loyalty to the one true God, have become increasingly hostile to both the man and Jesus. At first they recognize that a miracle has taken place (vv. 15-16), but they conclude by placing all their trust in Moses, and deciding that Jesus is a sinner, without recognizable origins (see vv. 24-29). Not unexpectedly for the reader, Jesus enters the story of "the Jews," as he had entered the story of the man born blind. He condemns them as blind (vv. 39-41), and draws a comparison between his role as the door of the sheep and the Good Shepherd and their performance as thieves and robbers, strangers and hirelings (10:1-13).

But what of the messianic question, so urgently raised during the earlier parts of the narrative dealing with events that took place during the feast of the Tabernacles (see 7:25-31, 40-44)? Jesus has not denied traditional messianic expectation, but he has spoken of his relationship with God, his Father (see 8:8, 12-20, 39-59), and of the mystery of his origins and his destiny (see 7:16-18, 32-36, 52; 8:14, 21-27). In a climax to the story of his presence at the feast of Tabernacles, Jesus recalls a traditional messianic image as he describes himself as the Good Shepherd (10:14-18; see Ezekiel 34). But Jesus' shepherding flows from his knowledge and love of the Father, reciprocated by the knowledge and the love that the Father has for him (10:15, 17). Accepting the charge that the Father has given him, he will lay down his life for his sheep, but he will take it up again, gathering scattered sheep into one fold (v. 16).

If the first days (1:19-51) and the journey from Cana to Cana (2:1—4:54) led the reader to wonder about Israel's traditional experience of the presence of God through the *zikkārôn* of the feasts, the story has—by now—provided an answer. The reader has been associated with Jesus, the disciples, the crowd, and "the Jews" through the celebration of Sabbath (5:1-47), Passover (6:1-71), and Tabernacles (7:1—10:21). But these are celebrations of "the Jews" (see 6:4; 7:2). The reader knows that Jesus transforms the signs and shadows of what was done in the Temple for Israel. Jesus is the life-giver and judge (5:1-47), and the bread from heaven (6:1-71). As postwar Judaism looked to the Torah for light, water, and shepherd (see *2 Baruch* 77:11, 13-16), Jesus is the living water, the light of the world, the revelation of the one true God, the messianic Good Shepherd (John 7:1—10:21). The Johannine story does not abandon the symbols, so intimately linked to the feast of Tabernacles. The reader has access to living water, to light, and to the shepherd. Jesus is living water for "any one who thirsts" (7:37), the light "of the world" (8:12; 9:5), and the Good Shepherd who lays down his life for his sheep, to gather into one many who, as yet, do not belong to his fold (10:15-16).

Finally, "It was the feast of the Dedication in Jerusalem" (10:22). As Israel recalled the consecration and the reestablishment of the visible presence of God in the Temple, Jesus affirms that he and the Father are one (10:30), the Father is in Jesus and Jesus is in the Father (v. 38). All that Jesus has said through the celebration of Sabbath, Passover, and Tabernacles

(5:1—10:21) makes sense because Jesus is the consecrated one (10:36), the living presence of God among his people (vv. 30, 38). Such claims can produce only violence and *schisma*. Jesus flees, returning to the place of the first day of the story (see 1:19-28): across the Jordan where John at first baptized (10:39-42).

The intended readers of the Johannine community can identify with the implied reader: embodied in the Son of God they can find the perfection of what was done in the Jewish Temple in signs and shadows. The Johannine story has conveyed the author's point of view with force. There have been two gifts from God. The former gift, which came through Moses, has been an essential part of God's dealings with the human story. This gift, however, has been perfected and fulfilled in the gift that comes through Jesus Christ, the fullness of a gift that is the truth (see 1:16-17). The conflict between "the Jews" and Jesus, as it is reported in these narratives, is not a conflict between Jesus and Israel, but rather a conflict between Jesus and some from Israel who had decided that Jesus was not the Christ and that anyone who confessed that he was must be put out of the synagogue (see 9:22). "The Jews" are people who have made a decision about Jesus, and it is the feasts of "the Jews" that have been transcended. As Jesus and "the Jews" are on a collision course, so also are "the Jews" and the Johannine Christians.

John 11:1—12:50 concludes Jesus' public ministry and points the reader toward the meaning of that collision course. The story of Jesus' coming to Bethany, his meeting with Martha and Mary, the raising of Lazarus, the anointing, the solemn entry into Jerusalem, and Jesus' final words in response to the coming of the Greeks belong together. They mark a turn in the narrative, as Jesus faces the crisis inevitably produced by the words and deeds of his ministry. Jesus makes a decisive journey to Bethany (see 11:1, 7, 17; 12:1) and then to Jerusalem (see 11:55-57; 12:12-15) on the occasion of the feast of Passover (see 11:55; 12:1, 12, 20). From the outset, the reader is informed that Jesus' journey will be for the glory of God, so that the Son of God might be glorified (see 11:4; see also v. 40). But disciples, "the Jews," Martha, and—despite an initially positive response to the call of the Good Shepherd—even Mary are unable to see beyond the death of their loved one, to believe that Jesus is the resurrection and the life (see vv. 25-26). But, still praying for the belief of these bystanders (see v. 42), Jesus' summoning the dead Lazarus to life shows that his deeds match his words of self-revelation (vv. 38-44). Some Jews believe in Jesus because of the great wonder of the resurrection of Lazarus, but others inform their leaders of the event, and the plot to kill Jesus becomes urgent—to save the nation but also to gather into one the children of God who are scattered abroad (vv. 45-53). In Jerusalem, Mary is the first to recognize the significance of the death of Jesus, extravagantly anointing him for burial, in the midst of disbelief and betrayal (12:1-8). As "the world" desires to see him, the hour of Jesus' glorification is announced (12:19-20, 23, 31-32).

Characters, place, and time combine to form a unified story throughout John 11–12. Through the interplay of Jesus, Lazarus, Martha, Mary, and "the Jews," within the spatial and temporal context of Jesus' movement to Jerusalem at the time of Passover, the reader is informed that this Passover will be marked by the death of Jesus. But his violent end is announced as the moment of the glory of God (11:4), the glorification of Jesus (11:4; 12:23, 31), and the hour of his being lifted up from the earth (12:32). The reader knows that the lifting up is not only for the glory of God and the glorification of the Son of Man. The death of Jesus is not *for himself.* Jesus will lay down his life *for others.* In the midst of increasing misunderstanding (see 11:8, 12, 16, 21-22, 24, 27, 33, 39, 47, 55; 12:9, 13, 29, 34) and mounting violence (see 11:8, 16, 47-50, 54, 57; 12:10-11), the theme of "gathering" has emerged. It has grown in importance from the promise of the Good Shepherd in 10:15-16 to the prophecy of Caiaphas, further expanded by the narrator in 11:50-52. As "the Jews" (12:9), "the world" (v. 19), and "the Greeks" seek Jesus (v. 20), the hour has come for Jesus to be lifted up from the earth, to gather everyone to himself (12:32). Despite the summaries that conclude the story of Jesus' public ministry (12:37-50), there is still much that the reader must be told before this particular story of Jesus can be regarded as satisfactorily concluded. The Johannine story indicates that ahead of the reader lies an account of a death that is also the drawing of *pantas* around the lifted up and glorified Son of Man (12:23, 32).

CONCLUSION

Recent Johannine scholarship has devoted an increasing amount of attention to a reading of the text of the Fourth Gospel as it has come to us in Christian tradition.[1] Some of this scholarship attempts to trace complex, concentric literary patterns across parts of the Gospel, and the Gospel as a whole, but they fail to do justice to the skills of the Johannine storyteller.[2]

---

[1] This affirmation is not a judgment on the historical-critical work that continues to make an essential contribution to Johannine studies, despite the increase of interest in a more holistic approach. See, for example, the two recent and important studies of Painter, *Quest*, and Schnelle, *Antidocetic Christology*.

[2] Such attempts are myriad. One should consult the recent works of P. Ellis, *The Genius of John: A Compositional-Critical Commentary on the Fourth Gospel* (Collegeville: Liturgical Press, 1984); Mlakuzhyil, *Christocentric*.

Too much attention is given to possible verbal inclusions, thematic statements and restatements, without devoting enough attention to the experience of a reader who encounters one event after another. Although at times the narrator prompts the reader to recall the message of an earlier moment in the reading experience (see, for example, 4:46, 54; 5:30; 6:59; 7:14, 39; 8:59; 10:21, 40-42), readers do not read in chiasms, however obvious they might be to the scholar.[3] There is every indication that the Gospel is a carefully designed dramatic narrative.[4]

The Fourth Gospel remains the magic pool in which an infant can paddle and an elephant can swim. Various threads are unraveled and again entwined as the author leads the reader through the story, and as the reader strives, "even if unconsciously, to fit everything together in a consistent pattern."[5] The reader who emerges at 12:50 knows that a remarkable ministry has been reported and that its telling creates a *krisis*: "I have come as light into the world, that whoever believes in me may not remain in darkness. . . . The one who rejects me and does not receive my word has a judge; the word that I have spoken will be his judge on the last day" (12:46, 48). Who will believe and have life? Who will reject Jesus, not receive his word, and be finally judged by that word? Where will this story lead Jesus and the other characters in the story, especially the disciples and "the Jews"? Where will it lead the reader? There is still more story to be told, and the reader looks forward as the questions posed by the Johannine account of the ministry of Jesus beg for resolution.

[3] See R. M. Fowler, *Let the Reader Understand: Reader-Response Criticism and the Gospel of Mark* (Minneapolis: Fortress Press, 1991) 150–52.

[4] See, for example, the early study of Kysar, *John's Story*, and the more recent work of L. Schenke, *Das Johannesevangelium: Einführung—Text—dramatische Gestalt* (Stuttgart: Kohlhammer, 1992) 202–23. Brodie, *John*, attempts a similar, but idiosyncratic, reading.

[5] W. Iser, *The Implied Reader: Patterns of Communication in Prose Fiction from Bunyan to Beckett* (Baltimore: Johns Hopkins University Press, 1978) 283.

Bibliography

REFERENCE WORKS AND SOURCES

Aland, K., and B. Aland, eds. *Novum Testamentum Graece*. 26th ed. Stuttgart: Deutsche Bibelstiftung, 1979.

Aland, B., K. Aland, J. Karavidopoulos, C. M. Martini, B. M. Metzger, eds. *The Greek New Testament*. 4th ed. Stuttgart: United Bible Societies, 1993.

Bauer, W., W. F. Arndt, and F. W. Gingrich. *A Greek-English Lexicon of the New Testament and Other Early Christian Literature*. 2nd ed. revised and augmented by F. W. Gingrich and F. W. Danker. Chicago: University of Chicago Press, 1979.

Bietenhard, H. *Midrasch Tanhuma B. R. Tanhuma über die Tora, genannt Midrasch Jelammenedu*. 2 vols. Judaica et Christiana 5–6. Bern: Peter Lang, 1980, 1982.

Blass, F., and A. Debrunner. *A Greek Grammar of the New Testament and Other Early Christian Literature*. Rev. and trans. R. W. Funk. Chicago: University of Chicago Press, 1961.

Boismard, M.-E., and A. Lamouille. *Synopsis Graeca Quattuor Evangeliorum*. Leuven/Paris: Peeters, 1986.

Braude, W. G. *Pesikta Rabbati: Discourses for Feasts, Fasts, and Special Sabbaths*. 2 vols. Yale Judaica Series. New Haven: Yale University Press, 1968.

Brown, F., S. R. Driver, and C. A. Briggs. *A Hebrew and English Lexicon of the Old Testament with an Appendix Containing the Biblical Aramaic*. Oxford: Clarendon Press, 1907.

Brown, R. E., J. A. Fitzmyer, and R. E. Murphy, eds. *The New Jerome Biblical Commentary*. Englewood Cliffs: Prentice Hall, 1989.

Charlesworth, J. H., ed. *The Old Testament Pseudepigrapha*. 2 vols. Garden City, N.Y.: Doubleday, 1983, 1985.

Colson, F. H., G. H. Whitaker, J. W. Earp, and R. Marcus, eds. *Philo*. 12 vols. The Loeb Classical Library. London: Heinemann; Cambridge: Harvard University Press, 1929–1953.

Danby, H. *The Mishnah Translated from the Hebrew with Introduction and Brief Expository Notes*. Oxford: Clarendon Press, 1933.

Elliger, K., and K. Rudolph. *Biblia Hebraica Stuttgartensia*. Stuttgart: Deutsche Bibelgesellschaft, 1983.

Epstein, I., ed. *The Babylonian Talmud*. 35 vols. London: Soncino, 1948–52.

Etheridge, J. W. *The Targums of Onkelos and Jonathan ben Uzziel on the Pentateuch with the Fragments of the Jerusalem Targum from the Chaldee*. Reprint of 1862 Publication. 2 vols. New York: KTAV, 1968.

Freedman, H., and M. Simon, eds. *Midrash Rabbah: Translated into English with Notes, Glossary and Indices*. 10 vols. London: Soncino, 1939.

Grossfeld, B. *The Targum Onqelos to Genesis: Translated, with a Critical Introduction, Apparatus, and Notes*. The Aramaic Bible 6. Edinburgh: T. & T. Clark, 1988.

Grossfeld, B. *The Targum Onqelos to Leviticus and the Targum Onqelos to Numbers: Translated, with Apparatus and Notes*. The Aramaic Bible 8. Edinburgh: T. & T. Clark, 1988.

Kittel, G., and G. Friedrich, eds. *Theological Dictionary of the New Testament*. 10 vols. Grand Rapids: Eerdmans, 1964–76.

Lake, K., ed. *The Apostolic Fathers: With an English Translation*. 2 vols. The Loeb Classical Library. London: Heinemann; Cambridge: Harvard University Press, 1912, 1913.

Lauterbach, J., ed. *Mekilta de Rabbi Ishmael*. 3 vols. Philadelphia: The Jewish Publication Society of America, 1961.

Liddell, H., R. Scott, and A. S. Jones. *A Greek-English Lexicon*. Oxford: Clarendon Press, 1968.

Lohse, E., ed. *Die Texte aus Qumran: Hebräisch und Deutsch*. 3rd ed. Munich: Kösel-Verlag, 1981.

McNamara, M. *Targum Neofiti 1: Genesis. Translated, with Apparatus and Notes*. The Aramaic Bible 1A. Edinburgh: T. & T. Clark, 1992.

Maher, M. *Targum Pseudo-Jonathan: Genesis. Translated, with Introduction and Notes*. The Aramaic Bible 1B. Edinburgh: T. & T. Clark, 1992.

Metzger, B. M., *A Textual Commentary on the Greek New Testament*. London/New York: United Bible Societies, 1971.

Minor, M. *Literary-Critical Approaches to the Bible: An Annotated Bibliography*. West Cornwall, Conn.: Locust Hill Press, 1992.

Moulton, J. H., W. F. Howard, and N. Turner. *A Grammar of New Testament Greek*. 4 vols. Edinburgh: T. & T. Clark, 1909–1976.

Neusner, J. *Sifré to Numbers: An American Translation and Explanation*. 2 vols. Brown Judaic Studies 118–119. Atlanta: Scholars Press, 1986.

Neusner, J. *The Tosefta Translated from the Hebrew: Second Division Moed (The Order of Appointed Times)*. New York: KTAV, 1981.

Pirot, L., A. Robert, and H. Cazelles, eds. *Dictionnaire de la Bible Supplément*. Paris: Letouzey, 1928–.

Powell, M. A., C. G. Gray, and M. C. Curtis. *The Bible and Modern Literary Criticism: A Critical Assessment and Annotated Bibliography*. New York: Greenwood, 1992.

Rahlfs, A. *Septuaginta: Id est Vetus Testamentum Graece iuxta LXX Interpretes*. 2 vols. 8th ed. Stuttgart: Württemburgische Bibelanstalt, 1965.

Schwab, M., ed. *Le Talmud de Jérusalem*. 11 vols. Paris: Maisonneuve et Cie., 1878–90.

Strack, H., and P. Billerbeck. *Kommentar zum Neuen Testament aus Talmud und Midrasch*. 6 vols. Munich: C. H. Beck, 1922–61.

Taylor, C., ed. *Sayings of the Fathers Comprising Pirque Aboth in Hebrew and English with Notes and Excursuses*. The Library of Jewish Classics. New York: KTAV, 1969.

Temporini, H., and W. Hasse, eds. *Aufstieg und Niedergang der Römischen Welt*. Berlin: Walter de Gruyter, 1981– .

Thackeray, H. St. J., R. Marcus, A. Wikgren, and L. H. Feldman, eds. *Josephus*. 9 vols. The Loeb Classical Library. London/Cambridge: William Heinemann/Harvard University Press, 1926–1965.

van Belle, G. *Johannine Bibliography 1966–1985: A Cumulative Bibliography on the Fourth Gospel*. BETL 82. Leuven: University Press, 1988.

Winter, J. *Sifra: Halachischer Midrasch zu Leviticus*. Breslau: Stefan Münz, 1938.

Zerwick, M. *Biblical Greek Illustrated by Examples*. Rome: Biblical Institute Press, 1963.

COMMENTARIES ON THE FOURTH GOSPEL

Barclay, W. *The Gospel of John*. 2nd ed. 2 vols. The Daily Study Bible. Edinburgh: The Saint Andrew Press, 1975.

Barrett, C. K. *The Gospel according to St John*. 2nd ed. London: SPCK, 1978.

Bauer, W. *Das Johannesevangelium erklärt*. 3rd ed. HKNT 6. Tübingen: J. C. B. Mohr (Paul Siebeck), 1933.

Beasley-Murray, G. R. *John*. WBC 36. Waco: Word Books, 1987.

Becker, J. *Das Evangelium des Johannes*. 2 vols. ÖTK 4/1–2. Gütersloh/Würzburg: Gerd Mohn/Echter, 1979–81.

Bernard, J. H. *A Critical and Exegetical Commentary on the Gospel according to St John*. 2 vols. ICC. Edinburgh: T. & T. Clark, 1928.

Boismard, M.-E., and A. Lamouille. *L'Evangile de Jean*. Synopse des Quatre Evangiles en Français III. Paris: Cerf, 1977.

Brodie, T. L. *The Gospel according to John: A Literary and Theological Commentary*. New York: Oxford University Press, 1993.

Brown, R. E. *The Gospel according to John*. 2 vols. AB 29–29a. New York: Doubleday, 1966–70.

Bultmann, R. *Das Evangelium des Johannes*. MeyerK. Göttingen: Vandenhoeck & Ruprecht, 1941.

Bultmann, R. *The Gospel of John: A Commentary*. Oxford: Blackwell, 1971.

Calloud, J., and F. Genuyt. *L'Evangile de Jean (II): Lecture sémiotique des chapitres 7 à 12*. Lyon: Centre Thomas More, 1987.

Carson, D. A. *The Gospel according to John*. Grand Rapids: Eerdmans, 1991.

Delebecque, E. *Evangile de Jean: Texte Traduit et Annoté*. CahRB 23. Paris: Gabalda, 1987.

Ellis, P. F. *The Genius of John: A Compositional-Critical Commentary on the Fourth Gospel*. Collegeville, Minn.: Liturgical Press, 1984.

Gnilka, J. *Johannesevangelium*. NEchtB 4. Würzburg: Echter Verlag, 1989.

Haenchen, E. *John*. 2 vols. Hermeneia; Philadelphia: Fortress Press, 1984.

Hoskyns, E. C. *The Fourth Gospel*, ed. F. N. Davey. London: Faber & Faber, 1947.

Lagrange, M.-J. *Évangile selon saint Jean*. Etudes Bibliques. Paris: Gabalda, 1936.

Léon-Dufour, X. *Lecture de l'évangile selon Jean*. 3 vols. Parole de Dieu. Paris: Seuil, 1988, 1990, 1993.

Lightfoot, R. H. *St. John's Gospel*, ed. C. F. Evans. Oxford: University Press, 1956.

Lindars, B. *The Gospel of John*. NCB. London: Oliphants, 1972.

Loisy, A. *Le quatrième évangile*. Paris: Emile Nourry, 1921.

Marsh, J. *Saint John*. The Pelican New Testament Commentaries. Harmondsworth: Penguin Books, 1968.

Moloney, F. J. *Belief in the Word: Reading John 1–4*. Minneapolis: Fortress Press, 1993.

Morris, L. *The Gospel according to John*. NICNT. Grand Rapids: Eerdmans, 1971.

Panimolle, S. A. *Lettura Pastorale del Vangelo di Giovanni*. 3 vols. Bologna: Dehoniane, 1978–84.

Perkins, P. "The Gospel according to John." In *NJBC*, 942–985.

Schnackenburg, R. *The Gospel according to St John*. 3 vols. HTCNT 4/1-3. London/New York: Burns & Oates/Crossroad, 1968–82.

Segalla, G. *Giovanni*. NVB 36. Roma: Edizioni Paoline, 1976.

Sloyan, G. *John*. Interpretation. Atlanta: John Knox, 1988.

Stibbe, M. W. G. *John*. Readings: A New Biblical Commentary. Sheffield: JSOT Press, 1993.

Talbert, C. H. *Reading John: A Literary and Theological Commentary on the Fourth Gospel and the Johannine Epistles*. London: SPCK, 1992.

van den Bussche, H. *Jean: Commentaire de l'Évangile Spirituel*. Bruges: Desclée de Brouwer, 1976.

Westcott, B. F. *The Gospel according to Saint John*. London: John Murray, 1908.

Zevini, G. *Vangelo secondo Giovanni*. 2 vols. Commenti Spirituali del Nuovo Testamento. Roma: Città Nuova, 1984, 1987.

OTHER LITERATURE

Abbott, E. A. *Johannine Grammar*. London: A. & C. Black, 1906.

Anderson, H. "Fourth Maccabees." *ABD* 4:452–54.

Ashton, J. *Understanding the Fourth Gospel*. Oxford: Clarendon Press, 1991.

Atal, D. "'Die Wahrheit wird euch freimachen' (Joh 8,32)." In *Biblische Rund-*

bemerken: Schülerfestschrift für Rudolf Schnackenburg zum 60. Geburtstag, ed. H. Merklein and J. Lange, 283–99. Würzburg: Echter Verlag, 1974.

Bammel, E. "'Ex illa itaque die consilium fecerunt . . .'." In *The Trial of Jesus: Cambridge Studies in Honour of C. F. D. Moule*, ed. E. Bammel, 11–40. SBT 14; London: SCM Press, 1970.

———. "John Did not Miracles: John 10:41." In *Miracles: Cambridge Studies in their Philosophy and History*, 197–202. London: Mowbray, 1965.

———. "The Feeding of the Multitude." In *Jesus and the Politics of His Day*, ed. E. Bammel and C. F. D. Moule, 211–40. Cambridge: Cambridge University Press, 1984.

———. "Zum jüdischen Märtyrerkult." In *Judaica: Kleine Schriften I*, 79–85. WUNT 37. Tübingen: J. C. B. Mohr (Paul Siebeck), 1986.

Barker, M. "John 11.50." In *The Trial of Jesus: Cambridge Studies in Honour of C. F. D. Moule*, ed. E. Bammel, 41–46. SBT 14. London: SCM Press, 1970.

Barrett, C. K. *Essays on John*. London: SCM Press, 1982.

———. "The Background of Mark 10:45." In *New Testament Essays: Studies in Memory of Thomas Walter Manson*, ed. A. J. B. Higgins, 1–18. Manchester: Manchester University Press, 1959.

Berger, K. *Formgeschichte des Neuen Testaments*. Heidelberg: Quelle & Meyer, 1984.

Bernard, J. "La guérison de Bethesda. Harmoniques judéo-hellénistiques d'un récit de miracle un jour de sabbat." *MSR* 33 (1976) 3–34; 34 (1977) 13–44.

———. "Témoignage pour Jésus Christ." *MSR* 36 (1979) 3–55.

Beutler, J. "Der alttestamentlich-jüdische Hintergrund der Hirtenrede in Johannes 10." In *The Shepherd Discourse of John 10 and Its Context*, ed. J. Beutler and R. T. Fortna, 18–32. SNTSMS 67. Cambridge: University Press, 1991.

———. "Greeks Come to See Jesus (John 12,20f)." *Bib* 71 (1990) 333–47.

———. *Martyria: Traditionsgeschichtliche Untersuchungen zum Zeugnisthema bei Johannes*. FThSt 10. Frankfurt: Josef Knecht, 1972.

———. "Psalm 42/43 im Johannesevangelium." *NTS* 25 (1978–79) 33–57.

Bienaimé, G. "L'annonce des fleuves d'eau vive en Jean 7:37-39." *RTL* 21 (1990) 281–310, 417–39.

———. *Moïse et le don de l'eau dans la tradition juive ancienne: targum et midrash*. AnBib 98. Rome: Biblical Institute Press, 1985.

Birsdall, J. N. "John x.29." *JTS* 11 (1960) 342–44.

Bishop, E. F. "The Door of the Sheep—John x.7-9." *ExpT* 71 (1959-60) 307–9.

Bittner, W. *Jesu Zeichen im Johannesevangelium: Die Messias-Erkenntnis im Johannesevangelium vor ihrem jüdischen Hintergrund*. WUNT 2, Reihe 26. Tübingen: J. C. B. Mohr (Paul Siebeck) 1987.

Bjerkelund, C. J. *Tauta Egeneto: Die Präzisierungssätze im Johannesevangelium*. WUNT 40. Tübingen: J. C. B. Mohr (Paul Siebeck), 1987.

Black, M. *An Aramaic Approach to the Gospels and Acts*. 3rd ed. Oxford: Clarendon Press, 1967.

Blank, J. *Krisis: Untersuchungen zur johanneischen Christologie und Eschatologie*. Freiburg: Lambertus-Verlag, 1964.

Boismard, M.-E. "De son ventre couleront des fleuves d'eau." *RB* 65 (1958) 523–46.

——. "Jesus, le Prophète par excellence, d'après Jean 10,24-39." In *Neues Testament und Kirche. Für Rudolf Schnackenburg*, ed J. Gnilka, 160–71. Herder: Freiburg, 1974.

——. "Les citations targumiques dans le quatrième évangile." *RB* 66 (1959) 374–78.

——. "Problèmes de critique textuelle concernant le Quatrième Evangile." *RB* 60 (1953) 347–71.

Bokser, B. M. "Unleavened Bread and Passover, Feasts of." *ABD* 6:755–65.

Borgen, P. *Bread from Heaven: An Exegetical Study of the Conception of Manna in the Gospel of John and the Writings of Philo*. NovTSup 10. Leiden: E. J. Brill, 1965.

——. "John 6: Tradition, Interpretation and Composition." In *From Jesus to John: Essays on Jesus and New Testament Christology in Honour of Marinus de Jonge*, ed. M. C. de Boer, 268–91. JSNTSup 84. Sheffield: JSOT Press, 1993.

——. "The Use of Tradition in John 12.44-50." *NTS* 26 (1979–80) 18–35.

Bornkamm, G. "Das Bekenntnis im Hebräerbrief." In *Studien zu Antike und Urchristentum: Gesammelte Aufsätze Band II*, 188–203. BEvT 28. Munich: Kaiser Verlag, 1959.

——. "Die eucharistische Rede im Johannesevangelium." *ZNW* 47 (1956) 161–69.

Brown, R. E. "Roles of Women in the Fourth Gospel." *TS* 36 (1975) 688–99.

——. *The Birth of the Messiah: A Commentary on the Infancy Narratives of Matthew and Luke*. 2nd ed. Garden City: Doubleday, 1993.

——. *The Community of the Beloved Disciple: The Life, Loves, and Hates of an Individual Church in New Testament Times*. London: Geoffrey Chapman, 1979.

——. "The Gospel of Thomas and St John's Gospel." *NTS* 9 (1962–63) 155–77.

Bruns, J. E. "A Note on John 12,3." *CBQ* 28 (1966) 219–22.

Bühner, J.-A. *Der Gesandte und sein Weg im 4. Evangelium: Die kultur- und religionsgeschichtlichen Grundlagen der johanneischen Sendungschristologie sowie ihre traditionsgeschichtliche Entwicklung*. WUNT 2. Reihe 2. Tübingen: J. C. B. Mohr (Paul Siebeck), 1977.

Bultmann, R. *"pisteuô ktl."* *TDNT* 6:174–228.

——. *The History of the Synoptic Tradition*. Oxford: Blackwell, 1968.

Burge, G. M. *The Anointed Community: The Holy Spirit in the Johannine Tradition*. Grand Rapids: Eerdmans, 1987.

Busse, U. "Open Questions on John 10." In *The Shepherd Discourse of John 10 and Its Context*, ed. J. Beutler and R. T. Fortna, 6–17. SNTSMS 67. Cambridge: University Press, 1991.

Byrne, B. J. *Lazarus: A Contemporary Reading of John 11:1-46*. Zacchaeus Studies: New Testament. Collegeville: Liturgical Press, 1991.

Carroll, J. T. "Present and Future in Fourth Gospel Eschatology." *BTB* 19 (1989) 63–69.

Cavaletti, S. "La visione messianica di Abramo (Giov. 8,58)." *BibOr* 3 (1961) 179–81.

Cavallin, H. C. "Leben nach dem Tod im Spätjudentum und frühen Christentum." *ANRW* 19/1 (1979) 240–345.

Charlesworth, J. H. (ed.). *The Messiah: Developments in Earliest Judaism and Christianity*. Minneapolis: Fortress Press, 1992.

Chenderlin, F. *"Do This as my Memorial": The Semantic and Conceptual Background and Value of Anamnêsis in 1 Corinthians 11:24-25*. AnBib 99. Rome: Biblical Institute Press, 1982.

Cilia, L. *La morte di Gesù e l'unità degli uomini (Gv 11,47-53; 12,32): Contributo allo studio della soteriologia giovannea*. Bologna: Private publication, 1992.

Collins, J. J. *Between Athens and Jerusalem*. New York: Crossroad, 1983.

Crossan, J. D. "It is Written: A Structuralist Analysis of John 6." *Sem* 26 (1983) 3-21.

Culpepper, R. A. *Anatomy of the Fourth Gospel: A Study in Literary Design*. Philadelphia: Fortress Press, 1983.

————. "John 5.1-18. A Sample of Narrative Critical Commentary." In *The Gospel of John as Literature: An Anthology of Twentieth-Century Perspectives*, ed. M. W. G. Stibbe, 193–207. NT Tools and Studies 17. Leiden: E. J. Brill, 1993.

Dacy, M. "Sukkot: Origins to 500 C. E." Unpublished M. Phil. Thesis; Department of Semitic Studies, Sydney University, August 1992.

Dahl, N. A. "'Do Not Wonder!' John 5:28-29 and Johannine Eschatology Once More." In *The Conversation Continues: Studies in Paul and John. In Honor of J. Louis Martyn*, ed. R. T. Fortna, and B. R. Gaventa, 322–36. Nashville: Abingdon Press, 1990.

Daube, D. *Collaboration with Tyranny in Rabbinic Law*. Oxford: University Press, 1966.

————. *The New Testament and Rabbinic Judaism*. London: Athlone, 1956.

Davies, W. D. *The Gospel and the Land: Early Christianity and Jewish Territorial Doctrine*. Berkeley: University of California Press, 1974.

————. *The Setting of the Sermon on the Mount*. Cambridge: Cambridge University Press, 1966.

de Dinechin, "*Kathôs*: La similitude dans l'évangile de saint Jean." *RSR* 58 (1970) 195–236.

de Jonge, M. "Jewish Expectations about the Messiah according to the Fourth Gospel." *NTS* 19 (1972–73) 246–70.

de la Potterie, I. *La vérité dans saint Jean*. 2 vols. AnBib 73–74. Rome: Biblical Institute Press, 1977.

————. "Le Bon Pasteur." In *Populus Dei: Studi in onore del Cardinale Alfredo Ottaviani per il cinquantesimo del sacerdozio, 19 marzo 1966*, 2:927–68. 2 vols. Rome: LAS, 1969.

————. "L'exaltation du Fils de l'homme (Jn. 12,31-36)." *Greg* 49 (1968) 460–78.

————. "'Oida' et '*ginôskô*'. Les deux modes de la connaissance dans le quatrième évangile." *Bib* 40 (1959) 709–25.

de Merode, M. "L'accueil triomphal de Jésus selon *Jean*, 11-12." *RTL* 13 (1982) 49–62.

de Villiers, J. L. "The Shepherd and his Flock." *Neot* 2 (1968) 89–103.

Dodd, C. H. "Behind a Johannine Dialogue." In *More New Testament Studies*, 41–57. Manchester: Manchester University Press, 1968.

————. *Historical Tradition in the Fourth Gospel*. Cambridge: Cambridge University Press, 1963.

————. *The Interpretation of the Fourth Gospel*. Cambridge: University Press, 1953.

——. "The Prophecy of Caiaphas: John 11:47-53." In *More New Testament Studies*, 58–68. Manchester: Manchester University Press, 1968.

Domeris, W. R. "The Confession of Peter according to John 6:69." *TynBul* 44 (1993) 155–67.

Duke, P. D. *Irony in the Fourth Gospel*. Atlanta: John Knox Press, 1985.

Dunn, J. D. G. "John 6—A Eucharistic Discourse?" *NTS* 17 (1971) 328–38.

Duprez, A. *Jésus et les dieux guérisseurs: A Propos de Jean V*. CahRB 12. Paris: Gabalda, 1970.

Evans, C. A. "Obduracy and the Lord's Servant: Some Observations on the Use of the Old Testament in the Fourth Gospel." In *Early Jewish and Christian Exegesis: Studies in Memory of William Hugh Brownlee*, ed. C. A. Evans and W. F. Stinespring, 221–36. Scholars Press Heritage Series. Atlanta: Scholars Press, 1987.

——. "The Voice from Heaven: A Note on John 12:28." *CBQ* 43 (1981) 405–8.

——. *To See and Not Perceive: Isaiah 6.9-10 in Early Jewish and Christian Interpretation*. JSOTSup 64. Sheffield: JSOT Press, 1989.

Farmer, W. F. "The Palm Branches in John 12,13." *JTS* 3 (1952) 62–66.

Fee, G. D. "On the Inauthenticity of John 5:3b-4." *EvQu* 54 (1982) 207–18.

Ferraro, G. "Giovanni 6,60-71. Osservazioni sulla struttura letteraria e il valore della pericope nel quarto vangelo." *RivBib* 26 (1978) 33–69.

——. "Il senso di *heôs arti* in Giov. 5,17." *RivBib* 20 (1972) 529–45.

——. *L' "ora" di Cristo nel Quarto Vangelo*. Aloisiana 10. Rome: Herder, 1974.

Feuillet, A. "Deux références évangéliques cachées au Serviteur martyrisé." *NRT* 106 (1984) 549–65.

——. "La signification du second miracle de Cana (Jean IV,46-54)." In *Etudes Johanniques*, 34–46. Bruges: Desclée, 1962.

——. "Les deux onctions faites sur Jésus et Marie Madeleine. Contribution à l'étude des rapports entre les Synoptiques et le quatrième évangile." *RThom* 75 (1975) 357–93.

——. "Les *Ego eimi* christologiques du quatrième évangile." *RevScRel* 54 (1966) 5–22.

Forestell, J. T. *The Word of the Cross: Salvation as Revelation in the Fourth Gospel*. AnBib 57. Rome: Biblical Institute Press, 1974.

Fortna, R. T. *The Gospel of Signs: A Reconstruction of the Narrative Source Underlying the Fourth Gospel*. SNTSMS 11. Cambridge: Cambridge University Press, 1970.

Foster, D. "John Come Lately: The Belated Evangelist." In *The Bible and the Narrative Tradition*, ed. F. McConnell, 113–31. New York: Oxford University Press, 1986.

Fowler, R. M. *Let the Reader Understand: Reader-Response Criticism and the Gospel of Mark*. Minneapolis: Fortress Press, 1991.

Freed, E. D. "*Egô eimi* in John VIII.24 in the Light of Its Context and Jewish Messianic Belief." *JTS* 33 (1982) 163–67.

——. *Old Testament Quotations in the Gospel of John*. NovTSup 11. Leiden: E. J. Brill, 1965.

——. "The Entry into Jerusalem in the Gospel of John." *JBL* 80 (1961) 329–38.

——. "Who or What Was before Abraham in John 8:58?" *JSNT* 17 (1983) 52–59.

Gärtner, B. *John 6 and the Jewish Passover*. ConNT 17. Lund: Gleerup, 1959.

Geiger, M. "Aufruf an Rückkehrende. Zum Sinn des Zitats von Ps 78,24b in Joh 6,31." *Bib* 65 (1984) 449–64.

Genette, G. *Narrative Discourse: An Essay in Method*. Ithaca: Cornell University Press, 1980.

Giblin, C. H. "Mary's Anointing for Jesus' Burial-Resurrection (John 12:1-8)." *Bib* 73 (1992) 560–64.

———. "Suggestion, Negative Response and Positive Action in St John's Portrayal of Jesus (John 2.1-11; 4.46-54; 7.2-14; 11.1-44.)." *NTS* 26 (1979–80) 197–211.

———. "The Miraculous Crossing of the Sea (John 6.16-21)." *NTS* 29 (1983) 96–103.

———. "The Tripartite Narrative Structure of John's Gospel." *Bib* 71 (1990) 449–68.

Girard, M. "L'unité de composition de Jean 6, au regard de l'analyse structurelle." *Église et Théologie* 13 (1982) 79–110.

Goodman, P. *The Sukkot and Simkah Torah Anthology*. Philadelphia: Jewish Publications Society of America, 1973.

Gourgues, M. "L'aveugle-né (Jn 9). Du miracle au signe: typologie des réactions à l'égard du Fils de l'homme." *NRT* 104 (1982) 381–95.

———. "Section christologique et section eucharistique en Jean VI. Une proposition." *RB* 88 (1981) 515–27.

Grässer, E. "Die Juden als Teufelssöhne in Joh 8,37-47." In *Der Alte Bund im Neuen*, 154–67. WUNT 35. Tübingen: J. C. B. Mohr (Paul Siebeck) 1985.

Grelot, P. "Jean VII,38: eau du rocher ou source du Temple?" *RB* 70 (1963) 43–51.

———. "Washing in the Pool of Siloam: A Thematic Interpretation of the Johannine Cross." *NovT* 27 (1985) 227–35.

Grimm, W. "Die Preisgabe eines Menschen zur Rettung des Volkes. Priesterliche Tradition bei Johannes und Joseph." In *Josephus-Studien: Untersuchungen zu Josephus, dem antiken Judentum und dem Neuen Testament. Otto Michel zum 70. Geburtstag gewidmet*, ed. O. Betz, K. Haacker and M. Hengel, 133–46. Göttingen: Vandenhoeck & Ruprecht, 1974.

Grob, F. "Vous me cherchez, non parce que vous avez vu des signes . . ." Essai d'explication cohérent de Jean 6/26." *RHPR* 60 (1980) 429–39.

Grundmann, W. "The decision of the Supreme Court to put Jesus to death (John 11:47-57) in its context: tradition and redaction in the Gospel of John." In *Jesus and the Politics of His Day*, ed. E. Bammel and C. F. D. Moule, 295–318. Cambridge: Cambridge University Press, 1984.

Haenchen, E. "Johanneische Probleme." *ZTK* 56 (1959) 19–54.

Hare, D. R. A. *The Son of Man Tradition*. Minneapolis: Fortress Press, 1990.

Hart, H. St. J. "Judea and Rome. The Official Commentary." *JTS* 3 (1952) 172–98.

Harvey, A. E. *Jesus on Trial: A Study in the Fourth Gospel*. London: SPCK, 1976.

Hasel, G. F. "Sabbath." *ABD* 5:849–56.

Hauck, F. "*agnos ktl.*" *TDNT* 1:122–24.

Heil, J. P. *Jesus Walking on the Sea: Meaning and Gospel Functions of Matt 14:22-33, Mark 6:45-52 and John 6:15b-21*. AnBib 87. Rome: Biblical Institute Press, 1981.

Hengel, M. *The Zealots: Investigations into the Jewish Freedom Movement in the Period from Herod I until 70 A.D.* Edinburgh: T. & T. Clark, 1989.

Hofius, O. "Die Sammlung der Heiden zur Herde Israels (Joh 10:16; 11:51f.)." *ZNW* 58 (1967) 289-91.

Hollenbach, B. "Lest They Should Turn and Be Forgiven: Irony." *BT* 34 (1983) 312-21.

Holleran, J. W. "Seeing the Light: A Narrative Reading of John 9." *ETL* 49 (1993) 5-26, 354-82.

Holst, R. "The One Anointing of Jesus: Another Application of the Form-Critical Method." *JBL* 95 (1976) 435-46.

Horsley, R. A. "'Messianic' Figures and Movements in First-century Palestine," in *The Messiah: Developments in Earliest Judaism and Christianity*, ed. J. H. Charlesworth, 276-95. Minneapolis: Fortress Press, 1992.

——. "Popular Messianic Movements around the Time of Jesus." *CBQ* 46 (1984) 471-95.

Iser, W. *The Act of Reading: A Theory of Aesthetic Response.* London: Routledge & Kegan Paul, 1978.

——. *The Implied Reader: Patterns of Communication in Prose Fiction from Bunyan to Beckett.* Baltimore: Johns Hopkins University Press, 1978.

Jacoby, A. "Zur Heilung des Blinden von Bethsaida." *ZNW* 10 (1909) 185-94.

Jeremias, J. "*Abraam.*" *TDNT* 1:8-9.

——. *Die Wiederentdeckung von Bethesda.* Göttingen: Vandenhoeck & Ruprecht, 1949.

——. *Heiligengräber in Jesu Umwelt: Eine Untersuchung zur Volksreligion der Zeit Jesu.* Göttingen: Vandenhoeck & Ruprecht, 1958.

——. *Jerusalem in the Time of Jesus: An Investigation into Economic and Social Conditions during the New Testament Period.* Philadelphia: Fortress Press, 1969.

——. *The Eucharistic Words of Jesus.* London: SCM Press, 1966.

——. "*thyra.*" *TDNT* 3:178-80.

Johnston, E. D. "The Johannine Version of the Feeding of the Five Thousand: An Independent Tradition?" *NTS* 8 (1961-62) 151-54.

Joubert, H. L. N. "'The Holy One of God' (John 6:69)." *Neot* 2 (1968) 57-69.

Käsemann, E. *The Testament of Jesus according to John 17.* Philadelphia: Fortress Press, 1968.

Karris, R. J. *Jesus and the Marginalized in John's Gospel.* Zacchaeus Studies: New Testament. Collegeville: Liturgical Press, 1990.

Kiefer, O. *Die Hirtenrede.* SBS 23. Stuttgart: Katholisches Bibelwerk, 1967.

Kilmartin, E. J. "Liturgical Influence on John 6." *CBQ* 22 (1960) 183-91.

Kleist, J. A. "A Note on the Greek Text of St. John 12,7." *Classical Journal* 21 (1925) 46-48.

Korteweg, J. "'You will seek me and you will not find me' (Jn 7,34): An Apocalyptic Pattern in Johannine Theology." In *L'Apocalypse johannique et l'Apocalyptique dans le Nouveau Testament*, ed. J. Lambrecht, 349-54. BETL 53. Gembloux: Duculot, 1980.

Kossen, H. B. "Who were the Greeks of John XII 20?" In *Studies in John: Presented to Dr. J. N. Sevenster on the Occasion of his Seventieth Birthday*, 97-110. NovTSup 24. Leiden: E. J. Brill, 1970.

Kremer, J. *Lazarus: Die Geschichte einer Auferstehung. Text, Wirkungsgeschichte und Botschaft von Joh 11:1-46*. Stuttgart: Katholisches Bibelwerk, 1985.

Kysar, R. "Johannine Metaphor: Meaning and Function: A Literary Case Study of John 10:1-8." *Sem* 53 (1991) 81–111.

———. *John's Story of Jesus*. Philadelphia: Fortress Press, 1984.

———. "Pursuing the Paradoxes of Johannine Thought. Conceptual Tensions in John 6. A Redactional-Critical Proposal." In *The Living Text: Essays in Honor of Ernest W. Sanders*, 189–206. Lanham: University Press of America, 1985.

Lategan, B. C. "The truth that sets man free. John 8:31-36." *Neot* 2 (1968) 70–80.

Lee, D. A. *The Symbolic Narratives of the Fourth Gospel: The Interplay of Form and Meaning*. JSNTSup 95; Sheffield: JSOT, 1994.

Legault, A. "An Application of the Form-Critique Method to the Anointings in Galilee (Luke 7,36-50) and Bethany (Mt. 26,6-13; Mk. 14,3-9; Jn. 12.1-8)." *CBQ* 16 (1954) 131–45.

Léonard, J.-M. "Multiplication des pains: 2 Rois 4/42-44 et Jean 6/1-13." *ETR* 55 (1980) 265–70.

Léon-Dufour, X. "Père, fais moi passer sain et sauf à travers cette heure! (Jean 12,27)." In *Neues Testament und Geschichte: Historisches Geschehen und Deutung im Neuen Testament: Oscar Cullmann zum 70. Geburtstag*, ed. B. Baltensweiler and Bo Reicke, 156–65. Tübingen: J. C. B. Mohr (Paul Siebeck), 1972.

Leroy, H. *Rätsel und Missverständnis: Ein Beitrag zur Formgeschichte des Johannesevangeliums*. BBB 30. Bonn: Peter Hanstein, 1968.

Levey, S. H. *The Messiah: An Aramaic Interpretation. The Messianic Exegesis of the Targum*. Cincinnati: Hebrew Union College Press, 1974.

Lieu, J. M. "Blindness in the Johannine Tradition." *NTS* 34 (1988) 83–95.

Lindars, B. *New Testament Apologetic: The Doctrinal Significance of the Old Testament Quotations*. London: SCM Press, 1961.

———. "Rebuking the Spirit: A New Analysis of the Lazarus Story of John 11." *NTS* 38 (1992) 89–104.

———. "Slave and Son in John 8:31-36." In *The New Testament Age: Essays in Honor of Bo Reicke*, ed. W. C. Weinrich, 1:270–86. 2 vols. Macon: Mercer University Press, 1984.

Loader, W. "The Central Structure of Johannine Theology." *NTS* 30 (1984) 188–216.

———. *The Christology of the Fourth Gospel*. BBET 23; Frankfurt: Peter Lang, 1989.

McNeil, B. "The Raising of Lazarus." *DRev* 92 (1974) 269–75.

MacRae, G. W. "The Meaning and Evolution of the Feast of Tabernacles." *CBQ* 22 (1960) 251–76.

Manns, F. *L'Evangile de Jean à la lumière du Judaïsme*. SBFA 33. Jerusalem: Franciscan Printing Press, 1991.

Marchadour, A. *Lazare: Histoire d'un récit. Récits d'une histoire*. LD 132; Paris: Cerf, 1988.

Martin, J. P. "History and Eschatology in the Lazarus Narrative." *SJT* 17 (1964) 332-43.

Martyn, J. L. *History and Theology in the Fourth Gospel*. Nashville: Abingdon, 1979.

Meeks, W. A. "Equal to God." In *The Conversation Continues: Studies in Paul and John. In Honor of J. Louis Martyn*, ed. R. T. Fortna and B. R. Gaventa, 309–21. Nashville: Abingdon Press, 1990.

———. *The Prophet-King: Moses Traditions and the Johannine Christology*. NovTSup 14. Leiden: E. J. Brill, 1967.

Meier, J. P. *A Marginal Jew: Rethinking the Historical Jesus*. ABRL. New York: Doubleday, 1991.

Menard, J. E. "L'interprétation patristique de Jo 7:38." *Revue de l'université d'Ottawa* 25 (1955) 5–25.

Menken, M. J. J. "Die Redaktion des Zitates aus Sach 9,9 in Joh 12,15." *ZNW* 80 (1989) 193–209.

———. "John 6,51c-58: Eucharist or Christology?" *Bib* 74 (1993) 1–26.

———. *Numerical Literary Techniques in John: The Fourth Evangelist's Use of Numbers of Words and Syllables*. NovTSup 55. Leiden: E. J. Brill, 1985.

———. "Some Remarks on the Course of the Dialogue: John 6,25-34." *Bijdragen* 48 (1987) 139–49.

———. "The Old Testament Quotation in John 6,45. Source and Redaction." *ETL* 64 (1988) 164–72.

———. "The Provenance and Meaning of the Old Testament Quotation of John 6,31." *NovT* 30 (1988) 39–56.

Michaels, J. R. "The Temple Discourse in John." In *New Dimensions in New Testament Study*, ed. R. N. Longenecker and M. C. Tenney, 200–12. Grand Rapids: Zondervan, 1974.

Miller, E. L. "The Christology of John 8:25." *TZ* 36 (1980) 257–65.

Mlakuzhyil, G. *The Christocentric Literary Structure of the Fourth Gospel*. AnBib 117. Rome: Biblical Institute Press, 1987.

Mörchen, R. "'Weggehen': Beobachtungen zu Joh 12,36b." *BZ* 28 (1984) 240–42.

Mollat, D. *Etudes Johanniques* (Paris: Seuil, 1979).

———. "Jugement." *DBS* 4:1382–1385.

Moloney, F. J. "Johannine Theology." *NJBC*, 1417–26.

———. "John 6 and the Celebration of the Eucharist." *DRev* 93 (1975) 243–51.

———. *The Johannine Son of Man*. 2nd ed. BibScRel 14. Rome: LAS, 1978.

———. "When Is John Talking about Sacraments?" *AusBR* 30 (1982) 10–33.

Moore, S. D. "Are There Impurities in the Living Water that the Johannine Jesus Dispenses? Deconstruction, Feminism, and the Samaritan Woman." *BibInt* 1 (1993) 207–27.

Morgan-Wynne, J. E. "The Cross and the Revelation of Jesus as *egô eimi* in the Fourth Gospel (John 8.28)." In *Studia Biblica 1978 II. Papers on the Gospels. Sixth International Congress on Biblical Studies. Oxford 3-7 April 1978*, ed. E. A. Livingstone, 219–26. JSNTSup 2. Sheffield: JSOT Press, 1980.

Morgenstern, J. "Sabbath." *IDB* 4:135–41.

Morris, L. *The New Testament and the Jewish Lectionaries*. London: Tyndale Press, 1964.

Moule, C. F. D. "A Neglected Factor in the Interpretation of Johannine Eschatology." In *Studies in John: Presented to Dr. J. N. Sevenster on the Occasion of his Seventieth Birthday*, 155–60. NovTSup 24. Leiden: E. J. Brill, 1970.

———. "A Note on Didache IX 4." *JTS* 6 (1955) 240–43.

———. "The Individualism of the Fourth Gospel." *NovT* 5 (1962) 171–90.

———. "The Meaning of 'Life' in the Gospel and Epistles of St John. A Study in the Story of Lazarus, John 11:1-44." *Theology* 78 (1975) 114–25.

Mowinckel, S. *He That Cometh.* Oxford: Blackwell, 1959.

Müller, K. "Joh 9 und das jüdische Verständnis des Siloh-Spruches." *BZ* 13 (1969) 251–56.

Müller, M. "Have You Faith in the Son of Man? (John 9.35)." *NTS* 37 (1991) 291–94.

Neirynck, F. "L'*epanalepsis* et la critique litteraire. A propos de l'évangile de Jean." *ETL* 56 (1980) 303–38.

Neugebauer, F. "Miszelle zu Joh 5,35." *ZNW* 52 (1961) 130.

Neusner, J. *Ancient Israel after Catastrophe: The Religious World View of the Mishnah.* Charlottesville: University Press of Virginia, 1983.

Neusner, J., W. Scott Green, and E. S. Frerichs (eds.), *Judaism and Their Messiahs at the Turn of the Christian Era.* Cambridge: Cambridge University Press, 1988.

Neyrey, J. H. *An Ideology of Revolt: John's Christology in Social-Science Perspective* (Philadelphia: Fortress Press, 1988).

———. "Jesus the Judge: Forensic Process in John 8,21-59." *Bib* 68 (1987) 409–42.

Nicholson, G. C. *Death as Departure: The Johannine Descent-Ascent Schema.* SBLDS 63. Chico: Scholars Press, 1983.

Nickelsburg, G. W. E. *Jewish Literature between the Bible and the Mishnah: A Historical and Literary Introduction.* Philadelphia: Fortress Press, 1981.

Nisin, A. *Histoire de Jésus.* Paris: Seuil, 1961.

Nodet, E. "La Dédicace, les Maccabées et le Messie." *RB* 93 (1986) 321–75.

O'Connell, M. J. "The Concept of Commandment in the Old Testament." *TS* 21 (1960) 351–403.

Odeberg, H. *The Fourth Gospel Interpreted in Its Relation to Contemporaneous Religious Currents in Palestine and the Hellenistic-Oriental World.* Uppsala: Almqvist, 1929.

Onuki, T. *Gemeinde und Welt im Johannesevangelium: Ein Beitrag zur Frage nach der theologischen und pragmatischen Funktion des johanneischen "Dualismus."* WMANT 56; Neukirchen-Vluyn: Neukirchener Verlag, 1984.

Osborne, B. "A Folded Napkin in an Empty Tomb: John 11:44 and 20:7 Again." *HeyJ* 14 (1973) 437–40.

Painter, J. *John: Witness and Theologian.* London: SPCK, 1975.

———. "The Church and Israel in the Gospel of John: A Response." *NTS* 25 (1978–79) 103–12.

———. "Text and Context in John 5." *AusBR* 35 (1987) 28–34.

———. *The Quest for the Messiah. The History, Literature and Theology of the Johannine Community.* 2nd ed. Edinburgh: T. & T. Clark, 1993.

Pancaro, S. "'People of God' in St John's Gospel." *NTS* 16 (1969–70) 114–29.

———. "The Metamorphosis of a Legal Principle in the Fourth Gospel: A Closer Look at 7,51." *Bib* 53 (1972) 340–61.

———. "The Relationship of the Church to Israel in the Gospel of John." *NTS* 21 (1974–75) 396–405.

———. *The Law in the Fourth Gospel: The Torah and the Gospel. Moses and Jesus,*

Judaism and Christianity according to John. NovTSup 42. Leiden: E. J. Brill, 1975.

Panimolle, S. "La dottrina eucaristica nel racconto giovanneo della moltiplicazione del pane (Gv 6,1-15)." In *Segni e Sacramenti nel Vangelo di Giovanni,* ed. P.-R. Tragan, 73–88. Studia Anselmiana 66, Sacramentum 3. Rome: Editrice Anselmiana, 1977.

Perry, J. M., "The Evolution of the Johannine Eucharist." *NTS* 39 (1993) 22–35.

Phillips, G. A. "'This Is a Hard Saying. Who Can Be Listener to It?' Creating a Reader in John 6." *Sem* 6 (1983) 23–56.

Pickering, S. R. (ed.). "John 7:53-8:11. The Woman Taken in Adultery." *New Testament Textual Research Update* 1 (1993) 6–7.

Pinto da Silva, A. "Giovanni 7:37-39." *Salesianum* 45 (1983) 575–92.

Pollard, T. E. "The Exegesis of John X, 30 in the Early Trinitarian Controversies." *NTS* 3 (1956–7) 334–39.

Porsch, F. "'Ihr hat den Teufel zum Vater' (Joh 8,44)." *BK* 44 (1989) 50–57.

Porter, C. L. "John 9,38,39a: A Liturgical Addition to the Text." *NTS* 13 (1966–67) 387–94.

Prete, B. "'I poveri' nel racconto giovanneo dell'unzione di Betania (Giov. 12,1-8)." In *Evangelizare Pauperibus: Atti della XXIV Settimana Biblica Associazione Biblica Italiana,* 429–44. Brescia: Paideia, 1978.

——. "Un'aporia giovannea: il testo di Giov. 12,3." *RivBib* 25 (1977) 353–73.

Rahner, H. "Flumina de ventre Christi. Die Patristische Auslegung von Joh 7:37-38." *Bib* 22 (1941) 269–309.

Rajak, T. *Josephus: The Historian and His Society.* Philadelphia: Fortress Press, 1984.

Rankin, O. S. *The Origins of the Festival of Hannukah: The Jewish New-Age Festival.* Edinburgh: T. & T. Clark, 1930.

Reim, G. "Johannesevangelium und Synagogengottesdienst—eine Beobachtung." *BZ* 27 (1983) 101.

——. "Joh 8.44—Gotteskinder/Teufelskinder. Wie antijudaistisch ist 'die wohl antijudaistische Äuserrung des NT'?" *NTS* 30 (1984) 619–24.

——. "Joh 9—Tradition und zeitgenenössische messianische Diskussion." *BZ* 22 (1978) 245–53.

——. *Studien zum alttestamentliche Hintergrund des Johannesevangeliums.* SNTSMS 22. Cambridge: Cambridge University Press, 1974.

Reinhartz, A. *The Word in the World: The Cosmological Tale in the Fourth Gospel.* SBLMS 45. Atlanta: Scholars Press, 1992.

Reiser, W. E. "The Case of the Tidy Tomb: The Place of the Napkins of John 11:44 and 20:7." *HeyJ* 14 (1973) 47–57.

Rengstorf, K. "*apostellô (pempô) ktl.*" *TDNT* 1:398–447.

——. "*didaskô ktl.*" *TDNT* 2:135–65.

——. "*lêistês.*" *TDNT* 4:257–62.

——. "*manthanô ktl.*" *TDNT* 4:415–60.

Rensberger, D. *Johannine Faith and Liberating Community.* Philadelphia: Westminster Press, 1988.

Repo, E. "Fünf Brote und zwei Fische." In *Probleme der Forschung,* ed. A. Fuchs, 99–113. SNTU 3. Munich: Verlag Harold Wien, 1978.

Riedl, J. "Wenn ihr den Menschensohn erhöht habt, werdet ihr erkennen (Joh 8,28)." In *Jesus und der Menschensohn: Für Anton Vögtle*, ed. R. Pesch and R. Schnackenburg, 355–70. Freiburg: Herder, 1975.

Rimmon-Kenan, S. *Narrative Fiction: Contemporary Poetics*. New Accents. London: Methuen, 1983.

Roberge, M. "Jean VI,22-24: Un problème de critique littéraire." *LTP* 35 (1979) 139–151.

———. "Jean VI,22-24: Un problème de critique textuelle." *LTP* 34 (1978) 275–89.

———. "Jean 6,26 et le rassasiement eschatologique." *LTP* 45 (1989) 339–49.

———. "Le discours sur le pain de vie (Jean 6,22-59). Problèmes d'interprétation." *LTP* 38 (1982) 265–99.

Robert, R. "Étude littéraire de Jean VIII, 21-59." *RevThom* 89 (1989) 71–84.

Robinson, J. A. T. "The Destination and Purpose of St John's Gospel." *NTS* 6 (1959–60) 117–31.

———. "The Parable of the Shepherd." *ZNW* 46 (1955) 233–40.

———. *The Priority of John*. London: SCM Press, 1985.

Rochais, G. "Jean 7: une construction littéraire dramatique, à la manière d'un scénario." *NTS* 39 (1993) 355–78.

———. *Les récits de résurrection des morts dans le Nouveau Testament*. SNTSMS 40. Cambridge: Cambridge University Press, 1981.

Roth, W. "Scriptural Coding in the Fourth Gospel." *BR* 32 (1987) 6–29.

Ruckstuhl, E. *Die literarische Einheit des Johannesevangeliums, der gegenwärtige Stand der einschlägigen Forschungen*. Studia Friburgensia, n.F. 3. Freiburg in der Schweiz: Ed. S. Paul, 1951.

Rylaarsdam, C. "Passover and Feast of Unleavened Bread." *IDB* 3:663–68.

Sabugal, S. *La curación del ciego de nacimiento (Jn 9,1-41): Análisis exegético y teológico*. BEB 2; Madrid: Biblia y Fe, 1977.

———. ". . . 'Y la Verdad os hará libres' (Jn 8,32 a la luz de TPI Gen 15,11)." *Aug* 14 (1974) 177–81.

Sandmel, S. "Feasts and Fasts." *IDB* 2:260–64.

Schaefer, K. "The Ending of the Book of Zechariah." *RB* 100 (1993) 165–238.

Schäfer, P. *Die Vorstellung vom Heiligen Geist in der rabbinischen Literatur*. SANT 28. Munich: Kösel-Verlag, 1972.

Schenke, L. "Das johanneische Schisma und die 'Zwölf' (Johannes 6.60-71)." *NTS* 38 (1992) 105–21.

———. *Das Johannesevangelium: Einführung—Text—dramatische Gestalt*. Stuttgart: Kohlhammer, 1992.

———. "Das Szenarium von Joh 6,1-25." *TTZ* 92 (1983) 191–203.

———. "Die formale und gedankliche Struktur von Joh 6,26-58." *BZ* 24 (1980) 21–41.

———. "Joh 7-10: Eine dramatische Szene." *ZNW* 80 (1989) 172–92.

Schnackenburg, R. "Joh 12,39-41. Zur christologischen Schriftauslegung des vierten Evangeliums." In *Neues Testament und Geschichte: Historisches Geschehen und Deutung im Neuen Testament: Oscar Cullmann zum 70. Geburtstag*, ed. H. Baltensweiler and Bo Reicke, 167–77. Tübingen: J. C. B. Mohr (Paul Siebeck), 1972.

——. "Offenbarung und Glaube im Johannesevangelium." *BuL* 7 (1966) 165–80.

Schneider, J. "Zur Komposition von Joh. 10." *ConNT* 11 (1947) 220–25.

Schneiders, S. M. "Death in the Community of Eternal Life: History, Theology and Spirituality in John 11." *Int* 41 (1987) 44–56.

——. "Women in the Fourth Gospel and the Role of Women in the Contemporary Church." *BTB* 12 (1982) 35–45.

Schnelle, U. *Antidocetic Christology in the Gospel of John: An Investigation of the Place of the Fourth Gospel in the Johannine School*. Minneapolis: Fortress Press, 1992.

Schuchard, B. G. *Scripture within Scripture: The Interrelationship of Form and Function in the Explicit Old Testament Citations in the Gospel of John*. SBLDS 133. Atlanta: Scholars Press, 1992.

Schürmann, H. "Joh 6,51c—Ein Schlüssel zur grossen Brotrede." *BZ* 2 (1958) 244–62.

Scott, M. *Sophia and the Johannine Jesus*. JSNTSup 71. Sheffield: JSOT Press, 1992.

Segalla, G. "La complessa struttura letteraria di Giovanni 6." *Teologia* 15 (1990) 68–89.

——. "Un appello alla perseveranza nella fede in Gv 8,31-32?" *Bib* 62 (1981) 387–89.

——. *Volontà di Dio e dell'uomo in Giovanni (Vangelo e Lettere)*. SuppRivB 6. Brescia: Paideia, 1974.

Segovia, F. F. "The Journey(s) of the Word of God: A Reading of the Plot of the Fourth Gospel." *Sem* 53 (1991) 23–54.

Simonis, A. J. *Die Hirtenrede im Johannesevangelium: Versuch einer Analyse von Johannes 10,1-18 nach Entstehung, Hintergrund und Inhalt*. AnBib 29. Rome: Biblical Institute Press, 1967.

Smith, D. M. *The Composition and Order of the Fourth Gospel: Bultmann's Literary Theory*. New Haven: Yale University Press, 1965.

——. "The Setting and Shape of a Johannine Narrative Source." In *Johannine Christianity: Essays on Its Setting, Sources, and Theology*, 80–93. Edinburgh: T. & T. Clark, 1984.

Spicq, C. "*Trôgein*: Est-il synonyme de *phagein* et d'*esthiein* dans le Nouveau Testament?" *NTS* 26 (1979–80) 414–19.

Stählin, G. "Zum Problem der johanneischen Eschatologie." *ZNW* 33 (1934) 225–59.

Staley, J. "Stumbling in the Dark, Reaching for the Light: Reading Characters in John 5 and 9." *Sem* 53 (1991) 55–80.

——. *The Print's First Kiss: A Rhetorical Investigation of the Implied Reader in the Fourth Gospel*. SBLDS 82. Atlanta: Scholars Press, 1988.

Stenger, W. "'Der Geist ist es, der lebendig macht, das Fleisch nützt nichts' (Joh 6,63)." *TTZ* 85 (1976) 116–22.

Stibbe, M. W. G. *John as Storyteller: Narrative Criticism and the Fourth Gospel*. SNTSMS 73. Cambridge: Cambridge University Press, 1992.

Stimpfle, A. *Blinde sehen: Die Eschatologie im traditionsgeschichtliche Prozess des Johannesevangeliums*. BZNW 57. Berlin: de Gruyter, 1990.

Stott, W. "Sabbath, Lord's Day." In *The New International Dictionary of New Testament Theology*, ed. C. Brown, 3:405–8. 3 vols. Exeter: Paternoster Press, 1978.

Stowasser, M. *Johannes der Täufer im Vierten Evangelium*. ÖBS 12, Klosterneuburg: Östereichisches Katholisches Bibelwerk, 1992.

Strachan, R. H. *The Fourth Gospel: Its Significance and Environment*. 3rd ed. London: SCM Press, 1941.

Strand, K. A. (ed.). *The Sabbath in Scripture and History*. Washington: Review and Herald Publishing Association, 1982.

Suggit, J. N. "The Raising of Lazarus." *ExpT* 95 (1983–84) 106–8.

Swetnam, J. "The Meaning of *pepisteukotas* in John 8,31." *Bib* 61 (1980) 106–7.

Talbert, C. H. "The Myth of a Descending-Ascending Redeemer in Mediterranean Antiquity." *NTS* 22 (1975–76) 418–39.

Taylor, J. "Why Were the Disciples First Called 'Christians' at Antioch? (Acts 11,26)." *RB* 101 (1994) 75–94.

Thomas, J. C. "The Fourth Gospel and Rabbinic Judaism." *ZNW* 82 (1991) 159–82.

Thüsing, W. *Die Erhöhung und Verherrlichung Jesu im Johannesevangelium*. 3rd ed. NTAbh 21/1–2. Münster: Aschendorff, 1979.

Thyen, H. "Johannes 10 im Context des vierten Evangeliums." In *The Shepherd Discourse of John 10 and Its Context*, ed. J. Beutler and R. T. Fortna, 116–34. SNTSMS 67. Cambridge: Cambridge University Press, 1991.

Tragan, P.-R. *La Parabole du "Pasteur" et ses explications: Jean 10,1-18. La genèse, les milieux littéraires*. Studia Anselmiana 67. Rome: Editrice Anselmiana, 1980.

——. "Le discours sur le pain de vie: Jean 6,26-71. Remarques sur sa composition littéraire." In *Segni e Sacramenti nel Vangelo di Giovanni*, ed. P.-R. Tragan, 89–119. Studia Anselmiana 66. Sacramentum 3. Rome: Editrice Anselmiana, 1977.

Tsuchido, K. "Tradition and Redaction in John 8:12-30." *Annual of the Japanese Biblical Institute* 6 (1980) 56–75.

——. "Tradition and Redaction in John 12.1-43." *NTS* 30 (1984) 609–19.

Tuñí Vancells, J. O. *La verdad os hará libres Jn 8,32: Liberación y libertad del creyente en el cuarto evangelio*. Barcelona: Herder, 1973.

van der Loos, H. *The Miracles of Jesus*. NovTSup 8. Leiden: E. J. Brill, 1961.

van der Watt, J. G. "A New Look at John 5:25-29 in the Light of the Term 'Eternal Life' in the Gospel according to John." *Neot* 19 (1985) 71–86.

——. "The Use of *aiônios* in the Concept *zôê aiônios* in John's Gospel." *NovT* 31 (1989) 217–28.

van Tilborg, S. *Imaginative Love in John*. BibIntS 2. Leiden: E. J. Brill, 1993.

van Unnik, W. C. *Das Selbstverständnis der jüdischen Diaspora in der hellenistisch-römischen Zeit*, ed. P. W. van der Horst. AGJU 17. Leiden: E. J. Brill, 1993.

——. "The Quotation from the Old Testament in John 12,34." *NovT* 3 (1959) 174–79.

Vanhoye, A. "La composition de Jn. 5,19-30." In *Mélanges Bibliques en hommage au R. P. Béda Rigaux*, ed. A. Descamps and A. de Halleux, 259–74. Gembloux: Duculot, 1970.

——. "L'oeuvre du Christ, don du Père (Jn. 5,36 et 17,4)." *RSR* 48 (1960) 377–419.

von Wahlde, U. C. "Faith and Works in Jn VI 28-29." *NovT* 22 (1980) 304–15.

——. "Literary Structure and Theological Argument in Three Discourses with the Jews in the Fourth Gospel." *JBL* 103 (1984) 575–84.

——. "The Witnesses to Jesus in John 5:31-40 and Belief in the Fourth Gospel." *CBQ* 43 (1981) 385–408.

Wallace, D. B. "John 5,2 and the Date of the Fourth Gospel." *Bib* 71 (1990) 177–205.

Weiand, D. J. "John V.2 and the Pool of Bethesda." *NTS* 12 (1966) 392–404.

Weiss, H. "The Sabbath in the Fourth Gospel." *JBL* 110 (1991) 311–21.

Whittaker, J. "A Hellenistic Context for John 10,29." *VC* 24 (1970) 241–60.

Wilcox, M. "The 'Prayer' of Jesus in John XI.41b-42." *NTS* 24 (1977–78) 128–32.

Willmes, B. *Die sogenannte Hirtenallegorie Ez 34: Studien zum Bild des Hirten im Alten Testament.* BBET 19. Frankfurt: Peter Lang, 1984.

Witkamp, L. T. "Some Specific Johannine Features in John 6.1-21." *JSNT* 40 (1990) 43–60.

——. "The Use of Traditions in John 5.1-18." *JSNT* 25 (1985) 19–47.

Wuellner, W. "Putting Life Back into the Lazarus Story and Its Reading: The Narrative Rhetoric of John 11 as the Narration of Faith." *Sem* 53 (1991) 114–32.

Yee, G. A. *Jewish Feasts and the Gospel of John.* Zacchaeus Studies: New Testament. Wilmington: Michael Glazier, 1989.

Zaiman, J. H. "The Traditional Study of the Mishnah." In *The Study of Ancient Judaism,* ed. J. Neusner, 2:27–36. 2 vols. New York: KTAV, 1981.

Zimmerman, H. "Das absolute *egô eimi* als neutestamentliche Offenbarungsformel." *BZ* 4 (1960) 54–69; 266–76.

Index